AQA Biology

AS

Exclusively endor

Glenn Toole
Susan Toole

Nelson Thornes

Published in 2008 by:
Nelson Thornes Ltd
Delta Place
27 Bath Road
CHELTENHAM
GL53 7TH
United Kingdom

09 10 11 12 / 10 9 8 7 6

A catalogue record for this book is available from the British Library

ISBN 978 0 7487 8275 8

Cover photograph by Corbis/Dennis Galante

Illustrations include artwork drawn by Barking Dog Art and GreenGate Publishing

Page make-up by GreenGate Publishing, Kent

Printed and bound in China by 1010 Printing International Ltd.

Contents

Introduction

Nelson Thornes has worked in partnership with AQA to ensure this book and the accompanying online resources offer you the best support for your GCSE course.

All resources have been approved by senior AQA examiners so you can feel assured that they closely match the specification for this subject and provide you with everything you need to prepare successfully for your exams.

These print and online resources together **unlock blended learning**; this means that the links between the activities in the book and the activities online blend together to maximise your understanding of a topic and help you achieve your potential.

These online resources are available on **kerboodle!** which can be accessed via the internet at http://www.kerboodle.com/live, anytime, anywhere. If your school or college subscribes to this service you will be provided with your own personal login details. Once logged in, access your course and locate the required activity.

For more information and help visit
http://www.kerboodle.com

Icons in this book indicate where there is material online related to that topic. The following icons are used:

💡 Learning activity

These resources include a variety of interactive and non-interactive activities to support your learning:

- Animations
- Simulations
- Maths skills
- Key diagrams
- Glossary

✅ Progress tracking

These resources include a variety of tests that you can use to check your knowledge on particular topics (Test yourself) and a range of resources that enable you to analyse and understand examination questions (On your marks...). You will also find the answers to the examination-style questions online.

🔁 Research support

These resources include WebQuests, in which you are assigned a task and provided with a range of web links to use as source material for research.

These are designed as stretch and challenge resources to stretch you and broaden your learning, in order for you to attain the highest possible marks in your exams.

These are designed as Extension resources to stretch you and broaden your learning, in order for you to attain the highest possible marks in your exams.

Weblinks

Our online resources feature a list of recommended weblinks, split by chapter. This will give you a head start, helping you to navigate to the best websites that will aid your learning and understanding of the topics in your course.

🔬 How science works

These resources are a mixture of interactive and non-interactive activities to help you learn the skills required for success in this new area of the specification.

🔧 Practical

This icon signals where there is a relevant practical activity to be undertaken, and support is provided online.

▨ How to use this book

This book covers the specification for your course and is arranged in a sequence approved by AQA.

The textbook will cover all three of the Assessment Objectives required in your AQA A Level Biology course.

The main text of the book will cover AO1 – Knowledge and understanding. This consists of the main factual content of the specification. The other Assessment Objectives (AO2 – Application of knowledge and understanding and AO3 – How science works) make up around 50% of the assessment weighting of the specification, and as such will be covered in the textbook in the form of the feature 'Applications and How science works' (see below). You will **not** be asked to recall the information given under these headings for the purpose of examinations.

The book content is divided into the two theory units of the AQA Biology AS specification; Unit 1 – Biology and disease and Unit 2 – The variety of living organisms. Units are then further divided into chapters, and then topics, making the content clear and easy to use.

Unit openers give you a summary of the content you will be covering, and a recap of ideas from GCSE that you will need.

The features in this book include:

Learning objectives

At the beginning of each section you will find a list of learning objectives that contain targets linked to the requirements of the specification. The relevant specification reference is also provided.

Key terms

Terms that you will need to be able to define and understand are highlighted in bold type within the text, e.g. **haemoglobin**. Where terms are not explained within the same topic, they are highlighted in bold blue type, e.g. **haemoglobin**. You can look up these terms in the glossary.

Sometimes a term appears in brackets. These are words that are useful to know but are not used on the specification. They therefore do not have to be learned for examination purposes.

Hint

Hints to aid your understanding of the content.

Link

Links highlight any key areas where sections relate to one another.

Applications and How science works

This feature may cover either or both of the assessment objectives AO2 – Application of knowledge and understanding and AO3 – How science works, both key parts of the new specification.

As with the specification, these objectives are integrated throughout the content of the book. This feature highlights opportunities to apply your knowledge and understanding and draws out aspects of 'How science works' as they occur within topics, so that it is always relevant to what you are studying. The ideas provided in these features intend to teach you the skills you will need to tackle this part of the course, and give you experience that you can draw upon in the examination. You will not be examined on the exact information provided in Applications and How science works.

For more information, see 'How science works' on page 1 for more detail.

Summary questions

Short questions that test your understanding of the subject and allow you to apply the knowledge and skills you have acquired to different scenarios. These questions mostly cover material in the same topic but may sometimes include information from previous topics. Answers are supplied at the back of the book. These answers are more than just a mark scheme. They often include explanations of the answers to aid learning and understanding. The answers are not exhaustive and there may be acceptable alternatives.

Examiner's tip

Hints from AQA examiners to help you with your studies and to prepare you for your exam.

AQA Examination-style questions

Questions from past AQA papers that are in the general style that you can expect in your exam. These occur at the end of each chapter to give practice in examination-style questions for a particular topic. They also occur at the end of each unit; the questions here may cover any of the content of the unit. These questions relate to earlier specifications but have been chosen because they are relevant to the new specification. Despite careful selection there may be certain terms that do not exactly match the new requirements. They should therefore be treated in the same way as Applications and used for examination practice and application of knowledge, rather than learning their content. Answers to these questions are supplied online.

AQA examination questions are reproduced by permission of the Assessment and Qualifications Alliance.

Nelson Thornes is responsible for the solution(s) given and they may not constitute the only possible solution(s).

Web links in the book

As Nelson Thornes is not responsible for third party content online, there may be some changes to this material that are beyond our control. In order for us to ensure that the links referred to in the book are as up-to-date and stable as possible, the web sites provided are usually homepages with supporting instructions on how to reach the relevant pages if necessary.

Please let us know at **kerboodle@nelsonthornes.com** if you find a link that doesn't work and we will do our best to correct this at reprint, or to list an alternative site.

Skills for starting AS Biology

Welcome to biology at AS level.

This book aims to make your study of biology successful and interesting.

The book is written to cover the content of the AS course for the AQA specification. Each chapter in the book corresponds exactly to the subdivisions of each unit of the specification.

AS course structure (% of total AS marks is shown in brackets)

Unit 1 Biology and disease
       (33.33%)   Chapters 1–6

Unit 2 The variety of living organisms
       (46.67%)   Chapters 7–17

Unit 3 Investigative and practical skills
       (20%)   Online resources

Using the book

You will find that the AS course builds on the skills and understanding you developed in your GCSE course. New ideas are presented in the book in a careful step by step manner to enable you to develop a firm understanding of concepts and ideas. Biology at AS level will require you to describe and explain facts and processes in detail and with accuracy. However, the course is also about developing skills so that you can apply what you have learned. Examination papers will test skills such as interpreting new information, analysing experimental data, and evaluating information. In the AQA specification you will see sections which begin 'candidates should be able to ….' These are the sections which set out the skills you will need to develop to achieve success. You will find 'Application and How science works' features in the book. These features present relevant and challenging information which will enable you to develop these skills. The factual content of these sections is **not** required for examination purposes.

The AQA specification also emphasises how scientists work and how their work affects people in their everyday lives. For example, information is often presented in newspapers and on TV on science issues such as the possible side-effects of vaccines or drugs. Such reports may even contain conflicting evidence. The validity of evidence and the accuracy of conclusions is constantly questioned by scientists. Information in the text and in the accompanying resources will enable you to analyse evidence and data and to evaluate the way scientists obtain new evidence.

Checking your progress

You will find questions at the end of each chapter so that you can check your progress as you complete each section. Each chapter represents a manageable amount of learning so that you do not try to achieve too much too quickly. At the end of each unit there are questions written by AQA examiners in the same style that you will meet in examinations.

Investigative and practical skills

There are two routes for the assessment of Investigative and Practical Skills:

Either, **Route T**: Practical Skills Assessment (PSA) + Investigative Skills Assignment (ISA), which will be marked by your teacher.

Or, **Route X**: Practical Skills Verification (PSV) (assessed by your teacher) + Externally Marked Practical Assessment (EMPA), which is set and marked by an external AQA appointed examiner.

Both routes form 20% of the total AS assessment and will involve carrying out practical work, collecting and processing data, and then using the data to answer questions in a written test. The resources which accompany the book provide examples of investigations so that you can develop your practical and investigative skills as you progress through the topics in Units 1 and 2.

The book and accompanying resources provide a wealth of material specifically written for your AS biology course. As well as helping you to achieve success, you should find the resources interesting and challenging.

How science works

You have already gained some skills through the 'How science works' component of your GCSE course. Through the 'How science works' component of your AS Biology course, you will develop your scientific skills further and learn about important new ideas and applications. These skills are a key part of how every scientist works. Scientists use them to probe and test new theories and applications in whatever area they are working. Now you will develop your scientific skills further and gain new ones as you progress through the course.

'How science works' is developed in this book through relevant features that are highlighted. The How science works' features will help you to develop the relevant 'How science works' skills necessary for examination purposes, but more importantly these features should give you a thorough grasp of how scientists work, as well as a deeper awareness of how science is used to improve the quality life for everyone.

When carrying out their work scientists:

A Use theories, models and ideas to develop scientific explanations and make progress when validated evidence is found that supports a new theory or model.

B Use their knowledge and understanding when observing objects or events, in defining a problem and when questioning the explanations of themselves or of other scientists.

C Make observations that lead to explanations in the form of hypotheses. In turn hypotheses lead to predictions that can be tested experimentally.

D Carry out experimental and investigative activities that involve making accurate measurements, and recording measurements methodically.

E Analyse and interpret data to look for patterns and trends, to provide evidence and identify relationships.

F Evaluate methodology, evidence and data, and resolve conflicting evidence.

G Appreciate that if evidence is reliable and reproducible and does not support a theory, the theory must be modified or replaced with a different theory.

H Communicate the findings of their research to provide opportunity for other scientists to replicate and further test their work.

I Evaluate and report on the risks associated with new technology and developments.

J Consider ethical issues in the treatment of humans, other organisms and effects on the environment.

K Appreciate the role of the scientific community in validating findings and developments.

L Appreciate how society in general uses science to inform decision making.

UNIT 1

Biology and disease

Introduction

Every individual and community will experience disease at some time. Diseases affect every system of the body. Therefore to begin to understand disease we must first have a thorough knowledge of these systems. Such knowledge helps us to explain the symptoms of diseases and to develop ways of controlling them.

This unit investigates the structure and functions of certain human systems, all in the context of some of the diseases that afflict them. Each chapter in turn explores the following:

Causes of disease looks at how some diseases are caused by microorganisms while others are the result of our lifestyle. It explains how to interpret data about disease and shows why this is essential in determining the risks posed by certain aspects of our behaviour.

Enzymes and the digestive system explains how enzymes break down the complex food we eat into simple molecules that can be absorbed into cells. It emphasises the significance of the shape of proteins, including enzymes, and how factors such as temperature and pH can influence the way they function.

Cells and movement in and out of them explores the role of diffusion, osmosis and active transport in the movement of molecules across membranes. It moves on to explain how the bacterial disease cholera adversely affects the movement of salts and water in and out of the epithelial cells of the small intestine.

Lungs and lung disease is an account of the human gas-exchange system and how the alveolar surface of the lungs exchanges respiratory gases between the blood and the environment. It also investigates the effects on the lungs of bacterial diseases such as tuberculosis and diseases like fibrosis, asthma and emphysema that can result from certain lifestyle choices.

The heart and heart disease covers the structure and function of the heart and shows how factors such as diet, smoking and high blood pressure can affect the risk of suffering coronary heart disease.

Immunity considers the defensive functions of the blood system and how cell-mediated and humoral immunity help fight disease and protect against future infections. It concludes by looking at antibodies and how immunity may be acquired artificially through vaccination.

This unit provides many opportunities to explore How science works, both within the main text as well as in specifically designed Applications. Among other areas of How science works, Applications cover the use of knowledge and understanding to pose scientific questions (Chapter 6), analysis and interpretation of data (Chapters 1 and 4), the applications of science and ethical issues (Chapters 3 and 6).

What you already know

While the material in this unit is intended to be self-explanatory, there is certain information from GCSE that will prove very helpful to the understanding of the content of this unit. A knowledge of the following elements of GCSE will be of assistance:

- The effects of a balanced diet and regular exercise on health.

- The effects of tobacco smoke on the functioning of the heart and lungs.

- The causes of infectious diseases and how the body defends against them.

- The use of vaccines in controlling bacterial diseases.

- The structure of plant and animal cells, including the major components within them.

- How dissolved substances get in and out of cells by diffusion and osmosis.

- What enzymes are and how they function. The importance of the shape of an enzyme molecule and how this is affected by temperature and pH. What the enzymes amylase, protease and lipase do in the body and where they are produced.

- How the alveoli of the lungs and the villi of the small intestine are adapted as exchange surfaces.

- The function of the heart.

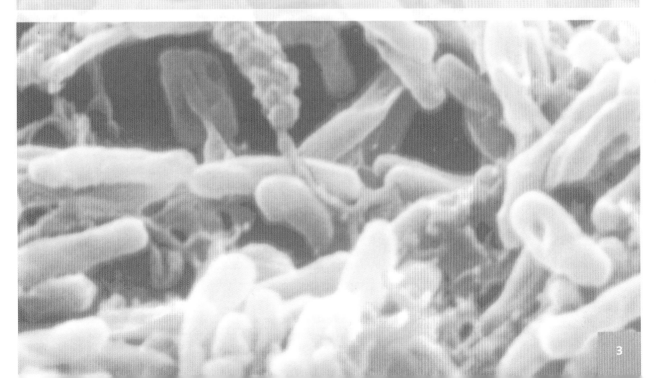

1.1 Pathogens

Causes of disease

Learning objectives:

▨ What are pathogens?

▨ How do pathogens enter the body?

▨ How do pathogens cause disease?

Specification reference: 3.1.1

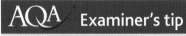

Examiner's tip

Be clear whether you are referring to a **bacterium** or a **virus**. Do not interchange the two terms.

'Microorganism' is a general term for a single-celled organism that is too small to be seen without a microscope. Microorganisms include bacteria and viruses. Many microorganisms live more or less permanently in our bodies benefiting from so doing, but causing us no harm. Some of these microorganisms are beneficial to us. Other microorganisms however, cause disease and these are called **pathogens**. Before we look at these it is worth considering what we mean by disease.

What is disease?

It is difficult to say what is meant by 'disease'. Disease is not a single thing, but rather a description of certain symptoms, either physical or mental, or both. Disease suggests a malfunction of body or mind which has an adverse effect on good health. It has mental, physical and social aspects.

Microorganisms as pathogens

For a microorganism to be considered a pathogen it must:

▨ gain entry to the host,

▨ colonise the tissues of the host,

▨ resist the defences of the host,

▨ cause damage to the host tissues.

Pathogens include bacteria, viruses and fungi (see Figures 1–3).

If a pathogen gets into the host and colonises its tissue an **infection** results. **Disease** occurs when an infection leads to recognisable symptoms

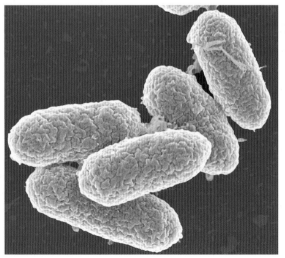

Figure 1 *Bacterial pathogen that causes salmonella food-poisoning*

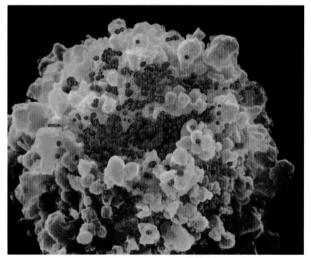

Figure 2 *False-colour scanning electron micrograph (SEM) of a T lymphocyte blood cell (green) infected with human immune deficiency virus (HIV; red), the agent that causes acquired immune deficiency syndrome (AIDS)*

in the host. When a pathogen is transferred from one individual to another it is known as **transmission.**

How do microorganisms get into the body?

Pathogens normally get into the body by penetrating one of the organism's interfaces with the environment. An interface is a surface or boundary linking two systems, in this case linking the external environment with the internal environment of the body. One of these interfaces is the skin. However, as the skin forms a thick, continuous layer, it is an effective barrier to infection. Invasion therefore normally occurs only when the skin is broken. This may happen as a result of cuts and abrasions or through the bites of insects and other animals. Some interfaces of the body have evolved to allow exchange of material between the internal and external environments. As a result the body linings at these points are thin, moist (and therefore sticky), have a large surface area and are well supplied with blood vessels. Just as these features make for easy entry of molecules, so they also make for easy entry of pathogenic microorganisms. Interfaces of the body are hence common points of entry and include:

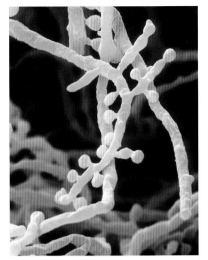
Figure 3 *False-colour scanning electron micrograph (SEM) of the fungus that causes athlete's foot*

- the **gas-exchange system**. Many pathogens enter the body through the gas exchange surfaces. Pathogens that cause influenza, tuberculosis and bronchitis infect in this way.
- the **digestive system**. Food and water may carry pathogens into the stomach and intestines via the mouth. Cholera, typhoid and dysentery pathogens enter the body by this means.

To help prevent the entry of pathogens the body has a number of natural defences. These include:

- a mucous layer that covers exchange surfaces and forms a thick sticky barrier that is difficult to penetrate,
- the production of enzymes that break down the pathogens,
- the production of stomach acid, which kills microorganisms.

How do pathogens cause disease?

Pathogens affect the body in two main ways:

- **by damaging host tissues**. Sometimes the sheer number of pathogens causes damage by, e.g. preventing tissues functioning properly. Viruses inhibit the synthesis of DNA, RNA and proteins by the host cells. Many pathogens break down the membranes of the host cells.
- **by producing toxins**. Most bacterial pathogens produce toxins. The cholera bacterium produces a toxin that leads to excessive water loss from the lining of the intestines.

Some diseases, like malaria, have a single cause, but others, like heart disease, have a number of causes. Pathogens, lifestyle and genetic factors can all cause disease.

How quickly a pathogen causes damage, and hence the onset of symptoms, is related to how rapidly the pathogen divides. Pathogens like those causing gastroenteritis divide about every 30 minutes and so symptoms of diarrhoea and vomiting become apparent within 24 hours of infection. The gastroenteritis pathogen also causes damage only if present in very large numbers. Other pathogens, such as the typhoid bacterium, cause harm when their numbers are relatively small.

AQA Examiner's tip

Remember that not all microorganisms cause disease. Therefore, when referring to a disease-causing organism, use the term 'pathogen', not 'microorganism'.

Hint

It is the pathogen that enters the body and causes the symptoms etc., **not** the disease. Do not write 'Cholera enters the body and this leads to diarrhoea' but rather write **'The bacterium that causes cholera** enters the body and this leads to diarrhoea'.

Summary questions

1. What is a pathogen?
2. Why are the digestive and respiratory systems often the sites of entry for pathogens?
3. In which **two** ways do pathogens cause disease?
4. Suggest **one** reason why oral antibiotics are not normally used to treat gastroenteritis and other diarrhoeal diseases.

1.2 Data and disease

Learning objectives:

▦ How are data on disease interpreted and analysed?

▦ What is a correlation and what does it mean?

▦ How is a causal link established?

Specification reference: 3.1.1

There is a considerable amount of information concerning disease and its possible causes. Newspapers, magazines, radio, TV and the internet bombard us with the latest statistics and research concerning the connection between various factors and the incidence of disease. Some of the information appears contradictory. So what can we believe? How can we tell if something is good or bad for us?

🔆 Analysing and interpreting data on disease

Epidemiology is the study of the incidence (number of cases) and pattern of a disease with a view to finding the means of preventing and controlling it. To do this, epidemiologists collect data on diseases and then look for a pattern or a relationship between these diseases and various factors in the lives of people who have them. As an example, let us look at at some of the epidemiological evidence that suggests drinking alcohol can cause breast cancer. What can we deduce from the graph in Figure 1?

▦ All the lines are, more or less, at zero at the age of 30. This shows that very few women in the survey, if any, had breast **cancer** before this age. (The scale makes it difficult to say categorically that **no one** had breast cancer by this age.)

▦ All the lines follow approximately the same pattern: they rise slowly at first and then at an increasing rate up to the age of 80. This describes their shape but what do they actually show? Namely that only a few women get breast cancer between the ages of 35 and 55, but that the incidence of the disease increases more rapidly after that age.

▦ What about the differences between the four coloured lines? The different colours represent four groups, which each consume a different number of alcoholic drinks each day. At every age beyond 35 years, the more drinks consumed each day, the more women in the group get breast cancer. This becomes more marked with increasing age.

▦ What is the overall interpretation? Namely that, when more alcoholic drinks are consumed each day, the risk of a woman developing breast cancer increases.

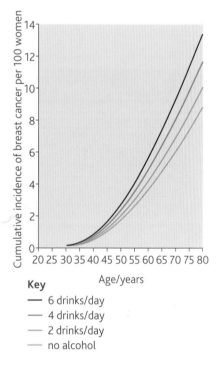

Key
— 6 drinks/day
— 4 drinks/day
— 2 drinks/day
— no alcohol

🔆 **Figure 1** *Estimated cumulative incidence of breast cancer per 100 women in developed countries, according to the number of alcoholic drinks consumed. Reprinted by permission from Macmillan Publishers Ltd:* British Journal of Cancer, *N. Hamajima et al. 87 (1), copyright 2002*

▦ Correlations and causal relationships

A **correlation** occurs when a change in one of two variables is reflected by a change in the other variable.

The interpretation of the data in Figure 1 shows that there is a correlation between drinking alcohol and breast cancer. What we **cannot** do, however, is to conclude that drinking alcohol is the **cause** of breast cancer. The data seem to suggest this is the case but there is no actual evidence here to prove it. There needs to be a clear causal connection between drinking alcohol and breast cancer before we can say that the case is proven. These data alone show only a correlation and not a cause. It could be that women who are stressed drink more alcohol and that it is the stress, rather than the alcohol, that causes breast cancer. To prove that drinking alcohol is the cause of breast cancer we would need experimental evidence to show that some component of the alcoholic drink led directly to women getting breast cancer. Recognising the distinction between a correlation and a causal relationship is a necessary and important skill.

Let us look at some different data. Figure 2 shows how the incidence of lung cancer changes with the number of cigarettes smoked a day. What can we conclude? Well, nothing really. We can see that the more cigarettes that are smoked, the greater are the number of deaths from lung cancer. In other words, there is a positive correlation between the two factors. However, we cannot conclude that it is the cigarette smoke that causes lung cancer. It may just be coincidence, or it could be that smokers are more stressed or drink more alcohol and these factors might be the cause of the cancer. Even though this graph does not itself establish a link, scientists have produced compelling experimental evidence to show that smoking tobacco definitely can cause lung cancer (see Topic 4.5).

Examiner's tip

It is important to be clear that a correlation does **not** mean that there is a causal link.

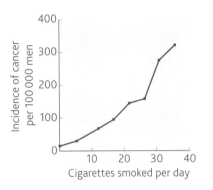

Figure 2 *Annual incidence of lung cancer per 100 000 men in the USA correlated to the daily consumption of cigarettes*

Looking critically at data

It is easy to accept data and other scientific information at face value when it should be looked at critically. To do this, consider the following questions when deciding how reliable the data are.

- Has the right factor been measured and have the correct questions been asked?
- How were the data gathered, were the methods reliable and was the right apparatus used?
- Do those collecting the data have a vested interest in the outcome of the research?
- Has the study been repeated, with the same results and conclusions, by other people?
- Are there still unanswered questions?

Summary questions

Study Figure 3 and answer the following questions.

1. State **two** correlations shown by the information in this bar chart.

2. Explain why the information provided does not show a causal relationship between the correlations you have identified.

3. The y-axis of the bar chart is labelled 'Relative risk of lung cancer'. Explain what this means. (It may help to refer to Topic 1.3.)

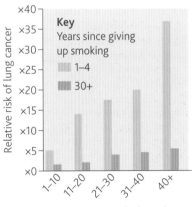

Figure 3 *The bar chart shows the risk of developing cancer in relation to the number of cigarettes smoked per day before stopping and the number of years since giving up smoking.*
Source: AQA, 2003

1.3 Lifestyle and health

Learning objectives:

▨ What is risk?

▨ How is risk measured?

▨ What factors affect the risk of contracting cancer?

Specification reference: 3.1.1

There are a number of disorders that result from an individual's lifestyle and the decisions they choose to make. In some cases the harmful consequences of their behaviour are known at the outset. Most people who begin smoking are aware of the increased risk of lung **cancer** and **emphysema**. In other cases, the damage may only become apparent later. Exercise, normally beneficial, can lead to **osteoarthritis** if it is excessive or inappropriate.

▨ What is risk?

Before we consider specific risk factors associated with cancer and coronary heart disease, let us consider what is meant by risk. Risk has many definitions depending on the context in which it is used. In respect of health, perhaps the simplest definition is:

> **a measure of the probability that damage to health will occur as a result of a given hazard**

The concept of risk has two elements:

▨ The probability that a hazardous event will occur.

▨ The consequences of that hazardous event.

This affects how we view risk. As an example, we may have a high probability of catching a cold, but as the consequences are minor we do not worry too much. The consequences of being struck by lightning are very severe but, as the probability of this occurring is very low, again it does not worry us much. It is when the probability is high and the consequences severe that we become concerned.

Measurement of risk

Risk can be measured as a value that ranges from 0 per cent (no harm will occur) to 100 per cent (harm will certainly occur).

Health risks need a timescale

To tell someone that their risk of dying is 100 per cent is meaningless because every one of us will die sometime. To state that their risk of dying **in the next month** is 100 per cent has an altogether different meaning.

Risk is often relative

Risk is measured by comparing the likelihood of harm occurring in those exposed to a hazard with those who are not exposed to it, e.g. smokers may be 15 times more likely to develop lung cancer than non-smokers.

Even when a risk is quantified, there are so many factors to consider that it is difficult to understand the risk. For example, take the figure above: smokers are 15 times more likely to develop lung cancer. To be able to understand the risk we need to know many other things:

▨ Over what time period does this occur?

▨ How does the number of cigarettes smoked a day affect the figure?

▨ Do stress levels, alcohol intake, occupation, gender, pollution or other factors have an influence?

▨ Does it change according to where the smokers live, e.g. in different countries, or in the city or countryside?

Hint

Remember that risk is about probabilities, **not** certainties. Some people may lead a lifestyle that would seem to put them at considerable risk and yet live well into old age. Conversely, others with few risk factors may become ill.

Misleading statistics

There is often so much more to a statistic, but reports in the media may be very misleading because they focus on a single figure. The impression given is that this figure applies to everyone, when often this is far from the case. In 2007 there were headlines such as 'HRT alert after more than 1000 women die' in national newspapers. This was certainly a disturbing statistic for the million or more women on hormone replacement therapy. A look behind the statistic showed that these extra deaths were over a 14-year period. The number of extra deaths each year was therefore 72. This is still a cause for concern but not nearly as alarming as the headlines would have us believe.

Risk factors and cancer

Cancer is not a single disease and, likewise, does not have a single cause. Some causal factors are beyond our individual control, e.g. age and genetic factors. Others are lifestyle factors and therefore within our power to change.

Lifestyle choices and cancer

We can do nothing about our genes or our age but our lifestyle can expose us to environmental and **carcinogenic** factors that put us at risk of contracting cancer. It is thought that about half the people who are diagnosed with cancer in the UK could have avoided getting the disease if they had changed their lifestyle. The specific lifestyle factors that contribute to cancer include:

- **smoking**. Not only smokers are in danger; those who passively breathe tobacco smoke also have an increased risk of getting cancer.

- **diet**. What we eat and drink affects our risk of contracting cancer. There is strong evidence that a low-fat, high-fibre diet, rich in fruit and vegetables, reduces the risk.

- **obesity**. Being overweight increases the risk of cancer.

- **physical activity**. People who take regular exercise are at lower risk from some cancers than those who take little or no exercise.

- **sunlight**. The more someone is exposed to sunlight or light from sunbeds, the greater is the risk of skin cancer.

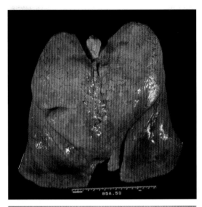

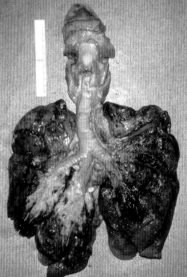

Figure 1 *Normal healthy lungs (top); smoker's lungs affected by cancer (bottom)*

Application

Smoking and lung cancer

Life insurance companies have calculated that, on average, smoking a single cigarette lowers an individual's life expectancy by 10.7 minutes – longer than it takes to smoke the cigarette! While this is a statistical deduction rather than a scientific one, there is now clear scientific evidence to support the view that smoking cigarettes damages your health and reduces life expectancy. One type of evidence comes from correlations between cigarette smoking and certain diseases.

Figure 2 on the next page shows deaths from lung cancer in the UK correlated to the number of cigarettes smoked per year during a period in the last century. Study it carefully and then answer the questions overleaf.

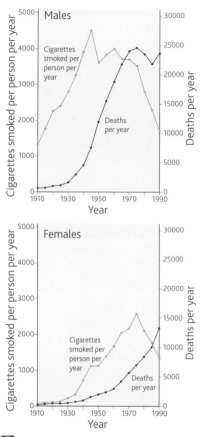

1 In which decade did smoking reach its peak for the following?

a males

b females

2 Explain how the graphs show that there is a correlation between the number of cigarettes smoked and deaths from lung cancer in both sexes.

3 In both sexes, the number of deaths per year from lung cancer increased over the period 1910 to 1970. Suggest **three** possible reasons for this.

4 Suggest a reason why there is a time lag between the number of cigarettes smoked and a corresponding change in the number of deaths from lung cancer.

💡 **Figure 2** *Incidence of deaths from lung cancer in the UK correlated to cigarettes smoked per year (1910–90)*

💡 Risk factors and coronary heart disease

Coronary heart disease (CHD) is the largest cause of death in the UK. There are a number of factors that increase the risk of an individual suffering from CHD. When combined together, four or five of these factors produce a disproportionately greater risk. Some factors, such as our genes, age and sex, are beyond our control, but there are others that we can do something about.

Factors we can control (lifestyle factors)

There are certain factors in our lives that we can control, such as:

▓ **smoking**. Smokers are between two and six times more likely to suffer from CHD. Giving up smoking is the single most effective way of increasing life expectancy.

▓ **high blood pressure**. Excessive prolonged stress, certain diets and lack of exercise all increase blood pressure and hence the risk of CHD.

▓ **blood cholesterol levels**. These can be kept lower by including fewer saturated fatty acids in the diet.

▓ **obesity**. A **body mass index** of over 25 brings an increased risk of CHD.

▓ **diet**. High levels of salt in the diet raise blood pressure while high levels of saturated fatty acids increase blood cholesterol concentration. Both therefore increase the risk of CHD. By contrast, foods such as dietary fibre reduce the risk of CHD by lowering blood cholesterol levels.

▓ **physical activity**. **Aerobic** exercise can lower blood pressure and blood cholesterol as well as helping to avoid obesity – all of which reduce the risk of CHD.

▓ Reducing the risk of cancer and CHD

There are measures that we can all take to reduce our chances of getting both cancer and CHD. These include:

▓ giving up or not taking up smoking,

▓ avoiding becoming overweight,

▓ reducing salt intake in the diet,

▓ reducing intake of cholesterol and **saturated fats** in the diet,

▓ taking regular aerobic exercise,

▓ keeping alcohol consumption within safe limits,

▓ increasing the intake of dietary fibre and **antioxidants** in the diet.

Summary questions

1 What single lifestyle change within the population of the UK would bring about the greatest reduction in cancer rates?

2 In what **three** ways would 30 minutes of brisk exercise each day reduce your chances of suffering coronary heart disease?

3 A friend asks how she can change her diet in order to live longer. What advice do you give her?

Application and How science works

Smoking and disease

Sixty years ago smoking was a highly popular pastime. Today, both individuals and governments worldwide are making strenuous efforts to eliminate it. How such a change was brought about illustrates the role that scientific knowledge can play in changing personal perceptions and public policy. This is an example of How science works (HSW: E, J and L).

History of smoking

When tobacco was first introduced to Britain in the 16th century it was usually smoked in pipes. At the end of the 19th century the invention of the cigarette-making machine made tobacco readily available to all. Initially, only men smoked, but women took up smoking in the 1920s. By 1945, the equivalent of 12 cigarettes a day for every British male was being smoked. At the time the public regarded smoking as a harmless pleasure. Doctors, however, were alarmed by a phenomenal increase in deaths from lung cancer. At a 1947 conference, a number of scientists suggested tobacco smoke as a possible cause of the increase. Their problem was how to convince the public, governments and the rest of the scientific world.

1 Scientists need to look at all possible explanations for the correlations that they have recognised. Suggest another possible cause of lung cancer, other than smoking, that they could have investigated.

Epidemiological evidence linking smoking to disease

Epidemiologists collect data on diseases and then look for correlations between these diseases and various factors in the lives of those who have them. The world's longest-running survey of smoking began in the UK in 1951. This survey, and others elsewhere in the world, has revealed a number of statistical facts about smokers.

- A regular smoker is three times more likely to die prematurely than a non-smoker.
- The more cigarettes smoked per day, the earlier, on average, a smoker dies.
- Smokers who give up the habit improve their life expectancy compared to those who continue to smoke.
- One in two long-term smokers will die early as a result of smoking.
- The incidence of pulmonary disease increases with the number of cigarettes smoked.
- Smokers make up 98 per cent of emphysema sufferers.

Data like those in Figure 3 were used to help establish a link between disease and smoking.

2 What correlation is shown by the data in Figure 3?

AQA Examiner's tip

Graphical data may be presented using a dual scale as shown in Figure 2. Look carefully at the labelling and units of each axis when analysing this type of data.

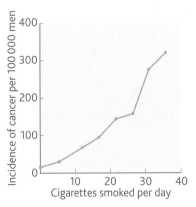

Figure 3 *Annual incidence of lung cancer per 100 000 men in the USA correlated to daily consumption of cigarettes*

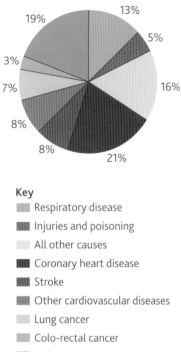

Key

▥ Respiratory disease

▥ Injuries and poisoning

▥ All other causes

▥ Coronary heart disease

▥ Stroke

▥ Other cardiovascular diseases

▥ Lung cancer

▥ Colo-rectal cancer

▥ Other cancer

Figure 4 *Causes of death in men in the UK in 2004. Source: National Statistics website: www.statistics.gov.uk Crown copyright material is reproduced with the permission of the Controller Office of Public Sector Information (OPSI)*

Epidemiological statistics show correlations between lung cancer and smoking. These include:

- A man smoking 25 cigarettes a day is 25 times more likely to die of lung cancer than a non-smoker.
- The longer a person smokes, the greater the risk of developing lung cancer. Smoking 20 cigarettes a day for 40 years increases the risk of lung cancer eight times more than smoking 40 cigarettes a day for 20 years.
- When a person stops smoking, the risk of developing lung cancer decreases and approaches that of a non-smoker after around 10–15 years (depending on age and amount of tobacco consumed).
- The death rate from lung cancer is 18 times greater in a smoker than in a non-smoker.

Cigarette manufacturers and some smokers argued that these epidemiological correlations were coincidental.

3 Much of the data linking smoking to lung cancer were collected from very large samples of the population. Suggest why this weakens the argument that the link is coincidental.

4 Do the data provide evidence of a causal link between lung cancer and smoking? Explain your answer.

Experimental evidence linking smoking to disease

Scientists carried out experiments in the 1960s in which dogs were made to inhale cigarette smoke. The smoke was either inhaled directly or first passed through a filter tip. Those dogs that inhaled the filtered smoke remained generally healthy. Those inhaling unfiltered smoke developed pulmonary disease and early signs of lung cancer. Scientists then carried out a further series of experiments that allowed them to formulate a new hypothesis from each result, which they could then test experimentally.

- Machines were used to simulate the action of smoking and to collect the harmful constituents that accumulated in the filters.
- These were then analysed chemically and each constituent was tested in the laboratory for its ability to damage epithelial cells and mutate the genes they contain. This was done by adding tar to the skin of mice or to cells that had been grown in culture.
- As a result of such tests it was shown that the tar found in cigarette smoke contained **carcinogens**.
- The constituent chemicals of the tar were each tested and one, benzopyrene (BP), was shown to mutate DNA.
- The scientists still had to demonstrate precisely **how** it caused cancer. They carried out experiments which showed that BP is absorbed by epithelial cells and converted to a derivative. This then binds with a **gene** and mutates it.
- Another experiment showed that this **mutation** led to uncontrolled cell division of epithelial cells and hence the growth of a **tumour**.
- Even this was not proof. In further experiments, scientists showed that the mutations of the gene in a cancer cell occurred at three specific points on the DNA. When the derivative of BP from tobacco smoke was used to mutate the gene, it caused changes to the DNA at precisely the same points.

5   What is the **key** evidence that smoking is a cause of lung cancer?

The evidence was now conclusive. Smoking tobacco could cause lung cancer. This is not to say that it always does, but simply that there is an increased risk – it is about probabilities not certainties.

This case study illustrates how scientists can suspect a correlation, collect the epidemiological evidence to demonstrate that the correlation exists, and then design and carry out a series of experiments to establish a causal link. We can never say absolutely that something is proven, only that there is proof within the bounds of our current scientific knowledge. That knowledge, and the theories based on it, are constantly being adapted in the light of new scientific evidence and discoveries.

These experiments convinced the public of the health risks of smoking and led to reduced use of tobacco in the UK (from 82 per cent of the male population in 1948 to 30 per cent in 2002). This changed view in turn persuaded the government to take measures designed to reduce smoking. These included:

■ progressively raising taxes on tobacco,

■ banning tobacco advertising,

■ placing health warnings on tobacco products,

■ banning smoking in work and public places, including bars, pubs and clubs.

6   'My father smoked 30 cigarettes a day and lived to be 95.' This type of argument is sometimes used to suggest that smoking is not harmful. Explain why scientists do not accept this reasoning.

The ethics of animal experimentation

The experiments described here will have indirectly prevented millions of premature deaths. However, the involvement of beagle dogs and mice in these experiments provoked a public outcry. This led to the 1986 Animal Act, which established a three-tier licensing system to limit and control animal experiments. The Act laid down a set of ethical standards to be followed and restricted the use of animals to cases where there is no realistic alternative.

Figure 5 *Smoking these 20 cigarettes would, on average, reduce your life expectancy by 3½ hours*

1 (a) What term is used to describe organisms which cause disease? *(1 mark)*

(b) Name **two** types of organism which cause disease. *(2 marks)*

(c) Disease-causing microorganisms gain entry into the body via one of its interfaces with the environment. **Figure 1** shows two of these interfaces. Copy and complete the diagram with two other examples of interfaces through which microorganisms may gain entry into the body. *(2 marks)*

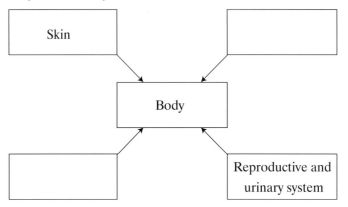

Figure 1

(d) Describe **two** ways in which the activity of microorganisms can give rise to disease symptoms.

(2 marks)

2 Lung cancer, chronic bronchitis and coronary heart disease (CHD) are associated with smoking. **Tables 1** and **2** give the total numbers of deaths from these diseases in the UK in 1974.

Table 1 Men

Age/years	Number of deaths (in thousands)		
	Lung cancer	**Chronic bronchitis**	**Coronary heart disease**
35–64	11.5	4.2	31.7
65–74	12.6	8.5	33.3
75+	5.8	8.1	29.1
Total (35–75+)	29.9	20.8	94.1

Table 2 Women

Age/years	Number of deaths (in thousands)		
	Lung cancer	**Chronic bronchitis**	**Coronary heart disease**
35–64	3.2	1.3	8.4
65–74	2.6	1.9	18.2
75+	1.8	3.5	42.3
Total (35–75+)	7.6	6.7	68.9

(a) (i) Using an example from the tables, explain why it is useful to give data for men and women separately.

(ii) Data like these are often given as percentages of people dying from each cause. Explain the advantage of giving these data as percentages. *(4 marks)*

(b) Give **two** factors, other than smoking, which increase the risk of coronary heart disease. *(2 marks)*

AQA, 2004

3 The graph in **Figure 2** gives information about the effects of cigarette smoking, plasma cholesterol concentrations and high blood pressure on the incidence of heart disease in American men.

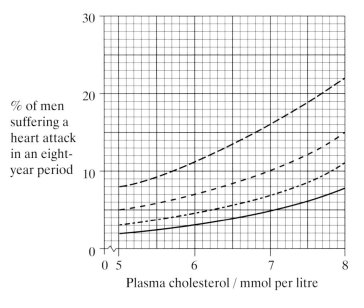

-·--- Smoker: high blood pressure

-·-·- Non-smoker: high blood pressure

--·--· Smoker: low blood pressure

——— Non-smoker: low blood pressure

Figure 2

(a) A non-smoker with low blood pressure has a plasma cholesterol concentration of 5 mmol per litre. Over a period of time this concentration increases to 8 mmol per litre. By how many times has this risk of heart disease increased? Show your working. *(2 marks)*

(b) Two non-smoking men with low blood pressure both have plasma cholesterol concentrations of 5 mmol per litre. One of them starts to smoke and the plasma cholesterol concentration of the other increases to 7 mmol per litre. Which man is now at the greater risk of heart disease? Explain your answer. *(3 marks)*

AQA, 2001

4 The table shows the number of deaths from various causes in a group of individuals of the same age. Individuals were identified as smokers or non-smokers.

Table 3

Cause of death	Number of deaths among smokers	Number of deaths among non-smokers
Total deaths (all causes)	7316	4651
Coronary artery disease	3361	1973
Strokes	556	428
Aneurysm	86	29
Lung cancer	397	37
Other causes	2916	2184

(a) Why was it necessary for the smokers and the non-smokers to be the same age? *(2 marks)*

(b) Do the figures in the table show that smokers were more likely to have died from a stroke than non-smokers? Use suitable calculations to support your answer. *(3 marks)*

(c) **Figure 3** and **Figure 4** show information from one study of lung cancer and lung diseases in adults of all ages in the UK.

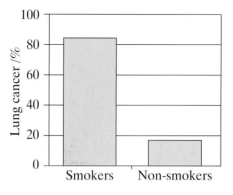

Figure 3 Proportion of lung cancer sufferers who are smokers or non-smokers

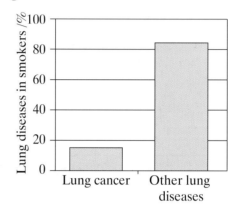

Figure 4 Proportion of types of lung disease in smokers who are suffering from lung disease

(i) Give **three** conclusions that can be drawn from the results of this study.

(ii) Suggest **two** reasons why conclusions made only on the basis of these data may not be reliable.

(5 marks)

AQA, 2003; AQA, 2002

5 (a) **Figure 5** shows the influence of different risk factors on the incidence of coronary heart disease in women. 7.5 mm Hg is equal to 1 kilopascal.

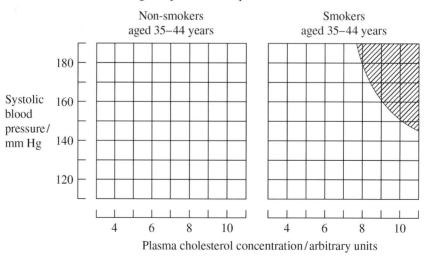

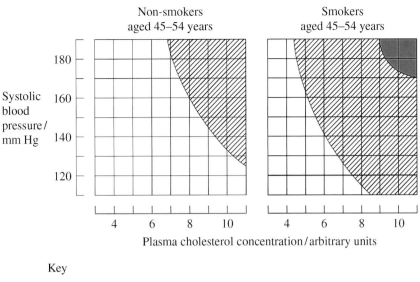

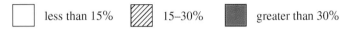

Key

Risk of developing coronary heart disease during next 10 years

less than 15%   15–30%   greater than 30%

Figure 5

(i) Use **Figure 5** to give the characteristics of women with the highest risk of developing coronary heart disease.

(ii) **Figure 5** only has limited value in predicting whether a particular woman might develop coronary heart disease. Explain why.   *(5 marks)*

(b) In an investigation, volunteers changed 5% of their energy intake from one food source to another. Their total energy intake remained constant. The effect of this change on their risk of developing coronary heart disease was measured. **Figure 6** shows the results of this investigation.

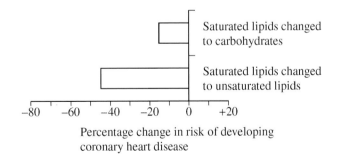

Percentage change in risk of developing
coronary heart disease

Figure 6

(i) Explain why it was necessary to ensure that the total energy intake remained constant.

(ii) Suggest an explanation for the results shown in **Figure 6**.   *(4 marks)*

AQA, 2007

Enzymes and the digestive system

2.1 Enzymes and digestion

Learning objectives:

▓ What are the structure and function of the major parts of the digestive system?

▓ How does the digestive system break down food both physically and chemically?

▓ What is the role of enzymes in digestion?

Specification reference: 3.1.2

AQA Examiner's tip

Digestion is the process in which **large** molecules are hydrolysed by enzymes into **small** molecules which can be absorbed and assimilated.

The human digestive system is made up of a long muscular tube and its associated glands. The glands produce **enzymes** that break down large molecules into small ones ready for absorption. The digestive system (Figure 1) therefore provides an interface with the environment because food substances enter the body through it.

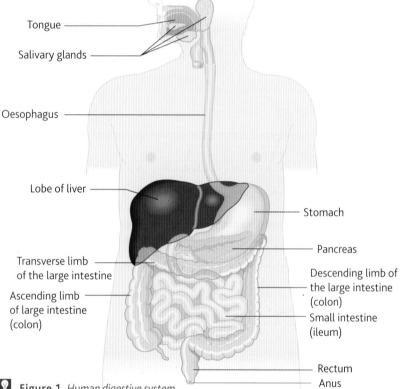

Tongue
Salivary glands
Oesophagus
Lobe of liver
Stomach
Pancreas
Transverse limb of the large intestine
Descending limb of the large intestine (colon)
Ascending limb of large intestine (colon)
Small intestine (ileum)
Rectum
Anus

💡 **Figure 1** *Human digestive system*

▓ Major parts of the digestive system

▓ The **oesophagus** carries food from the mouth to the stomach. It is therefore adapted for transport rather than for digestion or absorption. It is made up of a thick muscular wall.

▓ The **stomach** is a muscular sac with an inner layer that produces enzymes. Its role is to store and digest food, especially proteins. It has glands that produce enzymes which digest protein. Other glands in the stomach wall produce mucus. The mucus prevents the stomach being digested by its own enzymes.

▓ The **small intestine** is a long muscular tube. Food is further digested in the small intestine by enzymes that are produced by its walls and by glands that pour their secretions into it. The inner walls of the small intestine are folded into villi (Figure 2), which gives them a large surface area. The surface area of these villi is further increased

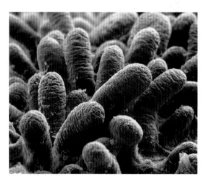

Figure 2 *False-colour scanning electron micrograph (SEM) of villi (brown) in the lining of the small intestine*

by millions of tiny projections, called microvilli, on the epithelial cells of each villus. This adapts the small intestine for its purpose of absorbing the products of digestion into the bloodstream.

- The **large intestine** absorbs water. Most of the water that is reabsorbed comes from the secretions of the many digestive glands. The food within the large intestine therefore becomes drier and thicker in consistency and forms faeces.
- The **rectum** is the final section of the intestines. The faeces are stored here before periodically being removed via the anus in a process called **egestion**.
- The **salivary glands** are situated near the mouth. They pass their secretions via a duct into the mouth. These secretions contain the enzyme amylase, which breaks down starch into maltose.
- The **pancreas** is a large gland situated below the stomach. It produces a secretion called pancreatic juice. This secretion contains proteases to digest proteins, lipase to digest lipids and amylase to digest starch.

What is digestion?

In humans, as with many organisms, digestion takes place in two stages:

1 physical breakdown,
2 chemical digestion.

Physical breakdown

If the food is large, it is broken down into smaller pieces by means of structures such as the teeth. This not only makes it possible to ingest the food but also provides a large surface area for chemical digestion. Food is churned by the muscles in the stomach wall and this also physically breaks it up.

Chemical digestion

Chemical digestion breaks down large, insoluble molecules into smaller, soluble ones. It is carried out by enzymes. All digestive enzymes function by **hydrolysis**. Hydrolysis is the splitting up of molecules by adding water to the chemical bonds that hold them together. The general term for such enzymes is **hydrolases**. Enzymes are specific (see Topic 2.7) and so it follows that more than one enzyme is needed to break down a large molecule. Usually one enzyme splits a large molecule into sections and these sections are then hydrolysed into smaller molecules by one or more additional enzymes. There are different types of digestive enzymes, three of which are particularly important:

- **Carbohydrases** break down carbohydrates, ultimately to monosaccharides.
- **Lipases** break down lipids (fats and oils) into glycerol and fatty acids.
- **Proteases** break down proteins, ultimately to amino acids.

Once the large food molecules have been hydrolysed into monosaccharides, glycerol, fatty acids and amino acids, they are absorbed by various means (see Topics 3.8 and 3.9) from the small intestine into the blood. They are carried to different parts of the body and are often built up again into large molecules, although these are not necessarily of the same type as the molecules from which they were derived. These molecules are incorporated into body tissues and/or used in processes within the body. This is called **assimilation**.

Hint

The contents of the intestines are **not** inside the body. Molecules and ions only truly enter the body when they cross the cells and cell-surface membranes of the epithelial lining of the intestines.

Hint

All organisms are made up of the same biological molecules and therefore our food consists almost entirely of other organisms, or parts of them. We must first break them down into molecules that are small enough to pass across cell-surface membranes.

AQA Examiner's tip

Make sure you distinguish between **absorption** (taking soluble molecules into the body) and **assimilation** (incorporating absorbed molecules into body tissues).

Summary questions

1 State **one** way in which the stomach is adapted:

   a to churn food

   b to prevent the enzymes it produces from digesting the surface of the stomach.

2 What is hydrolysis?

3 Which **two** structures produce amylase?

4 Suggest a reason why the stomach does not have villi or microvilli.

2.2 Carbohydrates – monosaccharides

Learning objectives:

- How are large molecules like carbohydrates constructed?

- What is the structure of a monosaccharide?

- How would you carry out the Benedict's test for reducing and non-reducing sugars?

Specification reference: 3.1.2

Hint

In biology certain prefixes are commonly used to indicate numbers. There are two systems, one based on Latin and the other on Greek. The Greek terms which are used when referring to chemicals are:

- mono – one
- di – two
- tri – three
- tetra – four
- penta – five
- hexa – six
- poly – many.

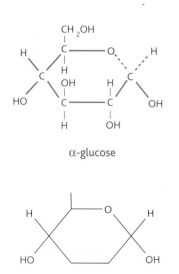

α-glucose

α-glucose (simplified)

Figure 1 *Molecular arrangement of α-glucose*

As the word suggests, carbohydrates are carbon molecules (carbo) combined with water (hydrate). Some carbohydrate molecules are small while others are large.

Life based on carbon

Carbon atoms have an unusual feature. They very readily form bonds with other carbon atoms. This allows a sequence of carbon atoms of various lengths to be built up. These form a 'backbone' along which other atoms can be attached. This permits an immense number of different types and sizes of molecule, all based on carbon. The variety of life that exists on Earth is a consequence of living organisms being based on the versatile carbon atom. As a result, carbon-containing molecules are known as organic molecules. In living organisms, there are relatively few other atoms that attach to carbon. Life is therefore based on a small number of chemical elements.

The making of large molecules

Many organic molecules, including carbohydrates, are made up of a chain of individual molecules. Each of the individual molecules that make up these chains is given the general name **monomer**. The carbon atoms of these monomers join to form longer chains. These longer chains of repeating monomer units are called **polymers**. How this happens is explained in Topic 2.3. Biological molecules like carbohydrates and proteins are often polymers. These polymers are based on a surprisingly small number of chemical elements. Most are made up of just four elements: carbon, hydrogen, oxygen and nitrogen.

In carbohydrates, the basic monomer unit is a sugar, otherwise known as a saccharide. A single monomer is therefore called a **monosaccharide**. A pair of monosaccharides can be combined to form a **disaccharide**. Monosaccharides can also be combined in much larger numbers to form **polysaccharides**.

Monosaccharides

Monosaccharides are sweet-tasting, soluble substances that have the general formula $(CH_2O)_n$, where n can be any number from 3 to 7.

Perhaps the best-known monosaccharide is glucose. This molecule is a hexose (6-carbon) sugar and has the formula $C_6H_{12}O_6$. However, the atoms of carbon, hydrogen and oxygen can be arranged in many different ways. Although the molecular arrangement is often shown as a straight chain for convenience, the atoms actually form a ring, Figure 1, which can take a number of forms.

💡 ⚠ Test for reducing sugars

All monosaccharides and some disaccharides (e.g. maltose) are reducing sugars. Reduction is a chemical reaction involving the gain of electrons. A reducing sugar is therefore a sugar that can donate electrons to (or reduce) another chemical, in this case Benedict's reagent. The test for a reducing sugar is therefore known as the Benedict's test. Benedict's reagent is an alkaline solution of copper(II) sulfate. When a reducing sugar is heated with Benedict's reagent it forms an insoluble red precipitate of copper(I) oxide. The test is carried out as follows:

▓ Add 2 cm³ of the food sample to be tested to a test tube. If the sample is not already in liquid form, first grind it up in water.

▓ Add an equal volume of Benedict's reagent.

▓ Heat the mixture in a gently boiling water bath for 5 minutes.

1 Food sample dissolved in water

2 Equal volume of Benedict's reagent added

3 Heated in water bath. If reducing sugar present solution turns orange–brown

Figure 2 *The Benedict's test*

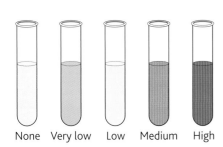

None   Very low   Low   Medium   High

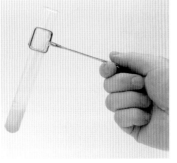

💡 **Figure 3** *Results of Benedict's test according to the concentration of reducing sugar present*

Figure 4 *If a reducing sugar is present an orange-brown colour is formed*

🔺 **Application**

Semi-quantitative nature of the Benedict's test

Table 1 shows the relationship between the concentration of reducing sugar and the colour of the solution and precipitate formed during the Benedict's test. The differences in colour mean that the Benedict's test is semi-quantitative, that is it can be used to estimate the approximate amount of reducing sugar in a sample.

The Benedict's test was carried out on five food samples. The results are shown in Table 2.

1 Place the letters in sequence of the increasing amount of reducing sugar in each sample.

2 Suggest a way, other than comparing colour changes, in which different concentrations of reducing sugar could be estimated.

3 Explain why it is not possible to distinguish between very concentrated samples, even though their concentrations are different.

AQA **Examiner's tip**

You only need to remember the simplified version of α-glucose. There are not many molecular structures that you have to remember for your AS examinations, but those that are required, like this, need to be learned.

AQA **Examiner's tip**

The Benedict's test may be a practical exercise but knowledge of the procedure is often tested in written examinations. Be certain to learn the **details**. 'Add Benedict's and look for a red colour' is not enough.

▓ **Summary questions**

1 Large molecules often contain carbon. Why is this?

2 What is the general name for a molecule that is made up of many similar repeating units?

3 Why does Benedict's reagent turn red when heated with a reducing sugar?

Table 1 *The Benedict's test*

Concentration of reducing sugar	Colour of solution and precipitate
None	Blue
Very low	Green
Low	Yellow
Medium	Brown
High	Red

Table 2

Sample	Colour of solution
A	Yellowish brown
B	Green
C	Red
D	Dark brown
E	Yellowish green

2.3 Carbohydrates – disaccharides and polysaccharides

Learning objectives:

- How are monosaccharides linked together to form disaccharides?

- How are α-glucose molecules linked to form starch?

- What is the test for non-reducing sugars?

- What is the test for starch?

Specification reference: 3.1.2

AQA Examiner's tip

Be clear about the difference between the terms 'condensation' and 'hydrolysis'. Both involve the use of water in reactions. However, condensation is the **giving out** of water in reactions while hydrolysis is the **taking in** of water to split molecules in reactions

Hint

To help you remember that condensation is **giving out** water, think of condensation on your bedroom window on cold mornings. This is water that you have **given out** in your breath.

Hint

Polysaccharides illustrate an important principle: that a few basic monomer units can be combined in a number of different ways to give a large range of different biological molecules.

In Topic 2.2, we saw that, in carbohydrates, the monomer unit is called a monosaccharide. Pairs of monosaccharides can be combined to form a **disaccharide**. Monosaccharides can also be combined in much larger numbers to form **polysaccharides**.

Disaccharides

When combined in pairs, monosaccharides form a disaccharide. For example:

- Glucose linked to glucose forms maltose.
- Glucose linked to fructose forms sucrose.
- Glucose linked to galactose forms lactose.

When the monosaccharides join, a molecule of water is removed and the reaction is therefore called a **condensation reaction**. The bond that is formed is called a **glycosidic bond**.

When water is added to a disaccharide under suitable conditions, it breaks the glycosidic bond releasing the constituent monosaccharides. This is called **hydrolysis** (addition of water that causes breakdown).

Figure 1a) illustrates the formation of a glycosidic bond by the removal of water (condensation reaction). Figure 1b) shows the breaking of the glycosidic bond by the addition of water (hydrolysis reaction).

a *Formation of glycosidic bond by removal of water (condensation reaction)*

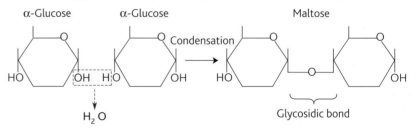

b *Breaking of glycosidic bond by addition of water (hydrolysis reaction)*

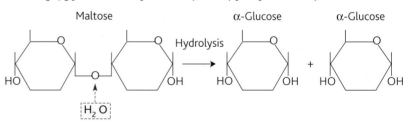

Figure 1 *Formation and breaking of a glycosidic bond by condensation and hydrolysis*

⚠ Test for non-reducing sugars

Some disaccharides (e.g. maltose) are reducing sugars. To detect these we use the Benedict's test, as described in Topic 2.2. Other disaccharides, such as sucrose, are known as non-reducing sugars because they do not change the colour of Benedict's reagent when they are heated with it. In order to detect a non-reducing sugar it must first be broken down into its monosaccharide components by hydrolysis. The process is carried out as follows:

- If the sample is not already in liquid form, it must first be ground up in water.
- Add $2\,cm^3$ of the food sample being tested to $2\,cm^3$ of Benedict's reagent in a test tube.
- Place the test tube in a gently boiling water bath for 5 minutes. If the Benedict's reagent does not change colour (the solution remains blue), then a reducing sugar is **not** present.
- Add another $2\,cm^3$ of the food sample to $2\,cm^3$ of dilute hydrochloric acid in a test tube and place the test tube in a gently boiling water bath for 5 minutes. The dilute hydrochloric acid will hydrolyse any disaccharide present into its constituent monosaccharides.
- Slowly add some sodium hydrogencarbonate solution to the test tube in order to neutralise the hydrochloric acid. (Benedict's reagent will not work in acidic conditions.) Test with pH paper to check that the solution is alkaline.
- Re-test the resulting solution by heating it with $2\,cm^3$ of Benedict's reagent in a gently boiling water bath for 5 minutes.
- If a non-reducing sugar was present in the original sample, the Benedict's reagent will now turn orange–brown. This is due to the reducing sugars that were produced from the hydrolysis of the non-reducing sugar.

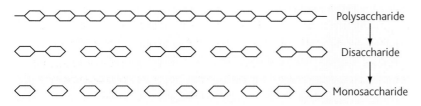

Figure 2 *The breakdown of a polysaccharide into disaccharides and monosaccharides*

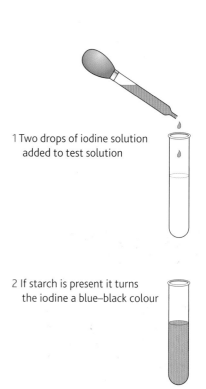

1 Two drops of iodine solution added to test solution

2 If starch is present it turns the iodine a blue–black colour

Figure 3 *Test for starch*

Polysaccharides

Polysaccharides are polymers, formed by combining together many monosaccharide molecules. The monosaccharides are joined by glycosidic bonds that were formed by **condensation reactions**. As polysaccharides are very large molecules, they are insoluble. This feature makes them suitable for storage. When they are hydrolysed, polysaccharides break down into disaccharides or monosaccharides (Figure 2). Some polysaccharides, such as cellulose (see Topic 10.3), are not used for storage but give structural support to plant cells.

Starch is a polysaccharide that is found in many parts of plants in the form of small granules or grains, e.g. starch grains in chloroplasts. It is formed by the linking of between 200 and 100 000 α-glucose molecules by glycosidic bonds in a series of condensation reactions. More details of starch and its functions are given in Topic 10.3.

Test for starch

Starch is easily detected by its ability to change the colour of the iodine in potassium iodide solution from yellow to blue–black (Figure 3). The test is carried out at room temperature. The test is carried out as follows:

- Place $2\,cm^3$ of the sample being tested into a test tube (or add two drops of the sample into a depression on a spotting tile).
- Add two drops of iodine solution and shake or stir.
- The presence of starch is indicated by a blue–black coloration.

Summary questions

1 Which one, or more, monomer units make up each of the following carbohydrates?
   a lactose
   b sucrose
   c starch

2 Glucose ($C_6H_{12}O_6$) combines with fructose ($C_6H_{12}O_6$) to form the disaccharide sucrose. From your knowledge of how disaccharides are formed, work out the formula of sucrose.

3 To hydrolyse a disaccharide it can be boiled with hydrochloric acid but if hydrolysis is carried out by an enzyme a much lower temperature (40°C) is used. Why is this?

2.4 Carbohydrate digestion

Learning objectives:

- How does salivary amylase act in the mouth to hydrolyse starch?

- How is starch digestion completed in the small intestine?

- How are disaccharides digested?

- What is lactose intolerance?

Specification reference: 3.1.2

Starch digestion

Enzymes are specific; therefore it usually takes more than one enzyme to completely break down a large molecule. Typically one enzyme breaks down the molecule into smaller sections and then other enzymes break down these sections further into their **monomers**. These enzymes are usually produced in different parts of the digestive system. This is because each enzyme works fastest at a different pH. It is obviously important that enzymes are produced in the correct sequence. This is true of starch digestion (Figure 1).

Firstly the enzyme **amylase** is produced in the mouth and the pancreas. Amylase **hydrolyses** the alternate glycosidic bonds of the starch molecule to produce the disaccharide maltose. The maltose is in turn hydrolysed into the monosaccharide α-glucose by a second enzyme, **maltase**. Maltase is produced by the lining of the intestine.

In humans the process takes place as follows.

- Food is taken into the mouth and chewed by the teeth. This breaks it into small pieces, giving it a large surface area.

- Saliva enters the mouth from the salivary glands and is thoroughly mixed with the food during chewing.

- Saliva contains **salivary amylase**. This starts hydrolysing any starch in the food to maltose. It also contains mineral salts that help to maintain the pH at around neutral. This is the optimum pH for salivary amylase to work.

- The food is swallowed and enters the stomach, where the conditions are acidic. This acid **denatures** the amylase and prevents further hydrolysis of the starch.

- After a time the food is passed into the small intestine, where it mixes with the secretion from the pancreas called pancreatic juice.

- The pancreatic juice contains **pancreatic amylase**. This continues the hydrolysis of any remaining starch to maltose. Alkaline salts are produced by both the pancreas and the intestinal wall to maintain the pH at around neutral so that the amylase can function.

- Muscles in the intestine wall push the food along the small intestine. Its epithelial lining produces the enzyme **maltase**. The maltase hydrolyses the maltose from starch breakdown into α-glucose.

Disaccharide digestion

In addition to the digestion of maltose described above, there are two other common disaccharides in the diet that need to be broken down.

Sucrose

In natural foods sucrose is usually contained within cells and these must be physically broken down by the teeth in order to release it. The sucrose passes through the stomach and into the small intestine, whose epithelial lining produces the enzyme **sucrase**. Sucrase hydrolyses the single glycosidic bond in the sucrose molecule to produce the two monosaccharides that make up sucrose, namely glucose and fructose.

> **Hint**
>
> We use the term **amylase** for convenience but in fact there are a number of different types of this enzyme. Secretions such as salivary amylase actually contain a number of different amylases that act on bonds at different points in the starch molecule.

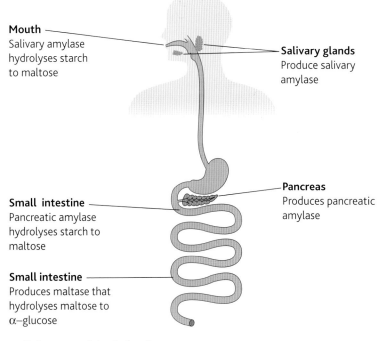

Mouth
Salivary amylase
hydrolyses starch
to maltose

Salivary glands
Produce salivary
amylase

Small intestine
Pancreatic amylase
hydrolyses starch to
maltose

Pancreas
Produces pancreatic
amylase

Small intestine
Produces maltase that
hydrolyses maltose to
α–glucose

Figure 1 *Summary of starch digestion*

Lactose

Lactose is the sugar found in milk, and hence in milk products, such as yoghurt and cheese. It is digested in the small intestine, whose epithelial lining produces the enzyme **lactase**. Lactase hydrolyses the glycosidic bond that links the glucose and galactose monosaccharides that make up lactose.

Lactose intolerance

We saw above that lactose is the sugar found in milk and that it is hydrolysed by the enzyme lactase. Milk is the only food of young babies and so they produce relatively large amounts of lactase. As milk forms a much smaller part of the diet in adults, the production of lactase naturally diminishes during childhood. However, in some people, this reduction is so great that they end up producing little or no lactase.

This was not too much of a problem for our ancestors because milk formed only a small part, if any part at all, of their diet. However, modern storage and distribution methods mean that adults now consume milk and milk products in greater quantities. As a result, some people do not produce sufficient lactase to digest all the lactose that they consume. When the undigested lactose reaches the large intestine, microorganisms break it down, giving rise to a large volume of gas. This may result in bloating, nausea, diarrhoea and cramps. Some people with this condition cannot consume milk or milk products at all, while others can drink only a little. Lactose intolerance is not life-threatening in adults and can be managed by avoiding foods containing lactose. The main difficulty is taking in sufficient calcium in the absence of milk. This can be resolved by taking in foods rich in calcium or by adding the enzyme lactase to milk before drinking it.

In young babies, whose sole food is milk, the condition is rare but more serious. These babies need to be fed special non-milk food that is rich in the calcium and vitamin D that natural milk provides.

Hint

Enzyme names usually end in '-ase' and start with the the first part of the name of their substrate (the substance on which they act). Hence maltase hydrolyses maltose, and sucrase hydrolyses sucrose.

Figure 2 *Milk and milk products*

Summary questions

1 What is the final product of starch digestion in the gut?

2 Name **three** enzymes produced by the epithelium of the small intestine.

3 In lactose-intolerant people, microorganisms in the large intestine convert the undigested lactose into gas, which accumulates and causes discomfort. By which process do microorganisms probably produce this gas?

4 Suggest a reason why the gas is unlikely to be carbon dioxide.

2.5 Proteins

Learning objectives:

- How are amino acids linked to form polypeptides – the primary structure of proteins?

- How are polypeptides arranged to form the secondary structure and then the tertiary structure of a protein?

- How is the quaternary structure of a protein formed?

- How are proteins identified?

Specification reference: 3.1.2

Proteins are very large molecules. The types of carbohydrates and lipids in all organisms are relatively few and they are very similar. However each organism has numerous proteins that differ from species to species. The shape of any one type of protein molecule differs from that of all other types of proteins. Proteins are the most important molecules to life. Indeed the word 'protein' is a Greek word meaning 'of first importance'. One group of proteins, enzymes, is involved in almost every living process. There is a vast range of different enzymes that between them perform a very diverse number of functions.

Structure of an amino acid

Amino acids are the basic **monomer** units which combine to make up a **polymer** called a polypeptide. Polypeptides can be combined to form proteins. About 100 amino acids have been identified, of which 20 occur naturally in proteins.

Every amino acid has a central carbon atom to which are attached four different chemical groups:

- amino group ($-NH_2$) – a basic group from which the amino part of the name amino acid is derived
- carboxyl group ($-COOH$) – an acidic group which gives the amino acid the acid part of its name
- hydrogen atom ($-H$)
- R group – a variety of different chemical groups. Each amino acid has a different R group.

The general structure of an amino acid is shown in Figure 1.

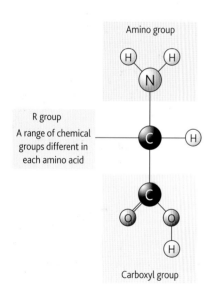

Amino group

R group
A range of chemical groups different in each amino acid

Carboxyl group

Figure 1 *The general structure of an amino acid*

The formation of a peptide bond

In the same way that monosaccharide monomers combine to form disaccharides (see Topic 2.3), so amino acid monomers can combine to form a dipeptide. The process is essentially the same: namely the removal of a water molecule in a **condensation** reaction. The water is made by combining an $-OH$ from the carboxyl group of one amino acid with an $-H$ from the amino group of another amino acid. The two amino acids then become linked by a new **peptide bond** between the carbon atom of one amino acid and the nitrogen atom of the other. The formation of a peptide bond is illustrated in Figure 2. In the same way as a glycosidic bond of a disaccharide can be broken by the addition of water (hydrolysis), so the peptide bond of a dipeptide can also be broken by hydrolysis to give its two constituent amino acids.

The primary structure of proteins – polypeptides

Through a series of condensation reactions, many amino acid monomers can be joined together in a process called **polymerisation**. The resulting chain of many hundreds of amino acids is called a **polypeptide**. The sequence of amino acids in a polypeptide chain forms the primary structure of any protein. As polypeptides have many (usually hundreds) of the 20

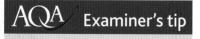

Examiner's tip

Distinguish between **condensation reactions** (molecules combine producing water) and **hydrolysis reactions** (molecules are split up by taking in water).

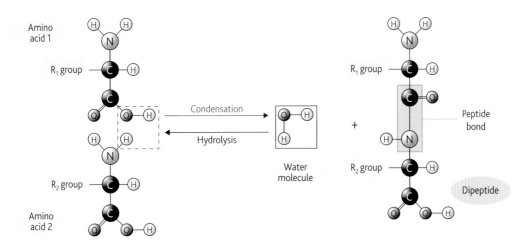

💡 **Figure 2** *The formation of a peptide bond*

naturally occurring amino acids joined in any sequence, it follows that there is an almost limitless number of possible combinations, and therefore types, of primary protein structure.

It is the primary structure of a protein that determines its ultimate shape and hence its function. A change in just a single amino acid in this primary sequence can lead to a change in the shape of the protein and may stop it carrying out its function. In other words, a protein's shape is very specific to its function. Change its shape and it will function less well, if at all.

A simple protein may consist of a single polypeptide chain. More commonly, however, a protein is made up of a number of polypeptide chains.

The secondary structure of proteins

The linked amino acids that make up a polypeptide possess both —NH and —C=O groups on either side of every peptide bond. The hydrogen of the —NH group has an overall positive charge while the O of the —C=O group has an overall negative charge. These two groups therefore readily form weak bonds, called **hydrogen bonds**. This causes the long polypeptide chain to be twisted into a 3-D shape, such as the coil known as an α-helix. Figure 3 illustrates the structure of an α-helix.

Tertiary structure of proteins

The α-helices of the secondary protein structure can be twisted and folded even more to give the complex, and often unique, 3-D structure of each protein (Figure 4). This is known as the tertiary structure. This structure is maintained by a number of different bonds, including:

▮ **disulfide bonds** – which are fairly strong and therefore not easily broken down.

▮ **ionic bonds** – which are formed between any carboxyl and amino groups that are not involved in forming peptide bonds. They are weaker than disulfide bonds and are easily broken by changes in pH.

▮ **hydrogen bonds** – which are numerous but easily broken.

It is the 3-D shape of a protein that is important when it comes to how it functions. It makes each protein distinctive and allows it to recognise, and be recognised by, other molecules. It can then interact with them in a very specific way.

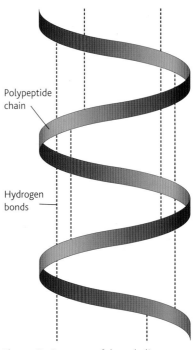

Polypeptide chain

Hydrogen bonds

Figure 3 *Structure of the α-helix*

▮ **Hint**

Remember that, although the 3-D structure is important to how a protein functions, it is the sequence of amino acids (primary structure) that determines the 3-D shape in the first place.

a The primary structure of a protein is the sequence of amino acids found in its polypeptide chains. This sequence determines its properties and shape. Following the elucidation of the amino acid sequence of the hormone insulin by Frederick Sanger in 1954, the primary structure of many other proteins is now known.

b The secondary structure is the shape which the polypeptide chain forms as a result of hydrogen bonding. This is most often a spiral known as the α-helix, although other configurations occur.

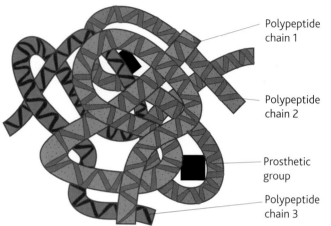

Polypeptide chain 1

Polypeptide chain 2

Prosthetic group

Polypeptide chain 3

c The tertiary structure is due to the bending and twisting of the polypeptide helix into a compact structure. All three types of bond, disulfide, ionic and hydrogen, contribute to the maintenance of the tertiary structure.

d The quaternary structure arises from the combination of a number of different polypeptide chains and associated non-protein (prosthetic) groups into a large, complex protein molecule.

Figure 4 *Structure of proteins*

▞▚ Quaternary structure of proteins

Large proteins often form complex molecules containing a number of individual polypeptide chains that are linked in various ways. There may also be non-protein (prosthetic) groups associated with the molecules (Figure 4d), such as the iron-containing haem group in haemoglobin. The structure and function of haemoglobin are considered in Topic 10.1.

🧪 Test for proteins

The most reliable protein test is the Biuret test, which detects peptide links. It is performed as follows.

▊ Place a sample of the solution to be tested in a test tube and add an equal volume of sodium hydroxide solution at room temperature.

▊ Add a few drops of very dilute (0.05%) copper(II) sulfate solution and mix gently.

▊ A purple coloration indicates the presence of peptide bonds and hence a protein. If no protein is present, the solution remains blue.

Summary questions

1 What type of bond links amino acids together?

2 What type of reaction is involved in linking amino acids together?

3 What **four** different components make up an amino acid?

Application

Protein shape and function

Proteins perform many different roles in living organisms. Their roles depend on their molecular shape, which can be of two basic types.

- Fibrous proteins, such as collagen, have structural functions.
- Globular proteins, such as enzymes and haemoglobin, carry out metabolic functions.

It is the very different structure and shape of each of these types of proteins that enables them to carry out their functions.

Fibrous proteins

Fibrous proteins form long chains which run parallel to one another. These chains are linked by cross-bridges and so form very stable molecules. One example is **collagen**. Its molecular structure is as follows:

- The primary structure is an unbranched polypeptide chain.
- In the secondary structure the polypeptide chain is very tightly wound.
- In the tertiary structure the chain is twisted into a second helix.
- Its quaternary structure is made up of three such polypeptide chains wound together in the same way as individual fibres are wound together in a rope.

Collagen is found in tendons. Tendons join muscles to bones. When a muscle contracts the bone is pulled in the direction of the contraction.

1   Explain why the quaternary structure of collagen makes it a suitable molecule for a tendon.

The individual collagen polypeptide chains in the fibres are held together by cross-linkages between amino acids of adjacent chains.

2   Suggest how the cross-linkages between the amino acids of polypeptide chains increase the strength and stability of a collagen fibre.

The points where one collagen molecule ends and the next begins are spread throughout the fibre rather than all being in the same position along it.

3   Explain why the arrangement of collagen molecules is necessary for the efficient functioning of a tendon.

Hint

Think of the polypeptide chain as a piece of string. In a fibrous protein many pieces of the string are twisted together into a rope, while in a globular protein the pieces of string, usually fewer, are rolled into a ball.

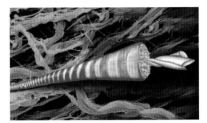

Figure 5 *Fine structure of the fibrous protein collagen*

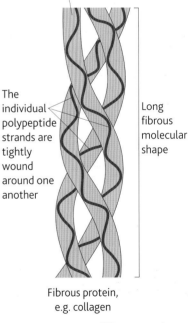

Each polypeptide forms a long, unfolded strand

The individual polypeptide strands are tightly wound around one another

Long fibrous molecular shape

Fibrous protein, e.g. collagen

Figure 6 *Structure of fibrous proteins*

2.6 Enzyme action

Learning objectives:

- How do enzymes speed up chemical reactions?

- How does the structure of enzyme molecules relate to their function?

- What is the lock and key model of enzyme action?

- What is the induced-fit model of enzyme action?

Specification reference: 3.1.2

Enzymes are globular proteins that act as catalysts. Catalysts alter the rate of a chemical reaction without undergoing permanent changes themselves. They can be reused repeatedly and are therefore effective in small amounts. Enzymes do not make reactions happen; they simply alter the speed of reactions that already occur, sometimes by a factor of many millions.

Enzymes as catalysts lowering activation energy

Let us consider a typical chemical reaction:

$$\text{sucrose} + \text{water} \longrightarrow \text{glucose} + \text{fructose}$$
$$\text{(substrates)} \qquad\qquad \text{(products)}$$

For reactions like this to take place naturally a number of conditions must be satisfied:

- The sucrose and water molecules must collide with sufficient energy to alter the arrangement of their atoms to form glucose and fructose.

- The energy of the products (glucose and fructose) must be less than that of the substrates (sucrose and water).

- An initial boost of energy is needed to kick start the reaction. The minimum amount of energy needed to activate the reaction in this way is called the **activation energy**.

There is an activation energy level, like an energy hill or barrier, which must initially be overcome before the reaction can proceed. Enzymes work by lowering this activation energy level (Figure 1). In this way enzymes allow reactions to take place at a lower temperature than normal. This enables some metabolic processes to occur rapidly at the human body temperature of 37 °C, which is relatively low in terms of chemical reactions. Without enzymes these reactions would proceed too slowly to sustain life as we know it.

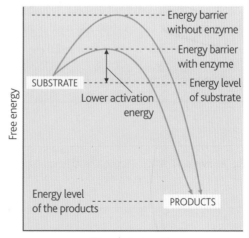

Figure 1 *How enzymes lower activation energy*

Enzyme structure

From Topic 2.5 you will be aware that enzymes, being globular proteins, have a specific 3-D shape that is the result of their sequence of amino acids (primary protein stucture). Although an enzyme molecule is large overall, only a small region of it is functional. This is known as the **active site** and is made up of a relatively small number of amino acids. The active site forms a small, hollow depression within the much larger enzyme molecule.

The molecule on which the enzyme acts is called the **substrate**. This fits neatly into this depression to form an **enzyme–substrate complex** (Figure 2). The substrate molecule is held within the active site by bonds that temporarily form between certain amino acids of the active site and groups on the substrate molecule.

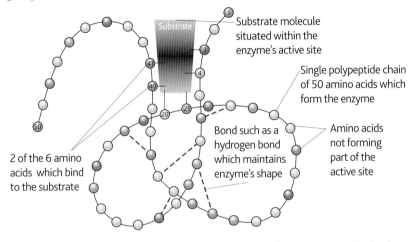

Figure 2 *Enzyme–substrate complex showing the six out of the 50 amino acids that form the active site*

⚠ 🔬 Lock and key model of enzyme action

Scientists often try to explain their observations by producing a representation of how something works. This is known as a scientific model. Examples include the physical models used to explain enzyme action. One model proposes that enzymes work in the same way as a key operates a lock; each key has a specific shape that fits and operates only a single lock. In a similar way, a substrate will only fit the active site of one particular enzyme. This model is supported by the observation that enzymes are specific in the reactions that they catalyse. The shape of the substrate (key) exactly fits the active site of the enzyme (lock). This is known as the **lock and key model** (Figure 3).

One limitation of this model is that the enzyme, like a lock, is considered to be a rigid structure. However, scientists had observed that other molecules could bind to enzymes at sites other than the active site. In doing so, they altered the activity of the enzyme (see Topic 2.7). This suggested that the enzyme's shape was being altered by the binding molecule. In other words, its structure was not rigid but flexible. In true scientific fashion this led to an alternative model being proposed, one that better fitted the current observations. This was the called the induced fit model.

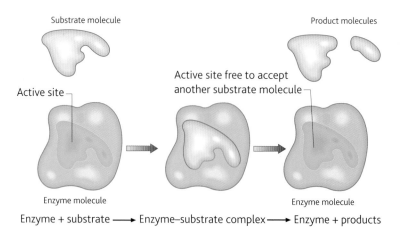

Substrate molecule

Product molecules

Active site free to accept
another substrate molecule

Active site

Enzyme molecule

Enzyme molecule

Enzyme + substrate ⟶ Enzyme–substrate complex ⟶ Enzyme + products

Figure 3 *Mechanism of enzyme action*

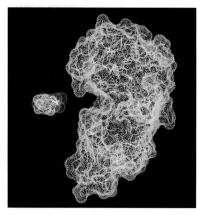

Figure 4 *Molecular computer graphics image of the enzyme ribonuclease A (right) and its substrate (left) approaching the enzyme's active site*

Induced fit model of enzyme action

Although the lock and key model describes the basic method of enzyme action, the induced fit model is more refined. Rather than being a rigid lock, it proposes that the enzyme actually changes its shape slightly to fit the profile of the substrate. In other words, the enzyme is flexible and can mould itself around the substrate in the way that a glove moulds itself to the shape of the hand. The enzyme has a certain general shape, just as a glove has, but this alters in the presence of the substrate. As it changes its shape, the enzyme puts a strain on the substrate molecule. This strain distorts a particular bond and consequently lowers the activation energy needed to break the bond.

The induced fit model is therefore a modified version of the lock and key model. It is a better explanation of the scientific observations because it explains:

▓ how other molecules can affect enzyme activity

▓ how the activation energy is lowered.

Any change in an enzyme's environment is likely to change its shape. The very act of colliding with its substrate is a change in its environment and so its shape changes – induced fit.

Summary questions

1 What is a catalyst?

2 Why are enzymes effective in tiny quantities?

3 Explain why changing one of the amino acids that make up the active site could prevent the enzyme from functioning.

4 Why might changing certain amino acids that are **not** part of the active site also prevent the enzyme from functioning?

2.7 Factors affecting enzyme action

Learning objectives:

- How is the rate of an enzyme-controlled reaction measured?

- How does temperature affect the rate of an enzyme-controlled reaction?

- How does pH affect the rate of an enzyme-controlled reaction?

- How does substrate concentration affect the rate of reaction?

Specification reference: 3.1.2

Before considering how pH and temperature affect enzymes, it is worth bearing in mind that, for an enzyme to work, it must:

- come into physical contact with its **substrate**,
- have an **active site** which fits the substrate.

Almost all factors that influence the rate at which an enzyme works do so by affecting one or both of the above. In order to investigate how enzymes are affected by various factors we need to be able to measure the rate of the reactions they catalyse.

Measuring enzyme-catalysed reactions

To measure the progress of an enzyme-catalysed reaction we usually measure its time-course, that is how long it takes for a particular event to run its course. The two 'events' most frequently measured are:

- the formation of the products of the reaction, e.g. the volume of oxygen produced when catalase acts on hydrogen peroxide (Figure 1),
- the disappearance of the substrate, e.g. the reduction in concentration of starch when it is acted upon by amylase (Figure 2).

Although the graphs in Figures 1 and 2 differ, the explanation for their shapes is the same:

- At first there is a lot of substrate (hydrogen peroxide or starch) but no product (water and oxygen, or maltose).
- It is very easy for substrate molecules to come into contact with the empty active sites on the enzyme molecules.
- All enzyme active sites are filled and the substrate is rapidly broken down into its products.
- The amount of substrate decreases as it is broken down, resulting in an increase in the amount of product.
- As the reaction proceeds, there is less and less substrate and more and more product.
- It becomes more difficult for the substrate molecules to come into contact with the enzyme molecules because there are fewer substrate molecules and also the product molecules may 'get in the way' of substrate molecules and prevent them reaching an active site.
- It therefore takes longer for the substrate molecules to be broken down by the enzyme and so its rate of disappearance slows, and consequently the rate of formation of product also slows. Both graphs 'tail off'.
- The rate of reaction continues to slow until there is so little substrate that any further decrease in its concentration cannot be measured.
- The graphs flatten out because all the substrate has been used up and so no new product can be produced.

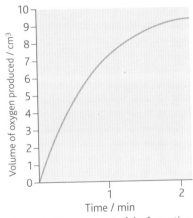

Figure 1 *Measurement of the formation of oxygen due to the action of catalase on hydrogen peroxide*

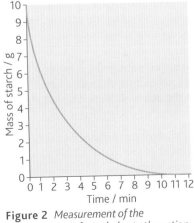

Figure 2 *Measurement of the disappearance of starch due to the action of amylase*

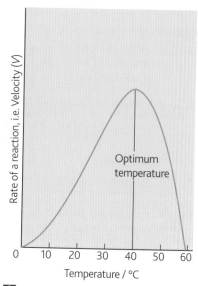

💡 **Figure 3** *Effect of temperature on the rate of an enzyme-controlled reaction*

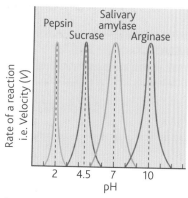

Figure 4 *Effect of pH on the rate of an enzyme-controlled reaction*

■ **Hint**

When considering how factors affect enzyme action, think 'shape change'.

AQA Examiner's tip

Enzymes are not alive and so cannot be 'killed'. Use the correct term: ...ured.

⊿ Effect of temperature on enzyme action

A rise in temperature increases the **kinetic energy** of molecules. As a result, the molecules move around more rapidly and collide with each other more often. In an enzyme-catalysed reaction, this means that the enzyme and substrate molecules come together more often in a given time, so that the rate of reaction increases.

Shown on a graph, this gives a rising curve. However, the temperature rise also begins to cause the hydrogen and other bonds in the enzyme molecule to break. This results in the enzyme, including its active site, changing shape. At first, the substrate fits less easily into this changed active site, slowing the rate of reaction. For many human enzymes this may begin at temperatures of around 45 °C.

At some point, usually around 60 °C, the enzyme is so disrupted that it stops working altogether. It is said to be denatured. **Denaturation** is a permanent change and, once it has occurred, the enzyme does not function again. Shown on a graph, the rate of this reaction follows a falling curve. The actual effect of temperature on the rate of an enzyme reaction is a combination of these two factors (Figure 3). The optimum working temperature differs from enzyme to enzyme. Some work fastest at around 10 °C, while others continue to work rapidly at 80 °C. Many enzymes in the human body have an optimum temperature of about 40 °C. Our body temperatures have, however, evolved to be 37 °C. The reasons for this are:

▦ Although higher body temperatures would increase the metabolic rate slightly, the advantages are offset by the additional energy (food) that would be needed to maintain the higher temperature.

▦ Other proteins, apart from enzymes, may be denatured at higher temperatures.

▦ At higher temperatures, any further rise in temperature, e.g. during illness, might denature the enzymes.

⊿ Effect of pH on enzyme action

The pH of a solution is a measure of its hydrogen ion concentration. Each enzyme has an optimum pH, that is a pH at which it works fastest (Figure 4). In a similar way to a rise in temperature, a change in pH reduces the effectiveness of an enzyme and may eventually cause it to stop working altogether, that is it becomes denatured.

The pH affects how an enzyme works in the following ways:

▦ A change in pH alters the charges on the amino acids that make up the active site of the enzyme. As a result, the substrate can no longer become attached to the active site and so the enzyme–substrate complex cannot be formed.

▦ A change in pH can cause the bonds that maintain the enzyme's tertiary structure to break. The enzyme therefore changes shape. These changes can alter the shape of the active site and the substrate may therefore no longer fit it. The enzyme has been denatured.

This is because even small changes in pH change the arrangement of the active site of an enzyme. The arrangement of the active site is partly determined by the hydrogen and ionic bonds between $—NH_2$ and —COOH groups of the polypeptides that make up the enzyme. The change in H^+ ions affects this bonding, causing the active site to change shape.

As pH fluctuations inside organisms are usually small, they are far more likely to reduce an enzyme's activity than to denature it.

Effects of substrate concentration on the rate of enzyme action

If the amount of enzyme is fixed at a constant level and substrate is slowly added, the rate of reaction increases in proportion to the amount of substrate that is added. This is because, at low substrate concentrations, the enzyme molecules have only a limited number of substrate molecules to collide with, and therefore the active sites of the enzymes are not working to full capacity. As more substrate is added, the active sites gradually become filled, until the point where all of them are working as fast as they can. The rate of reaction is at its maximum (V_{max}). After that, the addition of more substrate will have no effect on the rate of reaction. In other words, when there is an excess of substrate, the rate of reaction levels off. A summary of the effect of substrate concentration on the rate of enzyme action is given in Figure 6.

Hint

The active site and the substrate are not 'the same', any more than a key and a lock are the same – in some senses they are more like opposites. The correct term is **complementary**.

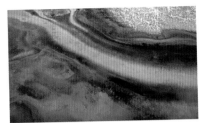

Figure 5 Enzymes in the algae in this hot spring remain functional at temperatures of 80 °C whereas in most organisms they are denatured at temperatures of 40 °C

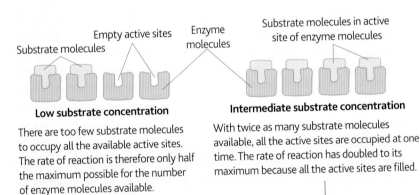
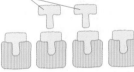

Low substrate concentration

There are too few substrate molecules to occupy all the available active sites. The rate of reaction is therefore only half the maximum possible for the number of enzyme molecules available.

Intermediate substrate concentration

With twice as many substrate molecules available, all the active sites are occupied at one time. The rate of reaction has doubled to its maximum because all the active sites are filled.

High substrate concentration

The addition of further substrate molecules has no effect as all active sites are already occupied at one time. There is no increase in the rate of reaction

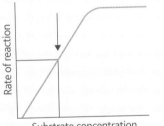
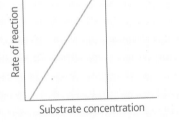
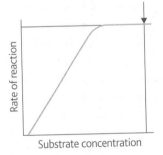

Figure 6 Effect of substrate concentration on the rate of an enzyme-controlled reaction

Summary questions

1 Explain why enzymes function less well at lower temperatures.

2 Explain how high temperatures may completely prevent enzymes from functioning.

3 Enzymes produced by microorganisms are responsible for spoiling food. Using this fact and your knowledge of enzymes, can you suggest a reason why the following procedures are carried out?

a Food is heated to a high temperature before being canned.

b Some foods, such as onions, are preserved in vinegar.

2.8 Enzyme inhibition

Learning objectives:

■ How do competitive inhibitors and non-competitive inhibitors affect the active site?

■ What is enzyme inhibition?

Specification reference: 3.1.2

Enzyme inhibitors are substances that directly or indirectly interfere with the functioning of the active site of an enzyme and so reduce its activity. Sometimes the inhibitor binds itself so strongly to the active site that it cannot be removed and so permanently prevents the enzyme functioning. Most inhibitors only make temporary attachments to the active site. These are called reversible inhibitors and are of two types:

■ competitive inhibitors – which bind to the active site of the enzyme

■ non-competitive inhibitors – which bind to the enzyme at a position other than the active site.

Competitive inhibitors

Competitive inhibitors have a molecular shape similar to that of the substrate. This allows them to occupy the active site of an enzyme. They therefore compete with the substrate for the available active sites (Figure 1). It is the difference between the concentration of the inhibitor and the concentration of the substrate that determines the effect that this has on enzyme activity. If the substrate concentration is increased, the effect of the inhibitor is reduced. The inhibitor is not permanently bound to the active site and so, when it leaves, another molecule can take its place. This could be a substrate or inhibitor molecule, depending on how much of each type is present. Sooner or later, all the substrate molecules will occupy an active site, but the greater the concentration of inhibitor, the longer this will take. An example of competitive inhibition occurs with an important respiratory enzyme that acts on succinic acid. Another compound, called malonic acid, can inhibit the enzyme because it has a very similar molecular shape to succinic acid. It therefore easily combines with the enzyme and blocks succinic acid from combining with the enzyme's active site.

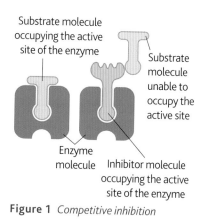

Figure 1 *Competitive inhibition*

Non-competitive inhibitors

Non-competitive inhibitors attach themselves to the enzyme at a site which is not the active site. Upon attaching to the enzyme, the inhibitor alters the

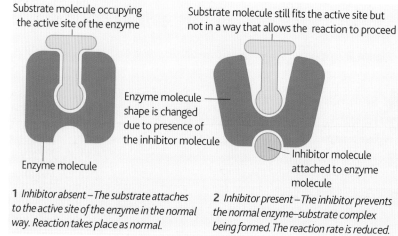

1 *Inhibitor absent – The substrate attaches to the active site of the enzyme in the normal way. Reaction takes place as normal.*

2 *Inhibitor present – The inhibitor prevents the normal enzyme–substrate complex being formed. The reaction rate is reduced.*

Figure 2 *Non-competitive inhibition*

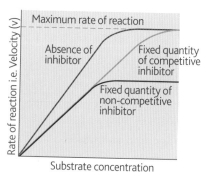

Figure 3 *Comparison of competitive and non-competitive inhibition on the rate of -controlled reaction at different concentrations*

shape of the enzyme's active site in such a way that substrate molecules can no longer occupy it, and so the enzyme cannot function (Figure 2). As the substrate and the inhibitor are not competing for the same site, an increase in substrate concentration does not decrease the effect of the inhibitor (Figure 3).

Application

Control of metabolic pathways

A metabolic pathway is a series of reactions in which each step is catalysed by an enzyme. In the tiny space inside a single cell, there are many hundreds of different metabolic pathways. The pathways are not at all haphazard, but highly structured. The enzymes that control a pathway are often attached to the inner membrane of a cell organelle in a very precise sequence. Inside each organelle optimum conditions for the functioning of particular enzymes may be provided. To keep a steady level of a particular chemical in a cell, the same chemical often acts as an inhibitor of an enzyme at the start of a reaction.

Let us look at the example illustrated in Figure 4. The end product inhibits enzyme A. If for some reason the quantity of end product increases above normal, then there will be greater inhibition of enzyme A. As a result, less end product will be produced and its level will return to normal. If the quantity of the end product falls below normal there will be less of it to inhibit enzyme A. Consequently, more end product will be produced and, again, its level will return to normal. In this way, the level of any chemical can be maintained at a relatively constant level. This is known as **end-product inhibition**. This type of inhibition is usually non-competitive.

Figure 4 *Inhibition*

Summary questions

1 Distinguish between a competitive and a non-competitve inhibitor

2 An enzyme-controlled reaction is inhibited by substance X. Suggest a simple way in which you could tell whether substance X is acting as a competitive or a non-competitive inhibitor.

---

1 Different conditions affect how enzymes work. Name one that might vary between one organelle and another.

2 Suggest why enzymes are attached to the inner membrane of an organelle 'in a very precise sequence'.

3 If an end product inhibits enzyme B rather than enzyme A, what would be:

   a The initial effect on the quantity of intermediate 1?

   b The overall longer term effect on the level of the end product?

4 What is the advantage of end-product inhibition being non-competitive rather than competitive? Explain your answer in terms of how the two types of inhibition take place.

1 **Figure 1** represents an enzyme molecule and three other molecules that could combine with it.

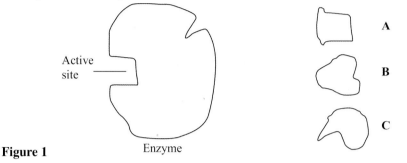

Figure 1

(a) Which molecule is the substrate for the enzyme? Give a reason for your answer. *(1 mark)*

(b) Use the diagram to explain how a **non-competitive** inhibitor would decrease the rate of the reaction catalysed by this enzyme. *(3 marks)*

(c) Lysozyme is an enzyme. A molecule of lysozyme is made up of 129 amino acid molecules joined together. In the formation of its active site, the two amino acids that are at positions 35 and 52 in the amino acid sequence need to be close together.

  (i) Name the bonds that join amino acids in the primary structure.

  (ii) Suggest how the amino acids at positions 35 and 52 are held close together to form the active site. *(3 marks)*

AQA, 2006

2 A student carried out an investigation into the mass of product formed in an enzyme-controlled reaction at three different temperatures. Only the temperature was different for each experiment. The results are shown in **Figure 2**.

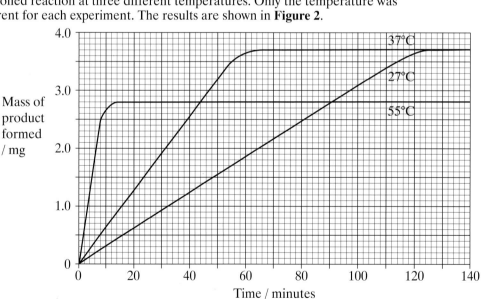

Figure 2

(a) Use your knowledge of enzymes to explain:

  (i) why the initial rate of reaction was highest at 55 °C;

  (ii) the shape of the curve for 55 °C after 20 minutes. *(5 marks)*

(b) Explain why the curves for 27 °C and 37 °C level out at the same value. *(2 marks)*

AQA, 2006

3 (a) Many reactions take place in living cells at temperatures far lower than those required for the same reactions in a laboratory.

Explain how enzymes enable this to happen. *(3 marks)*

(b) **Figure 3** shows the results of tests to determine the optimum temperature for the activity of this amylase.

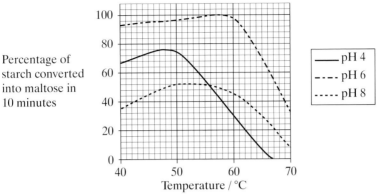

Figure 3

(i) Copy and complete the table with the optimum temperature for the activity of amylase at each pH value.

(ii) Describe and explain the effect of temperature on the rate of reaction of this enzyme at pH 4.

	pH		
	4	**6**	**8**
Optimum temperature / °C			

(7 marks)

AQA, 2004

4 In an investigation, the rate at which phenol was broken down by the enzyme phenol oxidase was measured in solutions with different concentrations of phenol. The experiment was then repeated with a non-competitive inhibitor added to the phenol solutions. **Figure 4** shows the results.

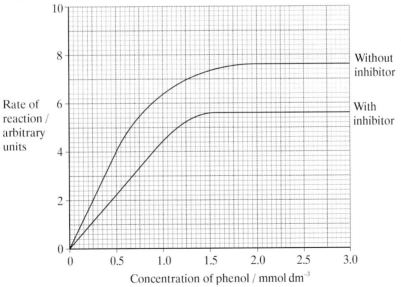

Figure 4

(a) Explain why an increase in concentration of phenol solution from 2.0 to 2.5 mmol dm^{-3} has no effect on the rate of the reaction without the inhibitor. *(2 marks)*

(b) Explain the effect of the non-competitive inhibitor. *(2 marks)*

(c) Calculate the percentage decrease in the maximum rate of the reaction when the inhibitor was added. Show your working. *(2 marks)*

(d) Make a copy of the graph and draw a curve on it to show the results expected if a competitive inhibitor instead of a non-competitive inhibitor had been used. *(1 mark)*

AQA, 2005

3 Cells and movement in and out of them

3.1 Investigating the structure of cells

The cell is the basic unit of life. However, with a few exceptions, cells are not visible to the naked eye and their structure is only apparent when seen under a microscope.

Microscopy

Microscopes are instruments that magnify the image of an object. A simple convex glass lens can act as a magnifying glass but such lenses work more effectively if they are in a compound light microscope. The relatively long wavelength of light rays means that a light microscope can only distinguish between two objects if they are $0.2\,\mu m$, or further, apart. This limitation can be overcome by using beams of **electrons** rather than beams of light. With their shorter wavelengths, the beam of electrons in the electron microscope can distinguish two objects as close together as $0.1\,nm$.

Magnification

The material that is put under a microscope is referred to as the **object**. The appearance of this material when viewed under the microscope is referred to as the **image**.

The magnification of an object is how many times bigger the image is when compared to the object.

$$\text{magnification} = \frac{\text{size of image}}{\text{size of object}}$$

In practice, it is more likely that you will be asked to calculate the size of an object when you know the size of the image and the magnification. In this case:

$$\text{size of object} = \frac{\text{size of image}}{\text{magnification}}$$

The important thing to remember when calculating the magnification is to ensure that the units of length (Table 1) are the same for both the object and the image.

Imagine, for example, that you know an object is actually $100\,nm$ in length and you are asked how much it is magnified in a photograph. You should first measure the object in the photograph. Suppose it is $10\,mm$ long. The magnification is:

$$\frac{\text{size of image}}{\text{size of object}} = \frac{10\,mm}{100\,nm}$$

Now convert the measurements to the same units – normally the smallest – which in this case is nanometres. There are $10\,000\,000$ nanometres in 10 millimetres and therefore the magnification is:

$$\frac{\text{size of image}}{\text{size of object}} = \frac{10\,000\,000\,nm}{100\,nm} = \frac{100\,000}{1} = \times 100\,000 \text{ times}$$

Table 1 *Units of length*

Unit	Symbol	Equivalent in metres
kilometre	km	10^3
metre	m	1
millimetre	mm	10^{-3}
micrometre	µm	10^{-6}
nanometre	nm	10^{-9}

AQA Examiner's tip

Careless language costs marks. Candidates sometimes state that optical microscopes have a longer wavelength than electron microscopes. What they mean to say is that **light** has a longer wavelength than a beam of electrons.

Resolution

The resolution, or resolving power, of a microscope is the minimum distance apart that two objects can be in order for them to appear as separate items. Whatever the type of microscope, the resolving power depends on the wavelength or form of radiation used. In a light microscope it is about 0.2 μm. This means that any two objects which are 0.2 μm or more apart will be seen separately, but any objects closer than 0.2 μm will appear as a single item. In other words, greater resolution means greater clarity, that is the image produced is clearer and more precise.

Increasing the magnification will increase the size of an image, but does not always increase the resolution. Every microscope has a limit of resolution. Up to this point increasing the magnification will reveal more detail but beyond this point increasing the magnification will not do this. The object, while appearing larger, will just be more blurred.

⬛ Cell fractionation

In order to study the structure and function of the various organelles that make up cells, it is necessary to obtain large numbers of isolated organelles.

Cell fractionation is the process where cells are broken up and the different organelles they contain are separated out.

Before cell fractionation can begin, the tissue is placed in a cold, **isotonic**, buffered solution for the following reasons. The solution is:

▒ cold – to reduce enzyme activity that might break down the organelles,
▒ isotonic – to prevent organelles bursting or shrinking as a result of osmotic gain or loss of water. An isotonic solution is one that has the same water potential as the original tissue,
▒ buffered – to maintain a constant pH.

There are two stages to cell fractionation:

Homogenation

Cells are broken up by a homogeniser (blender). This releases the organelles from the cell. The resultant fluid, known as homogenate, is then filtered to remove any complete cells and large pieces of debris.

Ultracentrifugation

Ultracentrifugation is the process by which the fragments in the filtered homogenate are separated in a machine called an ultracentrifuge. This spins tubes of homogenate at very high speed in order to create a centrifugal force. For animal cells, the process is as follows:

▒ The tube of filtrate is placed in the ultracentrifuge and spun at a slow speed.
▒ The heaviest organelles, the nuclei, are forced to the bottom of the tube, where they form a thin sediment or pellet.
▒ The fluid at the top of the tube (supernatant) is removed, leaving just the sediment of nuclei.
▒ The supernatant is transferred to another tube and spun in the ultracentrifuge at a faster speed than before.
▒ The next heaviest organelles, the mitochondria, are forced to the bottom of the tube.
▒ The process is continued in this way so that, at each increase in speed, the next heaviest organelle is sedimented and separated out (see Table 2 on the next page).

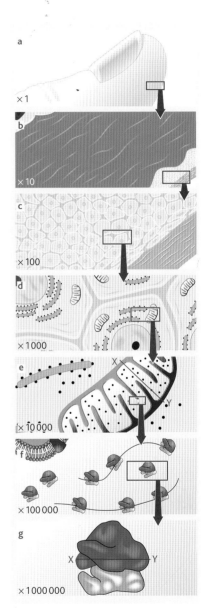

Figure 1 *The effect of progressive magnification of a portion of human skin*

Table 2 *Separation of organelles by ultracentrifugation*

Organelles to be separated out	Speed of centrifugation /gravitational force	Duration of centrifugation/min
Nuclei	1000	10
Mitochondria	3500	10
Lysosomes	16500	20
Ribosomes	100000	60

A summary of cell fractionation is given in Figure 2.

Summary questions

1 Distinguish between magnification and resolution.

2 An organelle that is 5 μm in diameter appears under a microscope to have a diameter of 1 mm. How many times has the organelle been magnified?

3 A cell organelle called a ribosome is typically 25 nm in diameter. If viewed under an electron microscope that magnifies it ×400 000, what would the diameter of the ribosome appear to be in millimetres?

4 At a magnification of ×12 000 a structure appears to be 6 mm long. What is its actual length?

5 Chloroplasts have a greater mass than mitochondria but a smaller mass than nuclei. Starting with a sample of plant cells, describe briefly how you would obtain a sample rich in chloroplasts. Use Table 2 to help you.

6 Using the magnifications given in Figure 1, calculate the actual size of the following organelles as measured along the line labelled X–Y. In your answer, use the most appropriate units from Table 1.

  a The organelle in box E

  b The organelle in box G

7 Using Table 2 and Figure 2 suggest which organelle or organelles (there may be more than one) would most likely be found in each of the following:

  a sediment 1

  b sediment 3

  c supernatant 1

  d supernatant 3.

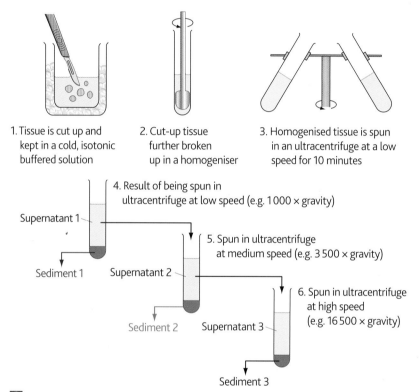

1. Tissue is cut up and kept in a cold, isotonic buffered solution

2. Cut-up tissue further broken up in a homogeniser

3. Homogenised tissue is spun in an ultracentrifuge at a low speed for 10 minutes

4. Result of being spun in ultracentrifuge at low speed (e.g. 1000 × gravity)

Supernatant 1

Sediment 1

5. Spun in ultracentrifuge at medium speed (e.g. 3500 × gravity)

Supernatant 2

Sediment 2

Supernatant 3

6. Spun in ultracentrifuge at high speed (e.g. 16500 × gravity)

Sediment 3

Figure 2 *Summary of cell fractionation*

The techniques of cell fractionation and ultracentrifugation enabled considerable advances in biological knowledge. They allowed a detailed study of the structure and function of organelles.

Figure 3 *An ultracentrifuge used to separate the various components of cell homogenate*

3.2 The electron microscope

Learning objectives:

▓ How do electron microscopes work?

▓ What are the differences between a transmission electron microscope and a scanning electron microscope?

▓ What are the limitations of the transmission and the scanning electron microscopes?

Specification reference: 3.1.3

Light microscopes have poor resolution as a result of the relatively long wavelength of light. In the 1930s, however, a microscope was developed that used a beam of electrons instead of light. This is called an electron microscope and it has two main advantages:

▓ The electron beam has a very short wavelength and the microscope can therefore resolve objects well – it has a high resolving power.

▓ As electrons are negatively charged the beam can be focused using electromagnets (Figure 2).

The best modern electron microscopes can resolve objects that are just 0.1 nm apart – 2000 times better than a light microscope. Because electrons are absorbed by the molecules in air, a near-vacuum has to be created within the chamber of an electron microscope in order for it to work effectively.

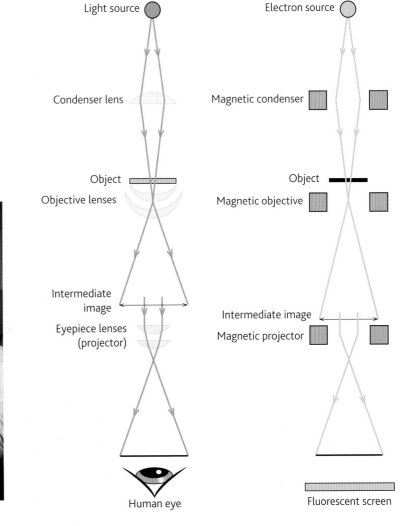

Figure 1 *Scientist looking at a sample using a transmission electron microscope (TEM)*

Figure 2 *Comparison of radiation pathways in light and electron microscopes*

There are two types of electron microscope:

- the transmission electron microscope (TEM)
- the scanning electron microscope (SEM).

The transmission electron microscope

The transmission electron microscope (TEM) consists of an electron gun that produces a beam of electrons that is focused onto the specimen by a condenser electromagnet. In a TEM, the beam passes through a thin section of the specimen. Parts of this specimen absorb electrons and therefore appear dark. Other parts of the specimen allow the electrons to pass through and so appear bright. An image is produced on a screen and this can be photographed to give a **photomicrograph**. The resolving power of a TEM is 0.1 nm, although problems with specimen preparation mean that this cannot always be achieved. The main limitations of the TEM are:

- The whole system must be in a vacuum and therefore living specimens cannot be observed.
- A complex 'staining' process is required and even then the image is only in black and white.
- The specimen must be extremely thin.
- The image may contain artefacts. Artefacts are things that result from the way the specimen is prepared. Artefacts may appear on the finished photomicrograph but are not part of the natural specimen. It is therefore not always easy to be sure that what we see on a photomicrograph really exists in that form.

In the TEM the specimens must be extremely thin to allow electrons to penetrate. The result is therefore a flat, 2-D image. We can partly get over this by taking a series of sections through a specimen. We can then build up a 3-D image of the specimen by looking at the series of photomicrographs produced. However, this is a slow and complicated process. One way in which this problem has been overcome is the development of the scanning electron microscope (SEM).

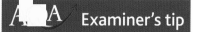

Examiner's tip

Remember that the greater resolving power of an electron microscope compared to a light microscope is due to the electron beam having a shorter wavelength than light.

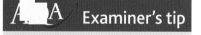

Examiner's tip

Look at photographs taken with an SEM and a TEM and make sure you can identify cell organelles. Don't just rely on diagrams.

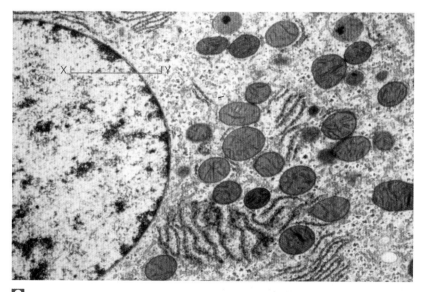

Figure 3 *Part of an animal cell seen under a transmission electron microscope (TEM)*

The scanning electron microscope

All the limitations of the TEM also apply to the scanning electron microscope (SEM), except that specimens need not be extremely thin as electrons do not penetrate. Basically similar to a TEM, the SEM directs a beam of electrons on to the surface of the specimen from above, rather than penetrating it from below. The beam is then passed back and forth across a portion of the specimen in a regular pattern. The electrons are scattered by the specimen and the pattern of this scattering depends on the contours of the specimen surface. We can build up a 3-D image by computer analysis of the pattern of scattered electrons and secondary electrons produced. The basic SEM has a lower resolving power than a TEM, around 20 nm, but is still ten times better than a light microscope.

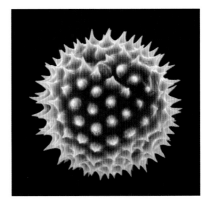

Figure 4 *False-colour scanning electron micrograph (SEM) of a pollen grain from a marigold plant*

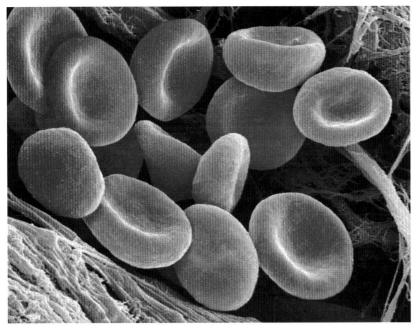

Figure 5 *False-colour scanning electron micrograph (SEM) of human red blood cells*

Summary questions

1 Why is the electron microscope able to resolve objects better than the light microscope?

2 Why do specimens have to be kept in a near-vacuum in order to be viewed effectively using an electron microscope?

3 Which of the biological structures in the following list:
plant cell (100 μm)   DNA molecule (2 nm)   virus (100 nm)
actin molecule (3.5 nm)   a bacterium (1 μm)
can, in theory, be resolved by the following?

  a a light microscope

  b a transmission electron microscope

  c a scanning electron microscope

4 In practice, the theoretical resolving power of an electron microscope cannot always be achieved. Why not?

5 In the photomicrograph of the animal cell in Figure 3, the line X–Y represents a length of 5 μm. What is the magnification of this photomicrograph?

3.3 Structure of an epithelial cell

▓ Hint

When you look at a group of animal cells, such as epithelial cells, under a light microscope you cannot see the cell-surface membrane because it is too small to be observed. What you actually see is the boundary between cells.

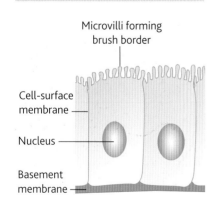

Figure 1 *Two adjacent epithelial cells from the lining of the small intestine*

Each cell can be regarded as a metabolic compartment, a separate place where the chemical processes of that cell occur. Cells are often designed to perform a particular function. Depending on that function, each cell type has an internal structure that suits it for its job. This is known as the **ultrastructure** of the cell. Epithelial cells are **eukaryotic** cells. Eukaryotic cells have a distinct nucleus and possess membrane-bounded organelles. They differ from **prokaryotic** cells, such as bacteria. More details of these differences are given in Topic 3.10. The function of epithelial cells is to absorb and secrete. Figure 1 shows the structure of an epithelial cell from the small intestine as viewed under a light microscope. Using an electron microscope, we can see the structure of organelles within this type of cell. The most important of these organelles are described below, with the exception of the cell-surface membrane, which is covered in Topic 3.5.

▓ The nucleus

The nucleus (Figure 3) is the most prominent feature of a eukaryotic cell, such as an epithelial cell. The nucleus contains the organism's hereditary material and controls the cell's activities. Usually spherical and between 10 and 20 μm in diameter, the nucleus has a number of parts.

▓ The **nuclear envelope** is a double membrane that surrounds the nucleus. Its outer membrane is continuous with the endoplasmic reticulum of the cell and often has ribosomes on its surface. It controls the entry and exit of materials in and out of the nucleus and contains the reactions taking place within it.

▓ **Nuclear pores** allow the passage of large molecules, such as messenger RNA, out of the nucleus. There are typically around 3000 pores in each nucleus, each 40–100 nm in diameter.

▓ **Nucleoplasm** is the granular, jelly-like material that makes up the bulk of the nucleus.

▓ **Chromatin** is the DNA found within the nucleoplasm. This is the diffuse form that chromosomes take up when the cell is not dividing.

▓ The **nucleolus** is a small spherical body within the nucleoplasm. It manufactures ribosomal RNA and assembles the ribosomes.

The functions of the nucleus are to:

▓ act as the control centre of the cell through the production of mRNA and hence protein synthesis

▓ retain the genetic material of the cell in the form of DNA or chromosomes

▓ manufacture ribosomal RNA and ribosomes.

▓ The mitochondrion

Mitochondria (Figures 4 and 5) are rod-shaped and 1–10 μm in length. They are made up of the following structures:

▓ A **double membrane** surrounds the organelle, the outer one controlling the entry and exit of material. The inner membrane is folded to form extensions known as cristae.

- **Cristae** are shelf-like extensions of the inner membrane, some of which extend across the whole width of the mitochondrion. These provide a large surface area for the attachment of enzymes involved in respiration.

- The **matrix** makes up the remainder of the mitochondrion. It is a semi-rigid material containing protein, lipids and traces of DNA that allows the mitochondria to control the production of their own proteins. The enzymes involved in respiration are found in the matrix.

Mitochondria are the sites of certain stages of respiration (the Krebs cycle and the oxidative phosphorylation pathway). They are therefore responsible for the production of the energy-carrier molecule, **ATP**, from carbohydrates. Because of this, the number and size of the mitochondria, and the number of their cristae, all increase in cells that have a high level of metabolic activity and therefore need a plentiful supply of ATP. Examples of metabolically active cells include muscle and epithelial cells. Epithelial cells use a lot of energy in the process of absorbing substances from the intestines by **active transport** (see Topic 3.8).

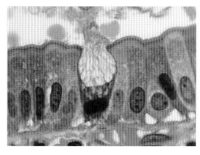

Figure 2 *Epithelial cells of the small intestine as seen under a light microscope*

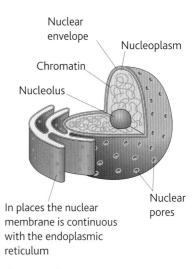

Figure 3 *The nucleus*

In places the nuclear membrane is continuous with the endoplasmic reticulum

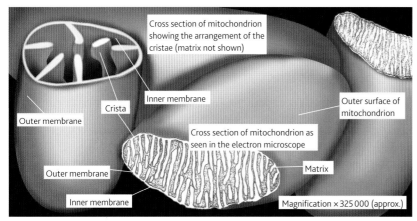

Figure 4 *Mitochondria*

Endoplasmic reticulum

The endoplasmic reticulum (ER) is an elaborate, three-dimensional system of sheet-like membranes, spreading through the cytoplasm of the cells. It is continuous with the outer nuclear membrane. The membranes enclose flattened sacs called cisternae (see Figure 6 on the next page). There are two types of ER:

- **Rough endoplasmic reticulum (RER)** has ribosomes present on the outer surfaces of the membranes. Its functions are to:
  a) provide a large surface area for the synthesis of proteins and glycoproteins,
  b) provide a pathway for the transport of materials, especially proteins, throughout the cell.

- **Smooth endoplasmic reticulum (SER)** lacks ribosomes on its surface and is often more tubular in appearance. Its functions are to:
  a) synthesise, store and transport lipids,
  b) synthesise, store and transport carbohydrates.

It follows that cells that need to manufacture and store large quantities of carbohydrates, proteins and lipids have a very extensive ER. Such cells include liver and secretory cells, e.g. the epithelial cells that line the intestines.

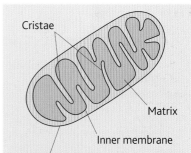
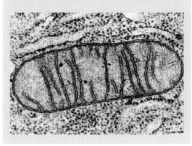

Figure 5 *The basic structure of a mitochondrion (top); false-colour transmission electron micrograph (TEM) of a mitochondrion (bottom)*

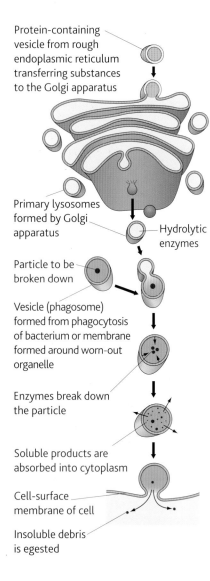

Protein-containing vesicle from rough endoplasmic reticulum transferring substances to the Golgi apparatus

Primary lysosomes formed by Golgi apparatus

Hydrolytic enzymes

Particle to be broken down

Vesicle (phagosome) formed from phagocytosis of bacterium or membrane formed around worn-out organelle

Enzymes break down the particle

Soluble products are absorbed into cytoplasm

Cell-surface membrane of cell

Insoluble debris is egested

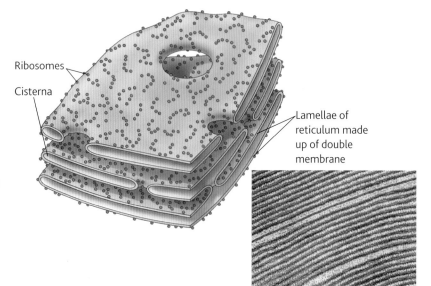

Ribosomes

Cisterna

Lamellae of reticulum made up of double membrane

Figure 6 *Structure of rough endoplasmic reticulum (RER) (above); false-colour transmission electron micrograph (TEM) of a section through rough endoplasmic reticulum (RER; red) (right)*

▌ Golgi apparatus

The Golgi apparatus occurs in almost all eukaryotic cells and is similar to the SER in structure except that it is more compact. It consists of a stack of membranes that make up flattened sacs, or **cisternae,** with small rounded hollow structures called vesicles. The proteins and lipids produced by the ER are passed through the Golgi apparatus in strict sequence. The Golgi modifies these proteins often adding non-protein components, such as carbohydrate, to them. It also 'labels' them, allowing them to be accurately sorted and sent to their correct destinations. Once sorted, the modified proteins and lipids are transported in vesicles which are regularly pinched off from the ends of the Golgi cisternae (Figure 7). These vesicles move to the cell surface, where they fuse with the membrane and release their contents to the outside.

The functions of the Golgi apparatus are to:

▌ add carbohydrate to proteins to form glycoproteins,

▌ produce secretory enzymes, such as those secreted by the pancreas,

▌ secrete carbohydrates, such as those used in making cell walls in plants,

▌ transport, modify and store lipids,

▌ form lysosomes.

Therefore the Golgi apparatus is especially well developed in secretory cells, such as the epithelial cells that line the intestines.

▌ Lysosomes

Lysosomes are formed when the vesicles produced by the Golgi apparatus contain enzymes such as proteases and lipases. As many as 50 such enzymes may be contained in a single lysosome. Up to 1.0 μm in diameter, lysosomes isolate these potentially harmful enzymes from the rest of the cell before releasing them, either to the outside or into a **phagocytic** vesicle within the cell (Figure 7).

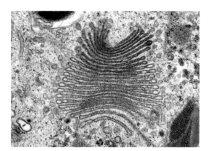

💡 **Figure 7** *The Golgi apparatus and the formation and functioning of a lysosome (top); false-colour transmission electron micrograph (TEM) of a Golgi apparatus (orange) (bottom)*

The functions of lysosomes are to:

▥ break down material ingested by phagocytic cells, such as white blood cells,

▥ release enzymes to the outside of the cell (exocytosis) in order to destroy material around the cell,

▥ digest worn out organelles so that the useful chemicals they are made of can be re-used,

▥ completely break down cells after they have died (autolysis).

Given the roles that lysosomes perform, it is not surprising that they are especially abundant in secretory cells, such as epithelial cells, and in **phagocytic** cells.

Ribosomes

Ribosomes are small cytoplasmic granules found in all cells. They may occur in the cytoplasm or be associated with the RER. There are two types, depending on the cells in which they are found:

▥ **80S type** – found in eukaryotic cells, is around 25 nm in diameter.

▥ **70S type** – found in prokaryotic cells, is slightly smaller.

Ribosomes have two subunits – one large and one small (Figure 8) – each of which contains ribosomal RNA and protein. Despite their small size, they occur in such vast numbers that they can account for up to 25 per cent of the dry mass of a cell. Ribosomes are important in protein synthesis.

Microvilli

Microvilli are finger-like projections of the epithelial cell that increase its surface area to allow more efficient absorption. They are described in more detail in Topic 3.9.

Relating cell ultrastructure to function

As each organelle has its own function, it is possible to deduce, with reasonable accuracy, the role of a cell by looking at the number and size of the organelles it contains. For example, as mitochondria produce ATP that is used as a temporary energy store, it follows that cells with many mitochondria are likely to require a lot of ATP and therefore have a high rate of metabolism. Even within each mitochondrion, the more dense and numerous the cristae, the greater the metabolic rate of the cell possessing these mitochondria.

> **▥ Hint**
>
> To help you understand the functions of the Golgi apparatus, think of it as the cell's post office, but receiving, sorting and delivering proteins and lipids, rather than letters.

> **▥ Hint**
>
> Lysosomes can be thought of as refuse disposal operatives. They remove useless and potentially dangerous material (e.g. bacteria) and reuse the useful parts, disposing of only that which cannot be recycled.

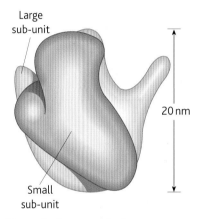

Figure 8 *Structure of a ribosome*

> **▥ Summary questions**
>
> **1** In which process are ribosomes important?
>
> **2** Name **three** carbohydrates that are absorbed by an epithelial cell of the small intestine.
>
> **3** Name the organelle which is being referred to in each of the following descriptions:
>
> a It possesses structures called cristae.
>
> b It contains chromatin.
>
> c It synthesises glycoproteins.
>
> d It digests worn out organelles.
>
> **4** The following list gives a type of cell and a brief description of its role. Suggest two organelles that might be numerous and/or well developed in each of the cells.
>
> a A sperm cell swims a considerable distance carrying the male chromosomes.
>
> b One type of white blood cell engulfs and digests foreign material.
>
> c Liver cells manufacture proteins and lipids at a rapid rate.

3.4 Lipids

Learning objectives:

- How are triglycerides formed?
- How can fatty acids vary?
- What is the structure of a phospholipid?
- How is the presence of a lipid identified?

Specification reference: 3.1.3

Hint

Fats are generally made of saturated fatty acids, while oils are made of unsaturated ones.

Saturated
(no double bonds between carbon atoms)

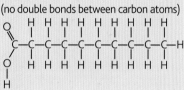

Mono-unsaturated
(one double bond between carbon atoms)

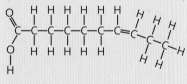

Polyunsaturated
(more than one double bond between carbon atoms)

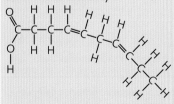

The double bonds cause the molecule to bend. They cannot therefore pack together so closely making them liquid at room temperature, i.e they are oils.

Figure 2 *Saturated and unsaturated fatty acids*

Lipids are a varied group of substances that share the following characteristics:

- They contain carbon, hydrogen and oxygen.
- The proportion of oxygen to carbon and hydrogen is smaller than in carbohydrates.
- They are insoluble in water.
- They are soluble in organic solvents such as alcohols and acetone.

The main groups of lipids are **triglycerides** (fats and oils), phospholipids and waxes.

Roles of lipids

The main role of lipids is in **plasma membranes**. Phospholipids contribute to the flexibility of membranes and the transfer of lipid-soluble substances across them. Other roles of lipids include:

- **an energy source**. When oxidised, lipids provide more than twice the energy as the same mass of carbohydrate.
- **waterproofing**. Lipids are insoluble in water and therefore useful as a waterproofing. Both plants and insects have waxy cuticles that conserve water, while mammals produce an oily secretion from the sebaceous glands in the skin.
- **insulation**. Fats are slow conductors of heat and when stored beneath the body surface help to retain body heat.
- **protection**. Fat is often stored around delicate organs, such as the kidney.

Fats are solid at room temperature (10–20 °C), whereas oils are liquid. Triglycerides are so called because they have three (tri) fatty acids combined with glycerol (glyceride). Each fatty acid forms a bond with glycerol in a **condensation reaction** (Figure 1). **Hydrolysis** of a triglyceride therefore produces glycerol and three fatty acids.

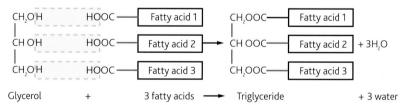

Figure 1 *Formation of a triglyceride.*
The three fatty acids may all be the same, thereby forming a simple triglyceride, or they may be different, in which case a mixed triglyceride is produced. In either case it is a condensation reaction.

As the glycerol molecule in all triglycerides is the same, the differences in the properties of different fats and oils come from variations in the fatty acids. There are over 70 fatty acids and all have a carboxyl (—COOH) group with a hydrocarbon chain attached. If this chain has no carbon–carbon double bonds, the fatty acid is then described as **saturated**, because all the carbon atoms are linked to the maximum possible number of hydrogen atoms, i.e. they are saturated with hydrogen atoms. If there is a single double bond, it is **mono-unsaturated**; if more than one double bond is present, it is **polyunsaturated**. These differences are illustrated in Figure 2.

Phospholipids

Phospholipids are similar to lipids except that one of the fatty acid molecules is replaced by a phosphate molecule (Figure 3). Whereas fatty acid molecules repel water (are hydrophobic), phosphate molecules attract water (are hydrophilic). A phospholipid is therefore made up of two parts:

- **a hydrophilic 'head'**, which interacts with water (is attracted to it) but not with fat
- **a hydrophobic 'tail'**, which orients itself away from water but mixes readily with fat.

Molecules that have two ends (poles) that behave differently in this way are said to be **polar**. This means that when these polar phospholipid molecules are placed in water they position themselves so that the hydrophilic heads are as close to the water as possible and the hydrophobic tails are as far away from the water as possible (Figure 4).

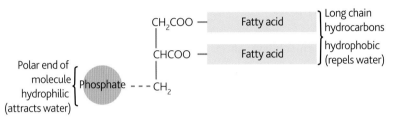

Figure 3 *Structure of a phospholipid*

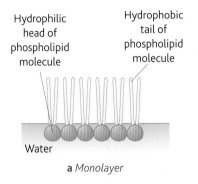

a *Monolayer*

b *Bilayered sheet*

Figure 4 *Two arrangements of phospholipid molecules in water*

⚠ Test for lipids

The test for lipids is known as the emulsion test and is carried out as follows:

1. Take a completely dry and grease-free test tube.
2. To $2\,cm^3$ of the sample being tested, add $5\,cm^3$ of ethanol.
3. Shake the tube thoroughly to dissolve any lipid in the sample.
4. Add $5\,cm^3$ of water and shake gently.
5. A cloudy-white colour indicates the presence of a lipid.
6. As a control, repeat the procedures using water instead of the sample; the final solution should remain clear.

The cloudy colour is due to any lipid in the sample being finely dispersed in the water to form an emulsion. Light passing through this emulsion is refracted as it passes from oil droplets to water droplets, making it appear cloudy.

Summary questions

1 In the following passage give the most suitable word for each of the letters **a** to **e**.

Fats and oils make up a group of lipids called **a** which, when hydrolysed, form **b** and fatty acids. A fatty acid with more than one carbon–carbon double bond is called **c**. In a phospholipid the number of fatty acids is **d**; these are described as **e** because they repel water.

2 State **two** differences between a triglyceride molecule and a phospholipid molecule.

3 Organisms that move, e.g. animals, and parts of organisms that move, e.g. plant seeds, use lipids rather than carbohydrates as an energy store. Suggest one reason why this is so.

3.5 The cell-surface membrane

Learning objectives:

▨ What is the structure of the cell-surface membrane?

▨ What are the functions of the various components of the cell-surface membrane?

▨ What is the fluid-mosaic model?

Specification reference: 3.1.3

Hint

Organelles such as mitochondria and chloroplasts are surrounded by two plasma membranes. The term 'cell-surface membrane' is reserved only for the plasma membrane around the cell.

AQA Examiner's tip

When representing a phospholipid it is important to be accurate. It has a **single** phosphate head and **two** fatty acid tails. All too often students show too many heads and/or too many tails.

Hint

All plasma membranes found around and inside cells have the same phospholipid bilayer structure. What gives plasma membranes their different properties are the different substances they contain – especially proteins.

All membranes around and within cells (including those around and within cell organelles) have the same basic structure and are known as **plasma membranes**.

The cell-surface membrane is the plasma membrane that surrounds cells and forms the boundary between the cell cytoplasm and the environment. It allows different conditions to be established inside and outside a cell. It controls the movement of substances in and out of the cell. Before we look at how the cell-surface membrane achieves this, we need first to look in more detail at the molecules that form its structure.

▨ Phospholipids

We looked at the molecular structure of a phospholipid in Topic 3.4. Phospholipids form a bilayer sheet. They are important components of cell-surface membranes for the following reasons:

▨ One layer of phospholipids has its hydrophilic heads pointing inwards (interacting with the water in the cell cytoplasm).

▨ The other layer of phospholipids has its hydrophilic heads pointing outwards (interacting with the water which surrounds all cells).

▨ The hydrophobic tails of both phospholipid layers point into the centre of the membrane – protected, as it were, from the water on both sides.

Lipid-soluble material moves through the membrane via the phospholipid portion. The functions of phospholipids in the membrane are to:

▨ allow lipid-soluble substances to enter and leave the cell,

▨ prevent water-soluble substances entering and leaving the cell,

▨ make the membrane flexible.

▨ Proteins

The proteins of the cell-surface membrane are arranged more randomly than the regular pattern of phospholipids. They are embedded in the phospholipid bilayer in two main ways:

▨ **Extrinsic proteins** occur either on the surface of the bilayer or only partly embedded in it, but they never extend completely across it. They act either to give mechanical support to the membrane or, in conjunction with glycolipids, as cell receptors for molecules such as hormones.

▨ **Intrinsic proteins** completely span the phospholipid bilayer from one side to the other. Some act as carriers to transport water-soluble material across the membrane while others are enzymes.

The functions of the proteins in the membrane are to:

▨ provide structural support

▨ act as carriers transporting water-soluble substances across the membrane

▨ allow active transport across the membrane by forming ion channels for sodium, potassium, etc.

- form recognition sites by identifying cells
- help cells adhere together
- act as receptors, e.g. for hormones.

Fluid-mosaic model of the cell-surface membrane

The way in which all the various molecules above are combined into the structure of the cell-surface membrane is shown in Figure 1. This arrangement is known as the **fluid-mosaic model** for the following reasons:

- **fluid** because the individual phospholipid molecules can move relative to one another. This gives the membrane a flexible structure that is constantly changing in shape.
- **mosaic** because the proteins that are embedded in the phospholipid bilayer vary in shape, size and pattern in the same way as the stones or tiles of a mosaic.

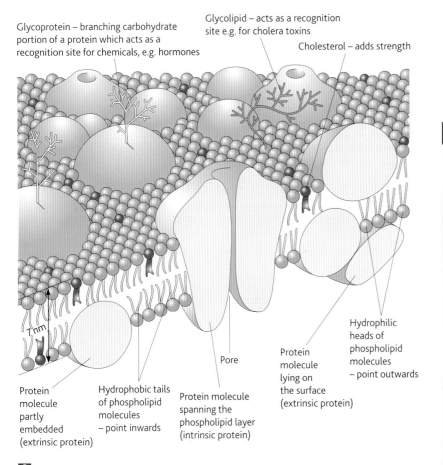

Glycoprotein – branching carbohydrate portion of a protein which acts as a recognition site for chemicals, e.g. hormones

Glycolipid – acts as a recognition site e.g. for cholera toxins

Cholesterol – adds strength

7 nm

Protein molecule partly embedded (extrinsic protein)

Hydrophobic tails of phospholipid molecules – point inwards

Protein molecule spanning the phospholipid layer (intrinsic protein)

Pore

Protein molecule lying on the surface (extrinsic protein)

Hydrophilic heads of phospholipid molecules – point outwards

Figure 1 *The fluid-mosaic model of the cell-surface membrane*

Summary questions

1 What is the overall function of the cell-surface membrane?

2 Which end of the phospholipid molecule lies towards the inside of the cell-surface membrane?

3 Through which molecule in the cell-surface membrane are each of the following likely to pass in order to get in or out of a cell?

   a a molecule that is soluble in lipids

   b a mineral ion

4 From your knowledge of the cell-surface membrane, suggest **two** properties that a drug should possess if it is to enter a cell rapidly.

3.6 Diffusion

Hint

Remember that diffusion is the **net** movement of particles. All particles move at random in diffusion; it is just that more move in one direction than in the other. This is due to concentration differences.

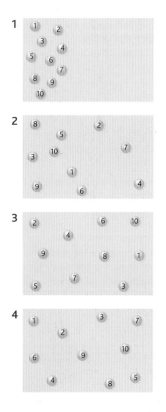

Figure 1 *Diffusion*

The exchange of substances between cells and the environment occurs in ways that require metabolic energy (active transport) and in ways that do not (passive transport). Diffusion is an example of passive transport.

Explanation of diffusion

As all movement requires energy, it is possibly confusing to describe diffusion as passive transport. In this sense, 'passive' means that the energy comes from the natural, inbuilt motion of particles, rather than from some external source. To help understand diffusion and other passive forms of transport it is necessary to understand that:

- all particles are constantly in motion due to the kinetic energy that they possess,

- this motion is random, with no set pattern to the way the particles move around,

- particles are constantly bouncing off one another as well as off other objects, e.g. the sides of the vessel in which they are contained.

Given these facts, Figure 1 shows how particles that are concentrated together in part of a closed vessel will, of their own accord, distribute themselves evenly throughout the vessel as a result of diffusion.

Diffusion is therefore defined as:

> the net movement of molecules or ions from a region where they are more highly concentrated to one where their concentration is lower.

1 If ten particles occupying the left-hand side of a closed vessel are in random motion, they will collide with each other and the sides of the vessel. Some particles from the left-hand side move to the right, but initially there are no available particles to move in the opposite direction, so the movement is in one direction only. There is a large concentration gradient and diffusion is rapid.

2 After a short time the particles (still in random motion) have spread themselves more evenly. Particles can now move from right to left as well as from left to right. However, with a higher concentration of particles (7) on the left than on the right (3), there is a greater probability of a particle moving to the right than in the reverse direction. There is a smaller concentration gradient and diffusion is slower.

3 Some time later, the particles will be evenly distributed throughout the vessel and the concentrations will be equal on each side. The system is in equilibrium. However, the particles are not static but remain in random motion. With equal concentrations on each side, the probability of a particle moving from left to right is equal to the probability of one moving in the opposite direction. There is no concentration gradient and no diffusion.

4 At a later stage, the particles remain evenly distributed and will continue to be so. Although the number of particles on each side remains the same, individual particles are continuously changing position. This situation is called **dynamic equilibrium**.

Rate of diffusion

There are a number of factors that affect the rate at which molecules or ions diffuse:

- **concentration gradient**. The greater the difference in the concentration of molecules or ions on either side of an exchange surface, the faster the rate of diffusion.
- **area over which diffusion takes place**. The larger the area of an exchange surface, the faster the rate of diffusion.
- **thickness of exchange surface**. The thinner an exchange surface, the faster the rate of diffusion.

The relationship between these three factors can be expressed as follows:

Diffusion is proportional to:

$$\frac{\text{surface area} \times \text{difference in concentration}}{\text{length of diffusion path}}$$

Although this expression gives a good guide to the rate of diffusion, it is not wholly applicable to cells because diffusion is also affected by:

- the nature of the plasma membrane – its composition and number of pores,
- the size and nature of the diffusing molecule, e.g. small molecules diffuse faster than large ones. Fat-soluble molecules, such as glycerol, diffuse faster than water-soluble ones and polar molecules diffuse faster than non-polar ones.

Hint

Diffusion only occurs between different concentrations of the **same** substance. For example, it may occur between different concentrations of oxygen or between different concentrations of carbon dioxide. It **never** occurs between different concentrations of oxygen and carbon dioxide.

Facilitated diffusion

Facilitated diffusion is a passive process. It relies only on the inbuilt motion (kinetic energy) of the diffusing molecules. There is no external input of energy. Like diffusion, it occurs down a concentration gradient, but it differs in that it occurs at specific points on the plasma membrane where there are special protein molecules. These proteins form water-filled channels (protein channels) across the membrane. These allow water-soluble ions and molecules, such as glucose and amino acids, to pass through. Such molecules would usually diffuse only very slowly through the phospholipid bilayer of the plasma membrane. The channels are selective, each opening only in the presence of a specific molecule. If the particular molecule is not present, the channel remains closed. In this way, there is some control over the entry and exit of substances.

An alternative form of facilitated diffusion involves carrier proteins that span the plasma membrane. When a particular molecule that is specific to the protein is present, it binds with the protein. This causes it to change shape in such a way that the molecule is released to the inside of the membrane (Figure 2). No external energy is needed for this. The molecules move from a region where they are highly concentrated to one of lower concentration, using only the kinetic energy of the molecules themselves.

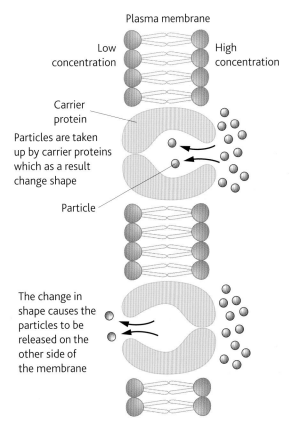

Figure 2 *Facilitated diffusion involving carrier proteins*

■ Summary questions

1 State **three** factors that affect the rate of diffusion.

2 How does facilitated diffusion differ from diffusion?

3 Explain why facilitated diffusion is a passive process.

■ Application

Diffusion in action

Starch in the diet is digested by the enzymes amylase and then maltase to form glucose. Glucose must be absorbed into the body so that it can be used by cells as a substrate for respiration. The glucose is absorbed from the exchange surface of the small intestine into the epithelial cells that line it. This absorption occurs partly by diffusion.

1 Glucose molecules mostly diffuse into cells through the pores in the proteins that span the phospholipid bilayer. Why do they not pass easily through the phospholipid bilayer?

2 State **two** changes to the structure of cell-surface membranes that would increase the rate at which glucose diffuses into a cell.

3 The other molecule required by cells for respiration is oxygen. This diffuses into the blood through the epithelial layers of the alveoli and blood capillaries. By how much would each of the following changes increase or decrease the rate of diffusion of oxygen?

 a The surface area of the alveoli is doubled.

 b The surface area of the alveoli is halved and the oxygen concentration gradient is doubled.

 c The oxygen concentration gradient is halved and the total thickness of the epithelial layers is doubled.

 d The oxygen concentration of the blood is halved and the carbon dioxide concentration of the alveoli is doubled.

3.7 Osmosis

Learning objectives:

- What is osmosis?
- What is the water potential of pure water?
- What is the effect of solutes on water potential?
- How does water potential affect water movement?
- What is the result of placing animal cells and plant cells into pure water?

Specification reference: 3.1.3

In the last topic we learned about diffusion. We now turn our attention to a special case of diffusion, known as osmosis. Osmosis only involves the movement of water molecules.

What is osmosis?

Osmosis is defined as:

the passage of water from a region where it has a higher water potential to a region where it has a lower water potential through a partially permeable membrane.

Cell-surface membranes and other plasma membranes such as those around organelles are partially permeable, i.e. they are permeable to water molecules and a few other small molecules, but not to larger molecules.

💡 Solutions and water potential

A solute is any substance that is dissolved in a solvent, e.g. water. The solute and the solvent together form a solution.

Water potential is represented by the Greek letter psi (Ψ), and is measured in units of pressure, usually kilopascals (kPa). Water potential is the pressure created by water molecules. Under standard conditions of temperature and pressure (25 °C and 100 kPa), pure water is said to have a water potential of zero.

It follows that:

- the addition of a solute to pure water will lower its water potential,
- the water potential of a solution (water + solute) must always be less than zero, i.e. a negative value,
- the more solute that is added (i.e. the more concentrated a solution), the lower (more negative) its water potential,
- water will move by osmosis from a region of higher (less negative) water potential (e.g. −20 kPa) to one of lower (more negative) water potential (e.g. −30 kPa).

One way of finding the water potential of cells or tissues is to place them in a series of solutions of different water potentials. Where there is no net gain or loss of water from the cells or tissues, the water potential inside the cells or tissues must be the same as that of the external solution.

Explanation of osmosis

Consider the hypothetical situation in Figure 1 overleaf, in which a partially permeable plasma membrane separates two solutions.

- The solution on the left has a low concentration of solute molecules while the solution on the right has a high concentration of solute molecules.
- Both the solute and water molecules are in random motion due to their **kinetic energy**.
- The partially permeable plasma membrane, however, only allows water molecules across it and not solute molecules.

▍ Hint

Remember that, while diffusion can be the movement of **any** molecule, osmosis is the movement of water molecules **only**.

▓ The water molecules diffuse from the left-hand side, which has the higher water potential, to the right-hand side, which has the lower water potential, i.e. along a water potential gradient (Figure 2).

▓ At the point where the water potentials on either side of the plasma membrane are equal, a dynamic equilibrium is established and there is no net movement of water.

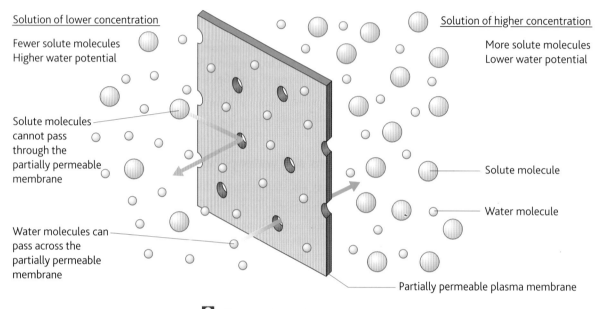

Solution of lower concentration
Fewer solute molecules
Higher water potential

Solution of higher concentration
More solute molecules
Lower water potential

Solute molecules cannot pass through the partially permeable membrane

Solute molecule

Water molecule

Water molecules can pass across the partially permeable membrane

Partially permeable plasma membrane

💡 **Figure 1** *Osmosis*

Understanding water potential

The highest value of water potential, that of pure water, is zero, and so all other values are negative. The more negative the value, the lower the water potential. Think of water potential as an overdraft at a bank. The bigger the overdraft, the more negative is the amount of money you have. The smaller the overdraft, the less negative is the amount of money you have.

Osmosis and animal cells

Animal cells, such as red blood cells, contain a variety of solutes dissolved in their watery cytoplasm. If a red blood cell is placed in pure water it will absorb water by osmosis because it has a lower water potential. Cell surface membranes are very thin (7 nm) and, although they are flexible, they cannot stretch to any great extent. The cell surface membrane will therefore break, bursting the cell and releasing its contents (in red blood cells this is called haemolysis). To prevent this happening, animal cells are normally bathed in a liquid which has the same water potential as the cells. In our example, the liquid is the blood plasma. This and red blood cells have the same water potential. If a red blood cell is placed in a solution with a water potential lower than its own, water leaves by osmosis and the cell shrinks and becomes shrivelled (see Table 1 on the next page).

Key

x kPa   water potential of cell
➡   direction of water movement

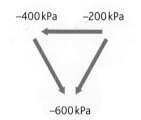

Water moves from higher water potential to lower water potential. The highest water potential is zero.

Figure 2 *Movement of water between cells along a water potential gradient*

Water potential (ψ) of external solution compared to cell solution	Higher (less negative)	Equal	Lower (more negative)
Net movement of water	Enters cell	Neither enters nor leaves	Leaves cell
State of cell	Swells and bursts	No change	Shrinks

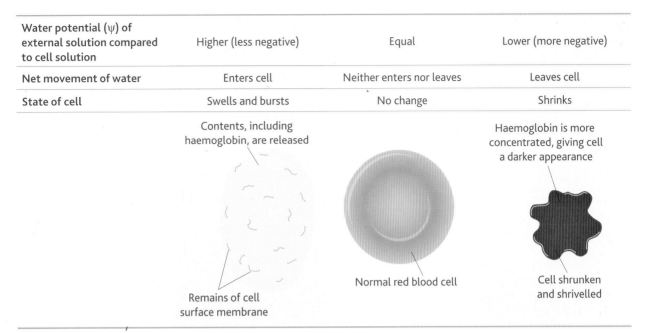

Contents, including haemoglobin, are released

Remains of cell surface membrane

Normal red blood cell

Haemoglobin is more concentrated, giving cell a darker appearance

Cell shrunken and shrivelled

Table 1 *Summary of osmosis in an animal cell, e.g. a red blood cell*

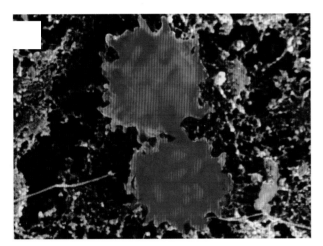

Figure 3 *Scanning electron micrograph (SEM) of red blood cells that have been placed in a solution of lower water potential. Water has left by osmosis and the cells have become shrunken and shrivelled.*

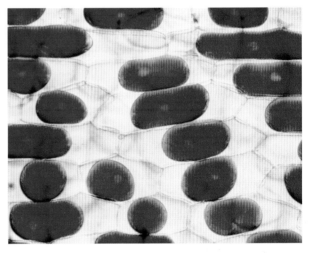

Figure 4 *Onion epidermal cells showing plasmolysis. The protoplasts, with their vacuoles containing red liquid, have shrunk and pulled away from the cell walls.*

Summary questions

1 What is meant by a partially permeable membrane?

2 Under standard conditions of pressure and temperature, what is the water potential of pure water?

3 Four cells have the following water potentials:

Cell A = −200 kPa
Cell B = −250 kPa
Cell C = −100 kPa
Cell D = −150 kPa.

In what order would the cells have to be placed for water to pass from one cell to the next if they are arranged in a line?

Water potential (ψ) of external solution compared to cell solution	Higher (less negative)	Equal	Lower (more negative)
Net movement of water	Enters cell	Neither enters nor leaves	Leaves cell
Protoplast	Swells	No change	Shrinks
Condition of cell	Turgid	Incipient plasmolysis	Plasmolysed

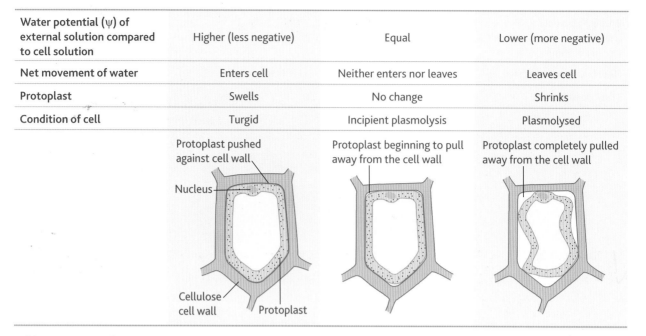

Table 2 *Summary of osmosis in a plant cell*

Application

Osmosis and plant cells

For the purposes of the following explanations, the plant cell can be divided into three parts:

- the **central vacuole**, which contains a solution of salts, sugars and organic acids in water
- the **protoplast**, consisting of the outer cell-surface membrane, nucleus, cytoplasm and the inner vacuole membrane
- the **cellulose cell wall**, a tough, inelastic covering that is permeable to even large molecules.

Like animal cells, plant cells also contain a variety of solutes, mainly dissolved in the water of the large cell vacuole that each possesses. When placed in pure water they also absorb water by osmosis because of their lower (more negative) water potential. Unlike animal cells, however, they are unable to control the composition of the fluid around their cells. Indeed, plant cells are normally permanently bathed in almost pure water, which is constantly absorbed from the plant's roots. Water entering a plant cell by osmosis causes the protoplast to swell and press on the cell wall. Because the cell wall is capable of only very limited expansion, a pressure builds up on it that resists the entry of further water. In this situation, the protoplast of the cell is kept pushed against the cell wall and the cell is said to be **turgid**.

If the same plant cell is placed in a solution with a lower water potential than its own, water leaves by osmosis. The volume of the cell decreases. A stage is reached where the protoplast no longer presses on the cellulose cell wall. At this point the cell is said to be at **incipient plasmolysis**. Further loss of water will cause the cell contents to shrink further and the protoplast to pull away from the cell wall. In this condition the cell is said to be **plasmolysed**. These events are summarised in Table 2.

1. Explain why an animal cell placed in pure water bursts while a plant cell placed in pure water does not.

2. Plant cells that have a water potential of −600 kPa are placed in solutions of different water potentials. State in each of the following cases whether, after 10 minutes, the cells would be turgid, plasmolysed or at incipient plasmolysis.

   a Solution A = −400 kPa

   b Solution B = −600 kPa

   c Solution C = −900 kPa

   d Solution D = pure water

3. If an animal cell with a water potential of −700 kPa was placed in each of the solutions, in which solutions is it likely to burst?

3.8 Active transport

Learning objectives:

▦ What is active transport?

▦ What does active transport require to take place?

Specification reference: 3.1.3

AQA ╱ Examiner's tip

Carrier proteins have a specific tertiary structure and will only transport particular substances across a membrane. They are not enzymes and do not have an active site.

Active transport allows cells to exchange molecules against a concentration gradient. Metabolic energy is required for the process. Once inside the cell the molecules are prevented from leaking back by the barrier of the cell-surface membrane's bilayer. In this way a different environment is maintained on either side of the membrane.

▦ What is active transport?

Active transport is:

the movement of molecules or ions into or out of a cell from a region of lower concentration to a region of higher concentration using energy and carrier molecules.

It differs from passive forms of transport in the following ways:

▦ Metabolic energy in the form of **ATP** is needed.

▦ Materials are moved against a concentration gradient, i.e. from a lower to a higher concentration.

▦ Carrier protein molecules which act as 'pumps' are involved.

▦ The process is very selective, with specific substances being transported.

Active transport uses ATP in one of two ways:

▦ by using ATP directly to move molecules,

▦ by using a concentration gradient that has already been set up by direct active transport. This is also known as **co-transport** and is explained in Topic 3.9.

Direct active transport of a single molecule or ion is described below.

▦ The carrier proteins span the cell-surface membrane and accept the molecules or ions to be transported on one side of it.

▦ The molecules or ions bind to receptors on the channels of the carrier protein.

▦ On the inside of the cell, ATP binds to the protein, causing it to split into ADP and a phosphate molecule. As a result, the protein molecule changes shape and opens to the opposite side of the membrane.

▦ The molecules or ions are then released to the other side of the membrane.

▦ The phosphate molecule is released from the protein and recombines with the ADP to form ATP.

▦ This causes the protein to revert to its original shape, ready for the process to be repeated.

These events are illustrated in Figure 1 on the next page. It is important to distinguish between active transport and facilitated diffusion. Both use carrier proteins but facilitated diffusion occurs **down** a concentration gradient, while active transport occurs **against** a concentration gradient. This means that facilitated diffusion does not require metabolic energy, while active transport does. The metabolic energy is provided in the form of ATP.

■ Hint

Carrier proteins are involved in both facilitated diffusion and active transport **but** any given protein carrier is very specific about what it carries and by which method.

■ Link

Link to A2 – Specification reference 3.5.2.

Sometimes more than one molecule or ion may be moved in the same direction at the same time by active transport. Occasionally, the molecule or ion is moved into a cell at the same time as a different one is being removed from it. One example of this is the **sodium–potassium pump**.

In the sodium–potassium pump, sodium ions are actively removed from the cell while potassium ions are actively taken in from the surroundings. This process is essential to a number of important processes in the organism, including the creation of a nerve impulse.

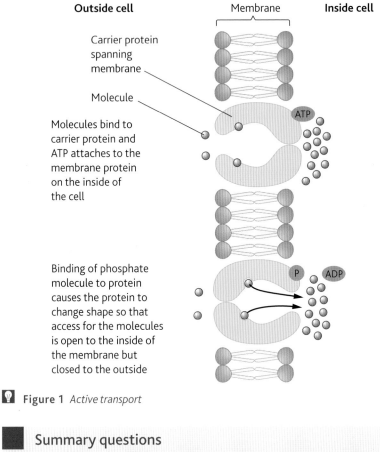

Outside cell   Membrane   **Inside cell**

Carrier protein spanning membrane

Molecule

Molecules bind to carrier protein and ATP attaches to the membrane protein on the inside of the cell

Binding of phosphate molecule to protein causes the protein to change shape so that access for the molecules is open to the inside of the membrane but closed to the outside

💡 **Figure 1** *Active transport*

■ Summary questions

1   State **one** similarity and **one** difference between active transport and facilitated diffusion.

2   The presence of many mitochondria is typical of cells that carry out active transport. Explain why this is so.

3   In the production of urine, glucose is initially lost from the blood but is then reabsorbed into the blood by cells in the kidneys. Explain why it is important that this reabsorption occurs by active transport rather than by diffusion.

3.9 Absorption in the small intestine

- What part do villi and microvilli play in absorption?

- How are the products of carbohydrate digestion absorbed in the small intestine?

- What are the roles of diffusion, active transport and co-transport in the process?

Specification reference: 3.1.3

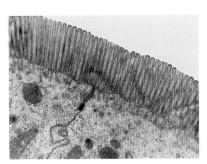

Figure 1 *Microvilli on an epithelial cell from the small intestine*

AQA Examiner's tip

Do not confuse villi and microvilli. Villi are 1 mm projections of the wall of the small intestine while microvilli are 0.6 µm projections of the cell-surface membrane of the epithelial cells that line this wall. Microvilli are therefore more than one thousand times smaller than villi.

Link

Link to A2 – Specification reference 3.5.4.

In Topic 2.4 we saw how carbohydrates in the diet are digested to form soluble products. We now turn our attention to how these soluble products are absorbed into the body. The soluble products in question are glucose, fructose and galactose. As these molecules are all absorbed in a similar way, we shall use glucose as our example.

Villi and microvilli

Glucose is absorbed through the walls of the small intestine. These are folded and possess finger-like projections, about 1 mm long, called **villi**. They have thin walls, lined with epithelial cells (see Topic 3.3), on the other side of which is a rich network of blood capillaries. The villi considerably increase the surface area of the small intestine and therefore accelerate the rate of absorption.

Villi are situated at the interface between the **lumen** (cavity) of the intestines (in effect outside the body) and the blood and other tissues inside the body. They are part of a specialised exchange surface adapted for the absorption of the products of digestion, such as glucose. Their properties increase the efficiency of absorption in the following ways:

- They increase the surface area for **diffusion**.
- They are very thin walled, thus reducing the distance over which diffusion takes place.
- They are able to move and so help to maintain a diffusion gradient (see below).
- They are well supplied with blood vessels so that blood can carry away absorbed molecules and hence maintain a diffusion gradient.

The epithelial cells lining the villi possess **microvilli** (see Figure 1). These are finger-like projections of the cell-surface membrane about 0.6 µm in length. They are collectively termed a 'brush border' because, under the light microscope, they look like the bristles on a brush.

The role of diffusion in absorption

Diffusion (Topic 3.6) is the net movement of molecules or ions from a region where they are highly concentrated to a region where their concentration is lower.

As carbohydrates are being digested continuously, there is normally a greater concentration of glucose within the small intestine than in the blood. There is therefore a concentration gradient down which glucose diffuses from inside the small intestine into the blood. Given that the blood is constantly being circulated by the heart, the glucose absorbed into it is continuously being removed by the cells as they use it up during respiration. This helps to maintain the concentration gradient between the inside of the small intestine and the blood (Figure 2).

Also, the villi contain muscles that regularly contract and relax, mixing the contents of the small intestine. This ensures that, as glucose is absorbed from the food adjacent to the villi, new glucose-rich food replaces it. This also helps to maintain the concentration gradient and allows diffusion to continue.

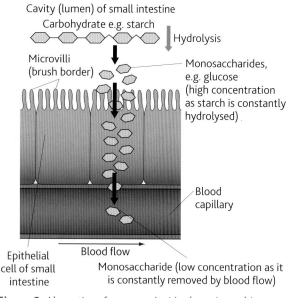

Figure 2 *Absorption of monosaccharides (e.g. glucose) by diffusion in the small intestine*

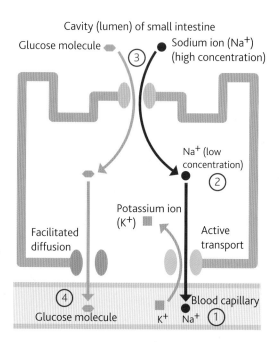

Figure 3 *Co-transport of a glucose molecule*

Role of active transport in absorption

At best, diffusion only results in the concentrations either side of the intestinal epithelium becoming equal. This means that not all the available glucose can be absorbed in this way and some may pass out of the body. The reason why this does not happen is because glucose is also being absorbed by active transport (see Topic 3.8). This means that all the glucose should be absorbed into the blood.

The actual mechanism by which glucose is absorbed from the small intestine is an example of co-transport because two molecules are involved. It entails glucose being drawn into the cells along with sodium **ions** that have been actively transported out by the sodium–potassium pump (see Topic 3.8). It takes place in the following manner (see Figure 3).

1   Sodium ions are actively transported out of epithelial cells, by the sodium–potassium pump, into the blood. This takes place in one type of protein-**carrier molecule** found in the cell-surface membrane of the epithelial cells.

2   There is now a much higher concentration of sodium ions in the lumen of the intestine than inside the epithelial cells.

3   The sodium ions diffuse into the epithelial cells down this concentration gradient through a different type of protein carrier (co-transport protein) in the cell-surface membrane. As the sodium ions flood back in through this second carrier protein, they couple with the glucose molecules which are carried into the cell with them.

4   The glucose passes into the blood plasma by facilitated diffusion using another type of carrier.

Both sodium ions and glucose molecules move into the cell, but while the sodium ions move **down** their concentration gradient, the glucose molecules move **up** their concentration gradient. It is the sodium ion concentration gradient, rather than **ATP** directly, that powers the movement of glucose into the cells. This makes it an indirect rather than a direct form of active transport.

Summary questions

1   State **two** ways in which a glucose concentration gradient is maintained between the inside of the small intestine and the capillaries in the villi.

2   Why is the term 'co-transport' used to describe the transport of glucose into cells?

3   In each of the following events in the glucose co-transport system, state whether the movements are active or passive.

a   Sodium ions move out of the epithelial cell.

b   Sodium ions move into the epithelial cell.

c   Glucose molecules move into the epithelial cell.

3.10 Cholera

Learning objectives:

▓ What are prokaryotic cells?

▓ How do prokaryotes differ from eukaryotes?

▓ What causes cholera and how does it produce the symptoms?

Specification reference: 3.1.3

Globally, cholera is of great significance, killing an estimated 120 000 people each year. The agent that causes the disease is a curved, rod-shaped bacterium called *Vibrio cholerae*. It is characterised by the presence of a flagellum at one end. Bacteria are examples of prokaryotic cells. The structure of a generalised prokaryotic cell is shown in Figure 1. The differences between prokaryotic and eukaryotic cells are listed in Table 1.

Table 1 *Comparison of prokaryotic and eukaryotic cells*

Prokaryotic cells	Eukaryotic cells
No true nucleus, only a diffuse area of nuclear material with no nuclear envelope	Distinct nucleus, with a nuclear envelope
No nucleolus	Nucleolus is present
Circular strands of DNA but no chromosomes	Chromosomes present, in which DNA is located
No membrane-bounded organelles	Membrane-bounded organelles, such as mitochondria, are present
No chloroplasts, only photosynthetic regions in some bacteria	Chloroplasts present in plants and algae
Ribosomes are smaller (70S type)	Ribosomes are larger (80S type)
No endoplasmic reticulum or associated Golgi apparatus and lysosomes	Endoplasmic reticulum present along with Golgi apparatus and lysosomes
Cell wall made of peptidoglycan	Where present, cell wall is made mostly of cellulose (or chitin or fungi)

▓ Structure of a bacterial cell

Bacteria occur in every habitat in the world; they are versatile, adaptable and very successful. Much of their success is a result of their small size, normally ranging from 0.1 to 10 μm in length. Their cellular structure is relatively simple (Figure 1). All bacteria possess a **cell wall**, which is made up of peptidoglycan. This is a mixture of polysaccharides and peptides. Many bacteria further protect themselves by secreting a **capsule** of mucilaginous slime around this wall. **Flagella** occur in certain types of bacteria. Their rigid corkscrew shape and rotating base enable bacteria to spin through fluids.

Inside the cell wall is the **cell-surface membrane**, within which is the cytoplasm that contains ribosomes of the 70S type. These ribosomes are smaller than those of eukaryotic cells (80S type), but nevertheless still synthesise proteins. Bacteria store food reserves as glycogen granules and oil droplets. The genetic material in bacteria is in the form of a **circular strand of DNA**. Separate from this are smaller circular pieces of DNA, called **plasmids**. These can reproduce themselves independently and may give the bacterium resistance to harmful chemicals, such as antibiotics. Plasmids are used extensively as vectors (carriers of genetic information) in genetic engineering. The roles of the main structures in a bacterial cell are summarised in Table 2.

Table 2 *Roles of structures found in a bacterial cell*

Cell structure	Role
Cell wall	Physical barrier that protects against mechanical damage and excludes certain substances
Capsule	Protects bacterium from other cells and helps groups of bacteria to stick together for further protection
Cell-surface membrane	Acts as a differentially permeable layer which controls the entry and exit of chemicals
Flagellum	Aids movement of bacterium because its rigid, corkscrew shape and rotating base help the cell spin through fluids
Circular DNA	Possesses the genetic information for the replication of bacterial cells
Plasmid	Possesses genes that aid the survival of bacteria in adverse conditions, e.g. produces enzymes which break down antibodies

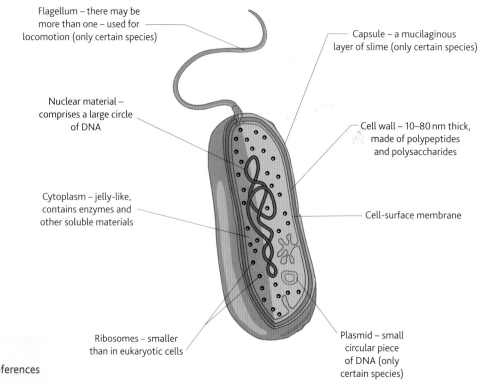

Flagellum – there may be more than one – used for locomotion (only certain species)

Capsule – a mucilaginous layer of slime (only certain species)

Nuclear material – comprises a large circle of DNA

Cell wall – 10–80 nm thick, made of polypeptides and polysaccharides

Cytoplasm – jelly-like, contains enzymes and other soluble materials

Cell-surface membrane

Ribosomes – smaller than in eukaryotic cells

Plasmid – small circular piece of DNA (only certain species)

💡 **Figure 1** *Structure of a generalised bacterial cell*

Link

Link to A2 – Specification references 3.5.8 and 3.5.9.

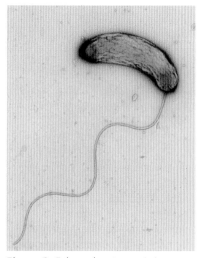

Figure 2 *False-colour transmission electron micrograph (TEM) of the cholera bacterium,* Vibrio cholerae

AQA Examiner's tip

Always write in **precise** scientific terms rather than in vague, generalised terms. For example, state that cholera may be spread 'by faecal contamination of the hands' rather than 'by not making sure your hands are clean after using the toilet'.

▓ How the cholera bacterium causes disease

The main symptoms of cholera are diarrhoea and consequently dehydration. Some people infected with the cholera bacterium show few if any symptoms. Some act as carriers, unwittingly spreading the disease.

Vibrio cholerae is transmitted by the ingestion of water, or more rarely food, that has been contaminated with faecal material containing this pathogen. Once ingested, it causes symptoms of the disease in the following ways.

▓ Almost all the *Vibrio cholerae* bacteria ingested by humans are killed by the acidic conditions in the stomach. However a few may survive, especially if the pH is above 4.5.

▓ When the surviving bacteria reach the small intestine they use their flagella to propel themselves, in a corkscrew-like fashion, through the mucus lining of the intestinal wall.

▓ They then start to produce a toxic protein. This protein has two parts. One part binds to specific carbohydrate receptors on the cell-surface membrane. As only the epithelial cells of the small intestine have these specific receptors, this explains why the cholera toxin only affects this region of the body. The other, the toxic part, enters the epithelial cells. This causes the **ion channels** of the cell-surface membrane to open, so that the chloride **ions** that are normally contained within the epithelial cells flood into the lumen of the intestine.

▓ The loss of chloride ions from the epithelial cells raises their **water potential**, while the increase of chloride ions in the lumen of the intestine lowers its water potential. Water therefore flows from the cells into the lumen.

The loss of ions from the epithelial cells establishes a concentration gradient. Ions therefore move by diffusion into the epithelial cells from the surrounding tissues, including the blood. This, in turn, establishes a water potential gradient that causes water to move by **osmosis** from the blood and other tissues into the intestine.

It is this loss of water from the blood and other tissues, into the intestine, that causes the symptoms of cholera, namely severe diarrhoea and dehydration.

Cholera is treated by restoring the water and ions that have been lost using oral rehydration therapy (see Topic 3.11).

Summary questions

1 Table 3 lists some of the features of cells. For the letter in each box, write down one of the following:
'present' if the feature always occurs
'absent' if it never occurs
'sometimes' if it occurs in some cells but not others.

2 How does the cholera toxin cause diarrhoea?

Table 3 *Features of prokaryotic and eukaryotic cells*

Feature	Prokaryotic cell	Eukaryotic cell
nuclear envelope	A	B
cell wall	C	D
flagellum	E	F
ribosomes	G	H
plasmid	I	J
cell-surface membrane	K	L
mitochondria	M	N

Application

Transmission of cholera

Cholera is transmitted by the ingestion of water, or more rarely food, that has been contaminated with faecal material containing the pathogen. Such contamination can arise because:

- drinking water is not properly purified,
- untreated sewage leaks into water courses,
- food is contaminated by people who prepare and serve it,
- organisms, especially shellfish, have fed on untreated sewage released into rivers or the sea.

1 Given that cholera is transmitted by food and water that is contaminated with faecal matter, suggest three measures that may be used to limit the spread of the disease.

2 Suggest a reason why, in countries where cholera is common, babies who are breast-fed are affected by cholera far less often than babies who are bottle-fed.

3 Suggest how inhibiting the development of a flagellum in the bacterium that causes cholera may prevent the disease.

4 Suggest a reason why injecting antibiotics into the blood can be effective in killing the cholera bacterium whereas the same antibiotics taken orally (by mouth) are not effective.

Figure 3 *Cholera is most easily transmitted where there is a lack of clean water, sanitation is poor and houses lack basic facilities*

3.11 Oral rehydration therapy

Learning objectives:

▨ What is oral rehydration therapy and how does it work?

▨ How have more effective rehydration solutions been developed?

▨ What are the advantages of using starch in place of some glucose in rehydration solutions?

▨ How do drug trials follow a regulated set of ethical procedures?

Specification reference: 3.1.3

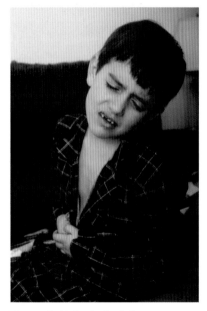

Figure 1 *Abdominal pain is a symptom of diarrhoea*

Cholera is just one of a number of diarrhoeal diseases that infect the intestines. Treatments for these diseases take a number of forms, of which oral rehydration therapy is one of the most important.

▨ What causes diarrhoea?

Diarrhoea is an intestinal disorder in which watery faeces are produced frequently. The causes include:

▨ damage to the epithelial cells lining the intestine,

▨ loss of **microvilli** due to toxins,

▨ excessive secretion of water due to toxins, e.g. cholera toxin.

As a result of diarrhoea, excessive fluid is lost from the body and/or insufficient fluid is taken in to make up for this loss. Either way, dehydration results and this may be fatal.

▨ ▨ What is oral rehydration therapy?

To treat diarrhoeal diseases it is vital to rehydrate the patient. Just drinking water is ineffective for two reasons:

▨ Water is not being absorbed from the intestine. Indeed, as in the case of cholera, water is actually being lost from cells.

▨ The drinking of water does not replace the electrolytes (**ions**) that are being lost from the epithelial cells of the intestine.

It is possible to replace the water and electrolytes intravenously by a drip, but this requires trained personnel. What is required is a suitable mixture of substances that can safely be taken by mouth and which will be absorbed by the intestine. But how can the patient be rehydrated if the intestine is not absorbing water? As it happens, there is more than one type of carrier protein in the cell-surface membranes of the epithelial cells that absorb sodium ions. The trick is to develop a rehydration solution that uses these alternative pathways. As sodium ions are absorbed, so the water potential of the cells falls and water enters the cells by **osmosis**. Therefore, a rehydration solution needs to contain:

▨ **water** – to rehydrate the tissues,

▨ **sodium** – to replace the sodium ions lost from the epithelium of the intestine and to make optimum use of the alternative sodium-glucose **carrier proteins**,

▨ **glucose** – to stimulate the uptake of sodium ions from the intestine and to provide energy,

▨ **potassium** – to replace lost potassium ions and to stimulate appetite,

▨ **other electrolyes** – such as chloride and citrate ions, to help prevent electrolyte imbalance.

These ingredients can be mixed and packaged as a powder, which can be made up into a solution with boiled water as needed. This can be administered by people with minimal training. The solution must be given regularly, and in large amounts, throughout the illness.

Application and How science works

Developing and testing improved oral rehydration solutions

The development of oral rehydration solutions resulted from a long process of scientific experimentation. This is an example of how science works (HSW: H, I & J).

- Early rehydration solutions led to side-effects, especially in children. These were caused by excess sodium.

- Mixtures with a lower sodium content, but more glucose, were tested. Unfortunately the additional glucose lowered the water potential in the lumen of the small intestine so much that it started to draw even more water from the epithelial cells. This made the dehydration even worse.

- Lowering the glucose content reduced this effect but, as glucose also acted as a respiratory substrate, it reduced the amount of energy being supplied to the patient. The problem then was how to supply the glucose without it having an osmotic effect.

- One answer was to use starch in place of some of the glucose. Starch is a large, insoluble molecule that consequently has no osmotic effect. It is, however, broken down steadily by amylase and maltase in the small intestine into its glucose **monomers** (see Topic 2.4). By experimenting with different concentrations of starch, a rehydration solution was developed that released glucose at the optimum rate, so it was taken up as it was produced, without adversely affecting the water potential. Further scientific research is being carried out to find the best source of starch.

Rice starch is a popular choice for two main reasons:

- It is readily available in many parts of the world, especially where diarrhoeal diseases are common.

- It provides other nutrients, such as amino acids. Not only are these nutrients nutritionally valuable but they also help the uptake of sodium ions from the small intestine.

As rice flour produces a very viscous solution, it is hard to swallow. One answer to this problem is to partly digest the starch with amylase. The smaller, and hence more soluble, starch components produce a less viscous drink.

Testing new drugs, including oral rehydration solutions

We have seen how the development of an improved medicine takes place in a number of stages, each of which must be tested for its safety. While initial testing can be done on tissue cultures and animals, to be sure of a drug's effectiveness and safety, it must eventually be tested on humans. This is normally carried out in four phases.

1. A small number (20–80) of usually healthy people are given a tiny amount of the drug to test for side-effects rather than to see if the drug is effective. The dose may be increased gradually in a series of such trials. This stage takes around 6 months.

2. The drug is then given to a slightly larger number of people (100–300) who have the condition the drug is designed to treat. This is to check that the drug works and to look at any safety issues. This stage takes up to 2 years.

Summary questions

1. The following inexpensive home-made rehydration solution is recommended when commercial products are not available:
   8 level teaspoons of sugar + 1 level teaspoon of table salt dissolved in 1 litre of boiled water.

   a Give **two** reasons why sugar (glucose) is included in the mixture.

   b Table salt is sodium chloride. Give **two** reasons why it is included in the mixture.

   c Why is it essential that the water is boiled?

2. Bananas are rich in potassium. It is sometimes recommended that mashed banana is added to the mixture. Give **two** reasons why this might help the patient recover.

3. Suggest another advantage of adding mashed banana to the mixture before drinking, especially in the case of children.

4. Sports drinks contain a high proportion of glucose to help replace the glucose used during strenuous exercise. Explain in terms of water potential why these drinks are therefore not suitable to rehydrate people with diarrhoea.

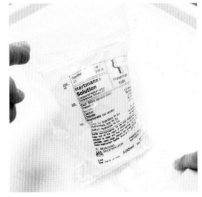

Figure 2 *Bag containing rehydration solution*

■ **Hint**

It is important to remember that oral rehydration solutions do not prevent or cure diarrhoea. They simply rehydrate and nourish the patient until the diarrhoea is cured by some other means.

3   A large-scale trial of many thousands of patients then takes place. Many are given a dummy drug, called a **placebo**. Often neither the scientists nor the patients know who has taken the real drug and who has taken the placebo until after the trial. This type of trial is known as a double-blind trial. These trials take many years.

4   If the drug passes all these stages it may be granted a licence, but its use and effects are still monitored over many years to check for any long-term effects.

1   Why must drugs ultimately be tested on humans?

2   Suggest a reason why a placebo is necessary to ensure that the results of a drug trial are reliable.

3   Suggest why the results of a 'double-blind' trial may be more reliable than a trial in which the patients know whether they are taking the real drug or a placebo.

Before a licence is granted, the results of the trials will be published in a scientific journal, such as *The Lancet*. This helps to ensure the validity of the results in three ways:

■   To be considered worthy of publication by the editors of such journals, any research must conform to accepted scientific standards.

■   Other scientists, especially those in the same field of research, are able to critically review the findings and challenge them if they feel they are inaccurate or misleading. This is known as **peer review**.

■   The experiments/trials can be replicated by others to see if the same results can be obtained.

These trials raise a number of ethical issues. Who should take part in such trials and how should they be recompensed? How can the participants be made aware of the dangers, especially when the trials themselves are designed to expose these dangers? What happens when things go wrong (as happened in March 2006, during a drug trial in London, when six young men became seriously ill)?

1   (a) Describe osmosis in terms of water potential.   *(3 marks)*

    (b) In an experiment, cylinders cut from a potato were placed in sucrose solutions
         of different concentrations. The cylinders were measured before and after
         immersion in sucrose solution. **Figure 1** shows the effect of the sucrose solutions
         on the length of the potato cylinders.

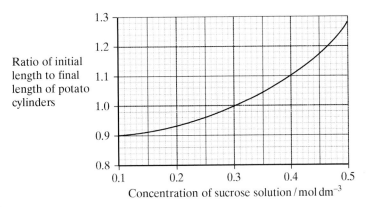

Figure 1

    (i) The initial length of the potato cylinder in $0.1 \, mol \, dm^{-3}$ sucrose solution was $5.0 \, cm$.
    Calculate the final length of this cylinder. Show your working.

    (ii) On a copy of **Figure 1**:
         1. mark with a **T** a point on the curve where the potato cells are turgid
         2. mark with a **W** a point on the curve where the potato cells have the same
             water potential as the sucrose solution.   *(3 marks)*

AQA, 2003

2   (a) **Figure 2** shows an electron micrograph of parts of epithelial cells from the small intestine.

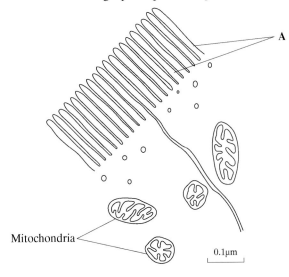

Figure 2

    (i) Name the structures labelled **A**.

    (ii) Explain how these structures help in the absorption of substances from the
          small intestine.   *(2 marks)*

(b) (i) The scale bar on this drawing represents a length of 0.1 μm. Calculate the magnification of the drawing. Show your working.

(ii) Explain why an electron microscope shows more detail of cell structure than a light microscope. *(4 marks)*

(c) The length of mitochondria can vary from 1.5 μm to 10 μm but their width never exceeds 1 μm. Explain the advantage of the width of mitochondria being no more than 1 μm. *(1 mark)*

AQA, 2004

3 (a) Oxygen and water move through cell-surface membranes into cells. Describe **two** ways in which these movements are similar. *(2 marks)*

Figure 3 shows the effect of concentration on the rate of uptake of magnesium ions by root hair cells.

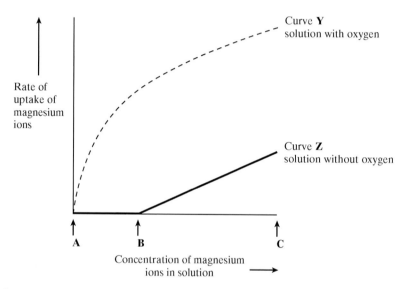

Figure 3

(b) For curve **Y** name the process the cells are using to absorb magnesium ions between concentrations **A** and **B**. Use information in the graph to explain your answer. *(2 marks)*

(c) In the solution without oxygen, explain why no magnesium ions are taken up between concentrations **A** and **B**. *(1 mark)*

(d) For curve Z explain why the rate of uptake increases between **B** and **C**. *(1 mark)*

AQA, 2004

4 **Figure 4** shows part of a cell-surface membrane.

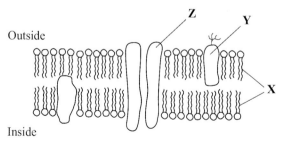

Figure 4

(a) Describe **two** functions of the structure made from the parts labelled **X**. *(2 marks)*

(b) Give **one** function of the molecule labelled **Y**. *(1 mark)*

(c) The part labelled **Z** is involved in facilitated diffusion of substances across the membrane.

   (i)   Give **one** similarity in the ways in which active transport and facilitated diffusion transport substances across the membrane.

   (ii) Give **one** way in which active transport differs from facilitated diffusion.

   (iii) **Figure 5** shows the relationship between the concentration of a substance outside a cell and the rate of entry of this substance into the cell.

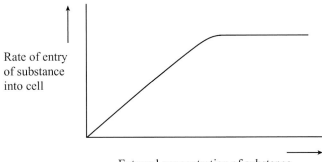

Figure 5

Explain the evidence from the graph that this substance is entering the cell by facilitated diffusion and not by simple diffusion.

(4 marks)

AQA, 2006

5   Mitochondria were isolated from liver tissue using differential centrifugation. The tissue was chopped in cold, isotonic buffer solution. A buffer solution maintains a constant pH. The first stages in the procedure are shown in **Figure 6**.

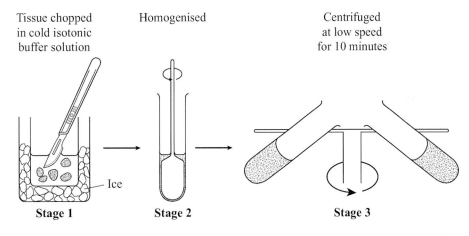

Figure 6

(a) The tissue was chopped in cold, isotonic buffer solution. Explain the reason for using:

   (i)   a cold solution

   (ii) an isotonic solution

   (iii) a buffer solution.   *(3 marks)*

(b) Why is the liver tissue homogenised?   *(1 mark)*

(c) Describe what should be done after **Stage 3** to obtain a sample containing only mitochondria.   *(2 marks)*

AQA, 2006

Lungs and lung disease

4.1 Structure of the human gas-exchange system

In this chapter we shall consider how lungs act as an interface for the exchange of gases and how their function can be affected by both pathogens and lifestyle.

All aerobic organisms require a constant supply of oxygen to release energy in the form of **ATP** during respiration. The carbon dioxide produced in the process needs to be removed as its build-up could be harmful to the body.

The volume of oxygen that has to be absorbed and the volume of carbon dioxide that must be removed are large in mammals because:

■ they are relatively large organisms with a large volume of living cells,

■ they maintain a high body temperature and therefore have high metabolic and respiratory rates.

As a result mammals have evolved specialised surfaces, called **lungs**, to ensure efficient gas exchange between the air and their blood.

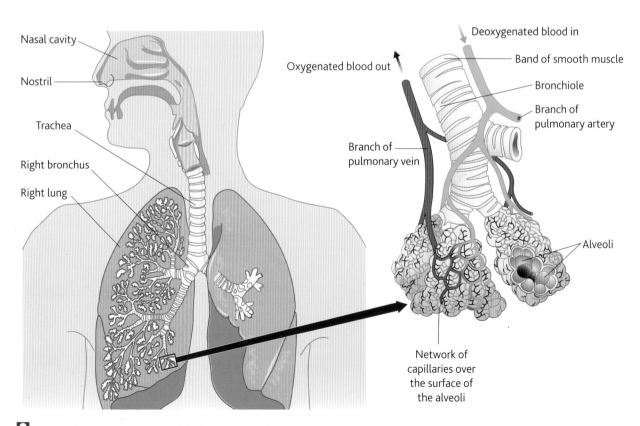

▼ **Figure 1** *The gross structure of the human gas-exchange system*

💡 Mammalian lungs

The lungs are the site of gas exchange in mammals. They are located inside the body because:

- air is not dense enough to support and protect these delicate structures,
- they would otherwise lose a great deal of water and dry out.

The lungs are supported and protected by a bony box called the **rib cage**. The ribs can be moved by the muscles between them. This enables the lungs to be ventilated by a tidal stream of air, thereby ensuring that the air within them is constantly replenished. The main parts of the human gas-exchange system and their structure and functions are described below.

- The **lungs** are a pair of lobed structures made up of a series of highly branched tubules, called bronchioles, which end in tiny air sacs called alveoli.
- The **trachea** is a flexible airway that is supported by rings of cartilage. The cartilage prevents the trachea collapsing as the air pressure inside falls when breathing in. The tracheal walls are made up of muscle, lined with ciliated epithelium and goblet cells. The goblet cells produce mucus that traps dirt particles and bacteria from the air breathed in. The cilia move the mucus, laden with dirt and microorganisms, up to the throat, from where it passes down the oesophagus into the stomach.
- The **bronchi** are two divisions of the trachea, each leading to one lung. They are similar in structure to the trachea and, like the trachea, they also produce mucus to trap dirt particles and have cilia that move the dirt-laden mucus towards the throat. The larger bronchi are supported by cartilage, although the amount of cartilage is reduced as the bronchi get smaller.
- The **bronchioles** are a series of branching subdivisions of the bronchi. Their walls are made of muscle lined with epithelial cells. This muscle allows them to constrict so that they can control the flow of air in and out of the alveoli.
- The **alveoli** are minute air-sacs, with a diameter of between $100\,\mu m$ and $300\,\mu m$, at the end of the bronchioles. They contain some **collagen** and elastic fibres, and they are lined with epithelium. The elastic fibres allow the alveoli to stretch as they fill with air when breathing in. They then spring back during breathing out in order to expel the carbon dioxide-rich air. The alveolar membrane is the gas-exchange surface.

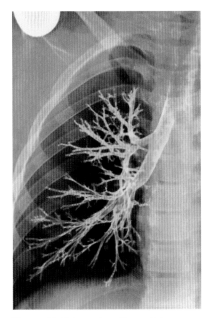

Figure 2 *False-colour X-ray of the bronchus and bronchioles of a healthy human lung*

Figure 3 *False-colour scanning electron micrograph (SEM) of a section of the epithelium of the trachea showing ciliated cells (green)*

▮ Summary questions

1 State **two** reasons why humans need to absorb large volumes of oxygen from the lungs.

2 List in the correct sequence all the structures that air passes through on its journey from the gas-exchange surface of the lungs to the nose.

3 Explain how the cells lining the trachea and bronchus protect the alveoli from damage.

4.2 The mechanism of breathing

Learning objectives:

■ How is air moved into the lungs when breathing in?

■ How is air moved out of the lungs when breathing out?

■ What is meant by pulmonary ventilation and how is it calculated?

Specification reference: 3.1.4

To maintain diffusion of gases across the alveolar epithelium, air must be constantly moved in and out of the lungs. We call this process breathing, or **ventilation**. When the air pressure of the atmosphere is greater than the air pressure inside the lungs, air is forced into the alveoli. This is called **inspiration** (inhalation). When the air pressure in the lungs is greater than that of the atmosphere, air is forced out of the lungs. This is called **expiration** (exhalation). The pressure changes within the lungs are brought about by the movement of two sets of muscles:

■ the diaphragm, which is a sheet of muscle that separates the thorax from the abdomen.

■ the intercostal muscles, which lie between the ribs. There are two sets of intercostal muscles:

   ■ the **internal intercostal muscles**, whose contraction leads to expiration

   ■ the **external intercostal muscles**, whose contraction leads to inspiration.

Figure 1 shows the arrangement of these various muscles.

Hint

There are two basic physical laws that will help you to understand the movement of air during breathing:

Within a closed container, as the volume of a gas increases its pressure decreases. Similarly, as the volume of a gas decreases so the pressure increases.

Gases move from a region where their pressure is higher to a region where their pressure is lower.

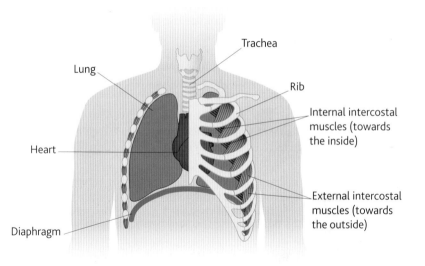

Figure 1 *The arrangement of the diaphragm and intercostal muscles*

AQA Examiner's tip

The volume of blood pumped by the heart in one minute is called the 'cardiac output'. Some examination candidates confuse this with 'pulmonary output'. Remember cardiac = heart and pulmonary = lungs, and don't confuse them.

Inspiration

Breathing in is an active process (it uses energy) and occurs as follows:

■ The external intercostal muscles contract, while the internal intercostal muscles relax.

■ The ribs are pulled upwards and outwards, increasing the volume of the thorax.

■ The diaphragm muscles contract, causing it to flatten, which also increases the volume of the thorax.

■ The increased volume of the thorax results in reduction of pressure in the lungs.

■ Atmospheric pressure is now greater than pulmonary pressure, and so air is forced into the lungs.

Expiration

Breathing out is a largely passive process (it does not require much energy) and occurs as follows:

■ The internal intercostal muscles contract, while the external intercostal muscles relax.

■ The ribs move downwards and inwards, decreasing the volume of the thorax.

■ The diaphragm muscles relax, making it return to its upwardly domed position, again decreasing the volume of the thorax.

■ The decreased volume of the thorax increases the pressure in the lungs.

■ The pulmonary pressure is now greater than that of the atmosphere, and so air is forced out of the lungs.

During normal quiet breathing, the recoil of the elastic lungs is the main cause of air being forced out (like air being expelled from a partly inflated balloon). Only under more strenuous conditions such as exercise do the various muscles play a part.

Pulmonary ventilation

It is sometimes useful to know how much air is taken in and out of the lungs in a given time. To do this we use a measure called pulmonary ventilation. Pulmonary ventilation is the total volume of air that is moved into the lungs during one minute. To calculate it we multiply together two factors:

■ tidal volume, which is the volume of air normally taken in at each breath when the body is at rest. This is usually around $0.5\,dm^3$.

■ ventilation (breathing) rate, i.e. the number of breaths taken in one minute. This is normally 12–20 breaths in a healthy adult.

Pulmonary ventilation is expressed as $dm^3\,min^{-1}$.

To summarise:

$$\text{pulmonary ventilation} = \text{tidal volume} \times \text{ventilation rate}$$
$$(dm^3\,min^{-1}) \qquad\qquad (dm^3) \qquad\qquad (min^{-1})$$

Summary questions

1 From the graphs in Figure 3, determine the tidal volume of this person.

2 From the graphs in Figure 3, calculate the rate of breathing of this person. Give your answer in breaths per minute. Show how you arrived at your answer.

3 If the volume of air in the lungs when the person inhaled was $3\,000\,cm^3$ what would the volume of air in the lungs be after the person had exhaled? Show your working.

4 Explain how muscles create the change of pressure in the alveoli over the period 0 to 0.5 s.

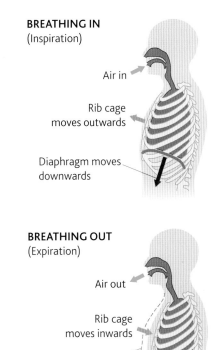

BREATHING IN
(Inspiration)

Air in

Rib cage moves outwards

Diaphragm moves downwards

BREATHING OUT
(Expiration)

Air out

Rib cage moves inwards

Position of rib cage when breathing in

Diaphragm moves upwards

Figure 2 *Position of ribs and diaphragm during inspiration and expiration*

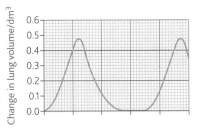
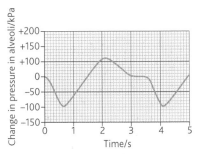

Figure 3 *The volume and pressure changes that occurred in the lungs of a person during breathing while at rest*

4.3 Exchange of gases in the lungs

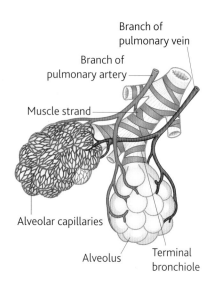 Learning objectives:

▓ What are the essential features of exchange surfaces?

▓ How are gases exchanged in the alveoli of humans?

Specification reference: 3.1.4

The site of gas exchange in mammals is the epithelium of the alveoli. These alveoli are minute air sacs some 100–300 μm in diameter and situated in the lungs. To ensure a constant supply of oxygen to the body, a diffusion gradient must be maintained at the alveolar surface.

▓ Essential features of exchange surfaces

To enable efficient transfer of materials across them by diffusion or active transport, exchange surfaces have the following characteristics:

▓ They have a **large surface area to volume ratio** – to speed up the rate of exchange.

▓ They are **very thin** – to keep the diffusion pathway short and so allow materials to cross rapidly.

▓ They are **partially permeable** – to allow selected materials to diffuse easily.

▓ There is **movement of the environmental medium**, e.g. air – to maintain a diffusion gradient.

▓ There is **movement of the internal medium**, e.g. blood – to maintain a diffusion gradient.

We saw in Topic 3.6 that the relationship between some of these factors is described in the following expression, known as Fick's Law:

diffusion is proportional to: $\dfrac{\text{surface area} \times \text{difference in concentration}}{\text{length of diffusion path}}$

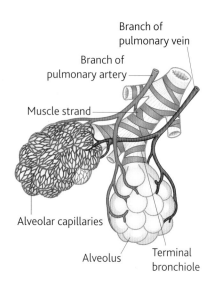

Branch of pulmonary vein

Branch of pulmonary artery

Muscle strand

Alveolar capillaries

Alveolus

Terminal bronchiole

Figure 1 *Alveoli*

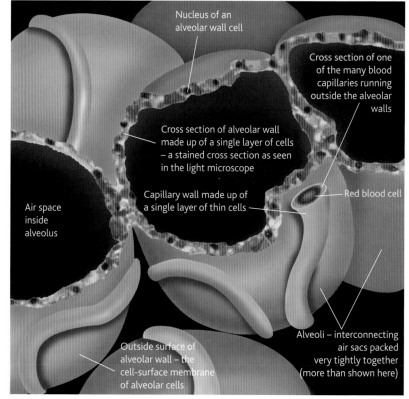

Nucleus of an alveolar wall cell

Cross section of one of the many blood capillaries running outside the alveolar walls

Cross section of alveolar wall made up of a single layer of cells – a stained cross section as seen in the light microscope

Capillary wall made up of a single layer of thin cells

Red blood cell

Air space inside alveolus

Outside surface of alveolar wall – the cell-surface membrane of alveolar cells

Alveoli – interconnecting air sacs packed very tightly together (more than shown here)

Figure 2 *External appearance of a group of alveoli*

Being thin, these specialised exchange surfaces are easily damaged and therefore are often located inside an organism for protection. Where an exchange surface, such as the lungs, is located inside the body, the organism needs to have some means of moving the external medium over the surface, e.g. a means of ventilating the lungs in a mammal.

Role of the alveoli in gas exchange

There are about 300 million alveoli in each human lung. Their total surface area is around $70\,m^2$ – about half the area of a tennis court. Their structure is shown in Figures 1 and 2. Each alveolus is lined mostly with epithelial cells only $0.05\,\mu m$ to $0.3\,\mu m$ thick. Around each alveolus is a network of pulmonary capillaries, so narrow $(7-10\,\mu m)$ that red blood cells are flattened against the thin capillary walls in order to squeeze through. These capillaries have walls that are only a single layer of cells thick $(0.04-0.2\,\mu m)$. Diffusion of gases between the alveoli and the blood will be very rapid because:

- red blood cells are slowed as they pass through pulmonary capillaries, allowing more time for diffusion,
- the distance between the alveolar air and red blood cells is reduced as the red blood cells are flattened against the capillary walls,
- the walls of both alveoli and capillaries are very thin and therefore the distance over which diffusion takes place is very short,
- alveoli and pulmonary capillaries have a very large total surface area,
- breathing movements constantly ventilate the lungs, and the action of the heart constantly circulates blood around the alveoli. Together, these ensure that a steep concentration gradient of the gases to be exchanged is maintained,
- blood flow through the pulmonary capillaries maintains a concentration gradient.

The diffusion of gases in an alveolus is illustrated in Figure 4.

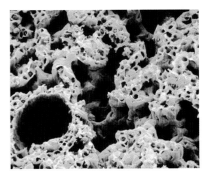

Figure 3 *False-colour scanning electron micrograph (SEM) of a section of human lung tissue showing alveoli surrounded by blood capillaries*

Hint

The diffusion pathway is short because the alveoli have only a single layer of epithelial cells and the blood capillaries have only a single layer of endothelial cells.

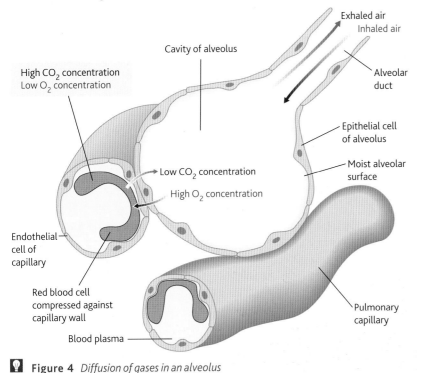

Figure 4 *Diffusion of gases in an alveolus*

Summary questions

1. How does each of the following features contribute to the efficiency of gas exchange in alveoli?

   a The wall of each alveolus is not more than $0.3\,\mu m$ thick.

   b There are 300 million alveoli in each lung.

   c Each alveolus is covered by a dense network of pulmonary blood capillaries.

   d Each pulmonary capillary is very narrow.

2. If the number of alveoli in each lung was increased to 600 million and the pulmonary ventilation was doubled, how many times greater would the rate of diffusion be?

4.4 Lung disease – pulmonary tuberculosis

Learning objectives:

■ What is the cause of pulmonary tuberculosis?

■ What are the symptoms of pulmonary tuberculosis?

■ How is pulmonary tuberculosis transmitted between individuals in the population?

■ How does disease develop within the body?

Specification reference: 3.1.4

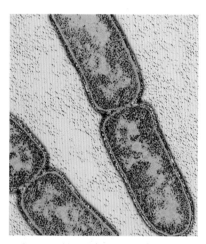

Figure 1 *False-colour transmission electron micrograph (TEM) of a cross-section through two pairs of recently divided* Mycobacterium tuberculosis *bacteria. The outer cell wall appears green. DNA – genetic material within the cell contents appears yellow.*

Tuberculosis (TB) is an infectious disease that can affect any part of the body although it is usually found in the lungs as these are the first site of infection. It is calculated that someone in the world is newly infected with TB every second. It kills approximately 2 million people each year; more than any other infectious disease.

Causes and symptoms

Tuberculosis is caused by one of two species of rod-shaped bacteria: *Mycobacterium tuberculosis* or *Mycobacterium bovis*. It is estimated that up to 30 per cent of the world's population have one or other form of the bacterium within their bodies. The symptoms of pulmonary tuberculosis initially include a persistent cough, tiredness and loss of appetite that leads to weight loss. As the disease develops, fever and coughing up of blood may occur.

Transmission

Pulmonary tuberculosis (TB) is spread through the air by droplets, released into the air when infected individuals cough, sneeze, laugh or even talk. *M. tuberculosis* is a resistant bacterium that can survive several weeks once the droplets have dried. It normally takes close contact with an infected person over a period of time rather than a casual meeting in the street to transmit the bacteria. TB is therefore usually spread between family members, close friends or work colleagues, especially in crowded and poorly ventilated conditions. TB can also be spread from cows to humans because *M. bovis* also infects cattle. Milk may contain the bacterium. Some groups are at greater risk of contracting TB. These include people who:

■ are in close contact with infected individuals over long periods, e.g. living and sleeping in overcrowded conditions,

■ work or reside in long-term care facilities where relatively large numbers of people live close together, e.g. old peoples' homes, care homes, hospitals or prisons,

■ are from countries where TB is common,

■ have reduced immunity, such as those listed in Table 1.

Course of infection

Once *Mycobacterium tuberculosis* has been inhaled by someone who is not immune to it, the infection follows a particular course.

■ The bacteria grow and divide within the upper regions of the lungs where there is a plentiful supply of oxygen.

■ The body's immune system responds and white blood cells accumulate at the site of infection to ingest the bacteria.

■ This leads to inflammation and the enlargement of the lymph nodes that drain that area of the lungs. This is called the **primary infection** and usually occurs in children.

■ In a healthy person there are few symptoms, if any, and the infection is controlled within a few weeks. However, some bacteria usually remain.

Many years later these bacteria may re-emerge to cause a second infection of TB. This is called **post-primary tuberculosis** and typically occurs in adults.

This infection also arises in the upper regions of the lungs but is not so easily controlled. The bacteria destroy the tissue of the lungs. This results in cavities and, where the lung repairs itself, scar tissue.

The sufferer coughs up damaged lung tissue containing bacteria, along with blood. Without treatment the TB spreads to the rest of the body and can be fatal.

Preventing the spread of TB depends largely on public services. These services are a compromise between current scientific understanding of TB and public, political and economic circumstances. Scientific knowledge may make vaccination an obvious preventive measure, but a lack of money, political will and public confidence in the process often makes it difficult to implement effectively.

Table 1 *Examples of groups with reduced immunity and therefore at increased risk of contracting TB*

The very young or very old
Those with AIDS
People with other medical conditions that make the body less able to resist disease, e.g. diabetes or a lung disease, such as silicosis
Those undergoing treatment with immunosuppressant drugs, e.g. following transplant surgery
The malnourished
Alcoholics or injecting drug-users
The homeless

Application and How science works

Prevention and control of TB

The main biological preventative measure for tuberculosis (TB) is vaccination. All children in the UK are routinely tested for their immunity to TB. Vaccination of those individuals who are already immune is unnecessary and dangerous. Those without immunity are given the vaccine. This is an attenuated (weakened) strain of *Mycobacterium bovis*, the organism that causes TB in cattle.

In addition to biological means of prevention, there are social and economic measures that can be introduced to reduce the number of TB cases. These include:

- better education about TB, particularly the need to complete all courses of drugs,
- more and better housing,
- improved health facilities and treatments,
- better nutrition to ensure that immune systems are not weakened by poor diet.

1 Suggest a reason why the bacteria in the vaccine are weakened before they are injected?

2 Explain how 'more and better housing' can help prevent TB.

Other means of controlling TB include treatment with drugs. One problem with all drug treatment for TB is the long period (6–9 months) for which the drugs must be taken. Another problem is the development of strains of *M. tuberculosis* that no longer respond to some drugs.

Despite all these measures, there has been a recent increase in TB in many developed countries. The reasons for this include the spread of HIV, the development of drug-resistant forms of *M.tuberculosis*, more people living 'rough' and a larger proportion of elderly people in the population.

3 To treat TB, a combination of four drugs is often given. Explain why this is necessary.

4 Suggest a reason why an increasingly elderly population might have led to an increase in TB infections.

Figure 2 *Poor, damp living conditions*

Summary questions

1 Which organisms can cause tuberculosis?

2 How is TB spread from infected to uninfected people?

3 Suggest reasons why TB is sometimes referred to as a 'disease of poverty'.

4 Suggest why heating milk to 72°C for 15 seconds (pasteurisation) might help to control the spread of TB.

4.5 Lung disease – fibrosis, asthma and emphysema

Learning objectives:

▨ What are fibrosis, asthma and emphysema?

▨ How do each of the above diseases affect lung function?

Specification reference: 3.1.4

We saw in Topic 4.2 that the alveolar epithelium of the lungs is the interface at which gas exchange takes place. To be efficient, this exchange surface needs to be thin, have a large surface area and be constantly ventilated. It follows that any factor that adversely affects one or more of these features will reduce the efficiency of gas exchange. Let us look at three lung diseases – pulmonary fibrosis, asthma and emphysema – each of which impairs the function of the lungs in different ways.

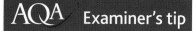

Pulmonary fibrosis

Pulmonary fibrosis arises when scars form on the epithelium of the lungs, causing them to become irreversibly thickened (Figure 1). To diffuse respiratory gases, the linings of the alveoli need to be thin. It follows that, in patients with fibrosis, oxygen cannot diffuse into the blood as efficiently because the diffusion pathway has been considerably lengthened and the volume of air that the lungs can contain has been reduced. The fibrosis also reduces the elasticity of the lungs. The expulsion of air when breathing out is due to the lungs springing back in the same way as a deflating balloon. To achieve this the lungs must be elastic. Fibrosis makes it difficult to breathe out and therefore ventilate the lungs. The effects of fibrosis on lung function, along with an explanation of their causes, are listed below.

Figure 1 *Honeycomb lung is a long-term consequence of pulmonary fibrosis. Areas of lung tissue are converted into multiple spaces, separated from each other by fibrous tissue.*

▨ **Shortness of breath, especially when exercising** is due to a considerable volume of the air space within the lungs being occupied by fibrous tissue. This means that less air, and hence oxygen, is being taken into the lungs at each breath. In addition, the thickened epithelium of the alveoli means that the diffusion pathway is increased and so the diffusion of oxygen into the blood is extremely slow. The loss of elasticity makes ventilating the lungs very difficult. This makes it hard to maintain a diffusion gradient across the exhange surface.

▨ **Chronic, dry cough** occurs because the fibrous tissue creates an obstruction in the airways of the lungs. The body's reflex reaction is to try to remove the obstruction by coughing. Since the tissue is more or less immovable, nothing is expelled and the cough is described as 'dry'.

▨ **Pain and discomfort in the chest** are the consequence of pressure, and hence damage, from the mass of fibrous tissue in the lungs and further damage and scarring due to coughing.

▨ **Weakness and fatigue** results from the reduced intake of oxygen into the blood. This means that the release of energy by cellular respiration is reduced, leading to tiredness.

The exact cause of fibrosis is unclear, but evidence suggests it is a reaction to microscopic lung injury, to which some individuals are genetically more susceptible.

Asthma

Asthma is an example of a localised allergic reaction. Asthma affects up to 10 per cent of the world population and accounts for 2000 deaths each year in the UK alone. Some of the most common **allergens** that stimulate asthma are pollen, animal fur and the faeces of the house dust mite (Figure 2). It can also be triggered, or made worse, by a range of factors,

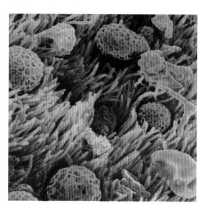

Figure 2 *Scanning electron micrograph (SEM) of allergens such as dust (pale blue) and pollen (pink) on the surface cilia of the trachea. These allergens may cause asthma and hay fever.*

including air pollutants (e.g. sulfur dioxide, nitrogen oxides and ozone), exercise, cold air, infection, anxiety and stress. One or more of these allergens causes white blood cells on the linings of the bronchi and bronchioles to release a chemical called histamine. This, in turn, has the following effects:

- The lining of these airways becomes inflamed.
- The cells of the epithelial lining secrete larger quantities of mucus than normal.
- Fluid leaves the capillaries and enters the airways.
- The muscle surrounding the bronchioles contracts and so constricts the airways.

Overall, there is a much greater resistance to the flow of air in and out of the alveoli. This makes it difficult to ventilate the lungs and so maintain a diffusion gradient across the exchange surface. The symptoms of asthma and their explanations are given below.

- **Difficulty in breathing** is due to the constriction of the bronchi and bronchioles, their inflamed linings and the additional mucus and fluid within them.
- **A wheezing sound when breathing** is caused by the air passing through the very constricted bronchi and bronchioles.
- **A tight feeling in the chest** is the consequence of not being able to ventilate the lungs adequately because of the constricted bronchi and bronchioles.
- **Coughing** is the reflex response to the obstructed bronchi and bronchioles in an effort to clear them.

Genetics appears to play a role, as asthma tends to run in families. The number of asthmatics continues to rise, and many explanations have been put forward for this. These include an increase in air pollution, an increase in stress and an increase in the variety of chemicals used in our food and manufactured products. There is also recent evidence that our 'cleaner' lifestyles mean that we are now exposed to fewer allergens as children and therefore become more easily sensitised to them in later life.

Emphysema

One in every five smokers will develop the crippling lung disease called emphysema. The disease develops over a period of 20 years or so and it is virtually impossible to diagnose until the lungs have been irreversibly damaged. Healthy lungs contain large quantities of elastic tissue, mostly made of the protein elastin. This tissue stretches when we breathe in and springs back when we breathe out. In emphysematous lungs the elastin has become permanently stretched and the lungs are no longer able to force out all the air from the alveoli. The surface area of the alveoli is reduced and they sometimes burst. As a result, little if any exchange of gases can take place across the stretched and damaged air sacs.

The symptoms of emphysema and their explanations are detailed below:

- **Shortness of breath** results from difficulty in exhaling air due to the loss of elasticity in the lungs. If the lungs cannot be emptied of much of their air, then it is difficult to inhale fresh air containing oxygen and so the patient feels breathless. The smaller alveolar surface area leads to reduced levels of oxygen in the blood and so the patient tries to increase the oxygen supply by breathing more rapidly.
- **Chronic cough** is the consequence of lung damage and the body's effort to remove damaged tissue and mucus that cannot be removed

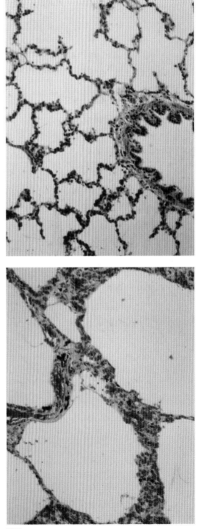

Figure 3 *Emphysematous and normal lung tissue (light micrograph). In normal lung tissue (top), there are a lot of small air spaces (alveoli). In the lung of a person with emphysema (bottom), the walls of the alveoli have broken down, making the spaces much larger.*

Hint

It can be helpful to think in terms of the different ways in which the lungs work to exchange gases and then consider how any lung disease interferes with these (see Table 1).

naturally because the cilia on the bronchi and bronchioles have been destroyed.

◼ **Bluish skin coloration** is due to low levels of oxygen in the blood as a result of poor gas diffusion in the lungs.

The only way to minimise the chances of getting emphysema is not to smoke at all, or to give up. The function cannot be restored to smoke-damaged lungs but giving up smoking can significantly reduce the rate of further deterioration.

Table 1 *Lung function and disease*

Lung function	Disease that interferes with function
to ventilate by inhalation	asthma
to ventilate by exhalation	fibrosis and emphysema
to provide a large surface area	emphysema
to provide a short diffusion pathway	fibrosis

◼ **Application and How science works**

Risk factors for lung disease

There are a number of specific risk factors that increase the probability of someone suffering from lung disease. In this context 'lung disease' refers to chronic obstructive pulmonary disease (COPD), which includes emphysema and chronic bronchitis. These risk factors include:

◼ **Smoking**. 90 per cent of people suffering from COPD are, or have been, heavy smokers.

◼ **Air pollution**. Pollutant particles and gases (e.g. sulfur dioxide) increase the likelihood of COPD, especially in areas of heavy industry.

◼ **Genetic make-up**. Some people are genetically more likely to get lung disease, others less so; this explains why some lifelong smokers never get lung disease while others die early.

◼ **Infections**. People who frequently get other chest infections also show a higher incidence of COPD.

◼ **Occupation**. People working with harmful chemicals, gases and dusts that can be inhaled have an increased risk of lung disease.

Let us analyse some data relating to the most significant risk factor – smoking.

The world's longest-running survey of smoking began in the UK in 1951. This survey and other ones elsewhere in the world have revealed a number of general statistical facts about smokers. Look at Figure 4. What does it tell us?

◼ All the lines start at 100 per cent. This shows that the whole of this group of the population were alive at the start of the survey. What else does this tell us? As the scale of the independent variable (age in years) has its origin at 35 it suggests that everyone in this group must have been at least 35 years old at the start of the survey.

Summary questions

1 Difficulty in breathing or shortness of breath are common symptoms of lung disease. For each of the following explain why the disease results in this symptom.

a asthma

b emphysema

c fibrosis

2 Link each of the following statements with **one** of the following diseases: fibrosis, asthma or emphysema.

a It is caused almost entirely by smoking.

b Thickening of the epithelium of alveoli leads to a lengthened diffusion pathway.

c It leads to a reduction in the surface area of the alveoli.

d It is a localised allergic reaction.

3 The photographs of normal lung tissue and emphysematous lung tissue (Figure 3 on page 83) are at the same magnification. Using the evidence in these photos and this topic, explain why an individual with emphysema has difficulty carrying out strenuous exercise.

- All the lines follow approximately the same pattern: they decline slowly at first and then at an increasing rate until at some point all lines cross the *x*-axis. This describes the shape but what does it actually show? Namely that only a few people die between the ages of 35 and 60 but that, after age 60, the death rate becomes increasingly rapid until, at some point everyone in the group has died.

- What about the differences between the four separate coloured lines? Each represents a different group distinguished by the number of cigarettes smoked each day. At every age beyond 35 years, the more cigarettes smoked, the fewer people remain alive. This difference is more marked the greater the age.

- At what age did the members of each group die? Well the line representing the group who smoked more than 25 cigarettes a day crosses the *x*-axis at 82 years, showing that no one in the group lived beyond that age. By contrast, some of the non-smokers lived beyond 90 years.

- What is the overall interpretation? Namely that the more cigarettes smoked per day, the earlier, on average, a smoker dies.

The interpretation of the data in Figure 4 shows there is a **correlation** between smoking and premature death. This does not, however, prove that smoking is the cause of an early death. The data seem to suggest this is the case but there is no evidence here to prove that it is so. There needs to be a clear causal connection between smoking and death before we can say that the case is proven. These data alone show only a correlation and not a cause. To prove that smoking is the cause of early death in smokers the correct scientific process needs to be followed. There are three main stages:

1 Establish a hypothesis to try to explain the correlation; this should be based on current knowledge.

2 Design and perform experiments to test the hypothesis.

3 Establish the causal link and formulate theories to explain it.

This is precisely what happened in establishing the causal link between smoking and lung cancer, as detailed in Topic 1.2.

Link

More information on correlations and causal relationships is given in Topic 1.2.

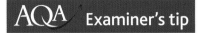

AQA **Examiner's tip**

It is important to be clear that a correlation does not mean that there is a causal link.

---

1 Name four risk factors associated with lung disease.

2 Using Figure 4, state what percentage of non-smokers are likely to survive to age 80.

3 How many times greater is the likelihood of a non-smoker living to age 70 than someone who smokes over 25 cigarettes a day?

4 About 10 to 15 years after giving up smoking the risk of death approaches that of non-smokers. Using this information and that in Figure 3 explain to a 40-year-old who smokes 30 cigarettes a day the likely impact on her life expectancy of giving up smoking immediately.

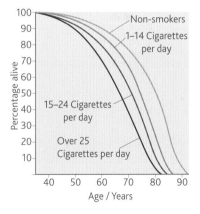

Figure 4 *Life expectancy related to the number of cigarettes smoked*

AQA Examination-style questions

1　**Figure 1** shows some of the structures involved in ventilating human lungs.

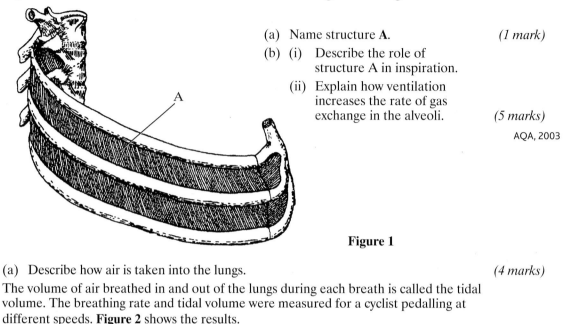

(a)　Name structure **A**. *(1 mark)*

(b)　(i)　Describe the role of structure A in inspiration.

　　(ii)　Explain how ventilation increases the rate of gas exchange in the alveoli. *(5 marks)*

AQA, 2003

Figure 1

2　(a)　Describe how air is taken into the lungs. *(4 marks)*

The volume of air breathed in and out of the lungs during each breath is called the tidal volume. The breathing rate and tidal volume were measured for a cyclist pedalling at different speeds. **Figure 2** shows the results.

(b)　Describe the **two** curves:

　　(i)　Tidal volume

　　(ii)　Breathing rate *(2 marks)*

(c)　Calculate the pulmonary ventilation when the cyclist is cycling at $20\,\text{km}\,\text{h}^{-1}$. Show your working. *(2 marks)*

AQA, 2005

Figure 2

3　A resting person breathed normally. The total volume of air in the lungs during each breath is shown in **Figure 3**.

(a)　(i)　The pulmonary ventilation rate is the volume of air taken into the lungs in one minute. Calculate the pulmonary ventilation rate of the person whose pattern of breathing is shown in the graph.

　　(ii)　Give **two** ways in which a change in the pattern of breathing may increase pulmonary ventilation rate during a period of exercise. *(2 marks)*

(b)　Describe the part played by the diaphragm in bringing about the movement of air over the part of the graph labelled **A**. *(3 marks)*

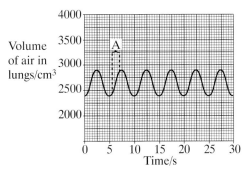

Figure 3

(c) The table shows the percentage of gases in samples of inhaled and exhaled air.

Gas	Percentage in	
	inhaled air	**exhaled air**
Nitrogen	78.47	74.40
Carbon dioxide	0.04	3.95
Oxygen	20.47	16.01
Other gases	0.38	0.36
Water vapour	0.42	4.20

Use the information in the table to explain why the percentage of nitrogen is lower in exhaled air than in inhaled air. *(1 mark)*

(d) (i) Name the structures in the lungs which an oxygen molecule will pass through on its way to an alveolus.

(ii) Describe how **two** features of an alveolus enable efficient exchange of gases in the lungs. *(5 marks)*

AQA, 2001

4 (a) Explain how emphysema reduces the efficiency of gas exchange in the lungs. *(4 marks)*

(b) Give **two** factors which could increase the incidence of emphysema. *(2 marks)*

(c) Give **three** differences between emphysema and asthma. *(3 marks)*

5 (a) Describe how pulmonary tuberculosis is transmitted from one person to another. *(2 marks)*

(b) Give **two** symptoms of pulmonary tuberculosis. *(2 marks)*

(c) The table shows the number of TB cases in the UK from 2000 to 2005.

Year	Number of TB cases in UK
2000	6 323
2001	6 652
2002	6 861
2003	6 970
2004	7 321
2005	8 113

(i) Suggest **two** reasons for the increase in the number of TB cases in the UK during this period.

(ii) Calculate the percentage increase in the number of TB cases in the UK between 2002 and 2005. *(4 marks)*

6 (a) Give **two** symptoms of pulmonary fibrosis. *(2 marks)*

(b) Explain how fibrosis affects the function of the lungs. *(4 marks)*

(c) Scientists investigated the effect of smoking cigarettes on the incidence of emphysema. The investigation included non-smokers and smokers who smoked 5, 10, 15 or 20 cigarettes per day.

(i) Give **three** other factors the scientists should take into consideration when choosing their sample for this investigation.

(ii) The results of the investigation showed a correlation between the number of cigarettes smoked and the incidence of emphysema. Using this example explain the distinction between a correlation and a causal relationship. *(5 marks)*

5.1   The structure of the heart

Learning objectives:

▥ What is the appearance of the heart and its associated blood vessels?

▥ Why is the heart made up of two adjacent pumps?

▥ How is the structure of the heart related to its functions?

Specification reference: 3.1.5

AQA Examiner's tip

Although the left ventricle has a thicker wall than the right ventricle, their internal volumes are the same. They have to be, otherwise more blood would be pumped out of one side of the heart than the other.

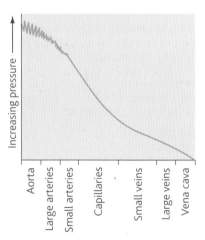

Figure 1 *Pressure changes in blood vessels*

AQA Examiner's tip

The left and right sides of the heart both contract together.

In this chapter we shall look at the structure of the heart, how it functions and the effects of lifestyle on heart disease.

The heart is a muscular organ that lies in the thoracic cavity behind the sternum (breastbone). It operates continuously and tirelessly throughout the life of an organism.

▥ ⚗ Structure of the human heart

The human heart is really two separate pumps lying side by side. The pump on the left deals with oxygenated blood from the lungs, while the one on the right deals with deoxygenated blood from the body. Each pump has two chambers:

▥ The **atrium** is thin-walled and elastic and stretches as it collects blood. It only has to pump blood the short distance to the ventricle and therefore has only a thin muscular wall.

▥ The **ventricle** has a much thicker muscular wall as it has to pump blood some distance, either to the lungs or to the rest of the body.

Why have two separate pumps? Why not just pump the blood through the lungs to collect oxygen and then straight to the rest of the body before returning it to the heart? The problem with such a system is that the blood has to pass through tiny capillaries in the lungs in order to present a large surface area for the exchange of gases (see Topic 4.3). In doing so, there is a very large drop in pressure and so the blood flow to the rest of the body would be very slow. This drop in pressure is illustrated in Figure 1. Mammals therefore have a system in which the blood is returned to the heart to increase its pressure before it is distributed to the rest of the body. It is essential to keep the oxygenated blood in the pump on the left side separate from the deoxygenated blood in the pump on the right.

Because the right ventricle pumps blood to the lungs, a distance of only a few centimetres, it has a thinner muscular wall than the left ventricle. The left ventricle, in contrast, has a thick muscular wall, enabling it to create enough pressure to pump blood to the extremities of the body, a distance of about 1.5 m. Although the two sides of the heart are separate pumps and, after birth, there is no mixing of the blood in each of them, they nevertheless pump in time with each other: both atria contract together and then both ventricles contract together.

Between each atrium and ventricle are valves that prevent the backflow of blood into the atria when the ventricles contract. There are two sets of valves:

▥ the **left atrioventricular (bicuspid) valves**, formed of two cup-shaped flaps on the left side of the heart,

▥ the **right atrioventricular (tricuspid) valves**, formed of three cup-shaped flaps on the right side of the heart.

Each of the four chambers of the heart is served by large blood vessels that carry blood towards or away from the heart. The ventricles pump blood away from the heart and into the arteries. The atria receive blood from the veins.

Vessels connecting the heart to the lungs are called **pulmonary** vessels. The vessels connected to the four chambers are therefore as follows:

- The **aorta** is connected to the left ventricle and carries oxygenated blood to all parts of the body except the lungs.
- The **vena cava** is connected to the right atrium and brings deoxygenated blood back from the tissues of the body.
- The **pulmonary artery** is connected to the right ventricle and carries deoxygenated blood to the lungs, where its oxygen is replenished and its carbon dioxide is removed. Unusually for an artery, it carries deoxygenated blood.
- The **pulmonary vein** is connected to the left atrium and brings oxygenated blood back from the lungs. Unusually for a vein, it carries oxygenated blood.

The structure of the heart and its associated blood vessels is shown in Figure 2.

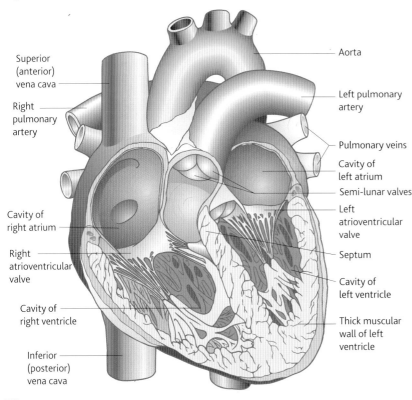

Figure 2 *Section through the human heart*

Supplying the heart muscle with oxygen

Although oxygenated blood passes through the left side of the heart, the heart does not use this oxygen to meet its own great respiratory needs. Instead, the heart muscle is supplied by its own blood vessels, called the **coronary arteries**, which branch off the aorta shortly after it leaves the heart. Blockage of these arteries, e.g. by a blood clot, leads to **myocardial infarction**, or heart attack, because an area of the heart muscle is deprived of oxygen and so dies.

> **Hint**
>
> An easy way to recall which heart chambers are attached to which type of blood vessel is to remember that A and V always go together. Hence: Atria link to Veins and Arteries link to Ventricles.

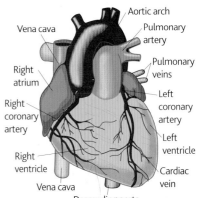

Figure 3 *External appearance of the human heart showing the blood supply to the heart muscle*

Summary questions

1. What is the name of the blood vessel that supplies the heart muscle with oxygenated blood?

2. State whether the blood in each of the following structures is oxygenated or deoxygenated:

   a vena cava

   b pulmonary artery

   c left atrium.

3. List the correct sequence of four main blood vessels and four heart chambers that a red blood cell passes through on its journey from the lungs, though the heart and body, and back again to the lungs.

4. Suggest why it is important to prevent mixing of the blood in the two sides of the heart.

5.2 The cardiac cycle

The heart undergoes a sequence of events that is repeated in humans around 70 times each minute when at rest. This is known as the **cardiac cycle**. There are two phases to the beating of the heart: contraction (systole) and relaxation (diastole). Contraction occurs separately in the ventricles and the atria and is therefore described in two stages. For some of the time, relaxation takes place simultaneously in all chambers of the heart and is therefore treated as a single phase in the account below, which is illustrated in Figure 1. The direction of blood flow through the heart is maintained by pressure changes and the action of valves.

■ Relaxation of the heart (diastole)

Blood returns to the atria of the heart through the pulmonary vein (from the lungs) and the vena cava (from the body). As the atria fill, the pressure in them rises, pushing open the atrioventricular valves and allowing the blood to pass into the ventricles. The muscular walls of both the atria and ventricles are relaxed at this stage. The relaxation of the ventricle wall reduces the pressure within the ventricle. This causes the pressure to be lower than that in the aorta and the pulmonary artery, and so the semi-lunar valves in the aorta and the pulmonary artery close, accompanied by the characteristic 'dub' sound of the heart beat.

1. Blood enters atria and ventricles from pulmonary veins and vena cava

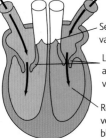

Semi-lunar valves closed

Left and right atrioventricular valves open

Relaxation of ventricles draws blood from atria

Relaxation of heart (diastole)

Atria are relaxed and fill with blood. Ventricles are also relaxed.

💡 **Figure 1** *The cardiac cycle*

2.

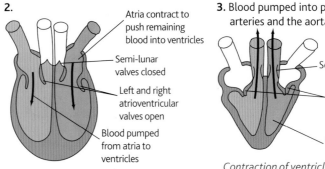

Atria contract to push remaining blood into ventricles

Semi-lunar valves closed

Left and right atrioventricular valves open

Blood pumped from atria to ventricles

Contraction of atria (atrial systole)

Atria contract, pushing blood into the ventricles. Ventricles remain relaxed.

3. Blood pumped into pulmonary arteries and the aorta

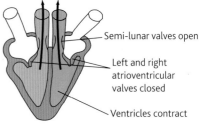

Semi-lunar valves open

Left and right atrioventricular valves closed

Ventricles contract

Contraction of ventricles (ventricular systole)

Atria relax. Ventricles contract, pushing blood away from heart through pulmonary arteries and the aorta.

■ Contraction of the atria (atrial systole)

The muscle of the atrial walls contracts, forcing the remaining blood that they contain (around 20 per cent of the total blood in the heart) into the ventricles. The blood has only to be pushed a very short distance and therefore the muscular walls of the atria are very thin. During this stage, the muscle of the ventricle walls remains relaxed.

■ Contraction of the ventricles (ventricular systole)

After a short delay to allow the ventricles to fill with blood, their walls contract simultaneously. This increases the blood pressure within them, forcing shut the atrioventricular valves and preventing backflow of blood into the atria. The 'lub' sound of these valves closing is a characteristic of the heart beat. With the atrioventricular valves closed, the pressure rises further, forcing open the semi-lunar valves and pushing blood into the pulmonary artery and aorta. The walls of the ventricles are much thicker than those of the atria as they have to pump the blood much further. The wall of the left ventricle has to pump blood to the extremities of the body and so is much thicker than that of the right ventricle, which only has to pump blood as far as the adjacent lungs.

Valves in the control of blood flow

It is important to keep blood flowing in the right direction through the heart and around the body. This is achieved mainly by the pressure created by the heart muscle. Blood, as with all liquids and gases, will always move from a region of higher pressure to one of lower pressure. There are, however, situations within the circulatory system when pressure differences would result in blood flowing in the opposite direction from that which is desirable. In these circumstances, valves are used to prevent any unwanted backflow of blood.

Valves in the cardiovascular system are designed so that they open whenever the difference in blood pressure either side of them favours the movement of blood in the required direction. When pressure differences are reversed, i.e. when blood would tend to flow in the opposite direction to that which is desirable, the valves are designed to close. Examples of such valves include:

- **Atrioventricular valves** between the left atrium and ventricle and the right atrium and ventricle. These prevent backflow of blood when contraction of the ventricles means that ventricular pressure exceeds atrial pressure. Closure of these valves ensures that, when the ventricles contract, blood within them moves to the aorta and pulmonary artery rather than back to the atria.
- **Semi-lunar valves** in the aorta and pulmonary artery. These prevent backflow of blood into the ventricles when the recoil action of the elastic walls of these vessels creates a greater pressure in the vessels than in the ventricles.
- **Pocket valves** in veins (see Topic 13.6) that occur throughout the venous system. These ensure that when the veins are squeezed, e.g. when skeletal muscles contract, blood flows back to the heart rather than away from it.

The design of all these valves is basically the same. They are made up of a number of flaps of tough, but flexible, fibrous tissue, which are cusp-shaped, i.e. like deep saucers or bowls. When pressure is greater on the convex side of these cusps, rather than on the concave side, they move apart to let blood pass between the cusps. However, when pressure is greater on the concave side than on the convex side, blood collects within the 'bowl' of the cusps. This pushes them together to form a tight fit that prevents the passage of blood (Figure 2). So great are the pressures created within the ventricles of the heart that the atrioventricular valves are at risk of becoming inverted. To prevent this, the valves have string-like tendons that are attached to pillars of muscle in the ventricle wall (see Topic 5.1, Figure 2).

⚠ Cardiac output

Cardiac output is the volume of blood pumped by one ventricle of the heart in one minute. It is usually measured in $dm^3\,min^{-1}$ and depends upon two factors:

- the heart rate (the rate at which the heart beats)
- the stroke volume (volume of blood pumped out at each beat).

Cardiac output = heart rate × stroke volume

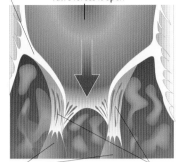

a *Valve open*

Cusp of valve

Higher blood pressure above valve forces it open

Pillar muscles

Lower blood pressure beneath valve

String-like tendons

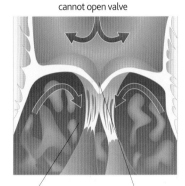

b *Valve closed*

Lower blood pressure cannot open valve

Higher blood pressure beneath valve forces it closed

Cusps of valves fit closely together

Figure 2 *Action of the valves*

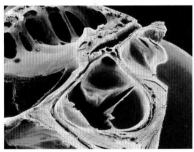

Figure 3 *False-colour scanning electron micrograph (SEM) of the semi-lunar valve of the aorta*

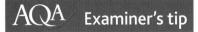

AQA **Examiner's tip**

Do not mix up **cardiac output** and **pulmonary ventilation** (see Topic 4.1). While both measure volumes, the first involves blood and the heart (cardiac) and the second involves air and the lungs (pulmonary).

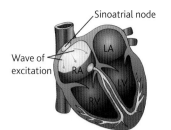

a Wave of electrical activity spreads out from the sinoatrial node

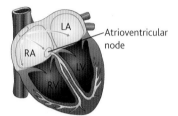

b Wave spreads across both atria causing them to contract and reaches the atrioventricular node

c Atrioventricular node conveys wave of electrical activity between the ventricles along the bundle of His and releases it at the apex, causing the ventricles to contract

Figure 4 *Control of the cardiac cycle*

How is the cardiac cycle controlled?

Cardiac muscle is **myogenic**, i.e. its contraction is initiated from within the muscle itself, rather than by nervous impulses from outside (neurogenic), as is the case with other muscles. Within the wall of the right atrium of the heart is a distinct group of cells known as the **sinoatrial node (SAN)**. It is from here that the initial stimulus for contraction originates. The sinoatrial node has a basic rhythm of stimulation that determines the beat of the heart. For this reason it is often referred to as the **pacemaker**. The sequence of events that controls the cardiac cycle is as follows:

- A wave of electrical activity spreads out from the SAN across both atria, causing them to contract.
- A layer of non-conductive tissue (the atrioventricular septum) prevents the wave crossing to the ventricles.
- The wave of electrical activity is allowed to pass through a second group of cells called the **atrioventricular node (AVN)**, which lies between the atria.
- The AVN, after a short delay, conveys a wave of electrical activity between the ventricles along a series of specialised muscle fibres called the **bundle of His**.
- The bundle of His conducts the wave through the atrioventricular septum to the base of the ventricles, where the bundle branches into smaller fibres.
- The wave of electrical activity is released from these fibres, causing the ventricles to contract quickly at the same time, from the apex of the heart upwards.

These events are summarised in Figure 4.

Pressure and volume changes of the heart

Mammals have a closed circulatory system, i.e. the blood is confined to vessels, and this allows the pressure within them to be maintained and regulated. Figure 5 illustrates the pressure and volume changes that take place in the heart during a typical cardiac cycle.

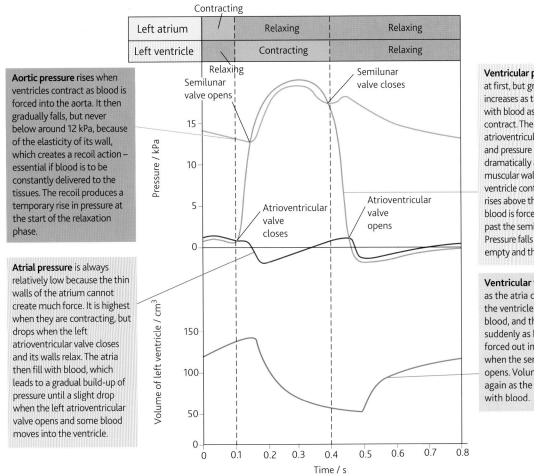

Aortic pressure rises when ventricles contract as blood is forced into the aorta. It then gradually falls, but never below around 12 kPa, because of the elasticity of its wall, which creates a recoil action – essential if blood is to be constantly delivered to the tissues. The recoil produces a temporary rise in pressure at the start of the relaxation phase.

Ventricular pressure is low at first, but gradually increases as the ventricles fill with blood as the atria contract. The left atrioventricular valves close and pressure rises dramatically as the thick muscular walls of the ventricle contract. As pressure rises above that of the aorta, blood is forced into the aorta past the semilunar valves. Pressure falls as the ventricles empty and the walls relax.

Atrial pressure is always relatively low because the thin walls of the atrium cannot create much force. It is highest when they are contracting, but drops when the left atrioventricular valve closes and its walls relax. The atria then fill with blood, which leads to a gradual build-up of pressure until a slight drop when the left atrioventricular valve opens and some blood moves into the ventricle.

Ventricular volume rises as the atria contract and the ventricles fill with blood, and then drops suddenly as blood is forced out into the aorta when the semilunar valve opens. Volume increases again as the ventricles fill with blood.

Figure 5 *Pressure and volume changes in the left side of the heart during the cardiac cycle*

Summary questions

1 Which chamber of the heart produces the greatest pressure?

2 Indicate whether each of the following statements is true or false.

   a The left and right ventricles contract together.

   b Heart muscle is myogenic.

   c Semi-lunar valves occur between the atria and ventricles.

   d The wave of electrical activity from the atrioventricular node is conveyed along the bundle of His.

   e The wave of electrical activity from the sinoatrial node directly causes the ventricles to contract.

3 In each case, name the structure being described.

   a On contraction it forces blood into the ventricles.

   b It acts as the heart's pacemaker.

   c It relays a wave of excitation to the apex of the heart.

4 After a period of training, the heart rate is often decreased when at rest although the cardiac output is unchanged. Suggest an explanation for this.

5 Using Figure 5, calculate the heart rate in beats per minute. Show your working.

Hint

Two facts will help you to understand the rather complex graph shown in Figure 5.

- Pressure and volume within a closed container are inversely related. When pressure increases, volume decreases, and vice versa.

- Blood, like all fluids, moves from a region where its pressure is greater to one where it is lower, i.e. it moves down a pressure gradient.

5.3 Heart disease

Learning objectives:

- What is an atheroma?
- What do thrombosis and aneurysm mean?
- Why does atheroma increase the risk of thrombosis and aneurysm?
- What is a myocardial infarction?
- What are the factors that affect the incidence of coronary heart disease?

Specification reference: 3.1.5

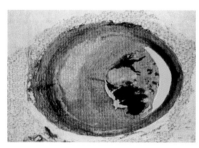

Figure 1 *Human coronary artery with a fatty atheroma partly blocking the interior*

Hint

Remember that plaques are formed **within** the artery wall. They are **not** deposits on the inner surface of the artery wall.

AQA Examiner's tip

Use the term 'atheroma' to describe the fatty deposits in an artery. Writing about 'furred-up arteries' will not gain credit.

Heart disease kills more people in the UK than any other disease. Almost half of heart disease deaths are from **coronary heart disease (CHD)**. CHD affects the pair of blood vessels, the **coronary arteries**, which supply the heart muscle with the glucose and oxygen that it requires for respiration. Blood flow through these vessels may be impaired by the build-up of fatty deposits known as **atheroma**. If blood flow to the heart muscle is interrupted, it can lead to **myocardial infarction**, in other words, a heart attack. Heart disease is not inevitable; most of it can be prevented.

Atheroma

Atheroma is a fatty deposit that forms within the wall of an artery. It begins as fatty streaks that are accumulations of white blood cells that have taken up **low-density lipoproteins (LDLs)**. These streaks enlarge to form an irregular patch, or **atheromatous plaque**. Atheromatous plaques most commonly occur in larger arteries and are made up of deposits of cholesterol, fibres and dead muscle cells. They bulge into the lumen of the artery, causing it to narrow so that the blood flow through it is reduced, as shown in Figure 1. The build-up of atheroma is shown in Figure 2. Atheromas increase the risk of two potentially very dangerous conditions: thrombosis and aneurysm.

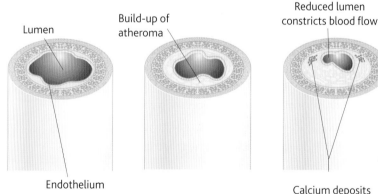

Figure 2 *Build-up of atheroma*

Thrombosis

If an atheroma breaks through the lining (endothelium) of the blood vessel, it forms a rough surface that interrupts the otherwise smooth flow of blood. This may result in the formation of a blood clot, or **thrombus**, in a condition known as thrombosis. This thrombus may block the blood vessel, reducing or preventing the supply of blood to tissues beyond it. The region of tissue deprived of blood often dies as a result of the lack of oxygen, glucose and other nutrients that the blood normally provides. Sometimes, the thrombus is carried from its place of origin and lodges in, and blocks, another artery. Figure 3 shows a thrombus in a coronary artery.

Aneurysm

Atheromas that lead to the formation of a thrombus also weaken the artery walls. These weakened points swell to form a balloon-like, blood-filled structure called an **aneurysm**. Aneurysms frequently burst, leading to haemorrhage and therefore loss of blood to the region of the body served by that artery. A brain aneurysm is known as a cerebrovascular accident (CVA), or stroke.

Myocardial infarction

More commonly known as a heart attack, the expression 'myocardial infarction' refers to a reduced supply of oxygen to the muscle (myocardium) of the heart. It results from a blockage in the coronary arteries. If this occurs close to the junction of the coronary artery and the aorta, the heart will stop beating because its blood supply will be completely cut off. If the blockage is further along the coronary artery, the symptoms will be milder, because a smaller area of muscle will suffer oxygen deprivation. In Britain, about half a million people a year have a heart attack, although fewer than one-third of them die as a result. Almost all show signs of atheroma and many have coronary thrombosis (clot-formation in the coronary arteries).

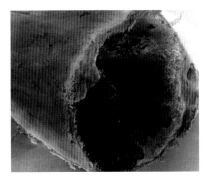

Figure 3 *Human coronary artery containing a thrombus*

Risk factors associated with coronary heart disease

There are a number of factors that seperately increase the risk of an individual suffering from heart disease. When combined together, four or five of these factors produce a disproportionately greater risk (Figure 4). These risk factors include the following.

Smoking

Smokers are between two and six times more likely to suffer from heart disease than non-smokers. Giving up smoking is the single most effective way of increasing life expectancy. There are two main constituents of tobacco smoke that increase the likelihood of heart disease:

- **Carbon monoxide** combines easily, but irreversibly, with the haemoglobin in red blood cells to form carboxyhaemoglobin. It thereby reduces the oxygen-carrying capacity of the blood. To supply the equivalent quantity of oxygen to the tissues, the heart must work harder. This can lead to raised blood pressure that increases the risk of coronary heart disease and strokes. In addition, the reduction in the oxygen-carrying capacity of the blood means that it may be insufficient to supply the heart muscle during exercise. This leads to chest pain (angina) or, in severe cases, a myocardial infarction.
- **Nicotine** stimulates the production of the hormone adrenaline, which increases heart rate and raises blood pressure. As a consequence there is a greater risk of smokers suffering coronary heart disease or a stroke. Nicotine also makes the red cells in the blood more 'sticky', and this leads to a higher risk of thrombosis and hence of strokes or myocardial infarction.

High blood pressure

If your genes cause you to have a high blood pressure, altering your lifestyle will not change this fact. Lifestyle factors such as excessive

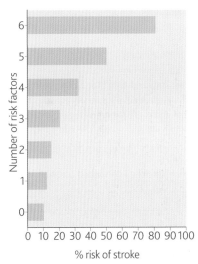

Figure 4 *The combined impact of six risk factors on the likelihood of a 70-year-old man experiencing a stroke in the next 10 years*

prolonged stress, certain diets and lack of exercise, increase the risk of high blood pressure. These are factors over which the individual can exert control. High blood pressure increases the risk of heart disease for the following reasons:

▥ As there is already a higher pressure in the arteries, the heart must work harder to pump blood into them and is therefore more prone to failure.

▥ Higher blood pressure within the arteries means that they are more likely to develop an aneurysm and burst, causing haemorrhage.

▥ To resist the higher pressure within them, the walls of the arteries tend to become thickened and may harden, restricting the flow of blood.

Blood cholesterol

Cholesterol is an essential component of membranes. As such, it is an essential biochemical which must be transported in the blood. It is carried in the plasma as tiny spheres of lipoproteins (lipid and protein). There are two main types:

▥ **high-density lipoproteins (HDLs)**, which remove cholesterol from tissues and transport it to the liver for excretion. They help protect arteries against heart disease

▥ **low-density lipoproteins (LDLs)**, which transport cholesterol from the liver to the tissues, including the artery walls, which they infiltrate, leading to the development of atheroma and hence heart disease.

Diet

There are a number of aspects of diet that increase the risk of heart disease, both directly and indirectly:

▥ **High levels of salt** raise blood pressure.

▥ **High levels of saturated fat** increase low-density lipoprotein levels and hence blood cholesterol concentration.

By contrast, foods that act as **antioxidants**, e.g. vitamin C, reduce the risk of heart disease, and so does non-starch polysaccharide (dietary fibre).

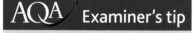

Examiner's tip

Use the terms 'high-density lipoproteins' and 'low-density lipoproteins', **not** 'good cholesterol' and 'bad cholesterol'.

▥ Hint

Always remember that risk factors increase the **probability** of getting heart disease, but they do not mean that someone will certainly get it. Heavy smokers, with high blood pressure and high blood cholesterol, may never develop heart disease, they are just more likely to (see Figure 5).

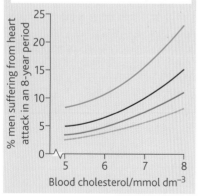

Figure 5 *Effects of blood pressure, smoking and blood cholesterol on the risk of heart attack in American men*

▥ Summary questions

1 Atheroma, thrombosis, aneurysm and myocardial infarction are four types of heart disease. Link each of the following descriptions to one of these diseases.

  a Commonly known as a heart attack.

  b Build-up of fatty deposits.

  c The formation of a blood clot.

  d Stretched region of an artery wall.

2 State **three** ways in which high blood pressure increases the risk of heart disease.

Application

A calculated risk

Figure 5 shows the effect of three of the above risk factors on the chance of heart attack in American men. Study the data and answer the questions:

1 A smoker with high blood pressure wishes to reduce his risk of heart attack. If he could only alter one factor, would he be better giving up smoking or reducing his blood pressure? Explain your answer.

2 A non-smoker with high blood pressure has a blood cholesterol level of 5 mmol dm^{-3}, over a period of 3 years this concentration increases to 8 mmol dm^{-3}. How many times greater is his risk of heart disease? Show your working.

3 Two non-smoking men with low blood pressure both have a blood cholesterol level of 5 mmol dm^{-3}. One of them starts to smoke and the blood cholesterol level of the other increases to 7 mmol dm^{-3}. Which man is now at the greater risk from heart disease? Explain your answer.

Application and How science works

Electrocardiogram

During the cardiac cycle, the heart undergoes a series of electrical current changes. These are related to the waves of electrical activity created by the sinoatrial node and the heart's response to these. If picked up by a cathode ray oscilloscope, these changes can produce a trace known as an **electrocardiogram**. Doctors can use this trace to provide a picture of the heart's electrical activity and hence its health. In a normal electrocardiogram (ECG) there is a pattern of large peaks and small troughs that repeat identically at regular intervals. An ECG produced during a heart attack shows less pronounced peaks and larger troughs that are repeated in a similar, but not identical, way. During a condition called fibrillation, the heart muscle contracts in a disorganised way that is reflected in an irregular ECG.

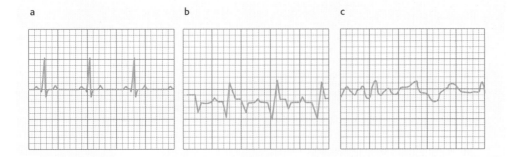

Figure 6 *Three different electrocardiogram (ECG) traces*

1 The three ECG traces shown in Figure 6 represent an ECG trace for a normal heart, one in fibrillation and one during a heart attack. Using the letters A, B and C, suggest which trace corresponds to which heart condition. Give reasons for your answers.

AQA Examination-style questions

1 **Figure 1** shows the pathways in the heart for the conduction of electrical impulses during the cardiac cycle.

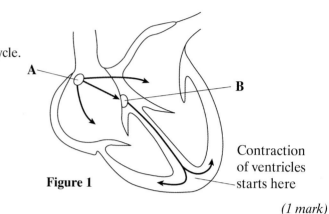

B

Contraction of ventricles starts here

Figure 1

(a) Name structure **A**. *(1 mark)*

(b) Explain why each of the following is important in pumping blood through the heart.
   (i) There is a short delay in the passage of impulses through part B.
   (ii) The contraction of the ventricles starts at the base. *(2 marks)*

(c) The table shows the blood pressure in the left atrium, the left ventricle and the aorta at different times during part of a cardiac cycle.

Time / s	Blood pressure / kPa		
	Left atrium	**Left ventricle**	**Aorta**
0.0	0.5	0.4	10.6
0.1	1.2	0.7	10.6
0.2	0.3	6.7	10.6
0.3	0.4	17.3	16.0
0.4	0.8	8.0	12.0

(i) At which time is blood flowing into the aorta?

(ii) Between which times are the atrioventricular valves closed? *(2 marks)*

(d) The maximum pressure in the left ventricle is higher than the maximum pressure in the right ventricle. What causes this difference in pressure? *(1 mark)*

AQA, 2004

2 **Figure 2** shows the left side of the heart at two stages in a cardiac cycle.

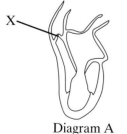 

X

Figure 2 Diagram A   Diagram B

(a) Name the structure labelled **X**. *(1 mark)*

(b) Describe **two** pieces of evidence in Diagram **B** which indicate that the ventricle is emptying. *(2 marks)*

(c) During exercise the rate of blood flow to heart muscle increases from 270 cm³ per minute to 750 cm³ per minute.
   (i) Calculate the percentage increase in rate of blood flow to heart muscle during exercise. Show your working.
   (ii) Explain the advantage of the increase in the rate of blood flow to heart muscle during exercise. *(4 marks)*

AQA, 2001

3 (a) The times taken in the various stages of a complete cardiac cycle are shown in the table.

Stage of cardiac cycle	Time taken / s
Contraction of the atria	0.1
Contraction of the ventricles	0.3
Relaxation of both atria and ventricles	0.4

  (i) Use the information in the table to calculate the heart rate in beats per minute.

  (ii) If the same rate of heartbeat were maintained throughout a 12-hour period, for how many hours would the ventricular muscle be contracting? *(2 marks)*

(b) Although the heart does have a nerve supply, the role of the nervous system is not to initiate the heartbeat but rather to modify the rate of contraction. The heart determines its own regular contraction.

Describe how the regular contraction of the atria and ventricles is initiated and coordinated by the heart itself. *(5 marks)*

(c) An interventricular septal defect is an opening in the wall (septum) that separates the left and right ventricles. Suggest and explain the effect of this defect on blood flow through the heart. *(2 marks)*

AQA, 2006

4 The table shows some information about the incidence of high blood pressure and heart attacks in the UK.

Sex	Condition	Percentage of people affected in each age group						
		16–24 years	25–34 years	35–44 years	45–54 years	55–64 years	65–74 years	75–84 years
Male	high blood pressure	0.5	1.5	3.5	6.0	17.0	22.5	18.5
	heart attack			0.1	0.2	1.1	2.4	3.2
Female	high blood pressure	0.7	1.6	3.8	7.8	20.5	27.9	26.9
	heart attack			0.1	0.3	0.6	0.7	1.8

(a) Use the pattern of data in the table to describe:

  (i) **two** similarities between males and females.

  (ii) **two** differences between males and females. *(4 marks)*

(b) People have been advised to reduce their cholesterol intake as a part of a healthy lifestyle. **Figure 3** shows information about mean daily intake of cholesterol.

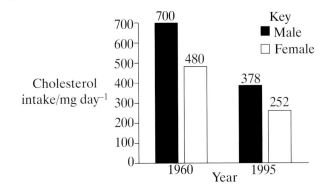

Figure 3

Calculate which group, male or female, shows the greater percentage reduction in cholesterol intake between 1960 and 1995. Show your working. *(2 marks)*

(c) Explain how smoking and a high blood cholesterol concentration increase the risk of developing coronary heart disease. *(6 marks)*

AQA, 2002

6.1 Defence mechanisms

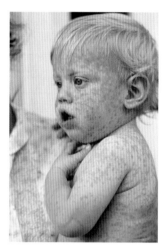

Figure 1 *Baby boy covered with measles rash. Measles is a highly infectious viral disease that mainly affects young children before they have acquired immunity to it*

Hint

The defensive mechanisms can be likened to the defences of a castle hundreds of years ago. The physical barrier is like the walls of the castle, the phagocytes are like the foot soldiers patrolling in the castle, who seek out and kill any intruders, and the lymphocytes are like specialised soldiers who respond to specific threats and use the intelligence gained from previous attacks to recognise, and quickly destroy, future intruders.

NB Don't use these descriptions in an examination!

We have seen in previous chapters some examples of infectious diseases and the damage they can do. Tens of millions of humans die each year from such infections. Many more survive and others appear never to be affected in the first place. Why are there these differences?

Any disease is, in effect, an interaction between the **pathogen** and the body's various defence mechanisms. Sometimes the pathogen overwhelms the defences and the individual dies. Sometimes the body's defence mechanisms overwhelm the pathogen and the individual recovers from the disease. Having overwhelmed the pathogen, however, the body's defences seem to be better prepared for a second infection from the same pathogen and can repel it before it can cause any harm. This is known as **immunity** and is the main reason why some people are unaffected by certain pathogens.

There is a complete range of intermediates between the stages described above. Much depends on the overall state of health of an individual. A fit, healthy adult will rarely succumb to an infection. Those in ill health, the young and the elderly are usually more vulnerable.

Defence mechanisms

The human body has a range of defences to protect itself from pathogens. They are of two main types:

▥ **Non-specific** mechanisms that do not distinguish between one type of pathogen and another, but respond to all of them in the same way. These mechanisms act immediately and take two forms:

(a) a barrier to the entry of pathogens,

(b) phagocytosis.

▥ **Specific** mechanisms that do distinguish between different pathogens. The responses are less rapid but provide long-lasting immunity. The responses involve a type of white blood cell called a **lymphocyte** and again take two forms:

(a) cell-mediated responses involving T lymphocytes,

(b) humoral responses involving B lymphocytes.

Before we look in detail at these defence mechanisms, let us first consider how the body distinguishes its own cells from foreign material.

Recognising your own cells

To defend the body from invasion by foreign material, lymphocytes must be able to distinguish the body's own cells and chemicals (self) from those that are foreign (non-self). If they could not do this, the lymphocytes would destroy the organism's own tissues.

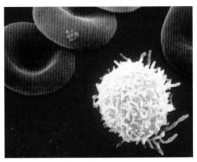

Chapter 6 Immunity

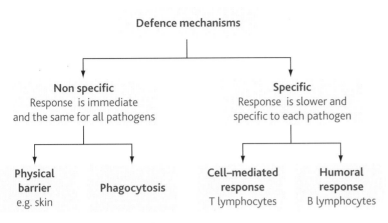

Defence mechanisms

Non specific — Response is immediate and the same for all pathogens

- **Physical barrier** e.g. skin
- **Phagocytosis**

Specific — Response is slower and specific to each pathogen

- **Cell–mediated response** T lymphocytes
- **Humoral response** B lymphocytes

Figure 2 *Summary of defence mechanisms*

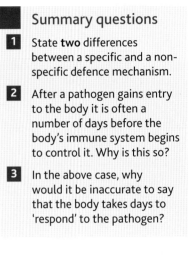

Figure 3 *False-colour scanning electron micrograph (SEM) of a single human lymphocyte (blue) and red blood cells (red)*

It is important to remember that specific lymphocytes are not produced in response to an infection, but that they already exist – all 10 million different types. Given that there are so many different types of lymphocytes, there is a high probability that, when a pathogen gets into the body, one of these lymphocytes will have a protein on its surface that is complementary to one of the proteins of the pathogen. In other words, the lymphocyte will 'recognise' the pathogen. Not surprisingly with so many different lymphocytes, there are very few of each type. When an infection occurs, the one type already present that has the complementary proteins to those of the pathogen is stimulated to build up its numbers to a level where it can be effective in destroying it. This explains why there is a time lag between exposure to the pathogen and body's defences bringing it under control.

Application

How lymphocytes recognise their own cells

- There are probably around 10 million different lymphocytes, each capable of recognising a different chemical shape.
- In the fetus, these lymphocytes are constantly colliding with other cells.
- Infection in the fetus is rare because it is protected from the outside world by the mother and, in particular, the placenta.
- Lymphocytes will therefore collide almost exclusively with the body's own material (self).
- Some of the lymphocytes will have receptors that exactly fit those of the body's own cells.
- These lymphocytes either die or are suppressed.
- The only remaining lymphocytes are those that fit foreign material (non-self), and therefore only respond to foreign material.

1 Distinguish between 'self' and 'non-self'.

Summary questions

1 State **two** differences between a specific and a non-specific defence mechanism.

2 After a pathogen gains entry to the body it is often a number of days before the body's immune system begins to control it. Why is this so?

3 In the above case, why would it be inaccurate to say that the body takes days to 'respond' to the pathogen?

101

6.2 Phagocytosis

If a pathogen is to infect the body it must first gain entry. Clearly then, the body's first line of defence is to form a physical or chemical barrier to entry. Should this fail, the next line of defence is the white blood cells. There are two types of white blood cell: **phagocytes** and **lymphocytes**. Phagocytes ingest and destroy the pathogen by a process called phagocytosis before it can cause harm. Lymphocytes are involved in immunity (see Topics 6.3 and 6.4).

▦ Barriers to entry

Barriers preventing the entry of pathogens take a number of different forms in humans, including:

▦ **a protective covering**. The skin covers the body surface, providing a physical barrier that most pathogens find hard to penetrate.

▦ **epithelia covered in mucus**. Many epithelial layers produce mucus, which acts as a further defence against invasion. In the lungs, pathogens stick to this mucus, which is then transported away by cilia, up the trachea, to be swallowed into the stomach.

▦ **hydrochloric acid in the stomach**. This provides such a low pH that the enzymes of most pathogens are denatured (see Topic 2.7) and therefore the organisms are killed.

Despite these various barriers, pathogens still frequently gain entry and the next line of defence is then phagocytosis.

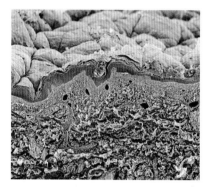

Figure 1 *Human skin forms a tough outer layer that forms a barrier to the entry of pathogens*

💡 Phagocytosis

Large particles, such as bacteria, are far too big to cross cell-surface membranes by diffusion or active transport. Instead they have to be engulfed by cells in the form of vesicles formed from the cell-surface membrane. This process is called phagocytosis. In the blood, the types of white blood cells that carry out phagocytosis are known as **phagocytes**. They provide an important defence against the pathogens that manage to enter the body. Some phagocytes travel in the blood but can move out of blood vessels into other tissues. Phagocytosis is illustrated in Figure 2 and is summarised below and in Figure 3.

▦ Chemical products of the pathogen act as attractants, causing phagocytes to move towards the pathogen (e.g. a bacterium).

▦ Phagocytes attach themselves to the surface of the pathogen.

▦ They engulf the pathogen to form a vesicle, known as a **phagosome**.

▦ Lysosomes (see Topic 3.3) move towards the vesicle and fuse with it.

▦ Enzymes within the lysosomes break down the pathogen. The process is the same as that for the digestion of food in the intestines, namely the hydrolysis of larger, insoluble molecules into smaller, soluble ones. (see Topic 2.1)

▦ The soluble products from the breakdown of the pathogen are absorbed into the cytoplasm of the phagocyte.

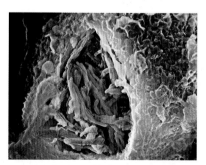

Figure 2 *False-colour scanning electron micrograph (SEM) of a phagocyte (red) engulfing tuberculosis bacteria (yellow), a process known as phagocytosis*

Phagocytosis causes inflammation at the site of infection. This swollen area contains dead pathogens and phagocytes, which are known as pus.

Inflammation is the result of the release of **histamine**, which causes dilation of the blood vessels. This, in turn, speeds up the delivery of phagocytes to the site of infection.

1 The phagocyte is attracted to the pathogen by chemoattractants. It moves towards the pathogen along a concentration gradient

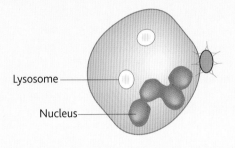

Pathogen (e.g. bacterium)

Chemical products of pathogen

Phagocyte

2 The phagocyte binds to the pathogen

Lysosome

Nucleus

3 Lysosomes within the phagocyte migrate towards the phagosome formed by engulfing the bacterium

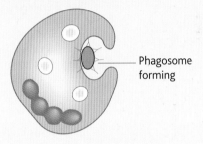

Phagosome forming

4 The lysosomes release their lytic enzymes into the phagosome, where they break down the bacterium

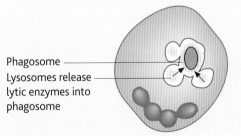

Phagosome
Lysosomes release lytic enzymes into phagosome

5 The breakdown products of the bacterium are absorbed by the phagocyte

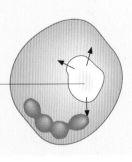

Breakdown debris of pathogen

Figure 3 *Summary of phagocytosis*

Summary questions

1 In the following passage, write down the missing word indicated by each letter a–f.

The first line of defence against disease is to prevent the entry of pathogens. The skin provides the main physical barrier, but the thinner coverings, such as the **a** layer in the lungs, also secrete **b** to provide a further barrier. Other means of preventing entry by pathogens include the secretion of **c** by the stomach. Pathogens that do invade the body may be engulfed by cells which carry out **d**. The engulfed pathogen forms a vesicle known as a **e**. Once engulfed the pathogen is broken down by enzymes released from organelles called **f**.

2 An enzyme called lysozyme breaks down the cell walls of bacteria. Among other places, it is found in tears. Suggest a reason why this is is so.

6.3 T cells and cell-mediated immunity

Learning objectives:

▦ What are antigens?

▦ What are the two main types of lymphocyte?

▦ What is the role of T cells (T lymphocytes) in cell-mediated immunity?

Specification reference: 3.1.6

Hint

An antigen is a molecule that triggers the production of an antibody. To avoid getting this the wrong way round, think of an anti**gen** as **gen**erating an antibody.

The initial response of the body to infection is non-specific (see Topic 6.2). The next phase is the specific response that confers immunity. Immunity is the ability of organisms to resist infection by protecting against disease-causing microorganisms that invade their bodies. It involves the recognition of foreign material (antigens).

▦ Antigens

An antigen is any part of an organism or substance that is recognised as non-self (foreign) by the immune system and stimulates an immune response. Antigens are usually proteins that are part of the cell-surface membranes or cell walls of invading cells, such as microorganisms, or diseased cells, such as cancer cells. The presence of an antigen triggers the production of an antibody as part of the body's defence system (see Topic 6.4).

▦ Lymphocytes

Immune responses such as phagocytosis are **non-specific** (see Topic 6.2) and occur whatever the infection. The body also has **specific** responses that react to individual forms of infection. These are slower in action at first, but they can provide long-term immunity. This specific immune response depends on a type of white blood cell called a **lymphocyte**. There are two types of lymphocyte, each with its own immune response:

▦ **B lymphocytes (B cells)** are associated with humoral immunity, i.e. immunity involving antibodies that are present in body fluids, or 'humour'. This is described in more detail in Topic 6.4.

▦ **T lymphocytes (T cells)** are associated with cell-mediated immunity, i.e. immunity involving body cells.

Both types of lymphocyte are formed from stem cells found in the bone marrow (Figure 1). Their names, however, indicate where they develop and mature:

▦ **B** lymphocytes mature in the **B**one marrow

▦ **T** lymphocytes mature in the **T**hymus gland.

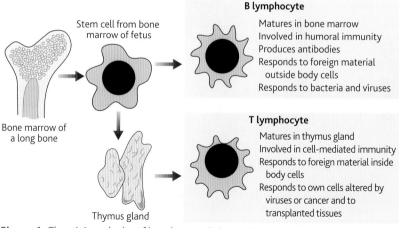

Figure 1 *The origin and roles of lymphocytes in immunity*

Cell-mediated immunity

T lymphocytes respond to an organism's own cells that have been invaded by non-self material, e.g. a virus or a cancer cell. They also respond to transplanted material, which is genetically different. T lymphocytes can distinguish these invader cells from normal cells because:

- phagocytes that have engulfed and broken down a pathogen present some of the pathogen's antigens on their own cell-surface membrane,
- body cells invaded by a virus also manage to present some of the viral antigens on their own cell-surface membrane, as a sign of distress,
- cancer cells likewise present antigens on their cell-surface membranes.

These cells are called **antigen-presenting cells** because they can present antigens of other cells on their own cell-surface membrane.

As T lymphocytes will only respond to antigens that are attached to a body cell (rather than to cells within the body fluids), this type of response is called **cell-mediated immunity**. There are a number of different types of T lymphocytes. The stages in the response of T lymphocytes to infection by a pathogen are summarised in Figure 2 and explained below.

1 Pathogens invade body cells or are taken in by phagocytes.
2 The phagocyte places antigens from the pathogen on its cell-surface membrane.
3 Receptors on certain T helper cells fit exactly onto these antigens.
4 This activates other T cells to divide rapidly by mitosis and form a clone.
5 The cloned T cells:

   a develop into memory cells that enable a rapid response to future infections by the same pathogen

   b stimulate phagocytes to engulf pathogens by phagocytosis

   c stimulate B cells to divide

   d kill infected cells.

The role of the receptors on T cells is important. The receptors on each T cell respond to a single antigen. It follows that there are a vast number of different types of T cell, each one responding to a different antigen.

Hint

Three terms that are frequently confused are 'antigen', 'antibody' and 'antibiotic'. When dealing with immunity put 'antibiotic' out of your mind – it has nothing to do with immunity (see Topic 16.2).

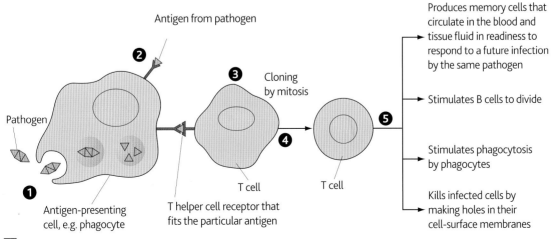

Figure 2 *Summary of the role of T cells in cell-mediated immunity*

How T cells kill infected cells

T cells kill body cells that are infected by pathogens. They do not kill by phagocytosis but by producing a protein that makes holes in the cell-surface membrane. These holes mean the cell becomes freely permeable to all substances and dies as a result. This illustrates the vital importance of cell-surface membranes in maintaining the integrity of cells and hence their survival. The action of T cells is most effective against viruses because they live inside cells. As viruses need living cells in which to reproduce, this sacrifice of body cells prevents them multiplying and infecting more cells.

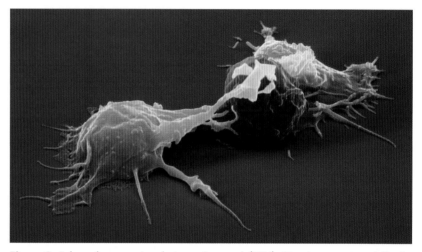

Figure 3 *False-colour scanning electron micrograph (SEM) of two human cytotoxic T cells (yellow) attacking a cancer cell (red)*

Summary questions

1. What is an antigen?

2. State **two** similarities between T cells and B cells.

3. State **two** differences between T cells and B cells.

Application

Bird flu

Avian (bird) flu is caused by one of many strains of the influenza virus. Although it is adapted primarily to infect birds, the H5N1 strain of the virus can infect other species, including humans. Avian flu affects the lungs and can cause the immune system to go into overdrive. This results in a massive overproduction of T cells.

1. From your knowledge of cell-mediated immunity and lung structure suggest why humans infected with the H5N1 virus may sometimes die from suffocation.

2. Suggest a reason why any spread of bird flu across the world is likely to be very rapid.

6.4 B cells and humoral immunity

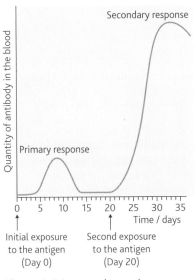

Learning objectives:

▦ What is the role of B cells (B lymphocytes) in humoral immunity?

▦ What are the roles of plasma cells and antibodies in the primary immune response?

▦ What is the role of memory cells in the secondary immune response?

▦ How does antigenic variation affect the body's response to infection?

Specification reference: 3.1.6

Hint

Remember that B cells with the appropriate antibody to bind to antigens of a pathogen are not produced in response to the pathogen. They are present from birth. Being present, they simply **multiply** in response to the pathogen.

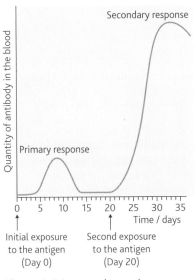

Figure 1 *Primary and secondary responses to an antigen*

We saw in Topic 6.3 that the first phase of the specific response to infection is the cloning of the relevant T cells to build up their numbers. Some of these T cells produce factors that stimulate B cells to divide. It is these B cells that are involved in the next phase of the specific response: humoral immunity.

🛈 💡 Humoral immunity

Humoral immunity is so called because it involves **antibodies** (see Topic 6.5), and antibodies are soluble in the blood and tissue fluid of the body. Another word for body fluids is 'humour'. There are many different types of B cells, possibly as many as 10 million, and each type produces a different antibody that responds to one specific antigen. When an **antigen**, e.g. a protein on the surface of a pathogen cell, enters the blood or tissue fluid, there will be one type of B cell that has an antibody on its surface whose shape exactly fits the antigen, i.e. they are complementary. The antibody therefore attaches to this complementary antigen. This type of B cell divides by **mitosis** (see Topic 11.3) to form a clone of identical B cells, all of which produce an antibody that is specific to the foreign antigen.

In practice, a typical pathogen, e.g. *Mycobacterium tuberculosis*, has many different proteins on its surface, all of which act as antigens. Some pathogens, such as the bacterium that causes cholera, also produce toxins. Each toxin molecule will also act as an antigen. Therefore many different B cells make clones, each of which produces its own type of antibody. For each clone, the cells produced develop into one of two types of cell:

▦ **Plasma cells** secrete antibodies directly. These cells survive for only a few days, but each can make around 2000 antibodies every second during its brief lifespan. These antibodies destroy the pathogen and any toxins it produces. The plasma cells are therefore responsible for the immediate defence of the body against infection. This is known as the **primary immune response**.

▦ **Memory cells** live considerably longer than plasma cells, often for decades. These cells do not produce antibodies directly, but circulate in the blood and tissue fluid. When they encounter the same antigen at a later date, they divide rapidly and develop into plasma cells and more memory cells. The plasma cells produce the antibodies needed to destroy the pathogen, while the new memory cells circulate in readiness for any future infection. In this way, memory cells provide long-term immunity against the original infection. This is known as the **secondary immune response**. It is both more rapid and of greater intensity than the primary immune response. It ensures that a new infection is repulsed before it can cause any harm – and individuals are often totally unaware that they have ever been infected. Figure 1 illustrates the relative amounts of antibody produced in the primary and secondary immune responses.

The role of B cells in immunity is explained on the next page and summarised in Figure 2.

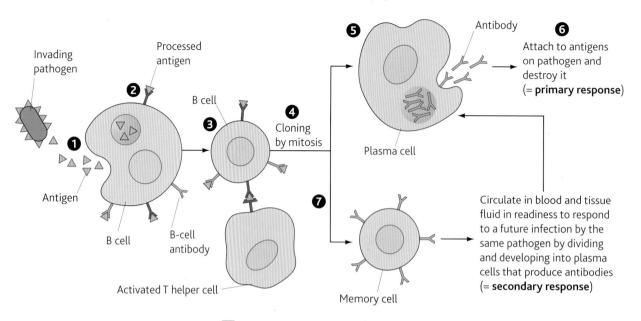

Figure 2 *Summary of role of B cells in humoral immunity*

1 The surface antigens of the invading pathogen are taken up by B cells.

2 The B cells process the antigens and present them on their surfaces.

3 T helper cells (activated in the process described in Topic 6.3) attach to the processed antigens on the B cells thereby activating them.

4 The B cells are now activated to divide by **mitosis** to give a clone of plasma cells.

5 The cloned plasma cells produce antibodies that exactly fit the antigens on the pathogen's surface.

6 The antibodies attach to antigens on the pathogen and destroy them. This is the primary immune response.

7 Some B cells develop into memory cells. These can respond to future infections by the same pathogen by dividing rapidly and developing into plasma cells that produce antibodies. This is the secondary immune response.

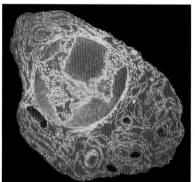

Figure 3 *False-colour transmission electron micrograph (TEM) of a plasma cell. Plasma cells are mature B lymphocytes that secrete antibodies. Note the well-developed rough endoplasmic reticulum (yellow dotted lines) where the antibodies are synthesised.*

Summary questions

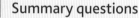

1 Explain why the secondary immune response is much more rapid than the primary one.

2 What are the differences between the cell-mediated and humoral responses to a pathogen?

3 Plasma cells can produce around 2000 protein antibodies each second. Suggest **three** cell organelles that you might expect to find in large quantities in a plasma cell, and explain why.

Antigenic variability

The way in which memory cells function explains why most of us only develop diseases like chickenpox and measles once during our lifetime. The pathogens causing each of these diseases are of a single type. Therefore they are quickly identified by the memory cells when they invade the body on subsequent occasions.

In contrast, influenza viruses, and some other pathogens, have over 100 different strains. The antigens that these viruses are made of, and those that they produce, are constantly changing. This is known as **antigenic variability**. Any subsequent infections are therefore highly likely to be caused by different varieties of the pathogen. Their antigens will not correspond to the antibodies or the memory cells formed during previous infections. With no appropriate memory cells to stimulate antibody production, the only means of overcoming the infection is the primary response. In other words, the body reacts as if each infection is a new one and the immune response is much slower. In the meantime, we develop the sore throat, high temperature and other symptoms typical of influenza.

6.5 Antibodies

Learning objectives:

▥ What is the structure of an antibody?

▥ How do antibodies function?

▥ What is a monoclonal antibody?

▥ How are monoclonal antibodies produced?

▥ How are monoclonal antibodies used to target specific substances and cells?

Specification reference: 3.1.6

Hint

One molecule fitting neatly with another is a recurring theme throughout biology. We met it with enzymes (see Topic 2.6) and with T cells (see Topic 6.3) and it features again here. While the 'lock and key' image is helpful, remember that, with the induced fit model of enzyme action, the molecules are flexible rather than rigid. This is the same for antibodies. The image of a hand fitting a glove is therefore perhaps a better one when it comes to understanding the process.

In Topic 6.4 we saw how B cells respond to **pathogens** by producing antibodies. Let us now look at antibodies and how they work in more detail.

Antibodies

Antibodies are proteins synthesised by B cells. When the body is invaded by non-self material, a B cell produces antibodies. These antibodies react with antigens on the surface of the non-self material by binding to them precisely, in the same way as a key fits a lock. Antibodies are therefore very specific, each antigen having its own individual antibody. This massive variety of antibodies is possible because they are made of proteins – molecules that occur in an almost infinite number of forms.

Antibodies are made up of four polypeptide chains. The chains of one pair are long and are called **heavy chains**, while the chains of the other pair are shorter and are known as **light chains**. To help the antibody fit around the antigens, they can change shape by moving as if they had a hinge at the fork of the Y-shape. Antibodies have a binding site that fits very precisely onto the antigen to form what is known as an **antigen–antibody complex**. The binding site is different on different antibodies and is therefore called the **variable region**. Each site consists of a sequence of amino acids that form a specific 3-D shape that binds directly to a single type of antigen. The rest of the antibody is the same in all antibodies and is known as the **constant region**. This binds to receptors on cells such as B cells. The structure of an antibody is illustrated in Figure 1.

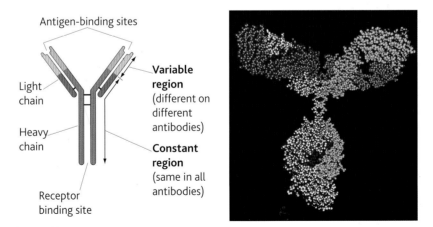

Antigen-binding sites

Light chain

Heavy chain

Receptor binding site

Variable region
(different on different antibodies)

Constant region
(same in all antibodies)

💡 **Figure 1** *Structure of an antibody (left); molecular model of an antibody (right). This Y-shaped protein is produced by B lymphocytes as part of the immune response.*

🛈 Monoclonal antibodies

We have seen that a bacterium or other microorganism entering the body is likely to have many hundreds of different antigens on its surface. Each antigen will induce a different B cell to multiply and clone itself (see Topic 6.4). Each of these clones will produce a different

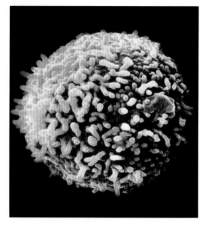

Figure 2 *False-colour scanning electron micrograph (SEM) of hybridoma cell used to produce monoclonal antibodies*

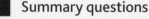

Summary questions

1 Suggest why proteins, rather than carbohydrates or fats, have evolved as the molecules of which all antibodies are made.

2 What is the difference between an antigen and an antibody?

antibody, collectively known as **polyclonal antibodies**. It is obviously of considerable medical value to be able to produce antibodies outside the body. It is even better if a single type of antibody can be isolated and cloned. Such antibodies are known as **monoclonal antibodies**.

Monoclonal antibodies have a number of useful functions in science and medicine.

■ **separation of a chemical from a mixture**.

■ **immunoassay**. This is a method of calculating the amount of a substance in a mixture. It is used in pregnancy testing kits, testing for drugs in the urine of athletes and detecting the human immunodeficiency virus (AIDS test).

■ **cancer treatment**. Monoclonal antibodies can be made that attach themselves only to cancer cells. These monoclonal antibodies can then be used to activate a cytotoxic drug (one that kills cells). This drug will only be activated by cells to which the monoclonal antibody is attached, i.e. the cancer cells. The cancer cells will then be destroyed, causing little damage, if any, to other cells.

■ **transplant surgery**. Even with close matching, a transplanted organ will normally suffer some rejection because of the action of the T cells. Monoclonal antibodies can be used to 'knock out' these specific T cells.

Application and How science works

Producing monoclonal antibodies

The production of a single type of antibody has long been recognised as useful. The problem had always been that B cells are short-lived and only divide inside a living organism. Nowadays, large quantities of a single antibody can be produced outside the body. This is another example of how science works (HSW: B and F).

There was much competition among scientific research teams to overcome the problem of getting B cells to grow indefinitely outside of the body and a variety of methods was investigated. Cesar Milstein and Georges Kohler evaluated these methods in relation to the behaviour of cancer cells. In 1975, they produced a solution to the problem by developing the following procedure:

■ A mouse is exposed to the non-self material against which an antibody is required.

■ The B cells in the mouse then produce a mixture of antibodies (polyclonal antibodies), which are extracted from the spleen of the mouse.

■ To enable these B cells to divide outside the body, they are mixed with cells that divide readily outside the body, e.g. cells from a cancer tumour.

■ Detergent is added to the mixture to break down the cell-surface membranes of both types of cell and enable them to fuse together.

■ The fused cells are separated under a microscope and each single cell is cultured to form a group (clone). Each clone is tested to see whether it is producing the required antibody.

■ Any clone producing the required antibody is grown on a large scale and the antibodies are extracted from the growth medium.

■ Because these antibodies come from cells cloned from a single B cell, they are called **monoclonal antibodies**.

As these monoclonal antibodies come from mouse tissue, they have to be modified to make them like human cells before they can be used. This process is called humanisation.

1 What is the purpose of adding detergent to the mixture of B cells and tumour cells?

2 When the detergent is added to the cells, the mixture is gently agitated. Suggest a reason why.

3 Why are cells from cancer tumours used to fuse with the B cells?

4 Some B cells and tumour cells fuse together. Suggest which other cells might also fuse together?

5 Why is it necessary to carry out 'humanisation' of the monoclonal antibodies?

Application and How science works

Ethical production and use of monoclonal antibodies

This is an example of how science works (HSW: J) The development of monoclonal antibodies has provided society with the power and opportunity to treat diseases in hitherto unknown ways. However, with this power and opportunity comes responsibility. The use of monoclonal antibodies raises some ethical issues.

■ Production involves the use of mice. These mice are used to produce both antibodies and tumour cells. The production of tumour cells involves deliberately inducing cancer in mice. Despite the specific guidelines drawn up to minimise any suffering, some people still have reservations about using animals in this way.

■ To eliminate the need for humanisation of the antibody, transgenic mice can be used. In this case, a human gene is placed in the mice so that they produce human antibodies rather than mouse antibodies. This raises the whole debate surrounding the ethics of genetic engineering.

■ Monoclonal antibodies have been used successfully to treat a number of diseases, including cancer and diabetes, saving many lives. There have also been some deaths associated with their use in the treatment of multiple sclerosis.

■ Testing for the safety of new drugs presents certain dangers. In March 2006, six healthy volunteers took part in the trial of a new monoclonal antibody (TGN1412) in London. Within minutes they suffered multiple organ failure, probably as a result of T cells overproducing chemicals that stimulate an immune response or attacking the body tissues. All the volunteers survived, but it raises issues about the conduct of drug trials (see Topic 3.11).

Society must use the issues raised here, combined with current scientific knowledge about monoclonal antibodies, to make decisions about their production and use. We must balance the advantages that a new medicine provides with the dangers that its production and use might bring. Only then can we make informed decisions at individual, local, national and global levels about the ethical use of drugs such as monoclonal antibodies.

Figure 3 *A scientist adding monoclonal antibodies to human tissue samples in order to detect cancer*

1 Another way to eliminate the need for humanisation would be to inject humans with an antigen and then extract the antibodies produced in response to it. Suggest reasons why this is considered unethical.

2 Should trials be limited to volunteers who are terminally ill with a condition that the monoclonal antibody is designed to treat?

6.6 Vaccination

Learning objectives:

▓ What is a vaccine?

▓ What are the features of an effective vaccination programme?

▓ Why does vaccination rarely eliminate a disease?

▓ What ethical issues are associated with vaccination programmes?

Specification reference: 3.1.6

Figure 1 *The development of new vaccines is a highly technological process requiring sterile conditions*

Immunity is the ability of an organism to resist infection. This immunity takes two forms.

▓ Passive **immunity** is produced by the introduction of antibodies into individuals from an outside source. As the antibodies are not being produced by the individuals themselves, they are not replaced when they are broken down in the body and so the immunity is generally short-lived.

▓ Active **immunity** is produced by stimulating the production of antibodies by the individuals' own immune system. It is generally long-lasting.

Vaccination is the introduction of a substance into the body with the intention of stimulating active immunity against a particular disease. When carried out on a large scale, this provides protection against disease not only for individuals, but also for whole populations.

▓ Features of a successful vaccination programme

Some programmes of vaccination against diseases have had considerable success. Yet, in other instances, similar measures have been less successful. The success of a vaccination programme depends on a number of factors:

▓ A suitable vaccine must be economically available in sufficient quantities to immunise all the vulnerable population.

▓ There must be few side-effects, if any, from vaccination. Unpleasant side-effects may discourage individuals in the population from being vaccinated.

▓ Means of producing, storing and transporting the vaccine must be available. This usually involves technologically advanced equipment, hygienic conditions and refrigerated transport.

▓ There must be the means of administering the vaccine properly at the appropriate time. This involves training staff with appropriate skills at different centres throughout the population.

▓ It must be possible to vaccinate the vast majority (all, if possible) of the vulnerable population. This is best done at one time so that, for a certain period, there are no individuals in the population with the disease and the transmission of the pathogen is interrupted. This is known as **herd immunity**.

▓ Why vaccination does not eliminate a disease

Even when these criteria for successful vaccination are met, it can still prove extremely difficult to eradicate a disease. The reasons are as follows:

▓ Vaccination fails to induce immunity in certain individuals, e.g. people with defective immune systems.

▓ Individuals may develop the disease immediately after vaccination but before their immunity levels are high enough to prevent it. These individuals may harbour the pathogen and reinfect others.

The pathogen may mutate frequently, so that its antigens change suddenly rather than gradually. This means that vaccines suddenly become ineffective because the new antigens on the pathogen are no longer recognised by the immune system. As a result the immune system does not produce the antibodies to destroy the pathogen. This **antigenic variability** happens with the influenza virus, which changes its antigens frequently. Immunity is therefore short-lived and individuals succumb to repeated bouts of influenza during their lifetime.

There may be so many varieties of a particular pathogen that it is almost impossible to develop a vaccine that is effective against them all. For example, there are over 100 varieties of the common cold virus.

Certain pathogens 'hide' from the body's immune system, either by concealing themselves inside cells, or by living in places out of reach, such as within the intestines, e.g. the cholera pathogen (see Topic 3.10).

Individuals may have objections to vaccination for religious, ethical or medical reasons. For example, concerns over the measles, mumps and rubella (MMR) triple vaccine has led a number of parents to opt for separate vaccinations for their children, or to avoid vaccination altogether.

Figure 2 *Vaccination programmes for children have considerably reduced deaths from infectious diseases*

The problems of controlling cholera and tuberculosis by vaccination

Control of cholera by means of vaccination is difficult because:

Cholera is an intestinal disease and therefore not easily reached by the immune system. Any oral treatment, e.g. antibiotics, rarely has time to be effective as it is too rapidly flushed from the intestines by the diarrhoea that is symptomatic of the disease.

The antigens of the cholera pathogen change rapidly (antigenic variability), making it difficult to develop an effective and lasting vaccine.

Mobile populations, resulting from global trade, tourism and refugees fleeing wars, spread cholera and make it difficult to ensure that individuals are vaccinated.

Control of TB by vaccination is difficult because:

The increase in HIV infection has led to more people with impaired immune systems. This makes them more likely to contract TB.

Poverty, wars and political unrest in some countries have created refugees who move around frequently and are often housed in overcrowded, temporary accommodation.

Mobile populations, resulting from global trade, tourism and refugees fleeing wars, have spread the disease worldwide and made it difficult to ensure that individuals are vaccinated.

The proportion of elderly people in the population is increasing. These people often have less effective immune systems and so vaccination is less effective at stimulating immunity.

Application and How science works

MMR vaccine

This is an example of how science works (HSW: I, K and L).

In 1988, a combined vaccine for measles, mumps and rubella (MMR) was introduced into the UK to replace three separate vaccines. All three diseases are potentially disabling and, in the case of measles, possibly lethal. Ten years later a study was

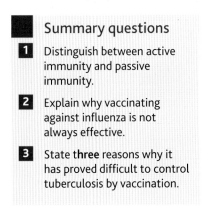

AQA Examiner's tip

When discussing ethical issues, always present a balanced view that reflects both sides of the debate and support your arguments with relevant biological information.

Summary questions

1. Distinguish between active immunity and passive immunity.

2. Explain why vaccinating against influenza is not always effective.

3. State **three** reasons why it has proved difficult to control tuberculosis by vaccination.

published in a well-respected medical journal. This suggested that there was a higher incidence of autism among children who had received the triple MMR vaccine than those who had received separate vaccinations. Autism is a condition in which individuals have impaired social interaction and communication skills.

In the wake of the media furore that followed, many parents decided to have their children vaccinated separately for the three diseases, while others opted for no vaccination at all. Parents of autistic children recalled that symptoms of the disorder emerged at around 14 months of age – shortly after the children had been given the MMR vaccination, adding to public concern about the MMR vaccine. The incidence of measles, mumps and rubella rose. Despite some public pressure to withdraw it, the Government continued to offer the MMR vaccination, insisting it was safe.

The vast majority of scientists now think that the vaccine is safe. A number of facts have emerged since the first research linking the MMR vaccine to autism.

- The author of the research had a conflict of interests. He was also being paid by the Legal Aid Board to discover whether parents who claimed their children had been damaged by MMR had a case. Some children were included in both studies.
- Further studies, including one in Japan involving over 30 000 children, have found no link between the MMR vaccine and autism.
- The sample size of the initial research was very small relative to later studies.
- The journal that published the initial research has publicly declared that, had it known all the facts, it would not have published the work.

1 Autism experts point out that many of the symptoms of autism first occur around the age of 14 months. Why is the information relevant to the debate on whether MMR vaccine and autism are linked?

2 How might an organisation funding research influence the outcome of that research without dishonestly altering the findings?

It was clearly a difficult choice for parents. Scientific evidence seemed to suggest a risk and the media publicised the dangers widely. Some parents, understandably, opted for separate vaccinations. Others, less understandably, mistrusted vaccinations in general and left their children unprotected. As a result, some children have developed disabilities that could have been avoided. On the other hand, had the research proved valid, it would have been those who held faith with the MMR vaccine who would have been putting their children's health at risk. It was a real dilemma, not least because there was disagreement among scientists about the risks. The parents had to weigh up the relative merits of conflicting evidence, data and opinion.

This case illustrates a difficulty with scientific evidence. The public sometimes believe that all such evidence must be true and accept it uncritically. However, all scientific evidence should be initially treated with caution – after all it is fellow scientists who are often quickest to criticise. There are various reasons for this caution:

- To be universally accepted, a scientific theory must first be critically appraised and confirmed by other scientists in the field. The confirmation of a theory takes time.

- Some scientists may have vested interests. They may not be acting totally independently but may be funded by other people or organisations who are anticipating a particular outcome from the research.

- Scientists' personal beliefs, views and opinions may influence the way they approach or represent their research.

- The facts, as presented by media headline writers, companies, governments and other organisations, may have been biased or distorted to suit their own interests.

- New knowledge may challenge accepted scientific beliefs; theories are being modified all the time.

Application and How science works

The ethics of vaccination programmes

This is an example of how science works (HSW: J). As vaccinations have saved millions of lives, it is easy to accept vaccination programmes without question. However, they do raise ethical issues that need to be addressed if such programmes are to command widespread support. The production and use of vaccines raises the following questions:

- The production of existing vaccines, and the development of new ones, often involves the use of animals. How acceptable is this?

- Vaccines have side-effects that may sometimes cause long-term harm. How can the risk of side-effects be balanced against the risk of developing a disease that causes even greater harm?

- On whom should vaccines be tested? How should such trials be carried out (see Topic 3.11)? To what extent should individuals be asked to accept risk in the interests of the public health?

- Is it acceptable to trial a new vaccine with unknown health risks only in a country where the targeted disease is common, on the basis that the population there has most to gain if it proves successful?

- To be fully effective the majority, and preferably all, of the population should be vaccinated. Is it right, in the interests of everyone's health, that vaccination should be compulsory? If so, should this be at any time, or just when there is a potential epidemic? Can people opt out? If so, on what grounds: religious belief, medical circumstances, personal belief?

- Should expensive vaccination programmes continue when a disease is almost eradicated, even though this might mean less money for the treatment of other diseases?

- How can any individual health risks from vaccination be balanced against the advantages of controlling a disease for the benefit of the population at large?

AQA Examination-style questions

1   (a)   Changes to the protein coat of the influenza virus cause antigenic variability. Explain how antigenic variability has caused some people to become infected more than once with influenza viruses.   *(2 marks)*

    (b)   **Figure 1** shows the changes in a B lymphocyte after stimulation by specific antigens.

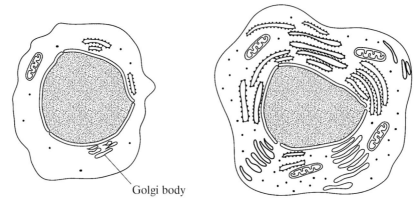

B lymphocyte before stimulation   B lymphocyte after stimulation

Figure 1

Explain how the changes shown in the drawings are related to the function of B lymphocytes.   *(4 marks)*

AQA, 2004

2   **Figure 2** shows one way in which white blood cells protect the body against disease.

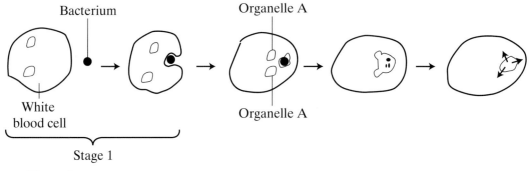

Figure 2

    (a)   Describe what is happening during Stage 1.   *(2 marks)*

    (b)   (i)   Name organelle **A**.

          (ii) Describe the role of organelle **A** in the defence against disease.   *(3 marks)*

AQA, 2001

3   (a)   What is vaccination?   *(2 marks)*

    (b)   A test has been developed to find out whether a person has antibodies against the mumps virus. The test is shown in **Figure 3**.

          (i)   Explain why this test will detect mumps antibodies, but not other antibodies in the blood.

          (ii) Explain why it is important to wash the well at the start of **Step 4**.

          (iii) Explain why there will be no colour change if mumps antibodies are not present in the blood.   *(5 marks)*

AQA, 2006

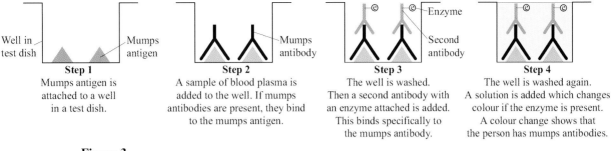

Step 1
Mumps antigen is attached to a well in a test dish.

Step 2
A sample of blood plasma is added to the well. If mumps antibodies are present, they bind to the mumps antigen.

Step 3
The well is washed. Then a second antibody with an enzyme attached is added. This binds specifically to the mumps antibody.

Step 4
The well is washed again. A solution is added which changes colour if the enzyme is present. A colour change shows that the person has mumps antibodies.

Figure 3

4   The box jellyfish produces a poison (venom) which enters the blood when a person is stung. A person who has been stung can be treated with an injection of antivenom. This antivenom is produced by injecting small amounts of venom from box jellyfish into a sheep, then extracting antibodies from the sheep's blood. These antibodies are then injected into the person who has been stung.

(a) If a sheep is injected with the box jellyfish venom on more than one occasion a higher yield of antivenom is obtained. Explain why.   *(2 marks)*

(b) Injecting antivenom does not give a person lasting protection against the venom of box jellyfish. Explain why.   *(2 marks)*

(c) Suggest **one** possible problem in injecting people with antivenom made in this way.   *(1 mark)*

AQA, 2006

5   People considered 'at risk' are offered a vaccination against influenza each year. **Figure 4** shows the number of people in the UK population aged 65 and over and the percentage of those who were vaccinated against influenza each winter.

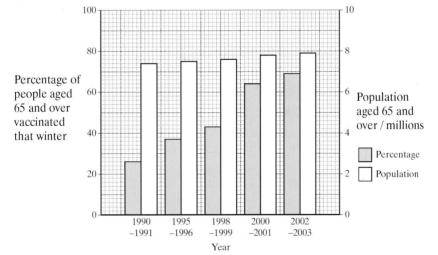

Figure 4

(a) Suggest **one** reason to explain the change in the percentage of people aged 65 and over being vaccinated.   *(1 mark)*

(b) (i) Calculate the change in the total number of people aged 65 and over being vaccinated between 1990/91 and 2000/01. Show your working.

   (ii) A student suggested that some people aged 65 and over were being vaccinated every year. Explain how the information in the bar chart supports this suggestion.

   (iii) Suggest why it is advisable for people to be vaccinated against influenza every year.   *(6 marks)*

(c) An influenza virus consists of a protein coat surrounding nucleic acid. The influenza vaccine consists only of the protein coat of the virus. Explain how the influenza vaccine produces immunity in the body.   *(2 marks)*

AQA, 2005

Unit 1 questions: Biology and disease

1   An increased concentration of cholesterol in the blood is one factor increasing the risk of myocardial infarction (heart attack). **Figure 1** shows the relationship between death from myocardial infarction and blood cholesterol concentration.

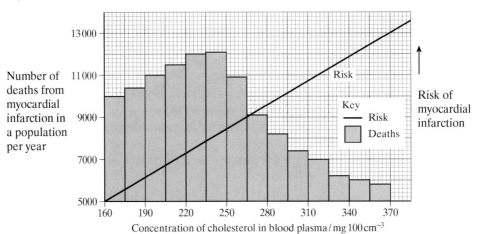

Figure 1

(a) (i)   Describe how high concentrations of cholesterol in the blood can lead to disease of the blood vessels supplying the heart.

    (ii)   Explain how disease of these blood vessels may lead to death from myocardial infarction.   *(5 marks)*

(b)   The number of deaths from myocardial infarction decreased at concentrations of cholesterol above 250 mg 100 cm^{-3} blood, whereas the risk of myocardial infarction continued to rise. Suggest an explanation for this difference.   *(2 marks)*

AQA, 2005

2   **Figure 2** shows the changes in pressure which take place in the aorta of a mouse during several heartbeats.

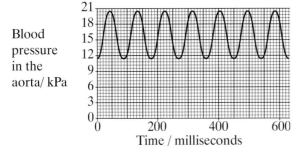

Figure 2

(a)   Which chamber of the heart produces the increase in pressure recorded in the aorta?   *(1 mark)*

(b)   The pressure of blood in the aorta decreases during each heartbeat but does not fall below 10 kPa. Explain what causes the pressure of blood to:

    (i)   decrease during each heartbeat

    (ii)   stay above 10 kPa.   *(3 marks)*

AQA, 2005

3 Cholera is a water-borne disease caused by the intestinal pathogen *Vibrio cholerae*. The pathogen produces an exotoxin which acts specifically on the epithelial cells of the small intestine causing changes in membrane permeability. Individuals with cholera suffer from severe diarrhoea which may result in death.

(a) Suggest **two** precautions which could be used to prevent the transmission of cholera. *(1 mark)*

(b) Explain how the effects of diarrhoea on the body can be treated. *(2 marks)*

(c) Suggest why the cholera exotoxin is specific to the epithelial cells of the small intestine. *(2 marks)*

(d) The cholera exotoxin affects the movement of ions through the intestinal wall. It causes the loss of chloride ions from the blood into the lumen of the small intestine. This prevents the movement of sodium ions from the lumen of the small intestine into the blood.

   (i) Describe how sodium ions normally enter the blood from the cells of the intestinal wall against a concentration gradient.

   (ii) Use the information provided to explain why individuals with cholera have diarrhoea. *(4 marks)*

AQA, 2004

4 **Figure 3** shows a bacterium.

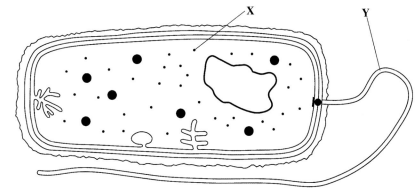

Figure 3

(a) Give the function of:

   (i) organelle **X**

   (ii) organelle **Y** *(2 marks)*

(b) (i) Give **two** ways in which the structure of this bacterium is similar to the structure of a cell lining the human small intestine.

   (ii) Give **two** ways in which the structure of this bacterium differs from the structure of a cell lining the human small intestine. *(4 marks)*

AQA, 2005

5 (a) What is an antigen? *(2 marks)*

(b) Describe how B cells respond when they are stimulated by antigens. *(4 marks)*

(c) A number of different species of bacteria can cause outbreaks of food poisoning. Explain how using monoclonal antibodies would enable a scientist to identify the species of bacterium involved in a particular outbreak of food poisoning. *(2 marks)*

6   Lactose is a disaccharide found in milk. In the human small intestine, the enzyme lactase catalyses the hydrolysis of lactose to the monosaccharides galactose and glucose. These monosaccharides are then absorbed into the blood.

(a)   Copy and complete the diagram in **Figure 4** to show the hydrolysis of lactose to galactose and glucose.

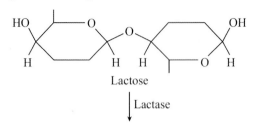

(2 marks)

Figure 4

(b)   Some people are lactose intolerant because they do not produce enough lactase enzyme in the small intestine. Lactose accumulates in the intestines and either remains unhydrolysed or is converted into other soluble substances by bacteria in the intestine. Explain how this could lead to diarrhoea in a lactose-intolerant individual.

(2 marks)

AQA, 2006

7   Some enzymes digest protein. They hydrolyse the peptide bonds between amino acids. The extent to which a protein is digested is called the degree of hydrolysis (DH). The DH value may be calculated from the equation:

$$DH = \frac{100 \times \text{Number of peptide bonds hydrolysed}}{\text{Total number of peptide bonds present}}$$

(a)   (i)   A protein molecule contains 151 amino acids. What is the total number of peptide bonds in this molecule?

(ii)   A molecule of this protein is digested. The DH value of the digested protein is 18. Calculate the number of peptide bonds that have been hydrolysed.

(2 marks)

(b)   What would be the DH value of a protein if it was completely hydrolysed to amino acids? Explain how you arrived at your answer.

(2 marks)

Enzymes A and B digest protein. **Figure 5** shows the effect of pH on the rates of reaction of these enzymes.

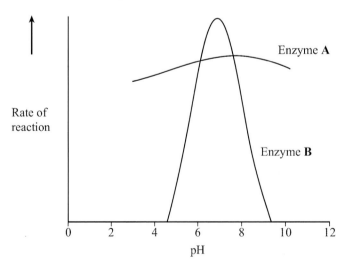

Figure 5

(c) Pepsin is a protein-digesting enzyme found in the stomach. It has an optimum pH of 2 and is fully denatured at pH 6. Sketch a curve on a copy of the graph to show the effect of pH on the rate of reaction of pepsin. *(1 mark)*

(d) Explain why the rate of reaction of enzyme B is low at pH 5. *(3 marks)*

(e) Enzyme A is present in some washing powders used for cleaning clothes. Use the graph to suggest why enzyme A would be of more use in washing clothes than enzyme B. *(1 mark)*

(f) Use your knowledge of protein structure to explain why enzymes are specific and can be affected by non-competitive inhibitors. *(6 marks)*

AQA, 2006

8   Liver was ground up to produce a homogenate. **Figure 6** shows how fractions containing different organelles were produced from the filtered homogenate.

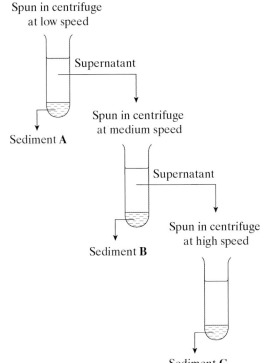

Figure 6

(a) Explain why the homogenate was filtered before spinning at low speed in the centrifuge. *(2 marks)*

(b) The main organelles present in sediment B were mitochondria. Suggest the organelles present in:
   (i) sediment A
   (ii) sediment C. *(2 marks)*

(c) What property of cell organelles allows them to be separated in this way? *(1 mark)*

(d) Explain why the organelles in sediment C could be seen with a transmission electron microscope but not with an optical microscope. *(2 marks)*

AQA, 2005

UNIT 2

The variety of living organisms

Chapters in this unit

There is not only immense variety between the members of different species but the individuals of a single species are equally diverse. This variety is the result of the DNA that each individual possesses and the influence of the environment upon organisms. To enable us to organise the millions of different species on Earth we classify them into groups. This classification is based not only on observable characters but also on genetic, biochemical and behavioural features. This unit looks at different aspects of biodiversity. Each chapter in turn explores the following:

▦ **Variation** explores how we investigate the diverse range of organisms on Earth and how variation is influenced by genetic and environmental factors.

▦ **DNA and meiosis** describes the structure of DNA and how genes are sections of DNA that determine the amino acid sequence in a polypeptide. It further shows how DNA is associated with proteins to form chromosomes and how the behaviour of these chromosomes during meiosis increases the variety among offspring.

▦ **Genetic diversity** looks at how the similarities and differences between organisms are the result of variation in DNA.

▦ **The variety of life** considers biochemical variety by looking at the diversity within two groups of molecules: haemoglobins and carbohydrates. It moves on to look at the structure of plant cells and how they differ from animal cells.

▦ **The cell cycle** is an account of how genetic information is copied and passed to genetically identical daughter cells during the process of mitosis.

▦ **Cellular organisation** shows how cells differentiate and become adapted for specific functions and how these cells are then aggregated into tissues which, in turn, form organs and organ systems.

▦ **Exchange and transport** considers how factors such as size and metabolic rate give rise to specialised exchange surfaces. Mass transport is explored by looking at the mammalian blood system and the movement of water in plants.

▦ **Classification** defines a species and looks at classification systems and the principles of taxonomy.

▦ **Evidence for relationships between organisms** covers the use of DNA, proteins and behaviour in clarifying relationships between organisms.

▦ **Adaptation and selection** uses antibiotic resistance to illustrate how evolution contributes to variety.

▦ **Biodiversity** explains how biodiversity may be measured and the influence of agriculture and deforestation on species diversity.

This unit further explores 'How science works', including the use of theories and ideas to develop scientific explanations, appreciating the tentative nature of scientific knowledge and the implications of science and their associated benefits and risks.

What you already know

While the material in this unit is intended to be self-explanatory, there is certain information from GCSE that will prove very helpful to the understanding of the content of this unit. A knowledge of the following elements of GCSE will be of assistance:

- Antibiotics and antibiotic resistance.

- The control of different characteristics by genes.

- The relationship of different types of cells to their function in a tissue or an organ.

- Structure of plant cells.

- Specialisation of cells to carry out particular functions.

- The roles of mitosis and meiosis in organisms.

- The meaning of chromosomes and genes.

- Gas exchange in plants.

- How dissolved substances are transported around the body of a mammal.

7 Variation

7.1 Investigating variation

Learning objectives:

▓ How is variation measured?

▓ What is sampling and why is it used?

▓ What are the causes of variation?

Specification reference: 3.2.1

Figure 1 *Variation between species (interspecific variation)*

One look around you and it is clear that living things differ. If one species differs from another this is called **interspecific variation** (Figure 1). But members of the same species also differ from each other. This is called **intraspecific variation** (Figure 2). Every one of the billions of organisms on planet Earth is unique. Even identical twins, who are born with the same DNA, vary as a result of their different experiences. How then do we measure the differences between these characteristics?

▓ Making measurements

All scientists measure things, but this is a particular problem for biologists. This is because they are usually measuring some aspect of living organisms and all living organisms are different. For this reason, biologists have to take many measurements of the same thing. They cannot reliably determine the height of buttercups or the number of red cells in 1 mm³ of human blood by taking a single measurement. Equally, they cannot measure every buttercup or human being in existence. What they do is take samples.

Sampling

Sampling involves taking measurements of individuals, selected from the population of organisms which is being investigated. In theory, if these individuals are representative of the population as a whole, then the measurements can be relied upon. But are the measurements representative? There are several reasons why they might not be, including:

▓ **sampling bias**. The selection process may be biased. The investigators may be making unrepresentative choices, either deliberately or unwittingly. Are they as likely to take samples of buttercups from a muddy area as a dry one? Will they avoid areas covered in cow dung or rich in nettles?

▓ **chance**. Even if sampling bias is avoided, the individuals chosen may, by pure chance, not be representative. The 50 buttercup plants selected might just happen to be the 50 tallest in the population.

The best way to prevent sampling bias is to eliminate, as far as possible, any human involvement in choosing the samples. This can be achieved by carrying out **random sampling**. One method is to:

1 Divide the study area into a grid of numbered lines,.e.g. by stretching two long tape measures at right angles to each other.

2 Using random numbers, from a table or generated by a computer, obtain a series of coordinates.

3 Take samples at the intersection of each pair of coordinates.

We cannot completely remove chance from the sampling process but we can minimise its effect by:

▓ **using a large sample size**. The more individuals that are selected the smaller is the probability that chance will influence the result. If we sample only five buttercups there is a high probability that they may all be taller than average. If we sample 500 there is a much lower probabilty that they will all be taller than average. The greater the sample size the more reliable the data will be.

- **analysis of the data collected**. Accepting that chance will play a part, the data collected can be analysed using statistical tests to determine the extent to which chance may have influenced the data. These tests allow us to decide whether any variation observed is the result of chance or is more likely to have some other cause.

Causes of variation

Variation is the result of two main factors: genetic differences and environmental influences. In most cases it is a combination of both.

Genetic differences

Genetic differences are due to the different genes that each individual organism possesses. These differences not only arise in living individuals but also change from generation to generation. Genetic variation arises as a result of:

- **mutations**. These sudden changes to genes and chromosomes may, or may not, be passed on to the next generation.
- **meiosis**. This special form of nuclear division forms the **gametes**. This mixes up the genetic material before it is passed into the gametes, all of which are therefore different (see Topic 8.4).
- **fusion of gametes**. In sexual reproduction the offspring inherit some characteristics of each parent and are therefore different from both of them. Which gamete fuses with which at fertilisation is a random process further adding to the variety of offspring two parents can produce.

Variety in asexually reproducing organisms can only be increased by mutation. Sexually reproducing organisms, in contrast, increase variation by all three methods. It follows that populations of sexually reproducing organisms are more varied than asexually reproducing organisms.

Environmental influences

The environment exerts an influence on all organisms. These influences affect the way the organism's genes are expressed. The genes set limits, but it is largely the environment that determines where, within those limits, an organism lies. In buttercups, for example, one plant may be determined by its genes to grow much taller than other plants. If, however, the seed germinated in an environment of poor light or low soil nitrogen, the plant may not grow properly and it will be short. Environmental influences include climatic conditions (e.g. temperature, rainfall and sunlight), soil conditions, pH and food availability.

In most cases variation is due to the combined effects of genetic differences and environmental influences. It is very hard to distinguish between the effects of the many genetic and environmental influences that combine to produce differences between individuals. As a result, it is very difficult to draw conclusions about the causes of variation in any particular case. Any conclusions that are drawn are usually tentative and should be treated with caution.

Link

Details of the process of meiosis are covered in Topic 8.4.

Figure 2 *Variation within a species (intraspecific variation): despite the immense variety that they show, all dogs, including this Pug and Great Dane, belong to the same species* – Canis familiaris

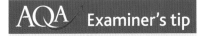
AQA Examiner's tip

Remember that intraspecific variation is variation within a species.

Summary questions

1 State **three** ways in which genetic variation can be increased in sexually reproducing organisms.

2 How is genetic variation increased in asexually reproducing organisms?

3 Give **two** reasons why a sample may not be representative of the population as a whole.

4 How may sampling bias be prevented?

7.2 Types of variation

Learning objectives:

- What are the types of variation?

- What is the mean of a normal distribution?

- What is standard deviation and how is it calculated?

Specification reference: 3.2.1

AQA Examiner's tip

A large standard variation means a lot of variety, while a small standard deviation means little variety.

Table 1

Height/cm	Frequency
140	0
144	1
148	23
152	90
156	261
160	393
164	458
168	413
172	177
176	63
180	17
184	4
188	1
190	0
192	0

Table 1 *Frequency of heights (measured to the nearest 2 cm)*

AQA Examiner's tip

You will **not** be asked to calculate standard deviation in written unit tests. You may, however, need to calculate it for the data collected as part of your investigative and practical skills unit.

Variation is the result of either genetic differences or the influence of the environment. In many cases it is a combination of both genetic and environmental factors.

Variation due to genetic factors

Where variation is the result of genetic factors organisms fit into a few distinct forms and there are no intermediate types. In the ABO blood grouping system, for example, there are four distinct groups: A, B, AB and O (Figure 1). A character displaying this type of variation is usually controlled by a single gene. This variation can be represented on a bar chart or pie graph. Environmental factors have little influence on this type of variation.

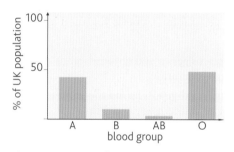

Figure 1 *Variation due to genetic factors illustrated by the percentage of the UK population with blood groups A, B, AB and O*

Variation due to environmental influences

Some characteristics of organisms grade into one another, forming a continuum. In humans, two examples are height and mass. Characters that display this type of variation are not controlled by a single gene, but by many genes (polygenes). Environmental factors play a major role in determining where on the continuum an organism actually lies. For example, individuals who are genetically predetermined to be the same height actually grow to different heights due to variations in environmental factors, such as diet. This type of variation is the product of polygenes and the environment. Table 1 shows the number of people in a particular sample (frequency) with various heights. If we take these data and plot them on a graph we obtain a bell-shaped curve known as a **normal distribution curve** (Figure 2).

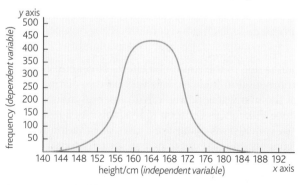

Figure 2 *Graph of frequency against height for a sample of humans*

Mean and standard variation

A normal distribution curve always has the same basic shape (Figure 2). It differs in two measurements: its maximum height and its width.

- The **mean** is the measurement at the maximum height of the curve. The mean of a sample of data provides an average value and is useful information when comparing one sample with another. It does not, however, provide any information about the range of values within the sample. For example, the mean number of children in a sample of eight families may be two. However, this could be made up of eight families each with two children or six families with no children and two families with eight children each.

- The **standard deviation** (s) is a measure of the width of the curve. It gives an indication of the range of values either side of the mean. A standard deviation is the distance from the mean to the point where the curve changes from being convex to concave (the point of inflexion). **68 per cent** of all the measurements lie within ± 1.0 standard deviation. Increasing this width to almost ± 2.0 (actually ± 1.96) standard deviations takes in 95 per cent of all measurements. These measurements are illustrated in Figure 3.

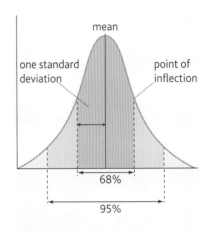

Figure 3 *The normal distribution curve showing values for standard deviation*

Calculating standard variation

At first sight, the formula for standard deviation can look complex:

$$\text{standard deviation} = \sqrt{\frac{\sum(x - \bar{x})^2}{n}}$$

Where:

- $\sum$ = the sum of
- x = measured value (from the sample)
- $\bar{x}$ = mean value
- n = total number of values in the sample.

However, it is straightforward to calculate and less frightening if you take it step by step. The following very simple example, using the six measured values (x) 4, 1, 2, 3, 5 and 0, illustrates each step in the process.

- Calculate the mean value ($\bar{x}$), i.e. $4 + 1 + 2 + 3 + 5 + 0 = 15$
  $$15 \div 6 = 2.5.$$

- Subtract the mean value from each of the measured values ($x - \bar{x}$). This gives: +1.5, −1.5, −0.5, +0.5, +2.5, −2.5.

- As some of these numbers are negative, we need to make them positive. To do this, square **all** the numbers $(x - \bar{x})^2$. Remember to square all the numbers and not just the negative ones. This gives: 2.25, 2.25, 0.25, 0.25, 6.25, 6.25.

- Add all these squared numbers together:
  $$\sum(x - \bar{x})^2 = 17.5$$

- Divide this number by the original number of measurements, i.e. 6:
  $$\frac{\sum(x - \bar{x})^2}{n} = \frac{17.5}{6} = 2.917$$

- As all the numbers have been squared, the final step is to take the square root in order to get back to the same units as the mean:
  $$\sqrt{\frac{\sum(x - \bar{x})^2}{n}} = \sqrt{2.917} = 1.708$$

> ### Hint
> Remember to square **all** the numbers, not just the negative ones.

Summary questions

1 In the following list of statements, decide whether each refers to variation due to genetic or environmental factors.

   a An example is the ABO blood grouping system in humans.

   b It can be represented by a line graph.

   c It is usually controlled by a single gene.

   d It can be represented as a bar graph.

   e A mean can be calculated.

   f An example is the length of the body in rats.

2 In a population of men the systolic blood pressure shows a normal distribution. The mean of the population is 125 (measured in mm Hg) and the standard deviation is 10. If the population was 1000, how many of them have a blood pressure between 115 and 135 mm Hg?

1 IQ test scores have been used as a measure of intelligence. Genetic and environmental factors may both be involved in determining intelligence. In an investigation of families with adopted children, the mean IQ scores of the adopted children were closer to the mean IQ scores of their adoptive parents than to that of their biological parents.

(a) Explain what the results of this investigation suggest about the importance of genetic and environmental factors in determining intelligence. *(1 mark)*

(b) Explain how data from studies of identical twins and non-identical twins could provide further evidence about the genetic control of intelligence. *(4 marks)*

AQA, 2006

2 Twin studies have been used to determine the relative effects of genetic and environmental factors on the development of a type of diabetes. The table shows the concordance (where both twins have the condition) in genetically identical and genetically non-identical twins.

Concordance in genetically identical twins /%	Concordance in genetically non-identical twins /%
85	35

(a) What do the data show about the relative effects of environmental and genetic factors on the development of diabetes? *(1 mark)*

(b) Suggest **two** factors which should be taken into account when collecting the data in order to draw valid conclusions. *(2 marks)*

AQA, 2005

3 Maize seeds were an important food crop for the people who lived in Peru. The seeds could be kept for long periods. Each year, some were sown to grow the next crop. Archaeologists have found well-preserved stores. The graph shows the lengths of seeds collected from three stores of different ages.

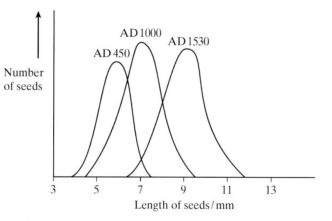

Within each store the maize seeds showed a range of different lengths. Give **two** causes of this variation and an explanation for each. *(4 marks)*

AQA, 2004

4   The graph shows the variation in length of 86 Atlantic salmon.

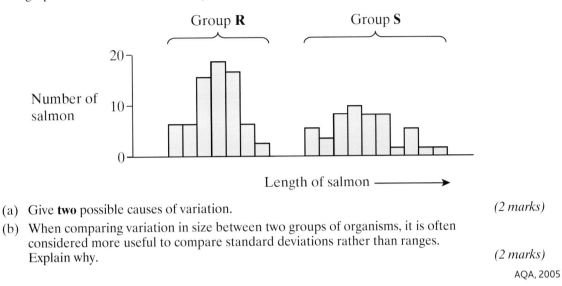

(a) Give **two** possible causes of variation.   *(2 marks)*

(b) When comparing variation in size between two groups of organisms, it is often
considered more useful to compare standard deviations rather than ranges.
Explain why.   *(2 marks)*

AQA, 2005

5   The graph shows variation in the number of spots on the wing-cases of a species of ladybird.

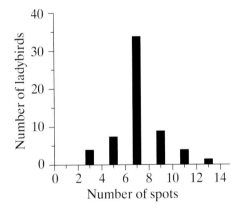

(a) The number of spots on the wing cases of this species of ladybird is determined by
genes. What does the graph suggest about the genetic control of spot number in
this species?   *(1 mark)*

(b) Give **one** piece of evidence from the graph that variation in the number of spots is
normally distributed.   *(1 mark)*

AQA, 2003

6   ABO blood groups in humans are an example of discontinuous variation, whereas
height in humans is an example of continuous variation.

(a) Describe how discontinuous variation differs from continuous variation in terms of:

   (i)   genetic control;
   (ii) the effect of the environment;
   (iii) the range of phenotypes.   *(3 marks)*

(b) Genetically identical twins often show slight differences in their appearance at birth.
Suggest **one** way in which these differences may have been caused.   *(1 mark)*

AQA, 2006

8 DNA and meiosis

8.1 Structure of DNA

Learning objectives:

■ What are the components of DNA?

■ How are these components arranged within the DNA double helix?

■ What is the function of DNA?

Specification reference: 3.2.2

In this chapter we shall learn the reasons why living organisms vary and how this variation is influenced by genetic and environmental factors. The double helix structure of deoxyribonucleic acid (DNA) makes it immediately recognisable. DNA is the chemical that determines inherited characteristics and it contains vast amounts of information in the form of the genetic code. The identification of this extraordinary molecule as the material that passes on the features of organisms from one generation to the next is one of the most remarkable feats of experimental biology. The discovery of the precise molecular arrangement of DNA was no less remarkable. Despite its complex structure, DNA is made up of just three basic components that combine to form a **nucleotide**.

Nucleotide structure

Individual nucleotides of DNA are made up of three components:

■ a sugar called deoxyribose,

■ a phosphate group,

■ an organic base belonging to one of two different groups:
  (a) single-ring bases – **cytosine (C)** and **thymine (T)**
  (b) double-ring bases – **adenine (A)** and **guanine (G)**.

The deoxyribose sugar, phosphate group and organic base are combined, as a result of **condensation reactions**, to give a single nucleotide (**mononucleotide**) as shown in Figure 1. Two mononucleotides may, in turn, be combined as a result of a condensation reaction between the deoxyribose sugar of one mononucleotide and the phosphate group of another. The new structure is called a **dinucleotide**. The continued linking of mononucleotides in this way forms a long chain known as a **polynucleotide**. In addition to DNA, some other biologically important molecules contain nucleotides. For simplicity the various components of nucleotides are represented by symbols, as shown in Table 1.

DNA structure

In 1953, James Watson and Francis Crick worked out the structure of DNA, following pioneering work by Rosalind Franklin on the X-ray diffraction patterns of DNA. This opened the door for many of the major developments in biology over the next half-century.

DNA is made up of two strands of nucleotides (polynucleotides). Each of the two strands is extremely long, and they are joined together by hydrogen bonds formed between certain bases. In its simplified form, DNA can be thought of as a ladder in which the phosphate and deoxyribose molecules alternate to form the uprights and the organic bases pair together to form the rungs (Figure 3).

Examiner's tip

Spelling can make a difference. 'Thymine' is a base in DNA but 'thiamine' is vitamin B$_1$.

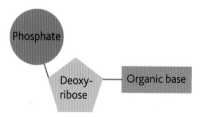

Figure 1 *Structure of a nucleotide*

Examiner's tip

Do not get confused between DNA and proteins. DNA is a sequence of **bases** but proteins are a sequence of **amino acids**. Nucleotides join to form a **polynucleotide**, amino acids join to form a **polypeptide**.

Pairing of bases

The organic bases contain nitrogen and are of two types. Those with a double-ring structure (adenine and guanine) have longer molecules than those with a single-ring structure (cytosine and thymine). It follows that, if the rungs of the DNA ladder are to be the same length, the base pairs must always be made up of one of each type. In fact, the pairings are even more precise than this:

▓ Adenine always pairs with thymine by means of two **hydrogen bonds**.

▓ Guanine always pairs with cytosine by means of three hydrogen bonds.

As a result of these pairings, adenine is said to be **complementary** to thymine and guanine is said to be complementary to cytosine.

It follows that the quantities of adenine and thymine in DNA are always the same, and so are the quantities of guanine and cytosine. However, the ratio of adenine and thymine to guanine and cytosine varies from species to species.

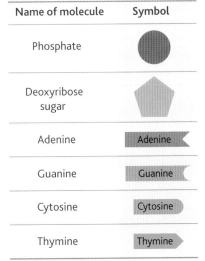

Name of molecule	Symbol
Phosphate	●
Deoxyribose sugar	⬠
Adenine	Adenine
Guanine	Guanine
Cytosine	Cytosine
Thymine	Thymine

Table 1 *Components of DNA*

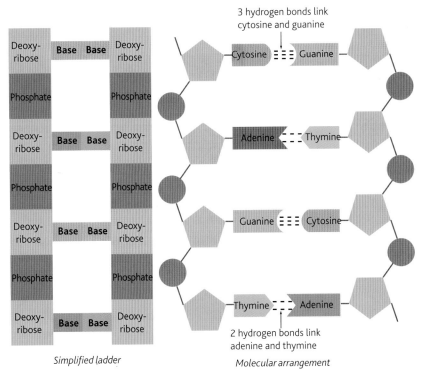

3 hydrogen bonds link cytosine and guanine

2 hydrogen bonds link adenine and thymine

Simplified ladder

Molecular arrangement

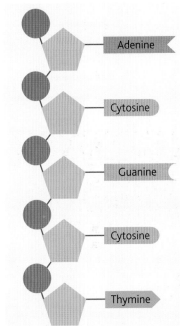

Figure 2 *Section of a polynucleotide*

💡 **Figure 3** *Basic structure of DNA*
DNA structure may be likened to a ladder in which alternating phosphate and deoxyribose molecules make up the 'uprights' and pairs of organic bases comprise the 'rungs'. Note the base pairings are always cytosine–guanine and adenine–thymine. This ensures a standard 'rung' length. Note also that the 'uprights' run in the opposite direction to each other (i.e. are antiparallel).

The double helix

In order to appreciate the structure of DNA, you need to imagine the ladder-like arrangement of the two polynucleotide chains being twisted. In this way, the uprights of phosphate and deoxyribose wind around one another to form a double helix. They form the structural backbone of the DNA molecule. For each complete turn of this helix, there are ten base pairs (see Figure 4 on the next page).

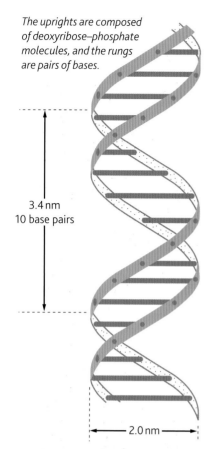

The uprights are composed of deoxyribose–phosphate molecules, and the rungs are pairs of bases.

3.4 nm
10 base pairs

←— 2.0 nm —→

Figure 4 *The double helix structure of DNA*

▓▓ **Hint**

In every molecule of DNA, the phosphate group, the deoxyribose and the four bases are always the same. What differs between one DNA molecule and another is the proportions, and more importantly the sequence, of each of the four bases.

▓▓ Function of DNA

DNA is the hereditary material responsible for passing genetic information from cell to cell and generation to generation. In total, there are around 3.2 billion base pairs in the DNA of a typical mammalian cell (Figure 6). This vast number means that there is an almost infinite variety of sequences of bases along the length of a DNA molecule. It is this variety that provides the immense genetic diversity within living organisms.

The DNA molecule is adapted to carry out its functions in a number of ways:

▓ It is very stable and can pass from generation to generation without change.

▓ Its two separate strands are joined only with hydrogen bonds, which allow them to separate during DNA replication (Topic 11.1) and protein synthesis.

▓ It is an extremely large molecule and therefore carries an immense amount of genetic information.

▓ By having the base pairs within the helical cylinder of the deoxyribose–phosphate backbone, the genetic information is to some extent protected from being corrupted by outside chemical and physical forces.

The function of the remarkable molecule that is DNA depends on the sequence of base pairs that it possesses. This sequence is important to everything it does and, indeed, to life itself.

▓ Summary questions

1 What are the three basic components of a nucleotide?

2 In terms of the structure of the DNA molecule, explain why the base pairings are not adenine with guanine and thymine with cytosine.

3 Suggest a reason why the base pairings of adenine with cytosine and guanine with thymine do not occur.

4 If the bases on one strand of DNA are TGGAGACT, what is the base sequence on the other strand?

5 If 19.9% of the base pairs in human DNA are guanine, what percentage of human DNA is thymine? Show your reasoning.

Unravelling the role of DNA

We now take for granted that DNA is the hereditary material that passes genetic information from cell to cell and generation to generation. This was not always the case because there were other contenders for this role, in particular proteins. How DNA, rather than proteins, was shown to be the hereditary material is a good example of how science works.

DNA versus protein

As chromosomes only become visible during cell division, scientists focused their attention on them as the sites of the hereditary material. Chromosomes were shown to be made up of proteins and DNA. To produce the extensive variety of cells and organisms that exists, the hereditary material clearly needed to be diverse so that each organism could have its own specific type. With the knowledge available at the time, scientists thought that proteins were the more likely candidate because of their considerable chemical diversity. In addition, proteins such as enzymes and antibodies showed great specificity. In contrast, DNA was considered to have too few components and to be too simple to fulfil the role. However, not all scientists were convinced and so they set about finding experimental evidence to determine the true nature of hereditary material.

1 What are the advantages of scientists questioning the validity of a current theory rather than automatically accepting it?

2 What is meant by the term 'hypothesis' in the scientific sense?

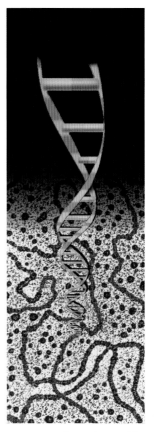

Figure 5 *Deoxyribonucleic acid (DNA)*

Evidence that DNA is the hereditary material

Scientists work by using **observations** and current knowledge to form a **hypothesis**. From this, they make **predictions** about the outcome of a particular **investigation**. By carrying out this investigation a number of times, they collect the experimental evidence that allows them to accept or reject their hypothesis.

By the early part of the 20th century, scientific observations and knowledge had revealed circumstantial evidence that DNA might be the hereditary material. It was present in chromosomes in the right amounts, it was very stable and its quantity halved in egg and sperm cells but not in other body cells. However, circumstantial evidence is not a scientific demonstration of cause and effect. Investigations were needed to test the hypothesis that DNA was the hereditary material.

Proving that DNA is the hereditary material

One investigation to test the hypothesis that DNA was the hereditary material involved experiments using mice and a bacterium that can cause pneumonia. The bacterium exists in two forms:

- a safe form that does not cause pneumonia, known as the R-strain,
- a harmful form that causes pneumonia, known as the S-strain.

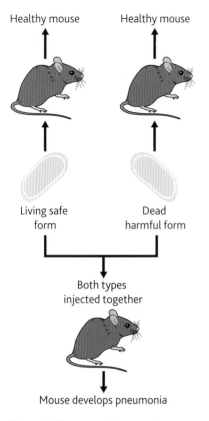

Healthy mouse   Healthy mouse

Living safe
form

Dead
harmful form

Both types
injected together

Mouse develops pneumonia

Figure 6 *Summary of an experiment to determine the nature of hereditary material in an organism*

Mice were separately injected with:

- ■ living bacteria of the safe form,
- ■ dead bacteria of the harmful form.

The group of mice injected with the living safe form of bacteria remained healthy, as did the group injected with the dead harmful form of bacteria. So, when mice were injected with both types together, it would not have been surprising to get a similar result. These mice, however, developed pneumonia. The experiment and the results are summarised in Figure 6.

Living bacteria of the harmful form were isolated from the mice with pneumonia. There are three possible explanations for this:

- ■ Experimental error, e.g. the harmful forms in the mixture were not all killed.
- ■ The living safe form had mutated into the harmful form. This is possible but extremely unlikely, especially given that the experiment was repeated many times with the same result.
- ■ Pneumonia is caused by a toxin. The harmful form of the bacterium has the information on how to make the toxin but, being dead, cannot do so. The safe form has the means of making the toxin but lacks the information on how to do so. The information on how to make the toxin may have been transferred from the harmful form to the safe form, which then produced it.

3 What simple procedure could be carried out to discount the first explanation?

4 Mutations happen very rarely. Explain why this helps to discount the second explanation.

The third explanation was considered worthy of further investigation and so a series of experiments was designed and carried out as follows:

- ■ The living harmful bacteria that were found in the mice with pneumonia, were collected.
- ■ Various substances were isolated from these bacteria and purified.
- ■ Each substance was added to suspensions of living safe bacteria to see whether it would transform them into the harmful form.
- ■ The only substance that produced this transformation was purified DNA.
- ■ When an enzyme that breaks down DNA was added, the ability to carry out the transformation ceased.

Other experiments provided further proof that DNA was the hereditary material and also suggested a mechanism by which it could be transferred from one bacterial cell to another.

- ■ It had been observed that viruses infect bacteria, causing the bacteria to make more viruses.
- ■ As viruses are made up of just protein and DNA, one or the other must possess the instructions that the bacteria use to make new viruses.

- The protein and DNA in the viruses were each labelled with a different radioactive element.
- One sample of bacteria was infected by viruses with radioactive protein while another sample was infected by viruses with radioactive DNA.
- In a later stage, the viruses and bacteria in both samples were separated from one another.
- Only the sample with bacteria that had been infected by viruses labelled with radioactive DNA showed signs of radioactivity.

This was evidence that DNA was the material that had provided the bacteria with the genetic information needed to make the viruses. It also showed how DNA can be passed from one bacterium to another, i.e. by viruses. If further proof were needed, this came from electron microscope studies that traced the movement of DNA from viruses into bacterial cells.

This sequence of experiments illustrates How science works.

- Observations lead to scientists proposing a theory that forms the basis for scientific work (HSW: A).
- A hypothesis is proposed to explain the observations (HSW: C).
- Experiments are designed, using appropriate methods, to test the hypothesis (HSW: C).
- Experiments are repeated many times to ensure the results are reliable (HSW: D).
- Results from the experiments are analysed and interpreted in order to accept or reject the hypothesis (HSW: E).
- The experimental techniques and results are critically reviewed by other scientists (HSW: K).
- In the light of these criticisms and new scientific knowledge, more refined experiments are designed that lead to the theory being accepted, modified or rejected (HSW: F).
- The knowledge obtained may be used in other aspects of science, often contributing to potential human benefits in technology and medicine (HSW: I).
- The benefits and risks of new discoveries are analysed by society at large before they are developed (HSW: I).
- The ethics of how experiments are carried out (e.g. the use of mice) and how the knowledge obtained is used (e.g. genetic engineering) are considered (HSW: J).

5 A new scientific discovery often presents moral, economic and ethical issues. Why is it important that society analyses the risks and benefits of these discoveries before they are developed?

8.2 The triplet code

Once it had been established that DNA was the means by which genetic information was passed from generation to generation, scientists puzzled as to exactly how DNA determined the features of organisms. Before we look at this problem, we need first to be clear about what we mean by a gene.

🛈 What is a gene?

Genes are sections of DNA that contain the coded information for making polypeptides. The coded information is in the form of a specific sequence of bases along the DNA molecule. Polypeptides combine to make proteins and so genes determine the proteins of an organism. Enzymes are proteins. As enzymes control chemical reactions they are responsible for an organism's development and activities. In other words, genes determine the nature and development of all organisms. A gene is a sequence of DNA bases that determines a polypeptide and a polypeptide is a sequence of amino acids (see Topic 2.5). So how exactly does a sequence of DNA bases determine a sequence of amino acids?

▐ Hint

Remember that the sequence of amino acids coded for by DNA is the primary structure of a protein. It is the primary structure that gives rise to the tertiary structure and hence the shape of the protein. So DNA codes indirectly for the shape of proteins, including enzymes.

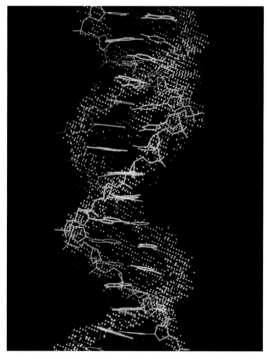

Figure 1 *Computer graphics representation of a short section of DNA*

▐ The triplet code

In trying to discover how DNA bases coded for amino acids, scientists suggested that there must be a minimum of three bases that coded for each amino acid. Their reasoning was as follows:

■ Only 20 amino acids regularly occur in proteins.

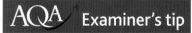 **Examiner's tip**

DNA codes for **amino acids** but it is made up of **nucleotides**. A common mistake found in answers on examination papers is to state that DNA is made up of amino acids.

- Each amino acid must have its own code of bases on the DNA.
- Only four different bases (adenine, guanine, cytosine and thymine) are present in DNA.
- If each base coded for a different amino acid, only four different amino acids could be coded for.
- Using a pair of bases, 16 (4^2) different codes are possible, which is still inadequate.
- Three bases produce 64 (4^3) different codes, more than enough to satisfy the requirements of 20 amino acids.

As the code has three bases it is called the **triplet code**. As there are 64 possible codes and only 20 amino acids, it follows that some amino acids have more than one code. In eukaryotes much of the nuclear DNA does not code for amino acids. These sections are called introns and can occur within genes and as muliple repeats between genes.

Application

Features of the triplet code

Further experiments have revealed the following features of the triplet code.

- A few amino acids have only a single triplet code.
- The remaining amino acids have between two and six triplet codes each.
- The code is known as a 'degenerate code' because most amino acids have more than one triplet code.
- The triplet code is always read in one particular direction along the DNA strand.
- The start of a sequence is always the same triplet code. This codes for the amino acid methionine. If this first methionine molecule does not form part of the final polypeptide, it is later removed.
- Three triplet codes do not code for any amino acid. These are called 'stop codes' and mark the end of a polypeptide chain. They act in much the same way as a full stop at the end of a sentence.
- The code is non-overlapping, i.e. each base in the sequence is read only once. Thus six bases numbered 123456 are read as triplets 123 and 456, rather than as triplets 123, 234, 345, 456.
- The code is universal, i.e. with a few minor exceptions it is the same in all organisms.

---

1 A section of DNA has the following sequence of bases along it: TACGCTCCGCTGTAC. All of the bases are part of the code for amino acids. The first base in the sequence is the start of the code.

a How many amino acids does the section of DNA code for?

b Two of the amino acids coded for will be the same. Which two?

c It is possible that this sequence codes for many different amino acids or many copies of the same amino acid. From your knowledge of the genetic code explain how this can happen.

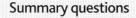

Summary questions

1 What is a gene?

2 How many bases are required to code for a chain of six consecutive amino acids?

3 Explain how a change in one base along a DNA molecule may result in an enzyme becoming non-functional.

8.3 DNA and chromosomes

Learning objectives:

▨ How does DNA in prokaryotic organisms differ from the DNA in eukaryotic organisms?

▨ What is a chromosome?

▨ How are genes arranged on a DNA molecule?

▨ What are homologous chromosomes?

▨ What is an allele?

Specification reference: 3.2.2

In Topic 3.10 we saw that, according to their organisation, there are two types of cell: **prokaryotic cells** and **eukaryotic cells**. We looked at some of the differences between the two. These differences extend to their DNA:

▨ In prokaryotic cells, such as bacteria, the DNA molecules are smaller, form a circle and are not associated with protein molecules. Prokaryotic cells therefore do not have chromosomes.

▨ In eukaryotic cells, the DNA molecules are larger, form a line (are linear) rather than a circle and occur in association with proteins to form structures called **chromosomes**.

▨ Chromosome structure

Chromosomes are only visible as distinct structures when a cell is dividing. For the rest of the time they are widely dispersed throughout the nucleus. When visible, chromosomes appear as two threads, joined at a single point (Figure 1). Each thread is called a chromatid.

The DNA in chromosomes is held in position by proteins. The considerable length of DNA found in each cell (around 2 m in every human cell) is highly coiled and folded as illustrated in Figure 2. Let us look carefully at this diagram.

We already know that DNA is a double helix. From the diagram you will see that this helix is wound around proteins to fix it in position. This

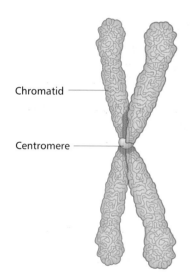

Figure 1 *Structure of a chromosome*

Chromatid

Centromere

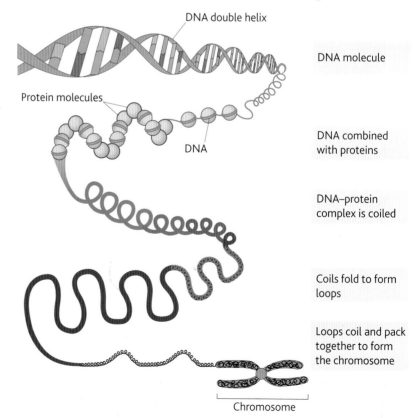

DNA double helix

DNA molecule

Protein molecules

DNA

DNA combined with proteins

DNA–protein complex is coiled

Coils fold to form loops

Loops coil and pack together to form the chromosome

Chromosome

Figure 2 *How DNA is packed into a chromosome*

DNA–protein complex is then coiled. The coil, in turn, is looped and further coiled before being packed into the chromosome. In this way a lot of DNA is condensed into a single chromosome. If you follow the diagram carefully you will see that a chromosome contains just a single molecule of DNA, although this is very long. This single DNA molecule has many genes along its length (see Topic 8.2). Each gene occupies a specific position along the DNA molecule.

Although the number of chromosomes is always the same for normal individuals of a species, it varies from one species to another. For example, while humans have 46 chromosomes, potato plants have 48 and dogs have 78. In almost all species, there is an even number of chromosomes in the cells of adults. This is because chromosomes occur in pairs called **homologous pairs**.

Homologous chromosomes

We saw above that chromosomes occur in pairs. There is an obvious reason for this. Sexually produced organisms, such as humans, are the result of the fusion of a sperm and an egg, each of which contributes a set of chromosomes to the offspring. Therefore, one of each pair is derived from the chromosomes provided by the mother in the egg (maternal chromosomes) and the other is derived from the chromosomes provided by the father in the sperm (paternal chromosomes). These are known as **homologous pairs** and the total number is referred to as the **diploid** number. In humans this is 46.

A homologous pair is always two chromosomes that determine the same genetic characteristics, but:

**'determining the same genetic characteristics' is not
the same as being identical.**

For instance, a homologous pair of chromosomes may each possess information on eye colour and blood group, but one chromosome may carry the codes (alleles) for blue eyes and blood group A, while the other carries the codes (alleles) for brown eyes and blood group B. During **meiosis**, the halving of the number of chromosomes is done in a manner which ensures that each daughter cell receives one chromosome from each homologous pair. In this way each cell receives one set of information for each characteristic of the organism. When these haploid cells combine, the diploid state, with paired homologous chromosomes, is restored.

What is an allele?

We have seen that genes are sections of DNA that contain coded information in the form of specific sequences of bases. Each gene exists in two, occasionally more, different forms. Each of these forms is called an **allele**. Each individual inherits one allele from each of its parents. These two alleles may be the same or they may be different. When they are different, each allele will code for a different polypeptide.

Any differences in the base sequence of an allele of a single gene may result in a different sequence of amino acids being coded for. This different amino acid sequence will lead to the production of a different polypeptide, and hence a different protein. Sometimes this different protein may not function properly or may not function at all. When the protein produced is an enzyme, it may have a different shape. The new shape may not fit the enzyme's substrate (see Topic 2.7). As a result the enzyme may not function and this can have serious consequences for the organism.

Hint

It is often mistakenly thought that humans have just 46 chromosomes throughout the body, rather than 46 in every single cell (except sperm and eggs). Remember that nearly every cell of your body needs to divide and so every cell needs DNA and hence chromosomes.

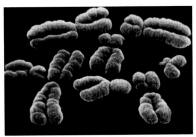

Figure 3 *False-colour scanning electron micrograph (SEM) of a group of human chromosomes*

Hint

Do not confuse genes and alleles. A **gene** refers to a particular characteristic such as eye colour. Genes usually exist in two different forms called **alleles**. The gene for eye colour has an allele that produces blue eyes and another allele that produces brown eyes.

Summary questions

1. In which **three** ways does the DNA of a prokaryotic cell differ from that of a eukaryotic cell?

2. What is the function of the protein found in chromosomes?

3. How is the considerable length of a DNA molecule compacted into a chromosome?

4. Suppose the total length of all the DNA in a single human muscle cell is 2.3 m.

   a If all the DNA were distributed equally between the chromosomes, what would be the length of DNA in each one?

   b What do you think the length of DNA is in a human brain cell?

8.4 Meiosis and genetic variation

Learning objectives:

■ Why is meiosis necessary?

■ What happens during meiosis?

■ How does meiosis create genetic variation?

Specification reference: 3.2.2

The division of cells involves, firstly, the division of the nucleus and, secondly, the division of the cell as a whole. The division of the nucleus of cells occurs in one of two ways:

■ **Mitosis** produces two daughter nuclei with the same number of **chromosomes** as the parent cell and as each other. We shall learn more about mitosis in Topic 11.2.

■ **Meiosis** produces four daughter nuclei, each with half the number of chromosomes as the parent cell.

■ Why is meiosis necessary?

In sexual reproduction two **gametes** fuse to give rise to new offspring. If each gamete has a full set of chromosomes (**diploid** number) then the cell that they produce has double this number. In humans, the diploid number of chromosomes is 46, which means that this cell would have 92 chromosomes. This doubling of the number of chromosomes would continue at each generation. It follows that, in order to maintain a constant number of chromosomes in the adults of a species, the number of chromosomes must be halved at some stage in the life cycle. This halving occurs as a result of meiosis.

Every diploid cell of an organism has two sets of chromosomes (see Topic 8.3): one set provided by each parent. During meiosis, the chromosome pairs separate, so that only one chromosome from each pair enters each gamete. This is known as the **haploid** number of chromosomes which, in humans, is 23. When two haploid gametes fuse at fertilisation, the diploid number of chromosomes is restored.

■ The process of meiosis

Meiosis involves two nuclear divisions that normally occur one after the other:

1 In the **first division (meiosis 1)** the **homologous chromosomes** pair up and their **chromatids** wrap around each other. Equivalent portions of these chromatids may be exchanged in a process called **crossing over**. We shall see the significance of this later. By the end of this stage the homologous pairs have separated, with one chromosome from each pair going into one of the two daughter cells.

2 In the **second meiotic division (meiosis 2)** the chromatids move apart. At the end of meiosis 2, four cells have been formed. In humans, each of these cells contains 23 chromatids.

This is summarised in Figure 1.

In addition to halving the number of chromosomes, meiosis also produces genetic variation among the offspring, allowing an organism to adapt and survive in a changing world. Meiosis brings about this genetic variation in the following two ways:

■ independent segregation of homologous chromosomes,

■ recombination of homologous chromosomes by crossing over.

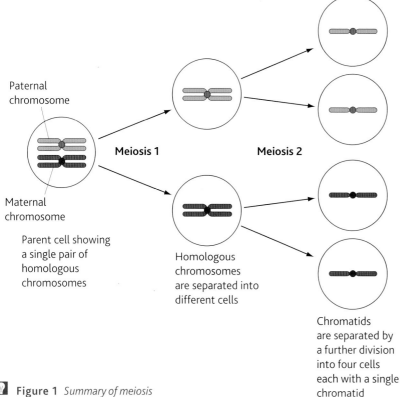

Paternal
chromosome

Maternal
chromosome

Parent cell showing
a single pair of
homologous
chromosomes

Meiosis 1

Meiosis 2

Homologous
chromosomes
are separated into
different cells

Chromatids
are separated by
a further division
into four cells
each with a single
chromatid

Figure 1 *Summary of meiosis*

Before we look at these two processes in more detail, let us remind ourselves of the meaning of three important terms:

- **gene** – a section of DNA that codes for a polypeptide,
- **locus** – the position of a gene on a chromosome or DNA molecule,
- **allele** – one of the different forms of a particular gene.

Independent segregation of homologous chromosomes

During meiosis 1, each chromosome lines up alongside its homologous partner (see Figure 2 overleaf). In humans, for example, this means that there will be 23 homologous pairs of chromosomes lying side by side. When these homologous pairs arrange themselves in this line they do so randomly. One of each pair will pass to each daughter cell. Which one of the pair goes into the daughter cell, and with which one of any of the other pairs, depends on how the pairs are lined up in the parent cell. Since the pairs are lined up at random, the combination of chromosomes that goes into the daughter cell at meiosis 1 is also random. This is called **independent segregation**.

Variety from new genetic combinations

Each member of a homologous pair of chromosomes has exactly the same genes and therefore determines the same characteristics (e.g. eye colour and blood group). However, the alleles of these genes may differ (e.g. they may code for brown or blue eyes, or blood group A or B). The random distribution, and consequent independent assortment, of these chromosomes therefore produces new genetic combinations. An example is shown in Figure 2 on the next page. In this diagram we look at just two homologous pairs. The stages shown on the figure are:

Hint

Imagine your chromosomes as two packs of 23 cards, red and blue, in which the cards are labelled from A to W. You were given the red pack by your mother and the blue pack by your father. Independent segregation is like dealing a card, of each letter in turn, at random from either of these two packs. Your final hand of 23 cards could contain any proportion of red and blue cards. In fact there are 2^{23} (over 8 million) different possible combinations.

■ Hint

Imagine your packs of blue and red cards again. Recombination is like taking a red card and a blue card, each with the same letter, and tearing an identical portion from each card and attaching it to the other card, so that you have new cards that are part red and part blue. You can do this in an almost infinite number of ways and all before you start to deal them as before!

■ **Stage 1**. One of the pair of chromosomes includes the gene for eye colour and carries one allele for brown eyes and one for blue eyes. The other chromosome carries the gene for blood group and also carries both the allele for blood group A and the allele for blood group B. There are two possible arrangements, P and Q, of the two chromosomes at the start of meiosis. Both are equally probable, but each produces a different outcome in terms of the characteristics that may be passed on via the gametes.

■ **Stage 2**. At the end of meiosis 1, the homologous chromosomes have segregated into two separate cells.

■ **Stage 3**. At the end of meiosis 2, the chromosomes have segregated into chromatids producing four gametes for each arrangement. The actual gametes are different, depending on the original arrangement (P or Q) of the chromosomes at stage 1.

Arrangement P produces the following types of gamete:

■ Brown eyes and blood group B

■ Blue eyes and blood group A.

Arrangement Q produces the following types of gamete:

■ Blue eyes and blood group B

■ Brown eyes and blood group A.

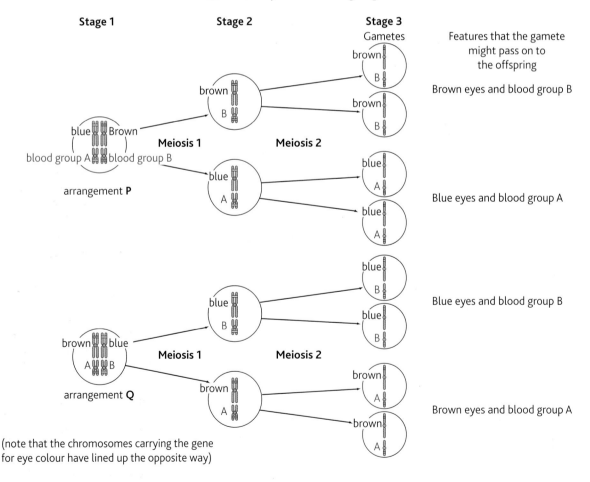

Figure 2 *Genetic variation produced as a result of independent segregation of chromosomes during meiosis. This diagram illustrates the independent segregation of two features, eye colour and blood group, that are carried on separate chromosomes*

Where the cells produced in meiosis are gametes these will be genetically different as a result of the different combinations of the maternal and paternal chromosomes they contain. These haploid gametes fuse randomly at fertilisation. The haploid gametes produced by meiosis must fuse to restore the diploid state. Each gamete has a different make-up and their random fusion therefore produces variety in the offspring. Where the gametes come from different parents (as is usually the case) two different genetic make-ups are combined and even more variety results.

Genetic recombination by crossing over

We saw above that, during meiosis 1, each chromosome lines up alongside its homologous partner. The following events then take place:

- The chromatids of each pair become twisted around one another.
- During this twisting process tensions are created and portions of the chromatids break off.
- These broken portions then rejoin with the chromatids of its homologous partner.
- Usually it is the equivalent portions of homologous chromosomes that are exchanged.
- In this way new genetic combinations are produced (Figure 3).

The chromatids cross over one another many times and so the process is known as **crossing over**. The broken-off portions of chromatid recombine with another chromatid, so this process is called **recombination**.

The effect of this recombination by crossing over on the cells produced at the end of meiosis is illustrated in Figure 4. Compare the four cells that result with those shown in Figure 1. If there is no recombination by crossing over only two different types of cell are produced. However, if recombination does occur, four different cell types are produced. Crossing over therefore increases genetic variety even further.

Chromatids of homologous chromosomes twist around one another, crossing over many times

Simplified representation of a single cross over

Point of breakage

Result of a single cross over showing equivalent portions of the chromatid having been exchanged

Figure 3 *Crossing over*

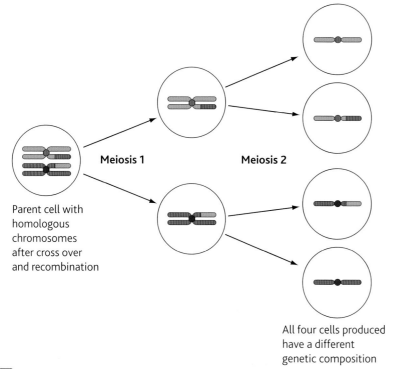

Parent cell with homologous chromosomes after cross over and recombination

Meiosis 1

Meiosis 2

All four cells produced have a different genetic composition

Figure 4 *Genetic variation as a result of recombination by crossing over*

Summary questions

1. A cell is examined and found to have 27 chromosomes. Is it likely to be haploid or diploid? Explain your answer.

2. In which **two** ways does meiosis lead to an increase in genetic variety?

3. Study Figure 2. Imagine that both alleles of the gene on the smaller chromosome are for blood group A (rather than blood groups A and B). List all the different combination of alleles in the gametes.

4. A mule is a cross between a horse (64 chromosomes) and a donkey (62 chromosomes). Mules therefore have 63 chromosomes. From your knowledge of meiosis, suggest why mules cannot produce gametes and are therefore sterile.

1   Explain how crossing over can contribute to genetic variation.   *(3 marks)*

AQA, 2004

2   **Figure 1** shows a short section of a DNA molecule.

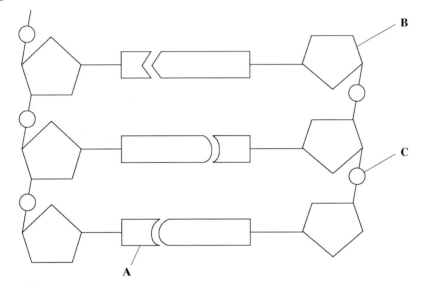

Figure 1

(a) Draw a diagram to show a single nucleotide using the information in **Figure 1**.   *(1 mark)*

(b) Use the letters in **Figure 1** to indicate a part of the molecule which:
  (i)   is a base
  (ii) contains nitrogen.   *(2 marks)*

(c) (i)   The sequence of bases on one strand of DNA is important for protein synthesis. What is its role?
  (ii) How are the two strands of the DNA molecule held together?
  (iii) Give **one** advantage of DNA molecules having two strands.   *(3 marks)*

AQA, 2005

3   (a) Explain what is meant by:
  (i)   an allele
  (ii) a gene.   *(2 marks)*

(b) Lysozyme is an enzyme consisting of a single polypeptide chain of 129 amino acids.
    What is the minimum number of nucleotide bases needed to code for this enzyme?   *(1 mark)*

AQA, 2005

4   (a) **Figure 2** shows two pairs of chromosomes from a plant cell. The letters represent alleles.

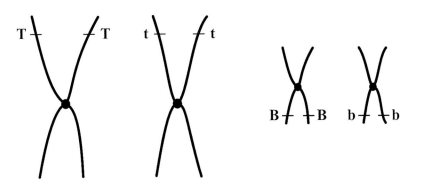

Figure 2

(i)   Give all the different types of the gametes which could be produced by this plant.

(ii) One chromosome has two copies of allele **T**. What occurs during meiosis which results in only one copy of the allele **T** being present in a gamete?   *(2 marks)*

(b) **Figure 3** shows another pair of chromosomes from the same plant cell. The table shows the numbers of gametes with each type produced by this plant.

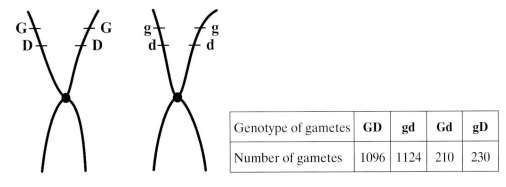

Genotype of gametes	GD	gd	Gd	gD
Number of gametes	1096	1124	210	230

Figure 3

(i)   Describe what happens during meiosis, which results in the new combinations of alleles, **Gd** and **gD**.

(ii) Suggest why there are fewer gametes with types **Gd** and **gD** than **GD** and **gd**.   *(4 marks)*

5   Copy and complete the table to show **three** differences between the structure of the DNA in a palisade cell in a leaf and a bacterium.   *(3 marks)*

A palisade cell in a leaf	A bacterium

9.1 Genetic diversity

Learning objectives:

■ Why are organisms different from one another?

■ What factors influence genetic diversity?

Specification reference: 3.2.3

Figure 1 *Examples of genetic diversity (from top to bottom): anemone; lichens; mountain goat; fritillary butterfly*

Hint

Remember that an allele is one alternative form of a gene and, as such, is a length of DNA on one chromosome of a homologous pair.

In this chapter we shall see how similarities and differences in DNA result in genetic diversity.

Organisms are varied. Around 1.8 million **species** of organisms on Earth have been identified and named. Many more are unnamed or undiscovered. Estimates of the total number of species on this planet range from 5 million to 100 million. All of these species are different.

Even between members of the same species there are a multitude of differences. Almost every one of the 6.5 billion people alive in 2008 are similar enough to be recognised as humans and yet different enough to be distinguished from one another. What makes us and other species similar and yet different?

■ Genetic diversity

We have seen in Topic 2.5 that it is proteins which make organisms different and, in Topic 8.2, that it is DNA which determines the considerable variety of proteins that make up each organism. Therefore similarities and differences between organisms may be defined in terms of variation in DNA. Hence it is differences in DNA that lead to the vast genetic diversity we find on Earth.

We also saw in Topic 8.2 that a section of DNA that codes for one or more polypeptides is called a gene. All members of the same species have the same genes. For example, all humans have a gene for blood group, just as all snapdragons (*Antirrhinum majus*) have a gene for petal colour. Which blood group humans have depends on which two **alleles** of the gene they possess. Likewise, the colour of a snapdragon's petals depends on which two alleles for petal colour it possesses. Organisms therefore differ in their alleles, not their genes. It is the combination of alleles they possess that makes species (and individuals within that species) different from one another.

The greater the number of different alleles that all members of a species possess, the greater the genetic diversity of that species. The greater the genetic diversity, the more likely that a species will be able to adapt to some environmental change. This is because it will have a wider range of alleles and therefore a wider range of characteristics. There is therefore a greater probability that some individual will possess a characteristic that suits it to the new environmental conditions. Genetic diversity is reduced when a species has fewer different alleles. Let us now look at some factors that influence genetic diversity.

■ Selective breeding

Selective breeding is also known as **artificial selection**. It involves identifying individuals with the desired characteristics and using them to parent the next generation. Offspring that do not exhibit the desired characters are killed, or at least prevented from breeding. In this way alleles for unwanted characteristics are bred out of the population. The variety of alleles in the population is deliberately restricted to a small number of desired alleles. Over many generations, this leads to a population all of which possess the desired qualities but which has reduced genetic diversity.

Selective breeding is commonly carried out in order to produce high-yielding breeds of domesticated animals and strains of plants. For example, in plants such as wheat, the features selected for include large grains with a high gluten content, short stems and resistance to disease.

The founder effect

The founder effect occurs when just a few individuals from a population colonise a new region. These few individuals will carry with them only a small fraction of the alleles of the population as a whole. These alleles may not be representative of the larger population. The new population that develops from the few colonisers will therefore show less genetic diversity than the population from which they came. The founder effect is often seen when new volcanic islands rise out of the sea. The few individuals that colonise these barren islands give rise to populations that are genetically distinct from the populations they left behind. The new populations may, in time, develop into a separate species. As these species have fewer alleles they are less able to adapt to changing conditions.

Genetic bottlenecks

Populations of a species may from time to time suffer a dramatic drop in numbers. Sometimes the reason for this drop is a chance event, such as a volcanic eruption or interference by man. The few survivors will possess a much smaller variety of alleles than the original population. In other words, their genetic diversity will be less. As these few individuals breed and become re-established, the genetic diversity of the new population will remain restricted. This effect can be illustrated by elephant seals. The population of northern elephant seals was hunted by mankind until, by about 1900, just 20 remained in a colony on the coast of Mexico. Their population has since increased but, when compared with the population of southern elephant seals in California, it shows considerably less genetic diversity. Less diversity means fewer alleles, making it less likely that the population can adapt to any change in its environment.

Application and How science works

Ethics of selective breeding in domesticated animals

Having outlined the background to selective breeding and the techniques involved, let us now consider some of the ethical issues surrounding it.

Almost all scientific progress has both benefits and risks. Scientists carry out research into various techniques of selective breeding from which they can report on the benefits and risks of each. Interested parties, such as government agencies, farmers, food producers, supermarkets and shopkeepers, and organisations such as animal welfare groups, can then debate the issues surrounding these reports. As part of this debate it is always worth bearing in mind that:

- Scientific research requires funding. Who funds the research may have an influence on its outcome. Consider how the type of research undertaken might differ according to whether a farming body, a food producer, a supermarket or an animal welfare group was funding the work.

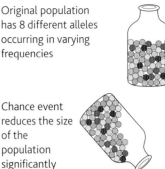

Original population has 8 different alleles occurring in varying frequencies

Chance event reduces the size of the population significantly

The individuals that survive have fewer alleles (just four types) and with different frequencies (green twice as frequent as yellow)

As the population recovers, the number and frequency of the alleles is the same as that of the population which came through the bottleneck. This is less diverse than that of the original population

Figure 2 *The bottleneck effect*

Summary questions

1 State whether each of the following is likely to **increase** or **decrease** genetic diversity:

a increasing the variety of alleles within a population

b breeding together closely related cats to develop varieties with longer fur

c a few seeds from a plant community on Iceland reaching the new volcanic island of Surtsey and establishing a new population

d mutation (permanent change to the DNA) of an allele.

2 Explain how a difference in its DNA might lead to an organism having a different appearance and hence the species showing greater genetic diversity.

3 Explain how genetic bottlenecks reduce genetic diversity.

Scientists are largely self-regulating. They help to make decisions on what experiments are carried out and how. Different scientists may have different codes of ethics depending on their personal, moral and religious beliefs. This may affect the experiments they perform.

Ethical implications

There is no doubt that selective breeding has produced livestock that gives greater yields. In turn, this has given us a reliable source of cheap food throughout the year. It has raised our standard of living. At the same time selective breeding of domesticated animals raises some ethical issues.

Is selective breeding interfering with nature? Do other species have 'rights'? Should the development of new varieties be allowed to take place naturally, as it has successfully done for millions of years. Do domesticated animals have value in themselves or only in terms of their usefulness to humans? Should we accept a lower standard of living in return for natural rather than artificial breeding of animals?

What features should be selected for and who decides? Is selective breeding of pets equally acceptable as selecting high-yielding food animals? Is it acceptable to select for features in cats, dogs and other pets simply because the features are fashionable or desirable to their owners?

How do we balance increased yield with animal welfare? At what point does a further increase in udder size become disabling for the cow rather than just inconvenient? Is it acceptable to inconvenience a cow anyway? Is it reasonable to selectively breed animals that are better suited to living in environmentally regulated sheds for long periods rather than in open fields?

Producing genetically uniform livestock by selective breeding leads to varieties of animals with a narrower range of alleles and hence less genetic diversity. Could we be losing forever some alleles that might be of benefit to the animals and mankind in the future?

In an effort to control global warming, should we select animals that produce less methane (a major greenhouse gas) and/or grow well at lower environmental temperatures and so do not need overwintering in heated sheds in colder climates?

Are we driven too much by consumerism? Should we stop trying to select increasingly higher-yielding varieties and simply be prepared to pay more for our food? Is this fair on the poorest people in our society?

Should we stop the traditional methods of selective breeding as these are still artificial? Is selective breeding an acceptable alternative to producing required characteristics by genetic engineering?

Scientists will continue to explore, and try to explain, aspects of the world about them, including research into selective breeding. It is up to society at large to decide how to use the information they provide. While scientists will inform us about what **can** be done, it is answering ethical questions like those above, that will help us decide what **ought** to be done.

1 Those who make decisions about whether a new scientific or technological discovery should be developed have a very difficult task. Suggest some of the factors that they need to take into account before making a decision.

2 Apart from ethical principles, suggest what other guidance any decision must comply with.

Selective breeding in cattle

The breeding of farm animals, such as cattle, has never been a random affair. For many thousands of years, farmers have chosen the most suitable domesticated animals and plants to parent the next generation. Selective breeding is therefore not new but traditional forms of selective breeding are slow and imprecise. What has changed is the pace and extent of selective breeding that has occurred over the past 50 years. What has prompted this change?

As consumers we want a reliable supply of a wide range of foods at minimum cost. We therefore create a highly competitive market that puts farmers under pressure to cut costs and supply cheap food in order to stay in business. As a result, food production has become ever more intensive. To meet our demand for cheap, plentiful food, scientists and farmers have worked together to breed higher-yielding varieties of domesticated plants and animals.

One method of increasing the pace of change by selective breeding is to use **artificial insemination (AI)**. AI is the collection of semen and its introduction into the vagina by artificial means. The semen of a single bull can be used to inseminate hundreds of cows. In the UK 80 per cent of insemination in cattle is by artificial means.

Cattle have been selectively bred for two main purposes:

- for meat – beef breeds (e.g. Herefords and Aberdeen Angus). Desirable characteristics include a high muscle to bone ratio and rapid growth and weight gain.
- for milk – dairy breeds (e.g. Friesians and Holstein). Desirable characteristics include high production of milk with a high fat and protein content, an udder that suits a milking machine and rapid delivery of milk.

The rapid change in cattle characteristics as a result of selection has raised a number of issues. For example, in dairy cattle it has had the following results:

- The genetic diversity of cattle has been reduced. Specialist breeds of cow, suited to local conditions, have disappeared, to be replaced by the highly bred Holstein–Friesian (the typical black-and-white cow) that now makes up 90 per cent of European dairy herds.
- The doubling of milk yield per cow over the past 50 years has put a strain on the animals' welfare. Mastitis (inflammation of the udder), lameness and infertility are all more common now.
- The natural lifespan of a cow is up to 25 years but most cows now go for slaughter after 5 years.
- Calves would normally suckle for 6–12 months but, so that the milk can be used by humans, they are removed from their mothers within 1–2 days.
- From the age of 2 years, dairy cows produce calves, and hence milk, continuously throughout their lives.

3 Traditional forms of selective breeding involve farmers choosing the most suitable animals to breed the next generation. Suggest reasons why this process is described as 'slow and imprecise'.

4 Suggest one possible danger of allowing the semen of a single bull to inseminate hundreds of cows.

5 Suggest two advantages of selective breeding in dairy cattle.

6 The Vegan Society opposes many aspects of the modern dairy industry. Suggest two ethical objections that groups like the Vegan Society might have to the selective breeding of dairy cattle.

Hint

Ethics are a set of standards that are followed by a particular group of individuals and are designed to regulate their behaviour. They determine what is acceptable and legitimate in pursuing the aims of the group.

Figure 3 *Cattle, such as the Highland variety (top) and Friesian variety (bottom), have been bred to produce different characteristics*

10.1   Haemoglobin

In this chapter we shall see how the variety of living organisms is reflected in the similarities and differences of the molecules and cells of which organisms are composed. In Topic 2.5 we looked at the structure of proteins and how the shape of a protein is important to how it functions. We have seen that the primary structure of a protein is the sequence of amino acids, determined by DNA, that makes up a polypeptide chain. It is this sequence that determines how the polypeptide is shaped into its tertiary structure. Linking together a number of polypeptides, sometimes along with non-protein groups, gives rise to a protein's quaternary structure. Let us now look at the haemoglobins – a group of protein molecules that have a quaternary structure.

Haemoglobin molecules

The haemoglobins are a group of chemically similar molecules found in a wide variety of organisms. The structure of a haemoglobin molecule is shown in Figure 1. It is made up as follows:

▓ **primary structure**, consisting of four polypeptide chains

▓ **secondary structure**, in which each of these polypeptide chains is coiled into a helix

▓ **tertiary structure**, in which each polypeptide chain is folded into a precise shape – an important factor in its ability to carry oxygen

▓ **quaternary structure**, in which all four polypeptides are linked together to form an almost spherical molecule. Each polypeptide is associated with a haem group – which contains a ferrous (Fe^{2+}) ion. Each Fe^{2+} ion can combine with a single oxygen molecule (O_2), making a total of four O_2 molecules that can be carried by a single haemoglobin molecule in humans.

β-polypeptide

α-polypeptide

Each chain is attached to a haem group that can combine with oxygen

Figure 1 *Quaternary structure of a haemoglobin molecule*

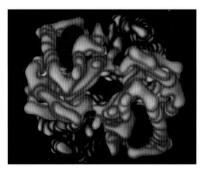

Figure 2 *Computer graphic representation of a haemoglobin molecule showing two pairs of polypeptide chains (orange and blue) associated with a haem group (red)*

The role of haemoglobin

The role of haemoglobin is to transport oxygen. To be efficient at transporting oxygen, haemoglobin must:

▓ readily associate with oxygen at the surface where gas exchange takes place

▓ readily dissociate from oxygen at those tissues requiring it.

These two requirements may appear to contradict each other, but they are achieved by a remarkable property of haemoglobin. It changes its affinity for oxygen under different conditions (Table 1). It achieves this because its shape changes in the presence of certain substances, such as carbon dioxide. In the presence of carbon dioxide, the new shape of the haemoglobin molecule binds more loosely to oxygen. As a result haemoglobin releases its oxygen.

Table 1 *Affinity of haemoglobin for oxygen under different conditions*

Region of body	Oxygen concentration	Carbon dioxide concentration	Affinity of haemoglobin for oxygen	Result
Gas exchange surface	High	Low	High	Oxygen is attached
Respiring tissues	Low	High	Low	Oxygen is released

Why have different haemoglobins?

Scientists long ago observed that many organisms possessed haemoglobin. They proposed that it carried oxygen from the gas-exchange surface to the tissues that required it for respiration. If so, this meant that it must readily combine with oxygen. Consequently they investigated the ability of haemoglobin from different organisms to combine with oxygen. Results showed that there were different types of haemoglobins. These exhibited different properties relating to the way they took up and released oxygen. Let's look at the haemoglobins at each end of a range:

- **Haemoglobins with a high affinity for oxygen**. These take up oxygen more easily but release it less readily.
- **Haemoglobins with a low affinity for oxygen**. These take up oxygen less easily but release it more readily.

Scientists questioned why this should happen. Further observation and experimentation showed a correlation between the type of haemoglobin in an organism and factors such as the environment in which it lived or its metabolic rate. Explanations for some of these correlations are as follows:

- An organism living in an environment with little oxygen requires a haemoglobin that readily combines with oxygen if it is to absorb enough of it. Provided that the organism's metabolic rate is not very high, the fact that this form of haemoglobin does not release its oxygen as readily into the tissues will not be a problem.
- An organism with a high metabolic rate needs to release oxygen readily into its tissues. Provided that there is plenty of oxygen in the organism's environment, it is more important to have a haemoglobin that releases its oxygen easily than one that takes it up easily.

Why do different haemoglobins have different affinities for oxygen?

The answer, scientists discovered, lies in the shape of the molecule. Different haemoglobin molecules have slightly different sequences of amino acids and therefore slightly different shapes. Depending on the shape, haemoglobin molecules range from those that have a high affinity for oxygen to those that have a low affinity for oxygen.

Loading and unloading oxygen

The process by which haemoglobin combines with oxygen is called **loading**, or **associating**. In humans this takes place in the lungs.

The process in which haemoglobin releases its oxygen is called **unloading**, or **dissociating**. In humans this takes place in the tissues.

Summary questions

1. Describe the quaternary structure of haemoglobin.

2. Explain how DNA leads to different haemoglobin molecules having different affinities for oxygen.

3. When the body is at rest, only one of the four oxygen molecules carried by haemoglobin is normally released into the tissues. Suggest why this could be an advantage when the organism becomes more active.

4. Carbon monoxide occurs in car exhaust fumes. It binds permanently to haemoglobin in preference to oxygen. Suggest a reason why a person breathing in car-exhaust fumes might lose consciousness.

10.2 Oxygen dissociation curves

Learning objectives:

▥ What is an oxygen dissociation curve?

▥ What is the effect of carbon dioxide concentration on the curve and why?

▥ How do the properties of the haemoglobins in different organisms relate to the environment and way of life of the organism concerned?

Specification reference: 3.2.4

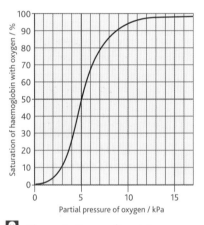

🔆 **Figure 1** *Oxygen dissociation curve for adult human haemoglobin*

Having looked at haemoglobin in topic 10.1, let us now consider its properties. How does it load and unload oxygen and what effect does carbon dioxide have on this process?

🔆 Oxygen dissociation curves

When haemoglobin is exposed to different partial pressures of oxygen (see Hint), it does not absorb the oxygen evenly. At very low concentrations of oxygen, the four polypeptides of the haemoglobin molecule are closely united, and so it is difficult to absorb the first oxygen molecule. However, once loaded, this oxygen molecule causes the polypeptides to load the remaining three oxygen molecules very easily. The graph of this relationship is known as the **oxygen dissociation curve** (see Figure 1). You will notice from this graph that a very small decrease in the partial pressure of oxygen leads to a lot of oxygen becoming dissociated from haemoglobin. The graph tails off at very high oxygen concentrations simply because the haemoglobin is almost saturated with oxygen.

We saw in Topic 10.1 that there are a number of different types of haemoglobin molecules, each with a different shape and hence a different affinity for oxygen. In addition, the shape of any one type of haemoglobin molecule can change under different conditions. These facts both mean that there are a large number of different oxygen dissociation curves. They all have a roughly similar shape but differ in their position on the axes.

The many different oxygen dissociation curves are better understood if two facts are always kept in mind:

▥ The further to the left the curve, the greater is the affinity of haemoglobin for oxygen (so it takes up oxygen readily but releases it less easily).

▥ The further to the right the curve, the lower is the affinity of haemoglobin for oxygen (so it takes up oxygen less readily but releases it more easily).

▥ Effects of carbon dioxide concentration

Haemoglobin has a reduced affinity for oxygen in the presence of carbon dioxide. The greater the concentration of carbon dioxide, the more readily the haemoglobin releases its oxygen (the Bohr effect). This explains why the behaviour of haemoglobin changes in different regions of the body.

▥ At the gas-exchange surface (e.g. lungs), the level of carbon dioxide is low because it diffuses across the exchange surface and is expelled from the organism. The affinity of haemoglobin for oxygen is increased, which, coupled with the high concentration of oxygen in the lungs, means that oxygen is readily loaded by haemoglobin. The reduced carbon dioxide level has shifted the oxygen dissociation curve to the left (Figure 2).

▥ In rapidly respiring tissues (e.g. muscles), the level of carbon dioxide is high. The affinity of haemoglobin for oxygen is reduced, which, coupled with the low concentration of oxygen in the muscles, means

■ Hint

Measuring oxygen concentration

The amount of a gas that is present in a mixture of gases is measured by the pressure it contributes to the total pressure of the gas mixture. This is known as the **partial pressure** of the gas and, in the case of oxygen, is written as pO_2. It is measured in kiloPascals (kPa). Normal atmospheric pressure is 100 kPa. As oxygen makes up 21 per cent of the atmosphere, its partial pressure is normally 21 kPa.

that oxygen is readily unloaded from the haemoglobin into the muscle cells. The increased carbon dioxide level has shifted the oxygen dissociation curve to the right (Figure 2).

We saw above that the greater the concentration of carbon dioxide, the more readily haemoglobin releases its oxygen. This is because dissolved carbon dioxide is acidic and the low pH causes haemoglobin to change shape. Let us see how this works in the transport of oxygen by haemoglobin.

Loading, transport and unloading of oxygen

- At the gas-exchange surface carbon dioxide is constantly being removed.
- The pH is raised due to the low level of carbon dioxide.
- The higher pH changes the shape of haemoglobin into one that enables it to load oxygen readily.
- This shape also increases the affinity of haemoglobin for oxygen, so it is not released while being transported in the blood to the tissues.
- In the tissues, carbon dioxide is produced by respiring cells.
- Carbon dioxide is acidic in solution, so the pH of the blood within the the tissues is lowered.
- The lower pH changes the shape of haemoglobin into one with a lower affinity for oxygen.
- Haemoglobin releases its oxygen into the respiring tissues.

The above process is a flexible way of ensuring that there is always sufficient oxygen for respiring tissues. The more active a tissue, the more oxygen is unloaded. This works as follows:

The higher the rate of respiration → the more carbon dioxide the tissues produce → the lower the pH → the greater the haemoglobin shape change → the more readily oxygen is unloaded → the more oxygen is available for respiration.

In humans, haemoglobin normally becomes saturated with oxygen as it passes through the lungs. In other words, most of the haemoglobin molecules are loaded with their maximum four oxygen molecules. When this haemoglobin reaches a tissue with a low respiratory rate, only one of these molecules will normally be released. The blood returning to the lungs will therefore contain haemoglobin that is still 75 per cent saturated with oxygen. If a tissue is very active, e.g. an exercising muscle, then three oxygen molecules will usually be unloaded from each haemoglobin molecule. These events are shown in Figure 3.

Application

Different lives – different haemoglobins
Where you live is important
If you walk along a sandy seashore when the tide is out, you may come across worm casts. Beneath these probably lies an organism called a lugworm. The lugworm is not very active, spending almost all its life in a U-shaped burrow. Most of the time the lugworm is covered by sea water, which it circulates through its burrow. Oxygen diffuses into the lugworm's blood from the water and it uses haemoglobin to transport oxygen to its tissues.

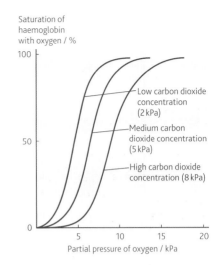

Figure 2 *The effect of carbon dioxide concentration on the oxygen dissociation curve*

Key
— Haemoglobin molecule is loaded with oxygen in the lungs
— Haemoglobin molecule in a resting tissue unloads only 25% of its oxygen
— Haemoglobin molecule in an active tissue unloads 75% of its oxygen

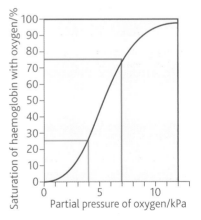

Figure 3 *The loading and unloading of haemoglobin with oxygen*

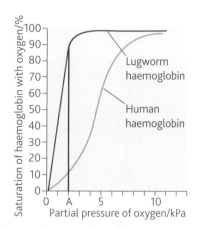

Figure 4 *Comparison of the oxygen dissociation curves of lugworm and human haemoglobin*

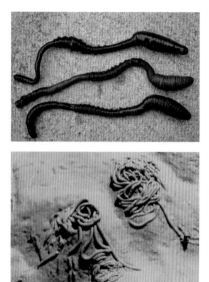

Figure 5 *Three lugworms lying on sand (top); lugworm casts at the entrances to their burrows (bottom)*

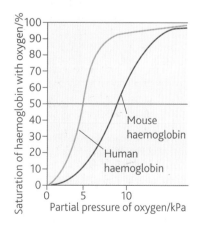

Figure 6 *Oxygen dissociation curves of mouse and human haemoglobin*

When the tide goes out, the lugworm can no longer circulate a fresh supply of oxygenated water through its burrow. As a result, the water in the burrow contains progressively less oxygen as the lugworm uses it up. The lugworm needs to extract as much oxygen as possible from the water in the burrow if it is to survive until the tide covers it again. Figure 4 shows the oxygen dissociation curve of lugworm haemoglobin compared to that of adult human haemoglobin.

1 In Figure 4, line A is drawn at a partial pressure of oxygen of 2 kPa. This is the partial pressure of oxygen found in lugworm burrows after the sea no longer covers them. Using figures from the graph, explain why a lugworm can survive at these concentrations of oxygen while a human could not.

2 Using the graphs in Figure 4, explain how the lugworm is able to obtain sufficient oxygen from an environment that contains so little.

3 Suggest one feature of a lugworm's way of life described in the passage that helps it to survive in an environment that has very little oxygen. Explain how this feature aids survival.

4 Haemoglobin usually loads oxygen less readily when the concentration of carbon dioxide is high (the Bohr effect). The haemoglobin of lugworms does not exhibit this effect. Explain why to do so could be harmful.

5 Suggest a reason why lugworms are not found higher up the seashore.

6 Llamas are animals that live at high altitudes. At these altitudes the atmospheric pressure is lower and so the partial pressure of oxygen is also lower. It is therefore difficult to load haemoglobin with oxygen. Suggest where the oxygen dissociation curve of llama haemoglobin is shifted to, relative to human haemoglobin. A sketch graph might help to clarify your answer.

Size matters

Mice are small mammals and therefore have a large surface area to volume ratio. As a result they tend to lose heat rapidly when the environmental temperature is lower than their body temperature. To compensate for this they have a high metabolic rate that generates heat and helps them to maintain their normal body temperature. Figure 6 shows the oxygen dissociation curve for the haemoglobin of a mouse compared to that of adult human haemoglobin.

7 The partial pressure of oxygen at which haemoglobin is 50 per cent saturated is known as the unloading pressure. Calculate the difference between the unloading pressure of human haemoglobin and that of mouse haemoglobin.

8 The oxygen dissociation curve of the mouse is shifted to the right of that for a human.

a What difference does this make to the way oxygen is unloaded from mouse haemoglobin compared to human haemoglobin?

b What advantage does this have for the maintenance of body temperature in mice?

c The position of the oxygen dissociation curve for a mouse means that its haemoglobin loads oxygen less readily than human haemoglobin. Given that the partial pressure of oxygen in air is normally 21 kPa, use the graph to explain why this is of no disadvantage to the mouse.

9 Using a sketch graph suggest the shapes and relative positions of the oxygen dissociation curves of the following mammals:

a a human

b an elephant

c a shrew

Activity counts
Flight in birds and swimming in fish are both energy-demanding processes. The muscles that move a bird's wings are powerful and require a lot of oxygen to enable them to respire at a sufficient rate to keep the body airborne. Flight muscles have a very high metabolic rate and, during flight, much of the blood pumped by the heart goes to these muscles. While birds use a great deal of energy opposing gravity in a medium that gives little support, fish have a different problem. They expend considerable energy swimming through a medium that is very dense and therefore difficult to move through.

10 Suggest whether the oxygen dissociation curve of a pigeon is shifted to the right or left of the curve for a human. Explain your answer.

11 The mackerel is a type of fish that swims freely in the surface waters of the sea. These fish rely on their ability to swim very fast in order to escape from predators. The plaice is a marine fish that uses a different strategy. These fish spend much of their lives stationary or moving very slowly on the sea bed, where they are camouflaged by their skin colour. The two fish are of relatively similar mass. Sketch a graph to show the relative positions of the oxygen dissociation curves of these two fish.

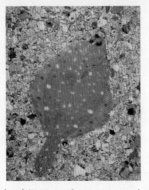

Figure 7 *Mackerel (top) live in surface waters and swim rapidly. Plaice (bottom) live on the sea bed and move very slowly*

12 Ice fish live in the Antarctic and are the only vertebrates to completely lack haemoglobin. Suggest a reason why they can survive without haemoglobin.

Summary questions

1 Study Figure 1 on page 152 and answer the following questions:

a At what partial pressure of oxygen is the haemoglobin 50 per cent saturated with oxygen?

b What is the percentage saturation of haemoglobin with oxygen when the partial pressure of oxygen is 9 kPa?

c In an exercising muscle the partial pressure of oxygen is 4 kPa while in the lungs it is 12 kPa. What percentage of the oxyhaemoglobin from the lungs will have released its oxygen to an exercising muscle?

2 a What is the effect of increased carbon dioxide concentration on oxygen dissociation?

b How does this change the saturation of haemoglobin with oxygen?

3 A rise in temperature shifts the oxygen dissociation curve to the right. Suggest how this enables an exercising muscle to work more efficiently.

10.3 Starch, glycogen and cellulose

In organisms, a wide range of different molecules with very different properties can be made from a limited range of smaller molecules. What makes the larger molecules different is the various ways in which the smaller molecules are combined to form them. Let us look at some of these larger molecules by considering three important polysaccharides.

▊ Starch

Starch is a polysaccharide that is found in many parts of a plant in the form of small grains. Especially large amounts occur in seeds and storage organs, such as potato tubers. It forms an important component of food and is the major energy source in most diets. Starch is made up of chains of α-glucose monosaccharides linked by glycosidic bonds that are formed by **condensation reactions**. The unbranched chain is wound into a tight coil that makes the molecule very compact. The structure of a starch molecule is shown in Figure 1.

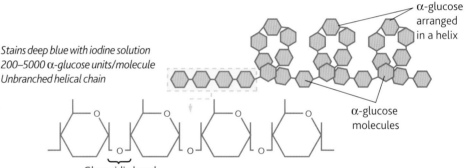

Stains deep blue with iodine solution
200–5000 α-glucose units/molecule
Unbranched helical chain

α-glucose arranged in a helix

α-glucose molecules

Glycosidic bond

🔋 **Figure 1** *Structure of a starch molecule*

The main role of starch is energy storage, something it is especially suited for because:

▊ it is insoluble and therefore does not tend to draw water into the cells by **osmosis**,

▊ being insoluble, it does not easily diffuse out of cells,

▊ it is compact, so a lot of it can be stored in a small space,

▊ when hydrolysed it forms α-glucose, which is both easily transported and readily used in respiration.

Starch is never found in animal cells. Instead a similar polysaccharide, called glycogen, serves the same role.

▊ Glycogen

Glycogen is very similar in structure to starch but has shorter chains and is more highly branched. It is sometimes called 'animal starch' because it is the major carbohydrate storage product of animals. In animals it is stored as small granules mainly in the muscles and the liver. Its structure suits it for storage for the same reasons as those given for starch. However, because it is made up of smaller chains, it is even more readily hydrolysed to α-glucose. Glycogen is found in animal cells but never in plant cells.

Figure 2 *False colour scanning electron micrograph (SEM) of starch grains (blue) in the cells of a potato. Starch is a compact storage material.*

Cellulose

Cellulose differs from starch and glycogen in one major respect: it is made of monomers of β-glucose rather than α-glucose. This seemingly small variation produces fundamental differences in the structure and function of this polysaccharide. The main reason for this is that, in the β-glucose units, the positions of the —H group and the —OH group on a single carbon atom are reversed. In β-glucose the —OH group is above, rather than below, the ring. This means that to form glycosidic links, each β-glucose molecule must be rotated by 180° compared to its neighbour. The result is that the —CH₂OH group on each β-glucose molecule alternates between being above and below the chain (Figure 3).

Rather than forming a coiled chain like starch, cellulose has straight, unbranched chains. These run parallel to one another, allowing hydrogen bonds (see Topic 2.5) to form cross-linkages between adjacent chains. While each individual hydrogen bond adds very little to the strength of the molecule, the sheer overall number of them makes a considerable contribution to strengthening cellulose, making it the valuable structural material that it is. The arrangement of β-glucose chains in a cellulose molecule is shown in Figure 3.

Simplified representation of the arrangement of glucose chains

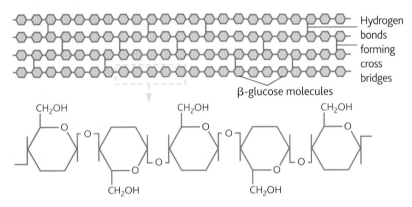

Figure 3 *Structure of a cellulose molecule*

The cellulose chain, unlike that of starch, has adjacent glucose molecules rotated by 180°. This allows hydrogen bonds to be formed between the hydroxyl (–OH) groups on adjacent parallel chains that help to give cellulose its structural stability.

The cellulose molecules are grouped together to form microfibrils which, in turn, are arranged in parallel groups called fibres (Figure 4).

Cellulose is a major component of plant cell walls and provides rigidity to the plant cell. The cellulose cell wall also prevents the cell from bursting as water enters it by osmosis. It does this by exerting an inward pressure that stops any further influx of water. As a result, living plant cells are turgid and push against one another, making herbaceous parts of the plant semi-rigid. This is especially important in maintaining stems and leaves in a turgid state so that they can provide the maximum surface area for photosynthesis.

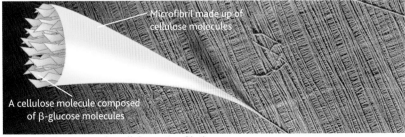

Figure 4 *Structure of a cellulose microfibril*

Summary questions

From the following list of carbohydrates choose one or more that most closely fit each of the statements below. Each carbohydrate may be used once, more than once, or not at all.

α-glucose	β-glucose
starch	glycogen
cellulose	

1. Stains deep blue with iodine solution.
2. Is known as 'animal starch'.
3. Found in plants.
4. Are polysaccharides.
5. Monosaccharide found in starch.
6. Has a structural function.
7. Can be hydrolysed.
8. Easily diffuses in and out of cells.

10.4　Plant cell structure

Learning objectives:

- What is the structure of leaf palisade cells?

- What is the structure of a choroplast and how is it related to its function?

- What is the plant cell wall composed of and what is its function?

- How do plant cells differ from animal cells?

Specification reference: 3.2.4

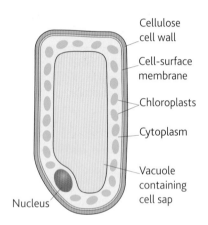

Figure 1 *Representation of a leaf palisade cell as seen under a light microscope*

Labels: Cellulose cell wall, Cell-surface membrane, Chloroplasts, Cytoplasm, Vacuole containing cell sap, Nucleus

Hint

Chloroplasts have DNA and may have evolved from free-living prokaryotic cells, but they are organelles, **not** cells.

Having looked at the variety of biological molecules, let us now turn our attention to variation between certain cells. In Unit 1 we looked at an epithelial cell from the intestines. This was an animal cell. Let us now look at plant cells. Plant cells are also **eukaryotic** cells. They therefore have a distinct nucleus and membrane-bound organelles, such as mitochondria and chloroplasts. An example of a plant cell is the leaf palisade cell.

Leaf palisade cell

The leaf palisade cell is a typical plant cell. Its function is to carry out photosynthesis. The structure of a leaf palisade cell is shown in Figure 1. From this you can observe the main features that suit it to its function of photosynthesis. These include:

- long, thin cells that form a continuous layer to absorb sunlight,

- numerous chloroplasts that arrange themselves in the best positions to collect the maximum amount of light,

- a large vacuole that pushes the cytoplasm and chloroplasts to the edge of the cell.

Chloroplasts are the organelles that carry out photosynthesis. Let us look at them in more detail.

Chloroplasts

Chloroplasts (Figure 2) vary in shape and size but are typically disc-shaped, 2–10 μm long and 1 μm in diameter. The following are their main features:

- **The chloroplast envelope** is a double plasma membrane that surrounds the organelle. It is highly selective in what it allows to enter and leave the chloroplast.

- **The grana** are stacks of up to 100 disc-like structures called **thylakoids**. Within the thylakoids is the photosynthetic pigment called **chlorophyll**. Some thylakoids have tubular extensions that join up with thylakoids in adjacent grana. The grana are where the first stage of photosynthesis takes place.

- **The stroma** is a fluid-filled matrix where the second stage of photosynthesis takes place. Within the stroma are a number of other structures, such as starch grains.

Chloroplasts are adapted to their function of harvesting sunlight and carrying out photosynthesis in the following ways:

- The granal membranes provide a large surface area for the attachment of chlorophyll, electron carriers and enzymes that carry out the first stage of photosynthesis. These chemicals are attached to the membrane in a highly ordered fashion.

- The fluid of the stroma possesses all the enzymes needed to carry out the second stage of photosynthesis.

- Chloroplasts contain both DNA and ribosomes so they can quickly and easily manufacture some of the proteins needed for photosynthesis.

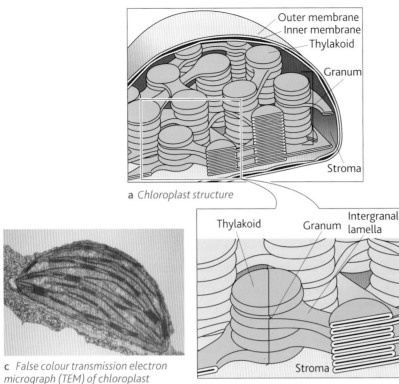

Outer membrane
Inner membrane
Thylakoid
Granum
Stroma

a *Chloroplast structure*

Thylakoid   Granum   Intergranal lamella

Stroma

b *Grana and thylakoids*

c *False colour transmission electron micrograph (TEM) of chloroplast (×44 000)*

Figure 2 *Chloroplast structure*

Link

Details of the role of chloroplasts in photosynthesis are covered in A2.

AQA Examiner's tip

Not all plant cells have chloroplasts. Think about root cells. These are below the soil surface where light rarely penetrates and so no photosynthesis is possible.

Cell wall

Characteristic of all plant cells, the cell wall consists of microfibrils of the polysaccharide cellulose (see Topic 10.3), embedded in a matrix. Cellulose microfibrils have considerable strength and so contribute to the overall strength of the cell wall. Cell walls have the following features:

▨ They consist of a number of polysaccharides, such as cellulose.
▨ There is a thin layer, called the **middle lamella**, which marks the boundary between adjacent cell walls and cements adjacent cells together.

The functions of the cellulose cell wall are:

▨ to provide mechanical strength in order to prevent the cell bursting under the pressure created by the osmotic entry of water (see Topic 3.7),
▨ to give mechanical strength to the plant as a whole,
▨ to allow water to pass along it and so contribute to the movement of water through the plant.

Differences between plant and animal cells

There are a few fundamental differences between plant and animal cells. These are shown in Table 1 on the next page.

AQA Examiner's tip

Plant cells have a cell-surface membrane **and** a cell wall, not just a cell wall.

Table 1 *Key differences between plant and animal cells*

Plant cells	Animal cells
Cellulose cell wall surrounds the cell as well as a cell-surface membrane	Only a cell-surface membrane surrounds the cell
Chloroplasts are present in large numbers in most cells	Chloroplasts are never present
Normally have a large, single, central vacuole filled with cell sap	If vacuoles are present they are small and scattered throughout the cell
Starch grains are used for storage	Glycogen granules are used for storage

Summary questions

1. Where are palisade cells found?
2. What is the function of chloroplasts?
3. Where in a chloroplast is chlorophyll found?
4. What **three** structures would you find in a plant cell but never in an animal cell?

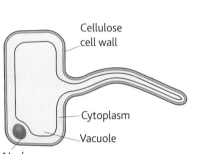

Cellulose cell wall

Cytoplasm

Vacuole

Nucleus

Application

Specialised plant cells

The root hair cell

Figure 3 shows the structure of a root hair cell. Each root hair is an extension of a root epidermal cell. Root hairs are the exchange surfaces in plants that are responsible for the absorption of water and mineral **ions**. These root hairs remain functional for a few weeks before dying back, to be replaced by others nearer the growing tip.

Root hairs absorb water by the process of osmosis. The soil solution surrounds the particles that make up soil. It contains a very low concentration of mineral ions dissolved in water. The root hairs, by comparison, have a relatively high concentration of ions and sugars within their vacuoles and cytoplasm. Because the root hairs are in direct contact with the soil solution, water moves by osmosis from the soil solution into the root hair cells.

The concentration of ions inside the root hair cell is normally greater than that in the soil solution. The uptake of mineral ions is therefore against the concentration gradient and, as a result, requires active transport. This is achieved using special **carrier proteins** that use **ATP**. This provides energy to transport particular ions from the soil solution (where they are in low concentrations), to the root hair cytoplasm and vacuole (where they are in higher concentrations).

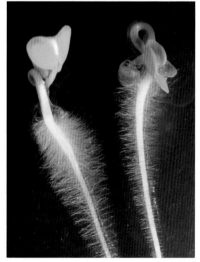

Figure 3 *A root hair cell (top); root hairs on radish seedlings provide a large surface area for the absorption of water and mineral ions (bottom)*

1. State two features shown in Figure 3 that suit a root hair cell to its function of absorbing water and mineral ions.

2. Define osmosis.

3. Explain in terms of water potential how water is absorbed into a root hair cell.

4. Suggest the name of an organelle that you might expect to occur in large numbers in a root hair cell.

5. Why do you think this organelle is found in such large numbers in a root hair cell?

Xylem vessels

In flowering plants, xylem vessels are the structures through which the vast majority of water is transported. Xylem vessels have thick cell walls. These vessels vary in appearance, depending on the type and amount of thickening of their cell walls. As they mature, their walls incorporate a substance called lignin and the cells die. The end walls break down, which allows the cells to form a continuous tube. The lignin often forms rings or spirals around the vessel. The structure of xylem vessels is shown in Figure 4.

6. The process of transporting water in plants in the transpiration stream involves water being pulled up the plant, which causes a negative pressure in the xylem vessels. How are xylem vessels adapted to cope with this?

7. Name two other features shown in Figure 4 that suit xylem vessels to their function of transporting water up a plant.

8. Suggest a reason why xylem vessels need to die in order to carry out their function effectively.

9. Suggest another feature of lignin, other than its mechanical strength, that would be useful in ensuring that water was carried up the plant.

10. The thickening of the cell wall in xylem vessels is often spiral. Suggest a reason why this is a better arrangement than having continuous thickening.

Other specialised cells

A large variety of plant cells are adapted to a particular function. Figure 5 shows three such cells (A–C) in transverse section. The structures in one cell are labelled and act as a key for the equivalent structures in the other two cells.

11. The functions of each of the three cells are given below. By stating the appropriate letter, suggest the cell that is best adapted to each function. Suggest one feature shown on the cell of your choice that is an adaptation to the function given.

a Carries out photosynthesis.

b Gives mechanical support.

c Divides repeatedly to give rise to other cells.

Longitudinal section

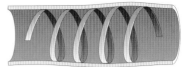

Transverse section

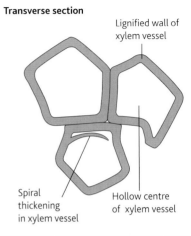

Lignified wall of xylem vessel

Spiral thickening in xylem vessel

Hollow centre of xylem vessel

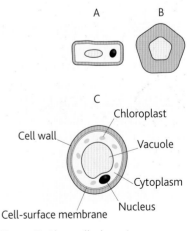

Figure 4 *Xylem vessels seen in longitudinal and transverse section (top); false-colour scanning electron micrograph (SEM) showing hollow, tubular xylem vessels adapted to transport water (bottom)*

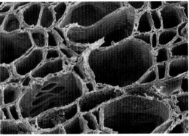

A   B

C

Chloroplast

Cell wall

Vacuole

Cytoplasm

Cell-surface membrane

Nucleus

Figure 5 *Plant cell adaptations*

Chapter 9 Genetic diversity

1   The National Vegetable Research Station stores a collection of seeds from many
     species and varieties of vegetables. These include old and rare varieties.

   (a) Why is it important to keep seeds from old and rare varieties of vegetables?   *(2 marks)*

   (b) Every few years, seeds of each variety in the collection are germinated and grown
        into mature plants. New seeds obtained from these plants are added to the collection.

        (i)   Suggest why it is necessary to obtain new seeds every few years.

        (ii) Within each variety, the scientists cross plants with different genes. Explain
              the advantage of this.   *(3 marks)*

AQA, 2004

Chapter 10 The variety of life

1   Haemoglobin is a protein

   (a) What is meant by the quaternary structure of a protein?   *(1 mark)*

   (b) The tertiary structure of haemoglobin allows it to carry oxygen. Explain how.   *(2 marks)*

2   **Figure 1** shows dissociation curves for haemoglobin in a fetus and in an adult.

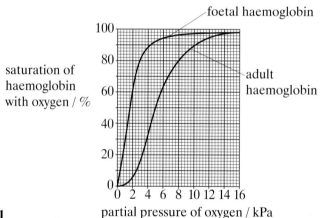

Figure 1

   (a) (i)   What is the difference in percentage saturation between fetal haemoglobin
              and adult haemoglobin at a partial pressure of 3 kPa?

        (ii) Explain the advantage of the curve for fetal haemoglobin being different
              from the curve for adult haemoglobin.   *(3 marks)*

   (b) The dissociation curve for adult haemoglobin changes during vigorous exercise.

        (i)   On a copy of the graph, sketch the position of the curve during vigorous exercise.

        (ii) Explain the advantage of this change in position.   *(3 marks)*

AQA, 2004

3   **Figure 2** shows the oxygen haemoglobin dissociation curves for three species of fish.

   (a) Species **A** lives in water containing a low partial pressure of oxygen. Species **C**
        lives in water with a high partial pressure of oxygen. The oxygen haemoglobin
        dissociation curve for species **A** is to the left of the curve for species **C**. Explain
        the advantage to species **A** of having haemoglobin with a curve in this position.   *(3 marks)*

   (b) Species **A** and B live in the same place but **B** is more active. Suggest an advantage
        to **B** of having an oxygen haemoglobin dissociation curve to the right of that for **A**.   *(2 marks)*

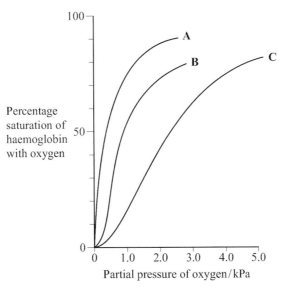

Figure 2

Percentage saturation of haemoglobin with oxygen

Partial pressure of oxygen/kPa

AQA, 2006

4 Cellulose is made from one type of monomer. The monomers are held together by bonds.
Figure 3 shows parts of three cellulose molecules in a cell wall.

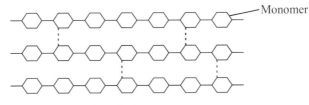

Monomer

Figure 3

(a) Name the monomer present in cellulose. *(1 mark)*

(b) Name the type of reaction that converts cellulose to its monomers. *(1 mark)*

(c) Cotton is a plant fibre used to make cloth. Explain how cellulose gives cotton its strength. *(3 marks)*

AQA, 2006

5 **Figure 4** shows a section through a leaf.

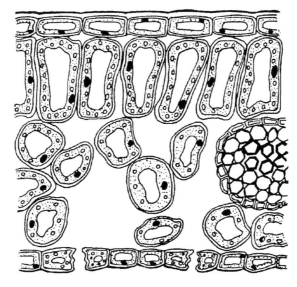

Figure 4

(a) Name **three** structures present only in plant cells. *(1 mark)*

(b) Explain how water enters a root hair cell. *(2 marks)*

AQA, 2003

11 The cell cycle

11.1 Replication of DNA

Learning objectives:

■ What happens during DNA replication?

■ How is a new polynucleotide strand formed?

■ Why is the process of DNA replication called semi-conservative?

Specification reference: 3.2.5

The cells that make up organisms are always derived from existing cells by the process of division. Cell division occurs in two main stages:

■ **Nuclear division** is the process by which the nucleus divides. There are two types of nuclear division, mitosis and **meiosis**.

■ **Cell division** follows nuclear division and is the process by which the whole cell divides.

Before a nucleus divides its DNA must be replicated (copied). This is to ensure that all the daughter cells have the genetic information to produce the enzymes and other proteins that they need.

The process of DNA replication is clearly very precise because all the new cells are more or less identical to the original one. This is a remarkable achievement when one considers the complexity of the DNA molecule. How then does DNA replication take place? Of the possible methods, it is the semi-conservative model that is universally accepted.

💡 Semi-conservative replication

For semi-conservative replication to take place there are four requirements:

■ The four types of nucleotide, each with their bases of adenine, guanine, cytosine and thymine, must be present.

■ Both strands of the DNA molecule must act as a template for the attachment of these nucleotides.

■ The enzyme DNA polymerase is needed to catalyse the reaction.

■ A source of chemical energy is required to drive the process.

The process of semi-conservative replication is illustrated in Figure 1. It takes place as follows:

■ The enzyme **DNA helicase** breaks the hydrogen bonds linking the base pairs of DNA.

■ As a result the double helix separates into its two strands and unwinds.

■ Each exposed polynucleotide strand then acts as a template to which complementary nucleotides are attracted.

■ Energy is used to activate these nucleotides.

■ The activated nucleotides are joined together by the enzyme **DNA polymerase** to form the 'missing' polynucleotide strand on each of the two original polynucleotide strands of DNA.

■ Each of the new DNA molecules contains one of the original DNA strands, i.e. half the original DNA has been saved and built into each of the new DNA molecules (Figure 2). The process is therefore termed 'semi-conservative replication'.

▉ Hint

It is a basic scientific principle that, when smaller molecules are built up into larger ones, energy is required. When larger molecules are broken down into smaller ones, energy is released.

▉ Link

The structure of DNA is covered in Topic 8.1

AQA Examiner's tip

Remember that DNA replication uses complementary base pairings to produce two identical copies.

a A representative portion of DNA, which is about to undergo replication.

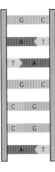

b An enzyme, DNA helicase, causes the two strands of the DNA to separate.

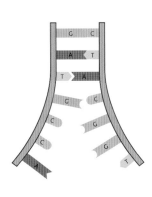

c DNA helicase completes the splitting of the strand. Meanwhile, free nucleotides that have been activated are attracted to their complementary bases.

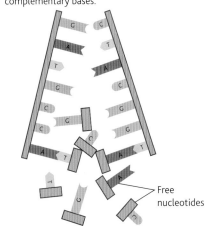

Free nucleotides

d Once the activated nucleotides are lined up, they are joined together by DNA polymerase (bottom three nucleotides). The remaining unpaired bases continue to attract their complementary nucleotides.

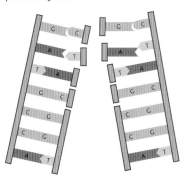

e Finally, all the nucleotides are joined to form a complete polynucleotide chain using DNA polymerase. In this way, two identical strands of DNA are formed. As each strand retains half of the original DNA material, this method of replication is called the semi-conservative method.

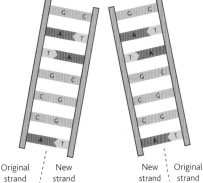

Original strand   New strand   New strand   Original strand

 **Figure 1** *The semi-conservative replication of DNA*

Summary questions

1 If the bases on a portion of the original strand of DNA are ATGCTACG, what would the equivalent sequence of bases be on the newly formed strand?

2 Why is the process of DNA replication described as semi-conservative?

3 If an inhibitor of DNA polymerase were introduced into a cell, explain what the effect would be on DNA replication.

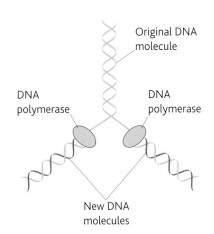

Original DNA molecule

DNA polymerase

DNA polymerase

New DNA molecules

Figure 2 *Role of DNA polymerase in the semi-conservative replication of DNA*

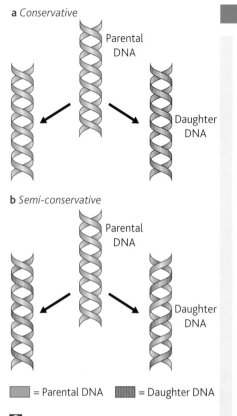

a *Conservative*

Parental
DNA

Daughter
DNA

b *Semi-conservative*

Parental
DNA

Daughter
DNA

▭ = Parental DNA   ▥ = Daughter DNA

Figure 3 *Different models of DNA replication*

Evidence for semi-conservative replication

This account illustrates how scientists use theories and models to attempt to explain observations. Scientific progress is made when experimental evidence is produced that supports a new theory or model (HSW: A).

When James Watson and Francis Crick worked out the structure of DNA in 1953, with the help of Rosalind Franklin's X-ray diffraction studies, they remarked in their paper:

> It has not escaped our notice that the specific pairing we have postulated immediately suggests a possible copying mechanism for the genetic material.

Their idea, namely the semi-conservative method, was, however, only one of two possible mechanisms. Both needed to be scientifically tested before a definite conclusion could be drawn. The two hypotheses were:

■ **The conservative model** suggested that the parental DNA remained intact and that a separate daughter DNA copy was built up from new molecules of deoxyribose, phosphate and organic bases. Of the two molecules present, one would be made of entirely new material while the other would be entirely original material (Figure 3).

■ **The semi-conservative model** proposed that the DNA molecule split into two separate strands, each of which then replicated its mirror image (i.e. the missing half). Each of the two new molecules would therefore have one strand of new material and one strand of original material (Figure 3).

If we look at Figure 3, we can see that the distribution of the 'old' DNA after replication is different in each model. To find out which mechanism was correct was therefore easy, at least in theory: simply label the old DNA in some way and then look at how it was distributed after replication. The next stage was to design an experiment to test which hypothesis was correct. Two scientists, Meselsohn and Stahl, achieved this in a neat and elegant experiment.

They based their work on three facts:

■ All the bases in DNA contain nitrogen.

■ Nitrogen has two forms: the lighter nitrogen ^{14}N and the **isotope** ^{15}N, which is heavier.

■ Bacteria will incorporate nitrogen from their growing medium into any new DNA that they make.

They reasoned that bacteria grown on a medium containing ^{14}N would have DNA that was lighter than bacteria grown on a medium containing ^{15}N. They labelled the 'old' DNA of bacteria by growing them on a medium of ^{15}N. They then transferred the bacteria to a medium of ^{14}N for a single generation to allow it to replicate once. The mass of each 'new' DNA molecule would depend upon which method of replication had taken place (Figure 3). To separate out the different DNA types, they centrifuged the extracted DNA in a special solution. The lighter the DNA, the nearer the top of the centrifuge tube it collected. The heavier the DNA, the nearer the bottom of the tube it collected (see Topic 3.1). They also analysed the DNA after two, then three, generations. By interpreting the results they could determine which hypothesis was correct. Their work is summarised in Figure 4.

1. Which part of the DNA molecule contains nitrogen?

2. Explain why, after one generation, all the DNA is made up of an equal mixture of ^{14}N and ^{15}N.

3. Suppose DNA were replicated by the conservative model. Sketch a tube showing the position of DNA after one generation.

4. From Figure 4, copy the chart for tube 4. Draw bars on the chart to show the percentage of each of the three possible types of DNA.

5. After three generations (tube 5), what percentage of the DNA will be made up of ^{14}N only?

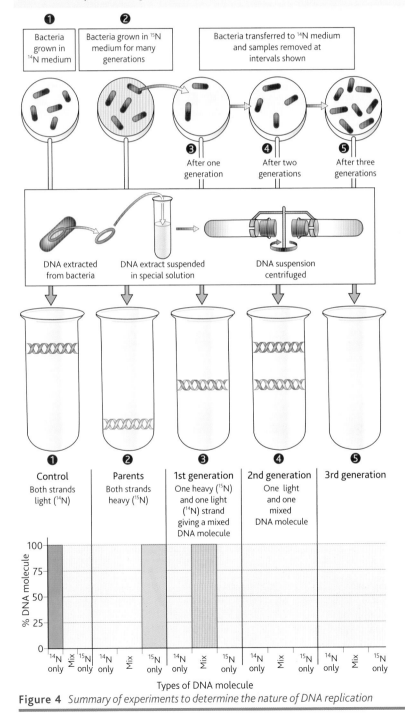

Figure 4 *Summary of experiments to determine the nature of DNA replication*

11.2 Mitosis

Learning objectives:

▓ What is mitosis?

▓ When does DNA replication take place?

▓ What is the importance of mitosis?

Specification reference. 3.2.5

▓ Link

Revising your knowledge about the structure of chromosomes (see Topic 8.3) will help you to understand mitosis.

AQA Examiner's tip

It is important to remember that the replication of DNA takes place during interphase before the nucleus and the cell divide.

Nuclear division can take place by either mitosis or meiosis:

▓ **Mitosis** produces two daughter nuclei that have the same number of **chromosomes** as the parent cell and each other.

▓ **Meiosis** produces four daughter nuclei, each with half the number of chromosomes of the parent cell.

After looking at meiosis in Topic 8.4, let us now turn our attention to mitosis.

▓ Mitosis

Mitosis is the division of the nucleus of a cell that results in each of the daughter cells having an exact copy of the DNA of the parent cell. Except in the rare event of a **mutation**, the genetic make-up of the two daughter nuclei is also identical to that of the parent nucleus. Mitosis is always preceded by a period during which the cell is not dividing. This period is called **interphase**. It is a period of considerable cellular activity that includes a very important event, the replication of DNA (see Topic 11.1). Although mitosis is a continuous process, it can be divided into four stages for convenience:

1 **prophase**, in which the chromosomes become visible and the nuclear envelope disappears,

2 **metaphase**, in which the chromosomes arrange themselves at the centre (equator) of the cell,

3 **anaphase**, in which each of the two threads of a chromosome (chromatid) migrates to an opposite pole,

4 **telophase**, in which the nuclear envelope reforms.

The process is illustrated and explained in Figure 1.

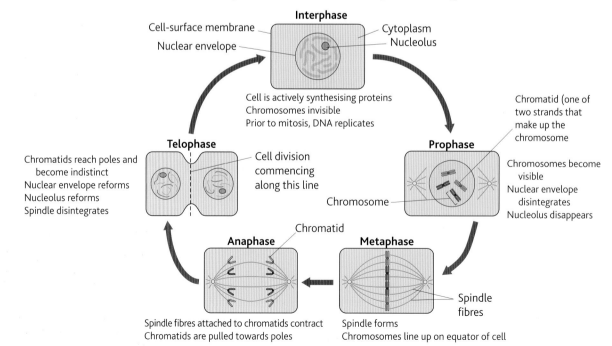

Figure 1 *The stages of mitosis in an animal cell*

💡 The importance of mitosis

Mitosis is important in organisms because it produces daughter cells that are genetically identical to the parent cells. Why then is it so essential to make exact copies of existing cells? There are three main reasons:

▦ **growth**. When two **haploid** cells (e.g. a sperm and an ovum) fuse together to form a **diploid** cell, this diploid cell has all the genetic information needed to form the new organism. If the new organism is to resemble its parents, all the cells that grow from this original cell must possess this same set of genetic information. Mitosis ensures that this happens. The cell firstly divides to give a group of identical cells.

▦ **differentiation**. These cells change, or differentiate, to give groups of specialised cells, e.g. epithelium in animals or xylem in plants (see Topic 12.1) These different cell types each divide by mitosis to give tissues made up of identical cells which perform a particular function. This is essential as the tissue can only function efficiently if all its cells have the same structure and perform the same function.

▦ **repair**. If cells are damaged or die it is important that the new cells produced have an identical structure and function to the ones that have been lost. If they were not exact copies the tissue would not function as effectively as before. Mitosis is therefore the means by which new cells replace damaged or dead ones.

▦ Summary question

1 In the following passage about mitosis, give the most appropriate word that is represented by each of the letters in red.

The period when a cell is not dividing is called **a** The stage of mitosis when the chromosomes are first visible as distinct structures is called **b** During this stage thin threads develop that span the cell from end to end and together form a structure called the **c** Towards the end of this stage, the **d** breaks down and the **e** disappears. The stage when the chromosomes arrange themselves across the centre of the cell is called **f** During the stage called **g** the chromatids move to opposite ends of the cell. Mitosis is important in **h** and **i** because it produces genetically identical cells.

▦ Application

Recognising the stages of mitosis

The photographs in Figure 2 show cells at various stages of mitosis.

Mitosis is a continuous process. When mitosis is viewed under a microscope, the observer only gets a snapshot of the process at one moment in time. In this snapshot, the number of cells at each stage of mitosis is proportional to the time each cell spends undergoing that stage. Table 1 shows the number of cells at each stage of mitosis during one observation.

1 State the names of the five different stages represented by the letters A–E in Figure 2. In each case give a reason for choosing your answer.

2 From Table 1, if one complete cycle takes 20 hours, how many minutes were spent in metaphase? Show your working.

3 In what percentage of the cells would the chromosomes have been visible? Show your working.

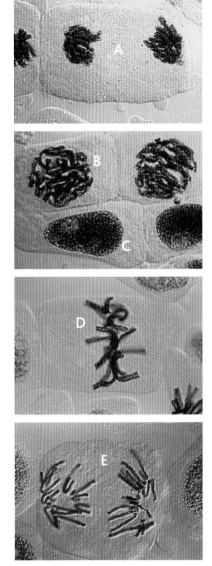

Figure 2 *Stages of mitosis*

Table 1

Stage	Number of cells
Interphase	890
Prophase	73
Metaphase	20
Anaphase	9
Telophase	8

AQA Examiner's tip

You must be able to recognise the stages of mitosis from drawings and photographs and explain the events occurring during each stage.

11.3 The cell cycle

Learning objectives:

▪ What are the three stages of the cell cycle?

▪ What happens during interphase?

▪ How does cancer and its treatment relate to the cell cycle?

Specification reference: 3.2.5

Hint

Interphase is sometimes known as the resting phase because no division takes place. In one sense, this description could hardly be further from the truth because interphase is a period of intense chemical activity.

Cells do not divide continuously, but undergo a regular cycle of division separated by periods of cell growth. This is known as the **cell cycle** and has three stages:

1 **interphase**, which occupies most of the cell cycle, and is sometimes known as the resting phase because no division takes place. It is divided into three parts:

  (a) First growth (G_1) phase, when the proteins from which cell organelles are synthesised are produced.

  (b) Synthesis (S) phase, when DNA is replicated.

  (c) Second growth (G_2) phase, when organelles grow and divide and energy stores are increased.

2 **nuclear division**, when the nucleus divides either into two (mitosis) or four (meiosis).

3 **cell division**, which follows nuclear division and is the process by which the whole cell divides into two (mitosis) or four (meiosis).

The length of a complete cell cycle varies greatly amongst organisms. Typically, a mammalian cell takes about 24 hours to complete a cell cycle, of which about 90 per cent is interphase.

The various stages of the cell cycle are shown in Figure 1.

Figure 2 shows the variations in mass of the cell and the DNA within it during the cell cycle.

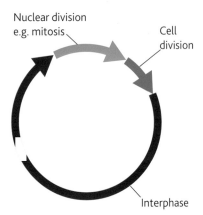

Figure 1 *The cell cycle*

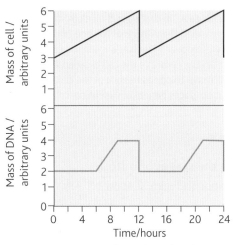

Figure 2 *Variations in cell and DNA mass during the cell cycle*

🛈 Cancer

Cancer is a group of diseases (around 200 in total) caused by a growth disorder of cells. It is the result of damage to the genes that regulate mitosis and the cell cycle. This leads to uncontrolled growth of cells. As a consequence, a group of abnormal cells, called a tumour, develops and constantly expands in size. Cancers can develop in any organ of the body, but are most commonly found in the lungs, prostate gland (male), breast and ovaries (female), large intestine, stomach, oesophagus and pancreas.

Summary questions

1 What are the three main stages of the cell cycle?

2 Using Figure 2, state at what time(s), or during which period, each of the following occur:

a cell division

b replication of DNA.

Application

Cancer and its treatment

The treatment of cancer often involves blocking some part of the cell cycle. In this way the cell cycle is disrupted and cell division, and hence cancer growth, ceases. Drugs used to treat cancer (chemotherapy) disrupt the cell cycle by:

- preventing DNA from replicating, e.g. cisplatin
- inhibiting the metaphase stage of mitosis by interfering with spindle formation, e.g. vinca alkaloids.

The problem with such drugs is that they also disrupt the cell cycle of normal cells. However, the drugs are more effective against rapidly dividing cells. As cancer cells have a particularly fast rate of division, they are damaged to a greater degree than normal cells. Those normal body cells, such as hair-producing cells, that divide rapidly are also vulnerable to damage. This explains the hair loss frequently seen in patients undergoing cancer treatment.

The graph in Figure 3 shows the effect of a chemotherapy drug that kills dividing cells. It was given to a cancer patient once every three weeks starting at time zero. The graph plots the changes in the number of healthy cells and cancer cells in a tissue over the treatment period of 12 weeks.

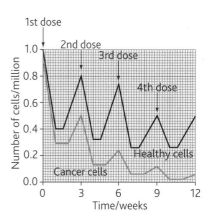

Figure 3 *Changes in the number of healthy cells and cancer cells in a tissue during a chemotherapy treatment of 12 weeks*

1 How many fewer healthy cells were there after 3 weeks compared to the start of the treatment?

2 What percentage of the original number of healthy cells were still present at 12 weeks?

3 How many times greater is the number of healthy cells compared to the number of cancer cells after 12 weeks?

4 Give a reason for the lower number of cancer cells compared to healthy cells at 12 weeks.

5 Describe two differences between the effect of the drug on cancer cells compared with healthy cells throughout the treatment.

6 Use the graph to explain why chemotherapy drugs have to be given a number of times if they are to be effective in treating cancer.

12.1 Cell differentiation and organisation

Learning objectives:

▨ What are the advantages of cellular differentiation?

▨ How are cells arranged into tissues?

▨ How are tissues arranged into organs?

▨ How are organs arranged into organ systems?

Specification reference: 3.2.6

In multicellular organisms, cells are specialised to perform specific functions. Similar cells are then grouped together into tissues, tissues into organs and organs into systems for increased efficiency.

▨ Cell differentiation

Single-celled organisms perform all essential life functions inside the boundaries of a single cell. Although they perform all functions adequately, they cannot be totally efficient at all of them, because each function requires a different type of cellular structure. One activity may be best carried out by a long, thin cell, while another might suit a spherically shaped cell. No one cell can provide the best conditions for all functions. For this reason, the cells of multicellular organisms are each adapted in different ways to perform a particular role. All cells in an organism are initially identical. As it matures, each cell takes on its own individual characteristics that suit it to the function that it will perform when it is mature. In other words, each cell becomes specialised in structure to suit the role that it will carry out. This is known as **cell differentiation**.

All the cells in an organism, such as a human, are derived by mitotic divisions of the fertilised egg. It follows that they all contain exactly the same **genes**. How then does the cell differentiate? Every cell contains the genes needed for it to develop into any one of the many different cells in an organism. But only a few of these genes are switched on (expressed) in any one cell. Different genes are switched on in each type of differentiated cell. The rest of the genes are switched off.

It is not just the shape of different cells that varies, but also the numbers of each of their organelles. For example, a muscle or sperm cell will have many mitochondria, while a bone cell has very few. White blood cells have many lysosomes while a muscle cell has very few.

The cells of a multicellular organism have therefore evolved to become more and more suited to one specialised function. In doing so, they have lost the ability to carry out other functions. They are therefore dependent on other cells to perform these activities for them. These other cells are specially adapted to their own particular function and perform it more effectively. As a result, the whole organism functions efficiently.

▨ Tissues

For working efficiency, cells are normally aggregated together. Such a collection of similar cells that perform a specific function is known as a **tissue**. Examples of tissues include:

▨ **epithelial tissues** (see Topic 3.3), which are found in animals and consist of sheets of cells. They line the surfaces of organs and often have a protective or secretory function. There are many types, including those made up of thin, flat cells that line organs where

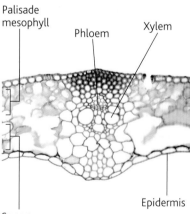

Palisade mesophyll

Phloem   Xylem

Epidermis

Spongy mesophyll

💡 **Figure 1** *Some of the various tissues that make up the organ called a leaf* diffusion takes place e.g. alveoli of the lungs (see Topics 4.1 and 4.3), and ciliated epithelium that lines a duct such as the trachea (see Topic 4.1). The cilia are used to move mucus over the epithelial surface.

▓ **xylem** (see Topic 10.4), which occurs in plants and is made up of a number of cell types. It is used to transport water and mineral ions throughout the plant and also gives mechanical support.

Organs

Just as cells are aggregated into tissues, so tissues are aggregated into organs. An organ is a combination of tissues that are coordinated to perform a variety of functions, although they often have one predominant major function. In animals, for example, the stomach is an organ that carries out the digestion of certain types of food (see Topic 2.1). It is made up of tissues such as:

▓ muscle to churn and mix the stomach contents,

▓ epithelium to protect the stomach wall and produce secretions,

▓ connective tissue to hold together the other tissues.

In plants, a leaf (Figure 1) is an organ made up of the following tissues:

▓ palisade mesophyll made up of leaf palisade cells (see Topic 10.4) that carry out photosynthesis,

▓ spongy mesophyll adapted for gaseous diffusion,

▓ epidermis to protect the leaf and allow gaseous diffusion,

▓ phloem to transport organic materials away from the leaf,

▓ xylem to transport water and ions into the leaf.

It is not always easy to determine which structures are organs. Blood capillaries, for example, are not organs whereas arteries and veins are both organs. All three structures have the same major function, namely the transport of blood. However, capillaries are made up of just one tissue – epithelium – whereas arteries and veins are made up of many tissues, e.g. epithelial, muscle and connective tissues.

Organ systems

Organs work together as a single unit known as an organ system. These systems may be grouped together to perform particular functions more efficiently. There are a number of organ systems in humans.

▓ The **digestive system** digests and processes food. It is made up of organs that include the salivary glands, oesophagus, stomach, duodenum, ileum, pancreas and liver.

▓ The **respiratory system** is used for breathing and gas exchange. It is made up of organs that include the trachea, bronchi and lungs.

▓ The **circulatory system** (Figure 2) pumps and circulates blood. It is made up of organs that include the heart, arteries and veins.

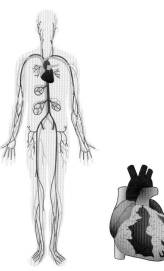

Circulatory system
Organ system

Heart
Organ

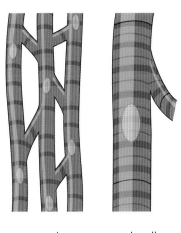

muscle
Tissue

muscle cell
Cell

Figure 2 *The circulatory system as an example of an organ system*

Summary questions

1 What is a tissue?

2 Why is an artery described as an organ whereas a blood capillary is not?

3 State whether each of the following is a tissue or an organ.
  a Heart   b Xylem   c Lungs   d Epithelium.

Chapter 11 The cell cycle

1. (a) Describe and explain how the structure of DNA results in accurate replication. *(4 marks)*

   (b) Describe the behaviour of chromosomes during mitosis and explain how this results in the production of two genetically identical cells. *(7 marks)*

   (c) A cancerous tumour is formed by uncontrolled mitotic division. This results in a mass of cells with an inadequate blood supply. Drugs are being developed which only kill cells in a low oxygen environment. Suggest how these drugs could be useful in the treatment of cancer. *(2 marks)*

   AQA, 2006

2. (a) **Figure 1** shows a stage of mitosis in an animal cell.

   (i) Name this stage of mitosis.

   (ii) Describe and explain what happens during this stage which ensures that two genetically identical cells are produced. *(3 marks)*

   Figure 1

   (b) **Figure 2** shows the relative amounts of DNA per cell during two successive cell divisions in an animal.

   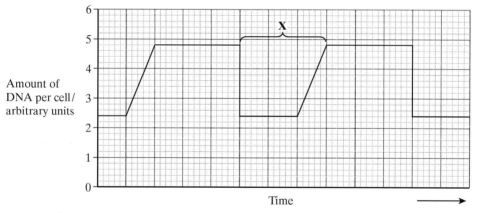

   Figure 2

   (i) What stage of the cell cycle is shown by **X**?

   (ii) Apart from an increase in the amount of DNA, give **one** process which occurs during stage **X** which enables nuclear division to occur. *(2 marks)*

   (c) The table shows the average duration of each stage of the cell cycle in the cells of a mammalian embryo. Give **one** piece of evidence from the table which indicates that these cells are multiplying rapidly. *(1 mark)*

Stage	Mean duration / minutes
Interphase	12
Prophase	50
Metaphase	15
Anaphase	10
Telophase	42

   AQA, 2005

3 (a) Explain why the replication of DNA is described as semi-conservative. *(2 marks)*

(b) Bacteria require a source of nitrogen to make the bases needed for DNA replication.

In an investigation of DNA replication some bacteria were grown for many cell divisions in a medium containing ^{14}N, a light form of nitrogen. Others were grown in a medium containing ^{15}N, a heavy form of nitrogen. Some of the bacteria grown in a ^{15}N medium were then transferred to a ^{14}N medium and left to divide once.

DNA was isolated from the bacteria and centrifuged. The DNA samples formed bands at different levels, as shown in the diagram.

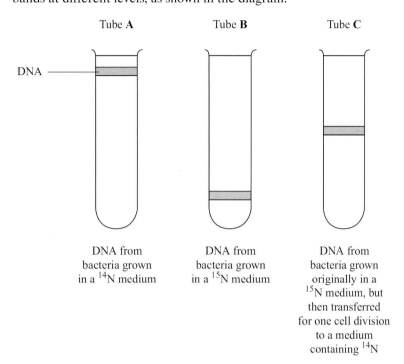

Figure 3

(i) What do tubes **A** and **B** show about the density of the DNA formed using the two different forms of nitrogen?

(ii) Explain the position of the band in tube **C**. *(3 marks)*

(c) In a further investigation, the DNA of the bacterium was isolated and separated into single strands. The percentage of each nitrogenous base in each strand was found. The table shows some of the results.

	Percentage of base present			
DNA sample	Adenine	Cytosine	Guanine	Thymine
Strand 1	26		28	14
Strand 2	14			

Copy the table and use your knowledge of base pairing to complete it. *(2 marks)*

AQA, 2006

Chapter 12 Cellular organisation

1 (a) Cells of multicellular organisms may undergo differentiation. What is meant by differentiation? *(1 mark)*

(b) (i) Explain what is meant by a tissue

(ii) Explain why skin is described as an organ. *(3 marks)*

(c) In mammals after fertilisation, cells divide by mitosis. Suggest how these cells develop into different tissues. *(2 marks)*

13.1 Exchange between organisms and their environment

Specification reference: 3.2.7

Learning objectives:

- How does the size of an organism and its structure relate to its surface area to volume ratio?
- How do larger organisms increase their surface area to volume ratio?
- How are surfaces specially adapted to facilitate exchange?

For survival, organisms must transfer materials between themselves and their environment. Once absorbed, materials must be rapidly distributed to the cells that require them and the waste products returned to the exchange surface for removal. This requires a transport system.

The size and metabolic rate of an organism will affect the amount of each material that needs to be exchanged. In turn this will influence the type of exchange surface and transport system that has evolved to meet the requirements of each organism. In this chapter we shall investigate the adaptations of exchange surfaces and transport systems in a variety of organisms.

Examples of things which need to be interchanged between an organism and its environment include:

- respiratory gases (oxygen and carbon dioxide)
- nutrients (glucose, fatty acids, amino acids, vitamins, minerals)
- excretory products (urea and carbon dioxide)
- heat.

This exchange can take place in two ways:

- passively (no energy is required), by **diffusion** and **osmosis**
- actively (energy is required), by **active transport**.

Surface area to volume ratio

Exchange takes place at the surface of an organism, but the materials absorbed are used by the cells that mostly make up its volume. For

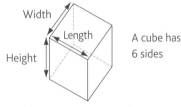

Figure 1 *Calculating volume*

Table 1 *How the surface area to volume ratio gets smaller as an object becomes larger*

Length of edge of a cube / cm	Surface area of whole cube (area of one side × 6 sides) / cm²	Volume of cube (length × width × height) / cm³	Ratio of surface area to volume (surface area ÷ volume)
1	$1 \times 6 = 6$	$1 \times 1 \times 1 = 1$	$\frac{6}{1} = 6.0$
2	$4 \times 6 = 24$	$2 \times 2 \times 2 = 8$	$\frac{24}{8} = 3.0$
3	$9 \times 6 = 54$	$3 \times 3 \times 3 = 27$	$\frac{54}{27} = 2.0$
4	$16 \times 6 = 96$	$4 \times 4 \times 4 = 64$	$\frac{96}{64} = 1.5$
5	$25 \times 6 = 150$	$5 \times 5 \times 5 = 125$	$\frac{150}{125} = 1.2$
6	$36 \times 6 = 216$	$6 \times 6 \times 6 = 216$	$\frac{216}{216} = 1.0$

exchange to be effective, the surface area of the organism must be large compared with its volume.

Small organisms have a surface area that is large enough, compared with their volume, to allow efficient exchange across their body surface. However, as organisms become larger, their volume increases at a faster rate than their surface area (Table 1). Because of this, simple diffusion of materials across the surface can only meet the needs of relatively inactive organisms. Even if the surface could supply enough material, it would still take too long for it to reach the middle of the organism if diffusion alone was the method of transport. To overcome this problem, organisms have evolved one or more of the following features:

- a flattened shape so that no cell is ever far from the surface (e.g. a flatworm)
- specialised exchange surfaces with large areas to increase the surface area to volume ratio (e.g. lungs in mammals, gills in fish).

Features of specialised exchange surfaces

To allow effective transfer of materials across them by diffusion or active transport, exchange surfaces show the following characteristics:

- a large surface area to volume ratio to increase the rate of exchange
- very thin so that the diffusion distance is short and therefore materials cross the exchange surface rapidly
- partially permeable to allow selected materials to cross without obstruction
- movement of the environmental medium, e.g. air, to maintain a diffusion gradient
- movement of the internal medium, e.g. blood, to maintain a diffusion gradient.

We saw in Topic 3.6 that the relationship between certain of these factors can be expressed as:

$$\text{Diffusion} \propto \frac{\text{surface area} \times \text{difference in concentration}}{\text{length of diffusion path}}$$

Being thin, specialised exchange surfaces are easily damaged. They are therefore often located inside an organism. Where an exchange surface is located inside the body, the organism needs to have a means of moving the external medium over the surface, e.g. a means of ventilating the lungs in a mammal.

Application

Significance of the surface area to volume ratio in organisms

The graph in Figure 2 shows the surface area to volume ratios of different-sized cubes.

1 Microscopic organisms obtain their oxygen by diffusion in across their body surface. Using the graph, explain how they are able to obtain sufficient oxygen for their needs.

2 The blue whale (Figure 3) is the largest organism on the planet. It spends much of its life in waters with temperatures between 0°C and 6°C. Using the graph, explain why large size is an advantage to blue whales.

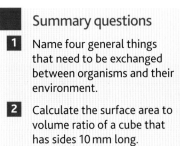

AQA Examiner's tip

In a cell the lowest oxygen concentration is inside the mitochondria, where oxygen is used up in respiration. Mitochondria also contain the highest concentration of carbon dioxide. This maintains the diffusion gradient for these gases in and out of the cell.

Summary questions

1 Name four general things that need to be exchanged between organisms and their environment.

2 Calculate the surface area to volume ratio of a cube that has sides 10 mm long.

3 Name three factors that affect the rate of diffusion of substances into cells.

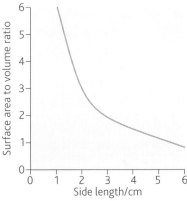

Figure 2 *Surface area to volume ratios*

Figure 3 *The blue whale is the largest organism on the planet*

13.2 Gas exchange in single-celled organisms and insects

Learning objectives:

▥ How do single-celled organisms exchange gases?

▥ How do terrestrial insects balance the need to exchange gases with the need to conserve water?

▥ How do insects exchange gases?

Specification reference: 3.2.7

▥ Gas exchange in single-celled organisms

Single-celled organisms are small and therefore have a large surface area to volume ratio. Oxygen is absorbed by diffusion across their body surface, which is covered only by a cell-surface membrane. In the same way, carbon dioxide from respiration diffuses out across their body surface. Where a living cell is surrounded by a cell wall, this is completely permeable and so there is no barrier to the diffusion of gases.

💡 Gas exchange in insects

Most insects are terrestrial (live on land). The problem for all terrestrial organisms is that water easily evaporates from the surface of their bodies and they can become dehydrated. They therefore need to conserve water. However, efficient gas exchange requires a thin, permeable surface with a large area. These features conflict with the need to conserve water. Overall, as a terrestrial organism, the insect has to balance the opposing needs of exchanging respiratory gases with reducing water loss.

To reduce water loss, terrrestrial organisms usually exhibit two features.

▥ **Waterproof coverings** over their body surfaces. In the case of insects this covering is a rigid outer skeleton that is covered with a waterproof cuticle.

▥ **Small surface area to volume ratio** to minimise the area over which water is lost.

These features mean that insects cannot use their body surface to diffuse respiratory gases in the way a single-celled organism does. Instead they have developed an internal network of tubes called **tracheae**. The tracheae are supported by strengthened rings to prevent them from collapsing. The tracheae divide into smaller tubes called **tracheoles**. The tracheoles extend throughout all the body tissues of the insect. In this way atmospheric air, with the oxygen it contains, is brought directly to the respiring tissues.

Respiratory gases move in and out of the tracheal system in two ways.

▥ **Along a diffusion gradient**. When cells are respiring, oxygen is used up and so its concentration towards the ends of the tracheoles falls. This creates a diffusion gradient that causes gaseous oxygen to diffuse from the atmosphere along the tracheae and tracheoles to the cells. Carbon dioxide is produced by cells during respiration. This creates a diffusion gradient in the opposite direction. This causes gaseous carbon dioxide to diffuse along the tracheoles and tracheae from the cells to the atmosphere. As diffusion in air is much more rapid than in water, respiratory gases are exchanged quickly by this method.

▥ **Ventilation**. The movement of muscles in insects can create mass movements of air in and out of the tracheae. This further speeds up the exchange of respiratory gases.

Gases enter and leave tracheae through tiny pores, called **spiracles**, on the body surface. The spiracles may be opened and closed by a valve. When the spiracles are open, water can evaporate from the insect. For

> **Hint**
>
> Every cell of an insect is only a very short distance from one of the tracheae or tracheoles and so the diffusion pathway is always short.

much of the time insects keep their spiracles closed to prevent this water loss. Periodically they open the spiracles to allow gas exchange. Part of an insect tracheal system is illustrated in Figure 1.

The tracheal system is an efficient method of gas exchange. It does, however, have some limitations. It relies mostly on diffusion to exchange gases between the environment and the cells. For diffusion to be effective, the diffusion pathway needs to be short. As a result this limits the size that insects can attain. Not that being small has hindered insects. They are one of the most successful groups of organisms on Earth.

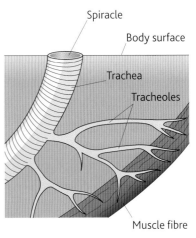

Figure 1 *Part of an insect tracheal system*

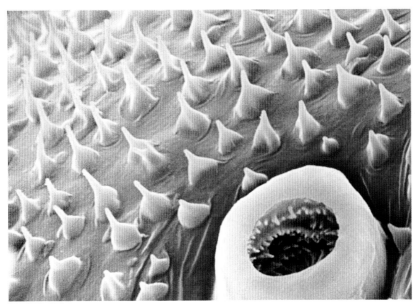

Figure 2 *Scanning electron micrograph (SEM) of a spiracle (or air pore, bottom right) of an insect*

Summary questions

1 By what process is carbon dioxide removed from a single-celled organism?

2 How do insects prevent excessive water loss from their tracheal system?

3 Explain why there is a conflict in terrestrial insects between the need for gas exchange and the need to conserve water.

4 Why does the tracheal system limit the size of insects?

■ Application

Spiracle movements

An experiment was carried out to measure the levels of oxygen and carbon dioxide in the tracheal system of an insect over a period of time. During the experiment the opening and closing of the insect's spiracles was observed and recorded. The results are shown in Figure 3.

1 Describe what happens to the level of oxygen in the tracheae when the spiracles are closed.

2 Suggest an explanation for this change in the level of oxygen when the spiracles are closed.

3 From the information provided by the graph, suggest what causes the spiracles to open.

4 What is the advantage of these spiracle movements to a terrestrial insect?

5 Fossil insects have been discovered that are larger than insects that occur on Earth today. What does this suggest about the composition of the atmosphere at the time when these fossil insects lived?

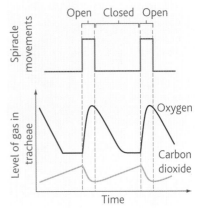

Figure 3

13.3 Gas exchange in fish

Fish have a waterproof, and therefore a gas-tight, outer covering. Being relatively large they also have a small surface area to volume ratio. Their body surface is therefore not adequate to supply and remove their respiratory gases and so, like insects and humans, they have developed a specialised internal gas exchange surface: the gills.

▦ Structure of the gills

The gills are located within the body of the fish, behind the head. They are made up of **gill filaments**. The gill filaments are stacked up in a pile, rather like the pages in a book. At right angles to the filaments are **gill lamellae**, which increase the surface area of the gills. Water is taken in through the mouth and forced over the gills and out through an opening on each side of the body. The position and arrangement of the gill filaments and gill lamellae are shown in Figure 1. From this figure you will notice that the flow of water over the gill lamellae and the flow of blood within them are in opposite directions. This is known as a **countercurrent flow**.

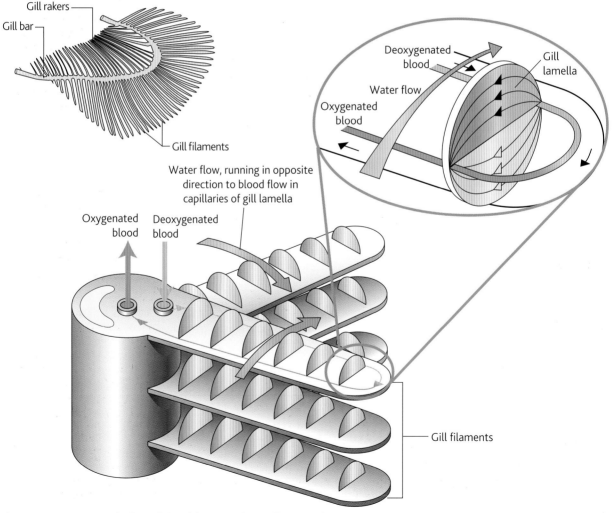

Figure 1 *Arrangement of gills in a fish and direction of water flow over them*

It is important for ensuring that the maximum possible gas exchange is achieved. If the water and blood flowed in the same direction, far less gas exchange would take place.

The countercurrent exchange principle

The essential feature of the countercurrent exchange system is that the blood and the water that flow over the gill lamellae do so in opposite directions. This arrangement means that:

- Blood that is already well loaded with oxygen meets water, which has its maximum concentration of oxygen. Therefore **diffusion** of oxygen from the water to the blood takes place.
- Blood with little or no oxygen in it meets water which has had most, but not all, of its oxygen removed. Again, diffusion of oxygen from the water to blood takes place.

There is therefore a fairly constant rate of diffusion across the entire length of the gill lamellae. In this way, about 80 per cent of the oxygen available in the water is absorbed into the blood of the fish. If the flow of water and blood had been in the same direction (parallel flow), the diffusion gradient would only be maintained across part of the length of the gill lamellae and only 50 per cent of the available oxygen would be absorbed by the blood.

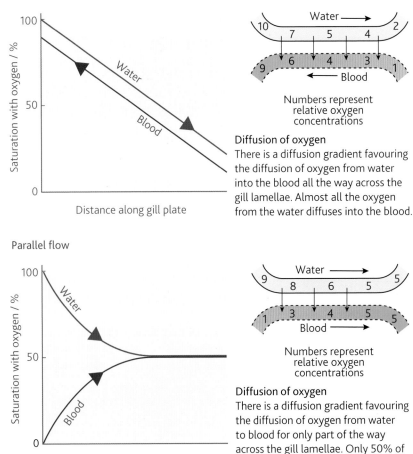

Figure 2 *Parallel and countercurrent flow in the gills of a fish*

Summary questions

1. In relation to fish gills, what is meant by countercurrent flow?

2. Why is countercurrent flow an efficient means of exchanging gases across the gills of fish?

3. Mackerel are active, fast-swimming fish while plaice spend most of their lives moving slowly on the sea bed. There are differences in the gills of these two types of fish. Suggest what these differences might be.

4. Water flow over fish gills is one-way whereas the flow of air in and out of the lungs is two-way. Suggest why one-way flow is an advantage to fish.

13.4 Gas exchange in the leaf of a plant

Learning objectives:

▨ How do plants exchange gases?

▨ What is the structure of a dicotyledonous plant leaf?

▨ How is the leaf adapted for efficient gas exchange?

Specification reference: 3.2.7

Like animal cells, all plant cells take in oxygen and produce carbon dioxide during respiration. When it comes to gas exchange, however, plants show one important difference from animals. Some plant cells carry out photosynthesis. During photosynthesis, plant cells take in carbon dioxide and produce oxygen. At times the gases produced in one process can be used for the other. This reduces the need for gas exchange with the external air. Overall, this means that the volumes and types of gases that are being exchanged by a plant leaf change. This depends on the balance between the rates of photosynthesis and respiration.

▨ When photosynthesis is taking place, although some carbon dioxide comes from respiration of cells, most of it has to be obtained from the external air. In the same way, some oxygen from photosynthesis is used in respiration but most of it **diffuses** out of the plant.

▨ When photosynthesis is not occurring, e.g. in the dark, oxygen diffuses into the leaf because it is constantly being used by cells during respiration. In the same way, carbon dioxide produced during respiration diffuses out.

▨ Structure of a plant leaf and gas exchange

In some ways, gas exchange in plants is not unlike that of insects (see Topic 13.2).

▨ No living cell is far from the external air, and therefore a source of oxygen and carbon dioxide.

▨ Diffusion takes place in the gas phase (air), which makes it more rapid than if it were in water.

Overall, therefore, there is a short, fast diffusion pathway. In addition, a plant leaf has a very large surface area compared with the volume of living tissue. For these reasons, no specialised transport system is needed for gases, which simply move in and through the plant by diffusion. Most gaseous exchange occurs in the leaves, which show the following adaptations for rapid diffusion:

▨ a thin, flat shape that provides a large surface area,

▨ many small pores, called **stomata**, mostly in the lower epidermis (Figure 1),

▨ numerous interconnecting air-spaces that occur throughout the mesophyll.

The structure of a leaf is shown in Figure 2.

▨ Stomata

Stomata are minute pores which occur mainly, but not exclusively, on the leaves, especially the underside. Each stoma (singular) is surrounded by a pair of special cells (guard cells). These cells can open and close the stomatal pore (Figure 3). In this way they can control the rate of gaseous exchange. This is important because terrestrial organisms lose water by

---

AQA Examiner's tip

The diffusion gradients in and out of the leaf are maintained by mitochondria carrying out respiration and chloroplasts carrying out photosynthesis.

Hint

Remember that plant cells respire all the time, but only plant cells with chloroplasts photosynthesise – and then only when the conditions are right.

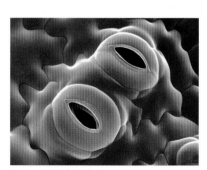

Figure 1 *False-colour scanning electron micrograph (SEM) of open stomata on the surface a leaf*

a *Leaf structure*

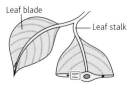

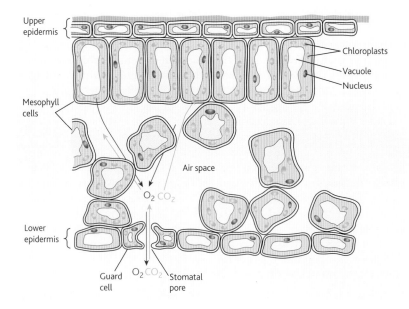

b *Vertical section through a dicotyledonous leaf*

Figure 2 *Section through a leaf of a dicotyledonous plant showing gas exchange when photosynthesis is taking place*

evaporation. Plants have to balance the conflicting needs of gas exchange and control of water loss. They do this by completely or partly closing stomata at times when water loss would be excessive.

Application

Exchange of carbon dioxide

The graph in Figure 4 shows the volume of carbon dioxide produced by a sample of tomato plants at different light intensities.

1 Which process produces carbon dioxide in the tomato plants?

2 Which process uses up carbon dioxide in the tomato plants?

3 Explain why, at point X, carbon dioxide is neither taken up nor given out by the tomato plants.

4 Some herbicides cause the stomata of plants to close. Suggest how these herbicides might lead to the death of a plant.

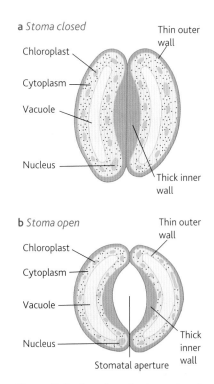

a *Stoma closed*

b *Stoma open*

Figure 3 *Surface view of a stoma closed and open*

Summary questions

1 State **two** similarities between gas exchange in a plant leaf and gas exchange in a terrestrial insect.

2 State **two** differences between gas exchange in a plant leaf and gas exchange in a terrestrial insect.

3 What is the advantage to a plant of being able to control the opening and closing of stomata?

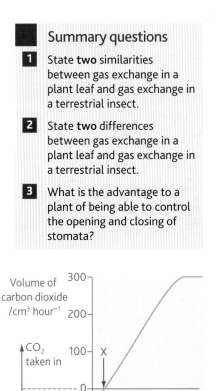

Figure 4

13.5 Circulatory system of a mammal

Learning objectives:

▓ How do large organisms move substances around their bodies?

▓ What are the features of the transport systems of large organisms?

▓ How is blood circulated in mammals?

Specification reference: 3.2.7

Figure 1 *Large organisms require a transport system to take materials from exchange surfaces to the cells that need them*

Diffusion is adequate for transport over short distances (see Topic 3.6). The efficient supply of materials over larger distances requires a mass transport system.

▓ Why large organisms need a transport system

All organisms need to exchange materials between themselves and their environment. We have seen that in small organisms this exchange takes place over the surface of the body (see Topic 13.2). However, with increasing size, the surface area to volume ratio decreases to a point where the needs of the organism cannot be met by the body surface alone (see Topic 13.1). A specialist exchange surface is therefore needed to absorb nutrients and respiratory gases, and to remove excretory products. These exchange surfaces are located in specific regions of the organism. A transport system is required to take materials from cells to exchange surfaces and from exchange surfaces to cells. Materials have to be transported between exchange surfaces and the environment. They also need to be transported between different parts of the organism. As organisms have evolved into larger and more complex structures, the tissues and organs of which they are made have become more specialised and dependent upon one another (see Topic 12.1). This makes a transport system all the more essential.

Whether or not there is a specialised transport medium, and whether or not it is circulated by a pump, depends on two factors:

▓ the surface area to volume ratio,

▓ how active the organism is.

The lower the surface area to volume ratio, and the more active the organism, the greater is the need for a specialised transport system with a pump.

▓ Features of transport systems

Any large organism encounters the same problems in transporting materials within itself. Not surprisingly, the transport systems of many organisms have many common features:

▓ A suitable medium in which to carry materials, e.g. blood. This is normally a liquid based on water because water readily dissolves substances and can be moved around easily.

▓ A form of mass transport in which the transport medium is moved around in bulk over large distances.

▓ A closed system of tubular vessels that contains the transport medium and forms a branching network to distribute it to all parts of the organism.

▓ A mechanism for moving the transport medium within vessels. This requires a pressure difference between one part of the system and another. It is achieved in two main ways:

(a) Animals use muscular contraction either of the body muscles or of a specialised pumping organ, such as the heart (see Topic 5.1).

(b) Plants do not possess muscles and so often rely on passive natural physical processes such as the evaporation of water (see Topic 13.9).

▨ A mechanism to maintain the mass flow movement in one direction, e.g. valves.

▨ A means of controlling the flow of the transport medium to suit the changing needs of different parts of the organism.

▨ Transport systems in mammals

Mammals have a closed blood system in which blood is confined to vessels. A muscular pump called the heart circulates the blood around the body. Mammals have a double circulatory system (Figure 2). This refers to the fact that blood passes twice through the heart for each complete circuit of the body. This is because, when blood is passed through the lungs, its pressure is reduced. If it were to pass immediately to the rest of the body its low pressure would make circulation very slow. Blood is therefore returned to the heart to boost its pressure before being circulated to the rest of the tissues. Substances are then delivered to the rest of the body quickly, which is necessary as mammals have a high body temperature and hence a high rate of **metabolism**. The vessels that make up the circulatory system of a mammal are divided into three types: arteries, veins and capillaries.

Although a transport system is used to move substances longer distances, the final part of the journey into cells is by diffusion. The final exchange from blood vessels into cells is rapid because it takes place over a large surface area, across short distances and there is a steep diffusion gradient.

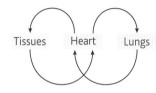

Figure 2 *Double circulation of a mammal*

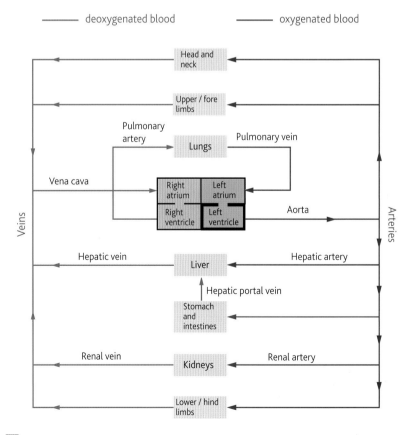

——— deoxygenated blood   ——— oxygenated blood

Figure 3 *Plan of the mammalian circulatory system*

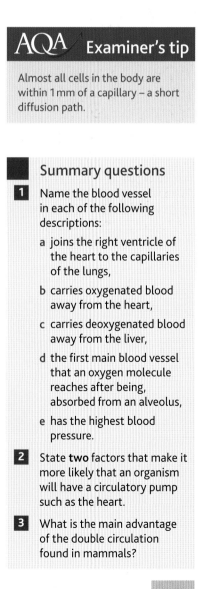

AQA Examiner's tip

Almost all cells in the body are within 1 mm of a capillary – a short diffusion path.

▨ Summary questions

1 Name the blood vessel in each of the following descriptions:

  a joins the right ventricle of the heart to the capillaries of the lungs,

  b carries oxygenated blood away from the heart,

  c carries deoxygenated blood away from the liver,

  d the first main blood vessel that an oxygen molecule reaches after being absorbed from an alveolus,

  e has the highest blood pressure.

2 State **two** factors that make it more likely that an organism will have a circulatory pump such as the heart.

3 What is the main advantage of the double circulation found in mammals?

13.6 Blood vessels and their functions

Learning objectives:

- What are the structures of arteries, arterioles and veins?

- How is the structure of each of the above vessels related to its function?

- What is the structure of capillaries and how is it related to their function?

Specification reference: 3.2.7

AQA Examiner's tip

Arteries, arterioles and veins carry out transport **not** exchange; only capillaries carry out exchange.

AQA Examiner's tip

The elastic tissue of arteries will stretch and recoil. It is not muscle and will not contract and relax.

In Topic 13.5 we saw that, in larger organisms, materials are transported around the body by the blood. To allow rapid transport of blood and to control its flow, the blood is confined to blood vessels.

Structure of blood vessels

There are different types of blood vessels:

- **Arteries** carry blood away from the heart and into arterioles.
- **Arterioles** are smaller arteries that control blood flow from arteries to capillaries.
- **Capillaries** are tiny vessels that link arterioles to veins.
- **Veins** carry blood from capillaries back to the heart.

Arteries, arterioles and veins all have the same basic layered structure. From the outside inwards, these layers are:

- **tough outer layer** that resists pressure changes from both within and outside
- **muscle layer** that can contract and so control the flow of blood
- **elastic layer** that helps to maintain blood pressure by stretching and springing back
- **thin inner lining (endothelium)** that is smooth to prevent friction and thin to allow diffusion
- **lumen** that is not actually a layer but the central cavity of the blood vessel through which the blood flows.

What differs between each type of blood vessel is the relative proportions of each layer. These differences are shown in Figure 1. Arterioles are not included because they are similar to arteries. They differ from arteries in being smaller in diameter and having a relatively larger muscle layer and lumen. The differences in structure are related to the differences in the function that each type of vessel performs.

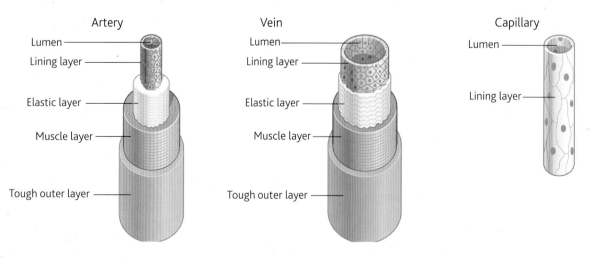

Figure 1 *Comparison of arteries, veins and capillaries*

Artery structure related to function

The function of arteries is to transport blood rapidly under high pressure from the heart to the tissues. Their structure is adapted to this function as follows:

- **The muscle layer is thick compared to veins**. This means smaller arteries can be constricted and dilated in order to control the volume of blood passing through them.
- **The elastic layer is relatively thick compared to veins** because it is important that blood pressure in arteries is kept high if blood is to reach the extremities of the body. The elastic wall is stretched at each beat of the heart (systole). It then springs back when the heart relaxes (diastole) in the same way as a stretched elastic band. This stretching and recoil action helps to maintain high pressure and smooth pressure surges created by the beating of the heart.
- **The overall thickness of the wall is large**. This also resists the vessel bursting under pressure.
- **There are no valves** (except in the arteries leaving the heart) because blood is under constant high pressure and therefore does not tend to flow backwards.

Arteriole structure related to function

Arterioles carry blood, under lower pressure than arteries, from arteries to capillaries. They also control the flow of blood between the two. Their structure is related to these functions as follows:

- **The muscle layer is relatively thicker than in arteries**. The contraction of this muscle layer allows constriction of the lumen of the arteriole. This restricts the flow of blood and so controls its movement into the capillaries that supply the tissues with blood.
- **The elastic layer is relatively thinner than in arteries** because blood pressure is lower.

Vein structure related to function

Veins transport blood slowly, under low pressure, from the tissues to the heart. Their structure is related to this function as follows:

- **The muscle layer is relatively thin** compared to arteries because veins carry blood away from tissues and therefore their constriction and dilation cannot control the flow of blood to the tissues.
- **The elastic layer is relatively thin** compared to arteries because the low pressure of blood within the veins will not cause them to burst and pressure is too low to create a recoil action.
- **The overall thickness of the wall is small** because there is no need for a thick wall as the pressure within the veins is too low to create any risk of bursting. It also allows them to be flattened easily, aiding the flow of blood within them (see below).
- **There are valves throughout** to ensure that blood does not flow backwards, which it might otherwise do because the pressure is so low. When body muscles contract, veins are compressed, pressurising the blood within them. The valves ensure that this pressure directs the blood in one direction only: towards the heart (Figure 3).

Capillary structure related to function

The function of capillaries (Figures 4 and 5) is to exchange metabolic materials such as oxygen, carbon dioxide and glucose between the

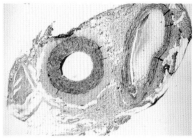

Figure 2 *Artery (left) and vein (right)*

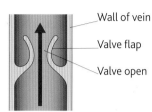

Wall of vein

Valve flap

Valve open

Blood flowing towards the heart passes easily through the valves

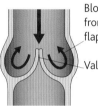

Blood flowing away from the heart pushes flaps of valve closed

Valve closed

Blood flowing away from the heart pushes valves closed and so blood is prevented from flowing any further in this direction

Figure 3 *Action of valves in veins in ensuring one-way flow of blood*

Figure 4 *False-colour scanning electron micrograph (SEM) of a section through a capillary with red blood cells passing through it*

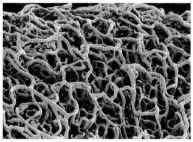

Figure 5 *Resin cast of a capillary network from the large intestine*

blood and the cells of the body. The flow of blood in capillaries is much slower. This allows more time for the exchange of materials.

The structure of capillaries is related to their function as follows:

▨ **Their walls consist only of the lining layer**, making them extremely thin, so the distance over which diffusion takes place is short. This allows for rapid diffusion of materials between the blood and the cells.

▨ **They are numerous and highly branched**, thus providing a large surface area for diffusion.

▨ **They have a narrow diameter** and so permeate tissues, which means that no cell is far from a capillary.

▨ **Their lumen is so narrow** that red blood cells are squeezed flat against the side of a capillary. This brings them even closer to the cells to which they supply oxygen. This again reduces the diffusion distance.

▨ **There are spaces between the lining (endothelial) cells** that allow white blood cells to escape in order to deal with infections within tissues.

Although capillaries are small, they cannot serve every single cell directly. Therefore the final journey of metabolic materials is made in a liquid solution that bathes the tissues. This liquid is called **tissue fluid**.

💡 Tissue fluid and its formation

Tissue fluid is a watery liquid that contains glucose, amino acids, fatty acids, salts and oxygen. Tissue fluid supplies all of these substances to the tissues. In return, it receives carbon dioxide and other waste materials from the tissues. Tissue fluid is therefore the means by which materials are exchanged between blood and cells and, as such, it bathes all the cells of the body. It is the immediate environment of cells and is, in effect, where they live. Tissue fluid is formed from blood plasma, and the composition of blood plasma is controlled by various homeostatic systems. As a result tissue fluid provides a mostly constant environment for the cells it surrounds.

Formation of tissue fluid

Blood pumped by the heart passes along arteries, then the narrower arterioles and, finally, the even narrower capillaries. This creates a pressure, called **hydrostatic pressure**, at the arterial end of the capillaries. This hydrostatic pressure forces tissue fluid out of the blood plasma. The outward pressure is, however, opposed by two other forces:

▨ hydrostatic pressure of the tissue fluid outside the capillaries, which prevents outward movement of liquid

▨ the lower **water potential** of the blood, due to the plasma proteins, that pulls water back into the blood within the capillaries.

However, the combined effect of all these forces is to create an overall pressure that pushes tissue fluid out of the capillaries. This pressure is only enough to force small molecules out of the capillaries, leaving all cells and proteins in the blood. This type of filtration under pressure is called **ultrafiltration**.

Return of tissue fluid to the circulatory system

Once tissue fluid has exchanged metabolic materials with the cells it bathes, it must be returned to the circulatory system. Most tissue fluid returns to the blood plasma directly via the capillaries. This return occurs as follows:

▨ The loss of the tissue fluid from the capillaries reduces the hydrostatic pressure inside them.

▨ As a result, by the time the blood has reached the venous end of the capillary network its hydrostatic pressure is less than that of the tissue fluid outside it.

▨ Therefore tissue fluid is forced back into the capillaries by the higher hydrostatic pressure outside them.

▨ In addition, the osmotic forces resulting from the proteins in the blood plasma pull water back into the capillaries.

The tissue fluid has lost much of its oxygen and nutrients by diffusion into the cells that it bathed, but it has gained carbon dioxide and waste materials in return. These events are summarised in Figure 6.

Not all the tissue fluid can return to the capillaries; the remainder is carried back via the lymphatic system. This is a system of vessels that begin in the tissues. Initially they resemble capillaries, but they gradually merge into larger vessels that form a network throughout the body. These larger vessels drain their contents back into the bloodstream via two ducts that join veins close to the heart.

The contents of the lymphatic system (lymph) are not moved by the pumping of the heart. Instead they are moved by:

▨ **hydrostatic pressure** of the tissue fluid that has left the capillaries

▨ **contraction of body muscles** that squeeze the lymph vessels – valves in the lymph vessels ensure that the fluid inside them moves away from the tissues in the direction of the heart.

A summary of the methods of tissue fluid formation and its return to the bloodstream is shown in Figure 7.

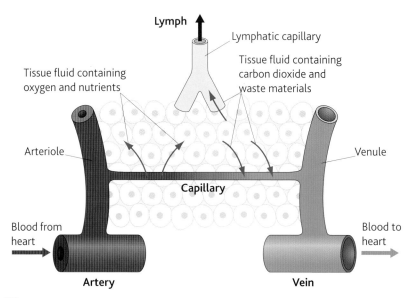

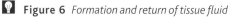

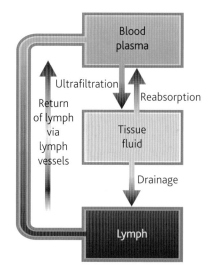

Figure 7 *Formation and return of tissue fluid to the bloodstream*

Figure 6 *Formation and return of tissue fluid*

Application and How science works

Blood flow in various blood vessels

The graph in Figure 8 shows certain features of the flow of blood from and to the heart through a variety of blood vessels.

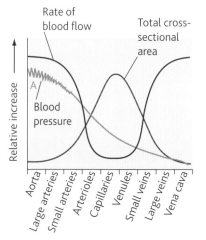

Figure 8 *Flow of blood to and from the heart*

1 Describe the changes in the rate of blood flow as blood passes from the aorta to the vena cava.

2 Explain why blood pressure in region A fluctuates up and down.

3 Why does the rate of blood flow decrease between the aorta and capillaries?

4 Explain how the rate of blood flow in the capillaries increases the rate of exchange of metabolic materials.

5 How does the structure of capillaries increase the efficiency of the exchange of metabolic substances?

Summary questions

1 Give **one** advantage of having:

a thick elastic tissue in the walls of arteries

b relatively thick muscle walls in arterioles

c valves in veins

d only a lining layer in capillaries.

2 Table 1 shows the mean wall thickness of different blood vessels in a mammal. Suggest the letter that is most likely to refer to a the aorta, b a capillary, c a vein, d an arteriole and e the renal artery.

Table 1

Blood vessel	Mean wall thickness / mm
A	1.000
B	0.001
C	2.000
D	0.500
E	0.030

3 What forces tissue fluid out of the blood plasma in capillaries and into the surrounding tissues?

4 By which **two** routes does tissue fluid return to the bloodstream?

13.7 Movement of water through roots

Learning objectives:

- How is water taken up by the root hairs?

- How does water pass through the cortex of a root?

- What are the apoplastic and symplastic pathways?

- How is water passed through the endodermis into the xylem?

Specification reference: 3.2.7

AQA Examiner's tip

Always refer to osmosis and to the water potential gradient when explaining how water enters a root-hair cell from the soil.

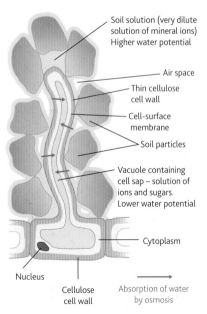

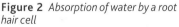

Figure 2 *Absorption of water by a root hair cell*

Link

If you are uncertain about osmosis or water potential it would be worth reading Topic 3.7 again.

The vast majority of plants are terrestrial organisms. As a result they need to conserve water and so they are covered by a waterproof layer. Therefore they cannot absorb water over the general body surface. Instead they have a special exchange surface in the soil: the **root hairs**. Before we look at how the root hairs absorb water and how water is transported, it is worth looking at the basic structure of a root. The arrangement of tissues in a **dicotyledonous** root is illustrated in Figure 1.

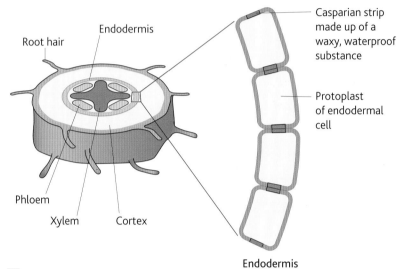

Figure 1 *Root of a dicotyledonous plant*

Uptake of water by root hairs

Root hairs are the exchange surfaces in plants that are responsible for the absorption of water and mineral ions. Plants constantly lose water by the process of **transpiration** (see Topic 13.9). This loss can amount to up to 700 dm³ per day in a large tree. All of this water must be replaced by water that is absorbed through the root hairs (Figure 2).

Each root hair is a long, thin extension of a root epidermal cell. These root hairs remain functional for a few weeks before dying back, to be replaced by others nearer the growing tip. They are efficient surfaces for the exchange of water and mineral ions because:

- they provide a large surface area as they are very long extensions and occur in thousands on each of the branches of a root,
- they have a thin surface layer (the cell-surface membrane and cellulose cell wall), across which materials can move easily.

Root hairs arise from epidermal cells a little way behind the tips of young roots. These hairs grow into the spaces around soil particles. In damp conditions they are surrounded by a soil solution which contains small quantities of mineral ions. The soil solution is, however, mostly water and therefore has a very high **water potential** – only slightly less than zero. In contrast, the root hairs, and other cells of the root, have sugars, amino acids and mineral ions dissolved inside them. These cells therefore have a much lower water potential. As a result, water moves by osmosis from the soil solution into the root-hair cells down this water potential gradient.

After being absorbed into the root-hair cell, water continues its journey across the root in two ways:

- the apoplastic pathway (the apoplast),
- the symplastic pathway (the symplast).

The apoplastic pathway

As water is drawn into endodermal cells, it pulls more water along behind it, due to the **cohesive** properties of the water molecules. This creates a tension that draws water along the cell walls of the cells of the root cortex. The mesh-like structure of the cellulose cell walls of these cells has many water-filled spaces and so there is little or no resistance to this pull of water along the cell walls (Figure 3).

The symplastic pathway

This takes place across the cytoplasm of the cells of the cortex as a result of **osmosis**. The water passes through the cell walls along tiny openings called plasmodesmata. Each plasmodesma (singular) is filled with a thin strand of cytoplasm. Therefore there is a continuous column of cytoplasm extending from the root-hair cell to the xylem at the centre of the root. Water moves along this column as follows:

- Water entering by osmosis increases the water potential of the root-hair cell.
- The root-hair cell now has a higher water potential than the first cell in the cortex.
- Water therefore moves from the root-hair cell to the first cell in the cortex by osmosis, down the water potential gradient.
- This first cell now has a higher water potential than its neighbour to the inside of the stem.
- Water therefore moves into this neighbouring cell by osmosis along the water potential gradient.
- This second cell now has a higher water potential than its neighbour to the inside, and so water moves from the second cell to the third cell by osmosis along the water potential gradient.
- At the same time, this loss of water from the first cortical cell lowers its water potential, causing more water to enter it by osmosis from the root-hair cell.
- In this way, a water potential gradient is set up across all the cells of the cortex, which carries water along the cytoplasm from the root-hair cell to the endodermis.

The apoplastic and symplastic pathways are summarised in Figure 4.

Passage of water into the xylem

When water reaches the endodermis by the apoplastic pathway, the waterproof band that makes up the Casparian strip in endodermal cells prevents it progressing further along the cell wall (Figure 5, next page). At this point, water is forced into the living protoplast of the cell, where it joins water that has arrived there by the symplastic pathway.

Active transport of salts is the most likely mechanism by which water now gets into the xylem. Endodermal cells actively transport salts into the xylem. This process requires energy and can therefore only occur

> ### Hint
>
> Remember that all water potential values of solutions are negative. Water moves from a higher (less negative) water potential to a lower (more negative) water potential.

> ### Hint
>
> Cohesion is the mutual attraction of molecules for one another. In other words, it is the ability of molecules (in this case water molecules) to stick to one another.

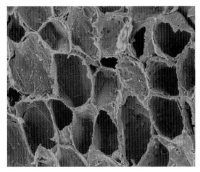

Figure 3 *Scanning electron micrograph (SEM) of plant cell walls showing the many spaces through which water can pass along the apoplastic pathway*

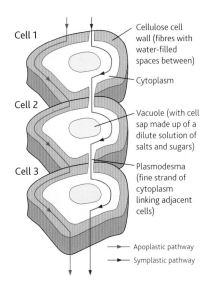

Figure 4 *Apoplastic and symplastic pathways across root cortex*

within living tissue. It takes place along **carrier proteins** in the cell-surface membrane. If water is to enter the xylem, it must first enter the cytoplasm of endodermal cells. This explains why the water from the apoplastic pathway is forced into the cytoplasm of the endodermal cells by the Casparian strip.

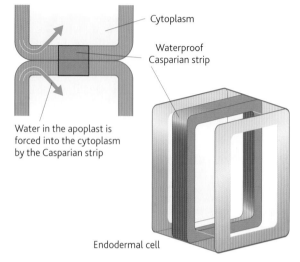

Figure 5 *Movement of water across the endodermis*

The active transport of mineral ions into the xylem by the endodermal cells creates a lower water potential in the xylem. Water now moves into the xylem, by osmosis, along a water potential gradient. This water potential gradient is the result of the active transport of salts into the xylem from the endodermal cells. This creates a force that helps to move water up the plant. This force is called **root pressure**. While its contribution to water movement up a large tree is minimal compared to the transpiration pull (see Topic 13.8), root pressure can make a significant contribution to water movement in small, herbaceous plants. Evidence for the existence of root pressure due to the active pumping of salts into the xylem includes the following:

- The pressure increases with a rise in temperature and decreases at lower temperatures.
- **Metabolic** inhibitors, such as cyanide, prevent most energy release by respiration and also cause root pressure to cease.
- A decrease in the availability of oxygen or respiratory substrates causes a reduction in root pressure.

Summary questions

1. Explain how water enters a root-hair cell.

2. State **two** differences between the apoplastic and symplastic pathways of water movement.

3. Why is water following the apoplastic pathway unable to cross the endodermis in the cell wall?

4. State whether each of the following processes is active or passive:

   a uptake of water by root hairs

   b movement of water from a cortex cell into an endodermal cell

   c movement of water from an endodermal cell into the xylem.

5. When seedlings are transplanted they sometimes wilt and die. Suggest **two** possible reasons for this.

13.8 Movement of water up stems

Learning objectives:

▦ What is transpiration?

▦ How does water move through the leaf?

▦ How does water move up the xylem?

Specification reference: 3.2.7

The main force that pulls water up the stem of a plant is the evaporation of water from leaves – a process called **transpiration** (see Topic 13.9). It is therefore logical to begin from the point where water molecules evaporate from the leaves, through the tiny openings, called **stomata**, on the surface of a leaf.

▦ Movement of water out through stomata

The humidity of the atmosphere is usually less than that of the air spaces next to the stomata. Provided the stomata are open, water vapour molecules diffuse out of the air spaces into the surrounding air. Water lost from the air spaces is replaced by water evaporating from the cell walls of the surrounding mesophyll cells. By changing the size of the stomatal pores, plants can control their rate of transpiration.

▦ Movement of water across the cells of a leaf

Water is lost from mesophyll cells by evaporation from their surfaces to the air spaces of the leaf. This is replaced by water reaching the mesophyll cells from the xylem by either the **apoplastic** or **symplastic** pathways (see Topic 13.7). In the case of the symplastic pathway, the water movement occurs because:

▦ mesophyll cells lose water to the air spaces,

▦ these cells now have a lower **water potential** and so water enters by **osmosis** from neighbouring cells,

▦ the loss of water from these neighbouring cells lowers their water potential,

▦ they, in turn, take in water from their neighbours by osmosis.

In this way, a water potential gradient is established that pulls water from the xylem, across the leaf mesophyll, and finally out into the atmosphere. These events are summarised in Figure 1 on the next page.

◩ Movement of water up the stem in the xylem

The two main factors that are responsible for the movement of water up the xylem, from the roots to the leaves, are cohesion–tension and root pressure. We looked at root pressure in Topic 13.7 so let us turn our attention to the cohesion–-tension theory. This operates as follows:

▦ Water evaporates from leaves as a result of transpiration (see Topic 13.9).

▦ Water molecules form hydrogen bonds between one another and hence tend to stick together. This is known as **cohesion**.

▦ Water forms a continuous, unbroken pathway across the mesophyll cells and down the xylem.

▦ As water evaporates from the mesophyll cells in the leaf into the air spaces beneath the stomata, more molecules of water are drawn up behind it as a result of this cohesion.

▦ Water is hence pulled up the xylem as a result of transpiration. This is called the **transpiration pull**.

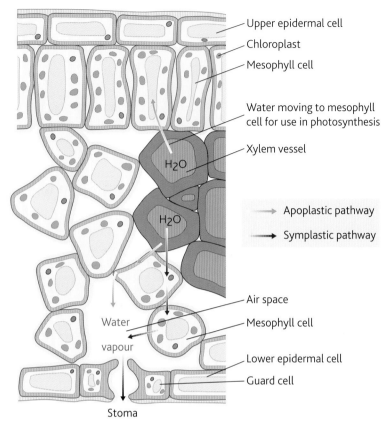

Figure 1 *Movement of water across leaf*

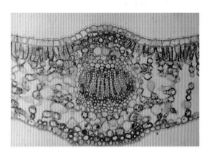

Figure 2 *Section through a leaf showing the tissues involved in the movement of water*

▌▌ Transpiration pull puts the xylem under tension, i.e. there is a negative pressure within the xylem, hence the name **cohesion–tension theory**.

Such is the force of the transpiration pull that it can easily raise water up the 100 m or more of the tallest trees. There are several pieces of evidence to support the cohesion–tension theory. These include:

▌▌ Change in the diameter of tree trunks according to the rate of transpiration. During the day, when transpiration is at its greatest, there is more tension (more negative pressure) in the xylem. This causes the trunk to shrink in diameter. At night, when transpiration is at its lowest, there is less tension in the xylem and so the diameter of the trunk increases.

▌▌ If a xylem vessel is broken and air enters it, the tree can no longer draw up water. This is because the continuous column of water is broken and so the water molecules can no longer stick together.

▌▌ When a xylem vessel is broken, water does not leak out, as would be the case if it were under pressure. Instead air is drawn in, which is consistent with it being under tension.

Transpiration pull is a passive process and therefore does not require metabolic energy to take place. Indeed, the xylem vessels through which the water passes are dead and so cannot actively move the water. As they are dead, their end walls can break down. This means that xylem forms a series of continuous, unbroken tubes from root to leaves, which is essential to the cohesion–tension theory of water flow up the stem. Energy is nevertheless needed to drive the process of transpiration. This energy is in the form of heat that ultimately comes from the Sun.

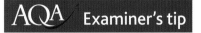

AQA Examiner's tip

Read the questions carefully. If a question says 'Explain how water in the xylem in the root reaches the leaves', don't describe uptake of water by root hairs and its movement through the endodermis.

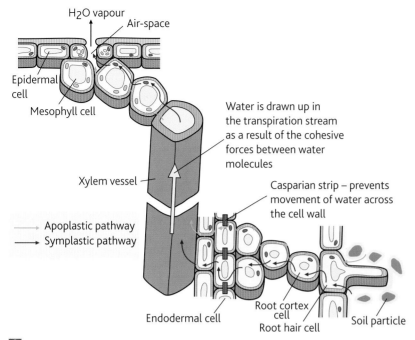

Figure 3 *Summary of water transport through a plant*

Figure 3 summarises the movement of water from the soil, through the plant, and into the atmosphere.

Application

Hug a tree

If you put your arms around a suitably sized tree trunk in the middle of the day your fingers will just touch on the far side of the tree. Try to hug the same tree at night and your fingers will probably no longer meet. The graph in Figure 4 shows why. It shows the rate of water flow up a tree and the diameter of the tree trunk over a 24 hour period.

1. At what time of day is transpiration rate greatest? Explain your answer.

2. Describe the changes in the rate of flow of water during the 24-hour period.

3. Explain in terms of the cohesion-tension theory the changes in the rate of flow of water during the 24-hour period.

4. Explain the changes in the diameter of the tree trunk over the 24-hour period.

5. If the tree was sprayed with ammonium sulfamate, a herbicide that kills living cells, the rate of water flow would be unchanged. Explain why.

Summary question

1. Give the most suitable word, or words, represented by **a–g** in the passage below.

Water evaporates from the air spaces in a plant by a process called **a**. This evaporation takes place mainly through pores called **b** in the epidermis of the leaf. Water evaporates into the air spaces from mesophyll cells. As a result these cells have a **c** water potential and so draw water by **d** from neighbouring cells. In this way, a water potential gradient is set up that draws water from the xylem. Water is pulled up the xylem because water molecules stick together – a phenomenon called **e**. During the night the diameter of a tree trunk **f**. Other forces helping to move water up the stem include **g**, which is the result of the movement of water into the xylem in the root following the active transport of ions into the xylem.

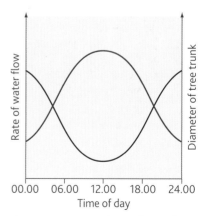

Figure 4 *Variation of rate of water flow and diameter of a tree trunk*

13.9 Transpiration and factors affecting it

Figure 1 *Transpiration pull is sufficient to transport water up plants such as this giant redwood tree, which is over 80 m tall*

We have seen in Topic 13.8 that transpiration is the evaporation of water vapour from plants. It takes place mostly through stomata in the leaves. Let us now look at why it occurs and what factors affect its rate.

Role of transpiration

Transpiration is sometimes referred to as 'a necessary evil'. This is because, although transpiration is universal in flowering plants, it is the unavoidable result of plants having leaves adapted for photosynthesis. Leaves have a large surface area to absorb light, and stomata to allow inward **diffusion** of carbon dioxide. Both features result in an immense loss of water: up to 700 dm³ per day in a large tree (Figure 1). Although transpiration helps bring water to the leaves, it is not essential because osmotic processes could achieve this. Less than 1 per cent of water moved in the transpiration stream is used by the plant. So what are the benefits of transpiration?

Materials such as mineral **ions**, sugars and hormones are moved around the plant dissolved in water. This water is carried up the plant by the transpiration pull. Without transpiration, water would not be so plentiful and the transport of materials would not be as rapid.

Factors affecting transpiration

A number of factors affect the rate of transpiration. These include the following.

Light

Stomata are the openings in leaves through which the carbon dioxide needed for photosynthesis diffuses. Photosynthesis only occurs in the light. It follows that the stomata of most plants open in the light and close in the dark. When stomata are open, water moves out of the leaf into the atmosphere. Consequently an increase in light intensity causes an increase in the rate of transpiration.

Temperature

Temperature changes affect two factors that influence the rate of transpiration.

■ how much water the air can hold, i.e. the **water potential** of air

■ the speed at which water molecules move.

A rise in temperature:

■ increases the kinetic energy and hence the speed of movement of water molecules. This increased movement of water molecules increases the rate of evaporation of water. This means that water evaporates more rapidly from leaves and so the rate of transpiration increases.

■ decreases the amount of water air can hold, i.e. it decreases its water potential.

Both these changes lead to an increase in transpiration rate. A reduction in temperature has the reverse effect; it reduces transpiration rate.

Humidity

Humidity is a measure of the number of water molecules in the air. The humidity of the air affects the water potential gradient between the air outside the leaf and the air inside the leaf. When the air outside the leaf has a high humidity, the gradient is reduced and the rate of transpiration is lower. Conversely, low humidity increases the transpiration rate.

Air movement

As water diffuses through stomata, it accumulates as vapour around the stomata on the outside of the leaf. The water potential around the stomata is therefore increased. This reduces the water potential gradient between the moist atmosphere in the air spaces within the leaf and the drier air outside. The transpiration rate is therefore reduced. Any movement of air around the leaf will disperse the humid layer at the leaf surface and so decrease the water potential of the air. This increases the water potential gradient and hence the rate of transpiration. The faster the air movement, the more rapidly the humid air is removed and the greater the rate of transpiration. These effects are shown in Figure 2.

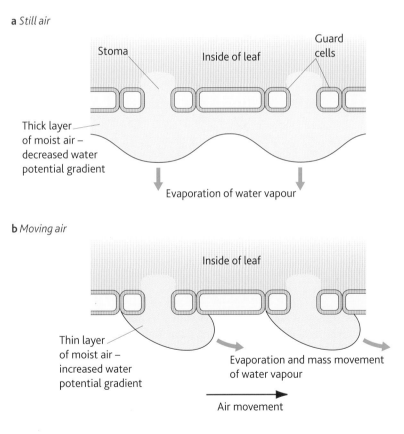

a *Still air*

b *Moving air*

Figure 2 *Effect of air movement on the rate of transpiration*

The factors affecting transpiration rate are summarised in Table 1 on the next page.

The energy for transpiration comes from the evaporation of water from leaves. We have seen that this evaporation depends on factors such as light, temperature, humidity and air movement. All these factors are either directly or indirectly the result of the Sun's energy. Therefore it is the Sun that ultimately drives transpiration.

Hint

The conditions inside the leaf are more constant than those outside it. Therefore it is changes to the **external** environment that largely affect transpiration rate.

Summary questions

1 Explain why transpiration is often described as a 'necessary evil'.

2 In each of the following cases, state whether the rate of transpiration increases or decreases:

a the temperature falls

b the wind speed increases

c the humidity decreases

d light intensity increases

e the water potential of the outside air is lowered.

3 When a potted plant is placed inside a black polythene bag, its transpiration rate falls. Give **two** reasons why this happens.

Table 1 *Summary of factors affecting transpiration rate*

Factor	How factor affects transpiration	Increase in transpiration caused by:	Decrease in transpiration caused by:
Light	Stomata open in the light and close in the dark	Higher light intensity	Lower light intensity
Temperature	Alters the **kinetic energy** of the water molecules and the relative humidity of the air	Higher temperatures	Lower temperatures
Humidity	Affects the water potential gradient between the air-spaces in the leaf and the atmosphere	Lower humidity	Higher humidity
Air movement	Changes the water potential gradient by altering the rate at which moist air is removed from around the leaf	More air movement	Less air movement

Application and How science works

Measurement of water uptake using a potometer

It is almost impossible to measure transpiration because it is extremely difficult to condense and collect all the water vapour that leaves all the parts of a plant. What we can easily measure, however, is the amount of water that is taken up in a given time by a part of the plant such as a leafy shoot. About 99 per cent of the water taken up by a plant is lost during transpiration, which means that the rate of uptake is almost the same as the rate at which transpiration is occurring. We can then measure water uptake by the same shoot under different conditions, e.g. various humidities, wind speeds or temperatures. In this way we get a reasonably accurate measure of the effects of these conditions on the rate of transpiration. This is an example of how science works (HSW: D).

The rate of water loss in a plant can be measured using a potometer (Figure 3). The experiment is carried out in the following stages:

■ A leafy shoot is cut under water. Care is taken not to get water on the leaves.

■ The potometer is filled completely with water, making sure there are no air bubbles.

■ Using a rubber tube, the leafy shoot is fitted to the potometer under water.

■ The potometer is removed from under the water and all joints are sealed with waterproof jelly.

■ An air bubble is introduced into the capillary tube.

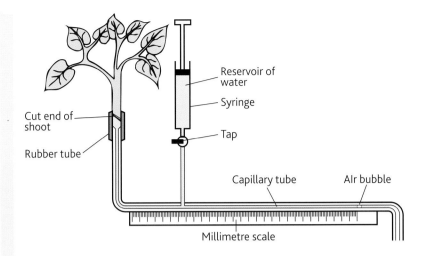

Figure 3 *A potometer*

■ The distance moved by the air bubble in a given time is measured a number of times and the mean is calculated.

■ Using this mean value, the volume of water lost is calculated.

■ The volume of water lost against the time in minutes can be plotted on a graph.

■ Once the air bubble nears the junction of the reservoir tube and the capillary tube, the tap on the reservoir is opened and the syringe is pushed down until the bubble is pushed back to the start of the scale on the capillary tube. Measurements then continue as before.

■ The experiment can be repeated to compare the rates of water uptake under different conditions, e.g. at different temperatures, humidity, light intensity, or the differences in water uptake between different species under the same conditions.

1 From your knowledge of how water moves up the stem, suggest a reason why each of the following procedures is carried out:

 a The leafy shoot is cut under water rather than in the air.

 b All joints are sealed with waterproof jelly.

2 What assumption must be made if a potometer is used to measure the rate of transpiration?

3 The volume of water taken up in a given time can be calculated using the formula $\pi r^2 l$ (where $\pi = 3.142$, r = radius of the capillary tube, and l = the distance moved by the air bubble). In an experiment the mean distance moved by the air bubble in a capillary tube of radius 0.5 mm during 1 min was 15.28 mm. Calculate the rate of water uptake in $mm^3\,h^{-1}$. Show your working.

4 If a potometer is used to compare the transpiration rates of two different species of plant, suggest one feature of both plant shoots that should, as far as possible, be kept the same.

5 Suggest reasons why the results obtained from a laboratory potometer experiment may not be representative of the transpiration rate of the same plant in the wild.

13.10 Limiting water loss in plants

In Topic 13.2 we looked at some of the problems created by the opposing needs of an efficient gas-exchange system and the requirement to conserve water in terrestrial organisms. The features that make a good gas-exchange system are the same features that increase water loss. In order to survive, terrestrial organisms must limit their water loss without compromising the efficiency of their gas-exchange systems. We saw in Topic 13.2 that insects reduce their water loss by having a waterproof covering and a relatively small surface area to volume ratio. While plants also have waterproof coverings, they cannot have a small surface area to volume ratio. This is because they photosynthesise, and photosynthesis requires a large surface area for the capture of light and for the exchange of gases. So how do plants limit water loss?

Xerophytic plants

Many plants can obtain enough water from the soil to enable them to survive without too many adaptations for reducing water loss. For these, a waterproof covering over parts of the leaves and the ability to close **stomata** when necessary are sufficient for them to survive. On the other hand, plants that do not have a plentiful water supply have developed a range of other adaptations to limit water loss through **transpiration**. These plants are called **xerophytes**.

Xerophytes are plants that are adapted to living in areas where their water losses due to transpiration may exceed their water uptake. Without these adaptations these plants would become desiccated and die. Xerophytic plants have modifications designed to increase water uptake, to store water and to reduce transpiration.

Figure 1 *Conifers have needle-like leaves to reduce water loss*

The main way of surviving in habitats with an unfavourable water balance is to reduce the rate at which water can be lost through transpiration. As the vast majority of transpiration occurs through the leaves, it is these organs that show most modifications. Examples of these modifications include:

■ **a thick cuticle**. Although the waxy cuticle on leaves forms a waterproof barrier, up to 10 per cent of transpiration can still occur by this route. The thicker the cuticle, the less water can escape by this means. Many evergreen plants, such as holly, have thick cuticles to reduce water loss, especially during the winter, when water is difficult to absorb because the soil is frozen.

■ **rolling up of leaves**. Most leaves have their stomata largely, or entirely, confined to the lower epidermis. The rolling of leaves in a way that protects the lower epidermis from the outside helps to trap a region of still air within the rolled leaf. This region becomes saturated with water vapour and so there is no **water potential** gradient between the inside and outside of the leaf. As there is no water potential gradient, transpiration is considerably reduced. Plants such as marram grass roll their leaves when transpiration rates are high, e.g. in hot or windy conditions.

Figure 2 *Holly has leaves with a thick waxy cuticle that reduces water loss*

■ **hairy leaves**. A thick layer of hairs on leaves, especially on the lower epidermis, traps moist air next to the leaf surface. The water potential gradient between the inside and the outside of the leaves is reduced and therefore less water is lost by transpiration. One type of heather plant has this modification.

stomata in pits or grooves. These again trap moist air next to the leaf and reduce the water potential gradient. Examples of plants using this mechanism include pine trees.

a reduced surface area to volume ratio of the leaves. We saw in Topic 3.6 that the smaller the surface area to volume ratio, the slower the rate of diffusion. By having leaves that are small and roughly circular in cross-section, as in pine needles, rather than leaves that are broad and flat, the rate of water loss can be considerably reduced. This reduction in surface area must always be balanced against the need for a sufficient area for photosynthesis to meet the requirements of the plant.

Summary questions

1. Insects and plants face the same problems when it comes to living on land. What is the main problem they share?

2. State **one** modification to reduce water loss that is shared by plants and insects.

3. Insects limit water loss by having a small surface area to volume ratio. Why is this not a feasible way of limiting water loss in plants?

4. Plants such as marram grass roll up their leaves, with the lower epidermis on the inside, to reduce transpiration.
   a Explain how rolling up their leaves helps to reduce transpiration.
   b Why would rolling the leaf the other way (with the upper epidermis on the inside) not be effective in reducing transpiration?

Application

Not only desert plants have problems obtaining water

Xerophytes are typically thought of as desert plants, and show a wide range of adaptations for coping with hot, dry conditions. However, similar adaptations may also be seen in plants found in sand dunes or other dry, windy places in temperate climates where rainfall is high and temperature relatively low. These adaptations are essential because the rain quickly drains away through the sand and out of the reach of the roots, making it difficult for these plants to obtain water. Plants living on salt marshes near the coast may have their roots drenched in water but find it difficult to absorb it. In addition, coastal regions are exposed to high wind speeds, which increase transpiration rates. Plants living in cold regions often have difficulty obtaining water for much of the year. Most plants living in these habitats show xerophytic modifications to enable them to reduce transpiration and so survive.

1. Give two reasons why plants growing on sand dunes need to have xerophytic features even though there is plentiful rainfall.

2. Explain in terms of water potential why salt marsh plants have difficulty absorbing water, despite having plenty around their roots.

3. Why do plants in cold regions 'have difficulty obtaining water from the soil for much of the year'?

4. Plants living in cold regions often reduce water loss by having leaves with a small surface area to volume ratio. This reduces the surface area available to capture light for photosynthesis. Photosynthesis is, in part, an enzyme-controlled process. Suggest a reason why having a smaller leaf area does not reduce the rate of photosynthesis in the same way as it would for plants in warmer climates.

Hint

Climate change affects rainfall and rate of transpiration. As a result, the distribution of plant species changes. As regions become drier, so the number of xerophytic plants in them increases.

Figure 3 *This cactus stores water in its swollen stem. It uses its stem to photosynthesise because it has fewer stomata. The leaves can therefore be needle-like to reduce their surface area and hence water loss.*

AQA Examiner's tip

When explaining adaptations of xerophytic plants to reduce water loss always relate these adaptations to reducing the water potential gradient and hence reduced evaporation of water and hence reduced transpiration.

1   (a) **Figure 1** shows part of the gill of a fish as seen through a light microscope. It is
         magnified 400 times.

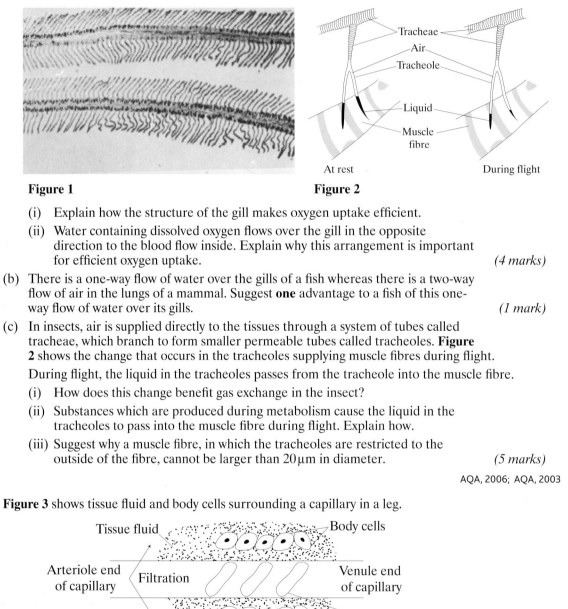

Figure 1   **Figure 2**

       (i)   Explain how the structure of the gill makes oxygen uptake efficient.
       (ii) Water containing dissolved oxygen flows over the gill in the opposite
             direction to the blood flow inside. Explain why this arrangement is important
             for efficient oxygen uptake.   *(4 marks)*
   (b) There is a one-way flow of water over the gills of a fish whereas there is a two-way
        flow of air in the lungs of a mammal. Suggest **one** advantage to a fish of this one-
        way flow of water over its gills.   *(1 mark)*
   (c) In insects, air is supplied directly to the tissues through a system of tubes called
        tracheae, which branch to form smaller permeable tubes called tracheoles. **Figure
        2** shows the change that occurs in the tracheoles supplying muscle fibres during flight.

        During flight, the liquid in the tracheoles passes from the tracheole into the muscle fibre.

       (i)   How does this change benefit gas exchange in the insect?
       (ii) Substances which are produced during metabolism cause the liquid in the
             tracheoles to pass into the muscle fibre during flight. Explain how.
       (iii) Suggest why a muscle fibre, in which the tracheoles are restricted to the
             outside of the fibre, cannot be larger than 20 µm in diameter.   *(5 marks)*

                                                                       AQA, 2006; AQA, 2003

2   **Figure 3** shows tissue fluid and body cells surrounding a capillary in a leg.

   (a) Name **two** substances which are at a higher concentration in the blood at the
        arteriole end of the capillary in a leg than at the venule end.   *(1 mark)*
   (b) Explain how fluid may be returned to the blood.   *(3 marks)*
   (c) (i)   People with high blood pressure often have swollen ankles and feet. This is
             the result of an accumulation of tissue fluid.

             Suggest an explanation for the link between high blood pressure and the
             accumulation of tissue fluid.

(ii) Suggest why tissue fluid accumulates more in the ankles and feet than in other parts of the body. *(3 marks)*

AQA, 2002

3 **Figure 4** shows part of a cross-section through a primary root.

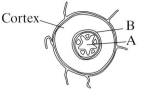

Figure 4

(a) Name the tissues labelled A and B. *(2 marks)*

(b) Water enters root-hair cells and moves across the cortex through both apoplastic and symplastic pathways.

    (i) Which part of the cortex cells forms the apoplastic pathway?

    (ii) Explain in terms of water potential how water enters root hair cells from the soil. *(3 marks)*

AQA, 2001

4 (a) Describe the roles of the following in moving water through the xylem:

    (i) root pressure

    (ii) cohesion–tension *(8 marks)*

(b) Describe and explain how **three** structural features reduce the rate of transpiration in xerophytic plants. *(3 marks)*

AQA, 2001

5 **Figure 5** shows an external view of a mammalian heart.

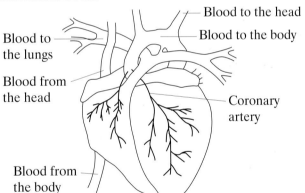

Figure 5

(a) Name the blood vessel which:

    (i) brings blood from the body

    (ii) takes blood to the lungs. *(2 marks)*

(b) (i) What is the function of the coronary artery?

    (ii) From which blood vessel does the coronary artery originate? *(2 marks)*

(c) The information below compares some features of different blood vessels.

		Blood vessel		
		Artery	**Capillary**	**Vein**
Property	Mean diameter of vessel	4.0 mm	8.0 μm	5.0 mm
	Mean thickness of wall	1.0 mm	0.5 μm	0.5 mm
		Relative thickness (shown by length of bar)		
Tissues present in wall	Endothelium	▬	▬	▬
	Elastic tissue	▬▬		▬▬
	Muscle	▬▬▬		▬▬

Use the information to explain how the structures of the walls of arteries, veins and capillaries are related to their functions. *(6 marks)*

AQA, 2004

14 Classification

14.1 Classification

Learning objectives:

■ What is a species?

■ How are species named?

■ What are the principles of classification?

■ How is classification related to evolution?

Specification reference: 3.2.8

Scientists have identified and named around 1.8 million different living organisms. No one knows how many types remain to be identified. Estimates for the total number of species on Earth vary from 10 million to 100 million. The figure is likely to be around 14 million. These represent only the species that exist today. Some scientists have estimated that 99 per cent of the species that have existed on Earth are now extinct, and almost all of them have left no fossil record. With such a vast number of organisms it is clearly important for scientists to name them and sort them into groups.

Classification is the organisation of living organisms into groups. This process is not random but is based on a number of accepted principles. Before we examine how organisms are grouped according to these principles, let us look at how scientists distinguish one type of organism from another.

■ The concept of a species

A species is the basic unit of classification. A definition of a species is not easy, but members of a single species have certain things in common:

■ **They are similar to one another but different from members of other species**. They have very similar genes and therefore closely resemble one another physically and biochemically. They have similar patterns of development and similar immunological features and they occupy the same **ecological niche**.

■ **They are capable of breeding to produce living, fertile offspring**. They are therefore able successfully to produce more offspring. This means that, when a species reproduces sexually, any of the genes of its individuals can, in theory, be combined with any other, i.e. they belong to the same **gene pool**.

■ Naming species – the binomial system

At one time scientists often gave new organisms a name that described their features, e.g. blackbird, rainbow trout. This practice resulted in the same names being used in different parts of the world for very different species. Therefore, it was difficult for scientists to be sure they were referring to the same organism. Over 200 years ago the Swedish botanist Linnaeus overcame this problem by devising a common system of naming organisms. This system is still in use today.

Organisms are identified by two names and hence the system is called the **binomial system**. Its features are as follows:

■ It is a universal system based upon Latin or Greek names.

■ The first name, called the **generic name**, denotes the genus to which the organism belongs. This is equivalent to the surname used to identify people and shared by their close relatives.

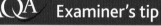

AQA Examiner's tip

A common error by candidates is to state that members of the same species are capable of breeding to produce viable offspring rather than fertile offspring.

The second name, called the **specific name**, denotes the species to which the organism belongs. This is equivalent to the first (or given) name used to identify people. However, unlike in humans, it is never shared by other species within the genus.

There are a number of rules that are applied to the use of the binomial system in scientific writing:

- The names are printed in italics or, if handwritten, they are underlined to indicate that they are scientific names.
- The first letter of the generic name is in upper case (capitals), but the specific name is in lower case (small letters).
- If the specific name is not known, it can be written as 'sp.', e.g. *Felix* sp.

The naming of organisms is in a constant state of change. Current names reflect the present state of scientific knowledge and understanding. In the same way, the classification of species is regularly changing as our knowledge of their evolution, physical features, biochemistry and behaviour increases.

Grouping species together – the principles of classification

With so many species, past and present, it makes sense to organise them into manageable groups. This allows better communication between scientists and avoids confusion. The grouping of organisms is known as **classification**, while the theory and practice of biological classification is called **taxonomy**.

There are two main forms of biological classification, each used for a different purpose.

- **Artificial classification** divides organisms according to differences that are useful at the time. Such features may include colour, size, number of legs, leaf shape, etc. These are described as analogous characteristics where they have the same function but do not have the same evolutionary origins. For example, the wings of butterflies and birds are both used for flight but they originated in different ways.

- **Natural classification**:
    a) is based upon the evolutionary relationships between organisms and their ancestors,
    b) classifies species into groups using shared features derived from their ancestors,
    c) arranges the groups into a hierarchy, in which the groups are contained within larger composite groups with no overlap.

Relationships in a natural classification are based upon homologous characteristics. Homologous characteristics have similar evolutionary origins regardless of their functions in the adult of a species. For example, the wing of a bird, the arm of a human and the front leg of a horse all have the same basic structure and all evolved from a common ancestor and are therefore homologous.

It must be remembered that all systems of classification are human inventions. They are developed for our convenience. The natural world does not follow any system of classification, nor is it is bound by our ideas.

Figure 1 *(From top to bottom) the fungus* Mucor mucedo *(bread mould); the plant* Lathyrus odoratus *(sweet pea); the animal* Felix tigris *(tiger). The classification of these organisms is shown in Table 1 on the next page.*

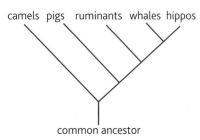

camels pigs ruminants whales hippos

common ancestor

The closer the branches, the closer the evolutionary relationship. Hippos and whales are more closely related than hippos and ruminants.

Figure 2 *A phylogenetic tree showing the evolutionary relationship between certain mammals*

■ Summary questions

1 What are the **two** main things that all members of a species share?

2 What are the **three** features of a natural system of classification?

3 *Rana temporaria* is the frog commonly found in Britain. Table 2, which is incomplete, shows part of its classification. Give the most appropriate name for each of the blanks represented by the numbers 1–7.

Table 2

Kingdom	Animalia
1	Chordata
2	Amphibia
3	Anura
4	Ranidae
Genus	5
6	7

■ Organising the groups of species – taxonomy

Each group within a natural biological classification is called a taxon (plural taxa). Taxonomy is the study of these groups and their positions in a hierarchical order, where they are known as taxonomic ranks. These are based upon the evolutionary line of descent of the group members. The largest group is a **kingdom** and each organism is placed into one of these. Within each kingdom the largest groups are known as **phyla**. Organisms in each phylum have a body plan radically different from organisms in any other phylum. Diversity within each phylum allows it to be divided into **classes**. Each class is divided into **orders** of organisms that have additional features in common. Each order is divided into **families** and at this level the differences are less obvious. Each family is divided into **genera** and each genus (singular) into **species**. As examples of how the system works (rather than names to be learnt), the classification of three organisms is given in Table 1.

Table 1 *Classification of three organisms from different kingdoms*

Rank	Pin mould	Sweet pea	Tiger
Kingdom	Fungi	Plantae	Animalia
Phylum	Zygomycota	Angiospermophyta	Chordata
Class	Zygomycetes	Dicotyledonae	Mammalia
Order	Mucorales	Rosales	Carnivora
Family	Mucoraceae	Fabaceae	Felidae
Genus	*Mucor*	*Lathyrus*	*Felix*
Species	*mucedo*	*odoratus*	*tigris*

▒ Phylogeny

We saw in the last section that the hierarchical order of taxonomic ranks is based upon the evolutionary line of descent of the group members. This evolutionary relationship between organisms is known as **phylogeny**. The term is derived from the word 'phylum', which, in classification, is a group of related or similar organisms. The phylogeny of an organism reflects the evolutionary branch that led up to it. The phylogenetic relationships of different species are usually represented by a tree-like diagram called a phylogenetic tree. In these diagrams, the oldest species is at the base of the tree while the most recent ones are represented by the ends of the branches. An example is shown in Figure 2.

■ Application

The difficulties of defining species

A species may be defined in terms of observable similarities and the ability to produce fertile offspring. There are, however, certain difficulties with this definition. These include:

■ Species are not fixed forever, but change and evolve over time. In time, some individuals may develop into a new species.

■ Within a species there can be considerable variation among individuals. All dogs, for example, belong to the same species, but **artificial selection** has led to a variety of different breeds.

- Many species are extinct and most of these have left no fossil record.
- Some species rarely, if ever, reproduce sexually.
- Members of different groups of the same species may be isolated, e.g. by oceans, and so never meet and therefore never interbreed.
- Groups of organisms that are isolated from one another may be classified as different species. These groups may turn out to be of the same species when their ability to interbreed is tested.
- Some species are sterile (see below).

Figure 3 *A horse (right) and a donkey (left), although different species, are capable of mating and producing offspring called mules*

1 Even where groups of extinct organisms have left fossil records, it is very difficult to distinguish different species. Suggest two reasons why.

2 Suggest reasons why it is often difficult to classify organisms as distinct species.

A horse and a donkey (Figure 3) are capable of mating and producing offspring, which are known as mules. A horse and a donkey are, however, different species and the resulting mules are infertile, i.e. they almost never produce offspring when mated with each other. Why are mules infertile? It is all down to the number of **chromosomes** and the first stage of **meiosis**. A horse has 64 chromosomes (32 pairs) and a donkey has 62 chromosomes (31 pairs). The **gametes** of a horse and a donkey therefore have 32 and 31 chromosomes respectively. When the gametes of a horse and a donkey fuse, the offspring (the mule) has 63 chromosomes. Gametes are formed by meiosis, which cannot take place if there is an odd number of chromosomes. So a mule cannot produce gametes and is therefore normally infertile. However, mitosis can take place and therefore a mule grows and develops normally.

There have been occasional cases of a fertile female mule. This event is very rare, so much so that the Romans had a saying that meant 'when a mule foals', which was the equivalent of our modern 'once in a blue moon'.

3 From your knowledge of the events during meiosis 1 (see Topic 8.4), suggest a reason why the cells of a mule with their 63 chromosomes are unable to undergo meiosis and so cannot produce gametes.

4 Does the fact that fertile mules occasionally occur make a mule a distinct species? Give reasons for your answer.

Application

Relationships

Figure 4 shows a phylogenetic tree for birds and certain reptiles.

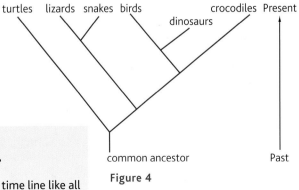

Figure 4

1 Which group is the closest relative of the snakes?

2 Are dinosaurs more closely related to crocodiles or birds?

3 Suggest a reason why dinosaurs are not shown along the time line like all the other groups.

15.1 Genetic comparisons using DNA and proteins

Learning objectives:

▪ How can comparisons of base sequences in DNA be used to investigate how closely related organisms are?

▪ What is DNA hybridisation and how is it used to determine relationships between organisms?

▪ How can comparisons of amino acid sequences in proteins be used to investigate the relationships between organisms?

▪ How are immunological comparisons used to investigate variations in proteins?

Specification reference: 3.2.9

Hint

As DNA determines the features of an organism, using the similarities in DNA as evidence for a close evolutionary relationship between species provides a direct record. Using similarities in the features themselves provides an indirect record. However, some DNA is non-functional and does not code for proteins. Analysis of this DNA can provide new evidence of relationships between organisms.

Link

An understanding of DNA hybridisation requires information found in Topic 11.1.

In Topic 14.1, we saw that classification systems were originally based on features that could easily be observed. As science has developed it has become possible to use a wider range of evidence to determine the evolutionary relationships between organisms.

When organisms evolve it is not only their visible internal and external features that adapt and change, but also the molecules of which they are made. DNA determines the proteins of an organism, including **enzymes** (see Topic 8.2) and proteins determine the features of an organism. It follows that changes in the features of an organism are due to changes in its DNA. Comparing the DNA and proteins of different **species** helps scientists to determine the evolutionary relationships between them.

Comparison of DNA base sequences

When one species gives rise to another species during evolution, the DNA of the new species will initially be very similar to that of the species that gave rise to it. Due to **mutations**, the sequences of nucleotide bases in the DNA of the new species will change. Consequently, over time, the new species will accumulate more and more differences in its DNA. As a result, we would expect species that are more closely related to show more similarity in their DNA base sequences than species that are more distantly related. As there are millions of base sequences in every organism, DNA contains a vast amount of information about the evolutionary history of all organisms.

One way to determine similarities between the DNA of different organisms is to use a technique called DNA hybridisation.

DNA hybridisation

DNA hybridisation depends upon a particular property of the DNA double helix. When DNA is heated, its double strand separates into its two complementary single strands. When cooled, the complementary bases on each strand recombine with each other to reform the original double strand. Given sufficient time, all strands in a mixture of DNA will pair up with their partners.

Using this property, DNA hybridisation can be used to compare the DNA of two species in the following manner:

▪ DNA from two species is extracted, purified and cut into short pieces.

▪ The DNA from one of the species is labelled by attaching a radioactive or fluorescent marker to it. It is then mixed with unlabelled DNA from the other species.

▪ The mixture of both sets of DNA is heated to separate their strands.

▪ The mixture is cooled to allow the strands to combine with other strands that have a complementary sequence of bases.

- Some of the double strands that reform will be made up of one strand from each species. This is called **hybridisation** and the new strands are called hybrid strands. These can be identified because they are 50 per cent labelled.
- These hybrid strands are separated out and the temperature is increased in stages.
- At each temperature stage the degree to which the two strands are still linked together is measured.
- If the two species are closely related they will share many complementary nucleotide bases.
- There will therefore be more **hydrogen bonds** linking them together in the hybrid strand.
- The greater the number of hydrogen bonds, the stronger the hybrid strand will be.
- The stronger the hybrid strand, the higher the temperature needed to separate it into its two single strands.
- The higher the temperature at which the hybrid strand splits, the more closely the two species are related.
- The lower the temperature at which it splits, the more distantly the species are related.

The process of DNA hydridisation is summarised in Figure 1.

Use of DNA base sequencing in classifying plants

Until recently the classification of flowering plants had been based on the appearance of a plant's physical features. This led to flowering plants being placed in one of two groups. The monocotyledons that have a single seed leaf (and generally have thin, narrow leaves) and the dicotyledons that have two seed leaves (and generally have broad leaves).

A team of scientists at The Royal Botanical Gardens, Kew recently devised a new classification of the families of flowering plants. This was based on the DNA sequences of three genes found in all plants. Their work was carried out as follows:

- They used 565 species that between them represented all the known families of flowering plants in the world.
- For each plant, the DNA sequences of all three genes were determined.
- The sequences for each species were compared using computer analysis.
- A phylogenetic tree for the families of flowering plants was devised based upon the DNA sequences of the species used.

The phylogenetic tree that the scientists produced showed how species have evolved into natural groups. These groupings represent evolutionary relationships better than any previous form of classification has ever done.

Comparison of amino acid sequences in proteins

The sequence of amino acids in proteins is determined by DNA. The degree of similarity in the amino acid sequence of the same protein in two species will therefore reflect how closely related the two species are. Once the amino acid sequence for a chosen protein has been determined for two species, the two sequences are compared. This can be done by

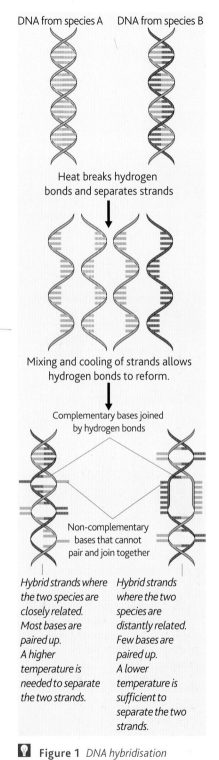

DNA from species A   DNA from species B

Heat breaks hydrogen bonds and separates strands

Mixing and cooling of strands allows hydrogen bonds to reform.

Complementary bases joined by hydrogen bonds

Non-complementary bases that cannot pair and join together

Hybrid strands where the two species are closely related. Most bases are paired up. A higher temperature is needed to separate the two strands.

Hybrid strands where the two species are distantly related. Few bases are paired up. A lower temperature is sufficient to separate the two strands.

💡 **Figure 1** *DNA hybridisation*

Link

An understanding of this immunological technique requires information found in Topic 6.5.

counting either the number of similarities or the number of differences in each sequence. An example is shown in Figure 2. Here there is a short sequence of seven amino acids of the same protein in six different species. The table on the right of the figure shows both the number of differences and the number of similarities.

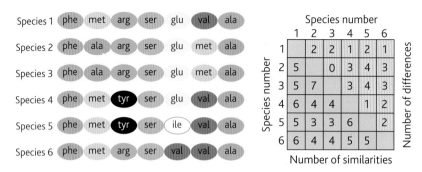

Figure 2 *Comparison of amino acid sequence in part of the same protein in six species*

Immunological comparisons of proteins

The proteins of different species can also be compared using immunological techniques. The principle behind this method is the fact that **antibodies** of one species will respond to specific **antigens** on proteins, such as albumin, in the blood **serum** of another. The process is carried out as follows:

▦ Serum albumin from species A is injected into species B.

▦ Species B produces antibodies specific to all the antigen sites on the albumin from species A.

▦ Serum is extracted from species B; this serum contains antibodies specific to the antigens on the albumin from species A.

▦ Serum from species B is mixed with serum from the blood of a third species C.

▦ The antibodies respond to their corresponding antigens on the albumin in the serum of species C.

▦ The response is the formation of a precipitate.

▦ The greater the number of similar antigens, the more precipitate is formed and the more closely the species are related.

▦ The fewer the number of similar antigens, the less precipitate is formed and the more distantly the species are related.

An example of this technique is illustrated in Figure 3. In this case, species A is a human, species B is a rabbit and species C is represented by a variety of other mammals.

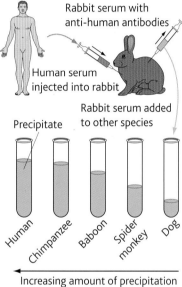

The results show that humans are very closely related to chimpanzees, less so to baboons and even less so to spider monkeys. They are only distantly related to dogs.

Figure 3 *Immunological comparisons of human serum with that of other species*

■ **Summary questions**

1 During the process of DNA hybridisation explain the following:

a why DNA is heated

b why some hybrid strands require a higher temperature to separate the two strands than others

c the significance of the difference, described in **b**, in determining the relationships between species.

2 Using the information in Figure 3, state, with reasons, which two species are most closely related.

Application

New classification of flowering plants

The phylogenetic tree in Figure 4 shows one proposed version of the classification of flowering plants that has been based on recent studies of DNA sequences in plant species.

1   What causes the DNA sequences of genes to change over a period of time?

2   Which of the groups shown has been present on Earth for the longest period of time?

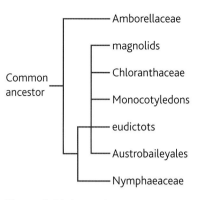

Figure 4 *Phylogenetic tree*

Application and How science works

Establishing relationships

The precise sequence of human evolution has long been a mystery. The evidence from different scientific techniques is often conflicting. Any conclusions drawn from the results of experiments are therefore tentative. Consequently scientists have been trying to refine their techniques in an attempt to clarify the evolutionary relationships of humans to other primates. As these new techniques have been adopted, our knowledge of primate evolution has changed as new evidence has provided a better explanation of the relationships between various primates. As a result the events in human evolution have been, and will continue to be, revised. This is an example of how science works (HSW: F and G). Some of the techniques and evidence that have led to these revisions are detailed below.

The proteins and DNA of organisms show differences between each species. These differences are thought to be due to changes that have occurred over long periods of time.

The sequences of amino acids in haemoglobin molecules have been used to clarify the evolution of primates. The amino acids found in seven specific positions in the haemoglobin molecules of six different primates were compared. The results of the study are shown in Table 1. Each amino acid is represented by a different letter.

Table 1

Primate	Position 1	Position 2	Position 3	Position 4	Position 5	Position 6	Position 7
Human	N	T	R	P	A	E	L
Gibbon	D	K	R	Q	T	D	H
Gorilla	N	T	K	P	A	D	L
Orang-utan	N	K	R	Q	T	D	L
Chimpanzee	N	T	R	P	A	E	L
Lemur	N	Q	T	A	T	E	H

1   Where the amino acid differs from that in human haemoglobin, the letter is shown in red. Use this information to list the evolutionary relationship of humans to the other primates shown. Start with the most closely related primate and end with the most distantly related one.

Another study compared the proteins found in a variety of primates using immunological techniques. The results of this study are illustrated in Figure 5.

2 Which two primates does this immunological study suggest are the most closely related? Give reasons for your answer.

3 Which primate does the study suggest is the nearest relative of the orang-utan? Give reasons for your answer.

4 The data in Figure 5 show the evolutionary relationships between humans and the five other primates. In what two ways do these relationships differ from that suggested by the haemoglobin study?

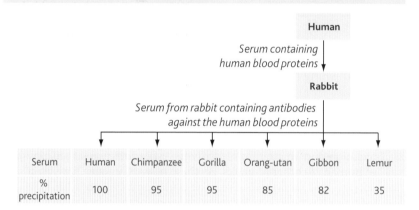

Serum	Human	Chimpanzee	Gorilla	Orang-utan	Gibbon	Lemur
% precipitation	100	95	95	85	82	35

Figure 5

A further study compared the number of base differences in the first 200 bases of a gene found in five species of primate. The results are shown in Table 2 below.

Table 2

	Human	Gorilla	Chimpanzee	Orang-utan	Lemur
Human	0				
Gorilla	12	0			
Chimpanzee	15	15	0		
Orang-utan	29	33	26	0	
Lemur	48	49	49	50	0

5 What evidence is there from the table to show humans are more closely related to orang-utans than lemurs?

6 Do these data support the evolutionary relationships of these primates suggested by the other two studies? Explain your answer.

The conflicting evidence for the relationships between different primates illustrates the need to use a variety of evidence from different sources in drawing valid scientific conclusions.

15.2 Courtship behaviour

Learning objectives:

- What is the role of courtship in ensuring successful mating?

- How does courtship help members of a species recognise each other?

Specification reference: 3.2.9

In Topic 15.1 we saw how similarities and differences can be used to establish evolutionary relationships. We saw that this is possible because, the differences between members of the same **species** are far fewer than the differences between members of different species. Similarities and differences in the physical and chemical make-up of organisms help them to distinguish members of their own species from those of other species. The same is true of behaviour. The behaviour of members of the same species is more alike than that of members of different species. Individuals can therefore recognise members of their own species by the way they act. Like the physical and chemical features of a species, most behaviour is genetically determined. It too has evolved and it influences the chances of survival. When it comes to survival of the species (as opposed to the individuals), courtship and mating are essential.

Why is courtship behaviour necessary?

No individual lives forever. Reproduction is therefore important to all organisms as it is the means by which a species can survive over time. Each individual tries to ensure that their DNA is passed on, through the reproductive process, to the next generation. The females of most species only produce eggs at specific times, often as little as once a year. It is therefore important to ensure that mating is successful and that the offspring have the maximum chance of survival. Courtship behaviour helps to achieve this by enabling individuals to:

- **recognise members of their own species** to ensure that mating only takes place between members of the same species because only members of the same species can produce fertile offspring (see Topic 14.1)
- **identify a mate that is capable of breeding** because both partners need to be sexually mature, fertile and receptive to mating
- **form a pair bond** that will lead to successful mating and raising of offspring
- **synchronise mating** so that it takes place when there is the maximum probability of the sperm and egg meeting.

The females of many species undergo a cycle of sexual activity during which they can only conceive during a very short time. They are often only receptive to mating for a period around the time when they produce eggs. Courtship behaviour is used by males to determine whether the female is at this receptive stage. If she responds with the appropriate behavioural response, courtship continues and is likely to result in the production of offspring. If she is not receptive, she exhibits a different pattern of behaviour and the male ceases to court her, turning his attentions elsewhere.

During courtship, animals use signals to communicate with a potential mate and with members of their own sex. Typically a male carries out some action. This action acts as a stimulus to the female, who responds with a specific action of her own. Her response acts as a stimulus to the male to carry out a further action. The ritual proceeds in this way in what is called a stimulus–response chain. The chain of actions is the same for all members of a species but differs for members of different species. In this way both individuals recognise that their partner is of the same species and that they may be prepared to mate. The longer the courtship sequence

Figure 1 *Courtship of great crested grebes – the weed presentation dance*

Examiner's tip

When considering animal behaviour always remember that animals do not think like humans.

Summary questions

1. Why is species recognition important in courtship?

2. Other than species recognition, what other functions does courtship perform?

3. If a female does not exhibit a typical behavioural response during courtship, the male will look elsewhere for a partner.

   a State **two** things that this suggests about the female.

   b How does the male's response help species survival in the long term?

4. Suggest a way in which the courtship behaviour of one species might be used to determine which of two other related species is most closely related to it.

Figure 3 *Male and female mallards during courtship display*

continues, the more likely it is that mating will result. If at any point one of the pair fails to respond appropriately, then the courtship sequence ends.

Application

Courting mallards

The courtship display of a male mallard duck has around ten display elements. These include shaking the tail, flicking the head, alternately raising the head and tail, shaking the bill and nodding the head while swimming. One particular display, called a grunt-whistle, involves lifting the breast out of the water while arching the head downwards followed by a sharp whistle and a deep grunt (Figure 2). These elaborate displays are found in closely related duck species. However in some species certain elements are omitted, while in others the order in which each element is performed is different.

Tail-shaking   Bill-shaking   Grunt-whistling   Head-flicking

Nod-swimming   Raising head/tail

Figure 2 *Some courtship displays of the male mallard*

1. Why do different species of duck have different courtship displays?

In Table 1 the courtship behaviour of six male ducks is summarised. The display elements are shown in sequence.

Table 1

Duck A	Shakes tail	Shakes bill	Grunt-whistles	Flicks head	Raises head/tail	Turns to female
Duck B	Shakes tail	Shakes bill	Grunt-whistles	Flicks head	Raises head/tail	Turns to female
Duck C	Shakes tail	Shakes bill	Grunt-whistles	Flicks head	Turns to female	–
Duck D	Shakes tail	Shakes bill	Grunt-whistles	Nods & swims	Raises head/tail	Turns to female
Duck E	Shakes tail	Shakes bill	Flicks head	Grunt-whistles	Raises head/tail	Turns to female
Duck F	Flicks head	Shakes tail	Nods & swims	Grunt-whistles	Turns to female	–

2. How many different species of duck are represented in the table?

3. Suggest why the courtship sequences provide evidence that ducks B and C are closely related.

4. Which duck does the evidence in the table suggest is only distantly related to the others? Give your reasoning.

5. When a female mallard chooses a male she performs characteristic head movements and calls. Suggest a possible reason for this behaviour.

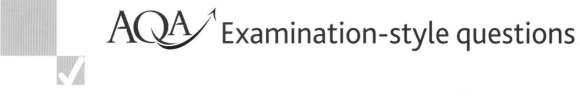

Chapter 14 Classification

1   The mammals form a class called the Mammalia within the animal kingdom. The grey wolf is a species of mammal. **Figure 1** shows the groups within the Mammalia to which the wolf (labelled **W**) belongs.

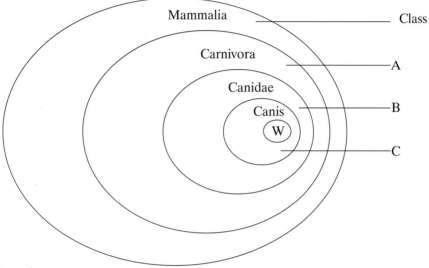

Figure 1

(a) (i)   Name the groups labelled A, B and C in **Figure 1**.

    (ii)   The lion, *Panthera leo*, belongs to another group in the Carnivora, called the Felidae. Describe how the information could be added to **Figure 1**, using the letter L to represent the lion species.   *(3 marks)*

(b)   The diagrams below show two systems of classification of mammals. **Figure 2** shows a simple hierarchy. **Figure 3** shows a phylogenetic system.

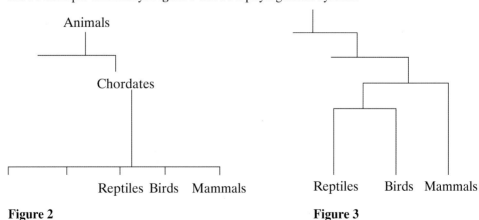

Figure 2   **Figure 3**

(i)   What is meant by a hierarchy?

(ii)   By reference to **Figures 2 and 3**, explain how a phylogenetic system differs from a simple hierarchy.   *(4 marks)*

AQA, 2004

Chapter 15 Evidence for relationships between organisms

1 The red grouse is a bird that lives on moorland. Each male fights for, and then defends, a territory into which he attracts females.

    (a) Male grouse vary in how aggressive they are. Suggest and explain **two** possible causes of this variation in aggressive behaviour. *(4 marks)*

    (b) **Figures 1 and 2** give information about aggressiveness of males, the size of their territories and the number of females they mate with.

        Use the information in **Figures 1 and 2** to describe how the defence of a territory by a male grouse affects his success in reproduction. *(3 marks)*

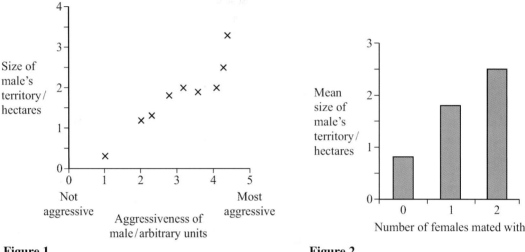

Figure 1　　　　　　　　　　　　　　　**Figure 2**

AQA, 2006

2 Cytochrome c is a protein with about 100 amino acids and is present in all eukaryotic organisms. It has the same three-dimensional shape in all species, but only 30 of the amino acids are the same in all species. The amino acid sequence of cytochrome c has been used to construct the phylogenetic tree shown in **Figure 3**.

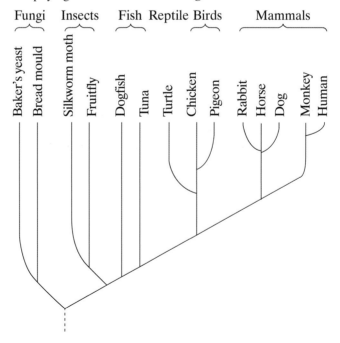

Figure 3

    (a) Name the kingdoms represented in this phylogenetic tree. *(1 mark)*

(b) What does the phylogenetic tree show about the evolutionary relationship between fungi and insects? *(2 marks)*

(c) Suggest how information on amino acid sequences is used to construct a phylogenetic tree. *(2 marks)*

(d) Suggest **one** advantage and **one** disadvantage of using cytochrome c to construct a phylogenetic tree. *(2 marks)*

AQA, 2005

3

(a) Courtship and mating in fruitflies can occur equally well in the light or dark. Fruitflies which mate in the dark are much more likely to produce offspring than those which mate in the light. Suggest an explanation for this. *(1 mark)*

Figure 4 shows the courtship sequence of males from two closely related species of fruitfly (species A and species B). The numbers show the probability of one courtship element following from another.

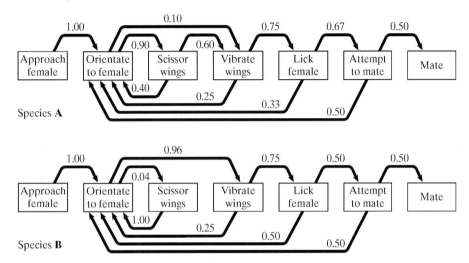

Figure 4

(b) Once a male of species A has orientated to the female, what is the probability that he will perform each courtship element once only and then attempt to mate? Show your working. *(2 marks)*

(c) Suggest how the courtship sequences provide evidence to support the claim that the two species are:

(i) closely related

(ii) separate species. *(2 marks)*

(d) During courtship, vibration of the wings creates a sound. The sound is different in the two species of fruitfly. Explain how this prevents mating between members of different species. *(2 marks)*

AQA, 2005

16.1 Genetic variation in bacteria

Learning objectives:

▥ What is the genetic material in bacteria?

▥ How does variation arise in bacteria?

▥ What are mutations?

▥ How does conjugation occur?

Specification reference: 3.2.10

Through the process of natural selection, organisms adjust to suit the changing environment in which they live. This is known as **adaptation**. Adaptation increases the long-term reproductive success of a species by helping its members to survive long enough to breed. Adaptation and selection are major factors in evolution. As such, they make a significant contribution to the diversity of living organisms.

One of the most diverse and adaptable groups of organisms is bacteria. Their adaptation to a changing environment can be seen in their ability to develop resistance to **antibiotics**. Before we look at **antibiotic resistance**, let us first consider how genetic variation can arise in bacteria.

We saw in Chapter 8 that DNA is the means by which genetic information is passed from generation to generation. Diversity in organisms arises from changes to its DNA. These changes occur in two ways:

▥ changing the quantity or structure of the DNA of an organism. This is known as a **mutation**.

▥ recombining the existing DNA of two individuals. This occurs during sexual reproduction.

As in other organisms, DNA is the genetic material in bacteria. Bacteria also increase diversity by changing their DNA in a similar manner to other organisms, namely by mutations and **conjugation**. Although conjugation recombines the DNA of two individuals, it is not strictly sexual reproduction.

▥ Mutations

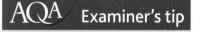

Mutations are changes in DNA that result in different characteristics. Mutations arise in many ways. For example, one or more bases in a DNA sequence may be added, deleted or replaced by others during replication (see Topic 11.1). In Topic 8.2 we learned that a triplet of bases on a DNA molecule codes for a single amino acid. Any differences in the base sequence of a DNA molecule may result in a different sequence of amino acids being coded for. This different amino acid sequence will lead to a different polypeptide, and hence a different protein, or no protein at all, being produced. If this protein is an enzyme it is likely to disrupt the metabolic pathway leading to the production of other substances, including proteins. As proteins are responsible for the characteristics of an organism, it follows that changes to DNA are likely to alter an organism's characteristics.

▥ Conjugation

Conjugation occurs when one bacterial cell transfers DNA to another bacterial cell. It takes place as follows:

▥ One cell produces a thin projection that meets another cell and forms a thin conjugation tube between the two cells.

The donor cell replicates one of its small circular pieces of DNA (plasmid).

The circular DNA is broken to make it linear before it passes along the tube into the recipient cell.

Contact between the cells is brief, leaving only time for a portion of the donor's DNA to be transferred.

In this way the recipient cell acquires new characteristics from the donor cell.

These events are illustrated in Figure 1 and Figure 2.

In conjugation, DNA in the form of genes can be passed from one species to another species. This is known as **horizontal gene transmission**. Where genes are passed down from one generation of a species to the next generation of the same species, the process is known as **vertical gene transmission**.

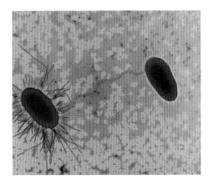

Figure 1 *Electron micrograph of* Escherichia coli (E. coli) *bacteria conjugating*

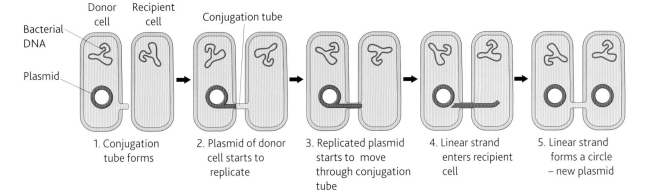

1. Conjugation tube forms
2. Plasmid of donor cell starts to replicate
3. Replicated plasmid starts to move through conjugation tube
4. Linear strand enters recipient cell
5. Linear strand forms a circle – new plasmid

Figure 2 *DNA transfer by conjugation in bacteria*

Application and How science works

Discovering conjugation in bacteria

Joshua Lederberg was a medical student whose observations led him to question the prevailing scientific view that bacteria passed down exact copies of genetic information to the next generation. In other words, they always produced genetically identical offspring, known as **clones**. In 1946 he teamed up with Edward Tatum to test his hypothesis that there was transfer of genetic information between the bacteria, thereby producing variety by a means other than mutation. They carried out experiments designed to demonstrate that genes could be transferred between different strains of the bacterium *Escherichia coli (E. coli)*. This is an example of how science works (HSW: C).

Lederberg and Tatum used two different strains of *E. coli* that were grown in dishes of a jelly-like substance (growth medium) that contained certain nutrients. Neither of the two strains could grow on a growth medium that contained only the basic nutrients (minimal medium). This was because each strain was unable to synthesise for itself two different nutrients that were essential for its growth.

Strain 1 could not synthesise the amino acid methionine and the vitamin biotin. Strain 1 would therefore only grow if these were added to the growth medium.

Strain 2 could not synthesise the amino acids threonine and leucine. Strain 2 would only grow if these were added to the growth medium.

Summary questions

1 In which **two** ways does genetic diversity occur in living organisms?

2 What is a mutation?

3 Albinism can be caused by a mutation that results in organisms being unable to produce an enzyme involved in the manufacture of a chemical called melanin. Suggest a possible sequence of events, starting with a mutation and ending with cells being unable to produce melanin.

4 Distinguish between horizontal and vertical gene transmission.

They mixed the two strains of *E. coli* together and grew them for several hours in a medium that contained supplements of all the missing nutrients (methionine, biotin, threonine and leucine).

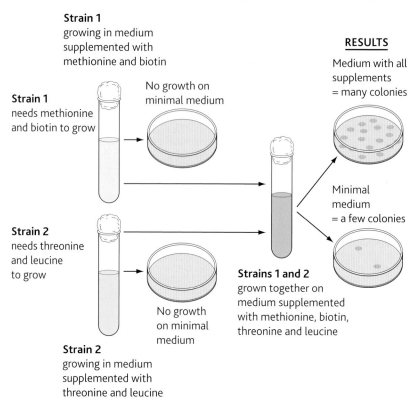

Strain 1
growing in medium supplemented with methionine and biotin

Strain 1
needs methionine and biotin to grow

No growth on minimal medium

RESULTS

Medium with all supplements = many colonies

Minimal medium = a few colonies

Strain 2
needs threonine and leucine to grow

No growth on minimal medium

Strains 1 and 2
grown together on medium supplemented with methionine, biotin, threonine and leucine

Strain 2
growing in medium supplemented with threonine and leucine

Figure 3 *Experiment to show transfer of DNA between two strains of* E. coli

1 Which of the strains of *E. coli* should grow on the medium that contained all the missing nutrients?

The bacteria were then removed from the medium by centrifugation (see Topic 3.1) and washed. Next they were transferred either to a medium with all the supplements or to a minimal medium without the supplements (methionine, biotin, threonine and leucine).

2 Which strains would you expect to grow on the minimal medium?

Lederberg and Tatum found that, while most cells did not grow, around 1 in 10 million did divide and develop into a colony of cells. The experiment and its results are summarised in Figure 3.

In further experiments, they were able to show that DNA had passed from one strain (the donor) to the other (the recipient) by conjugation.

3 What information had the DNA from the donor strain transferred to the recipient strain?

4 These further experiments were carried out to disprove explanations other than conjugation. Suggest one alternative explanation that might account for the growth of a few colonies on the minimal medium.

16.2 Antibiotics

Learning objectives:

- What are antibiotics and how do they work?

- How do bacteria become resistant to antibiotics?

- How is resistance passed on to subsequent generations and other species?

Specification reference: 3.2.10

The word 'antibiotic' is derived from Greek words meaning 'against life'. Antibiotics are substances produced by living organisms that can destroy or inhibit the growth of microorganisms. Although most are produced by bacteria, a few, such as penicillin, are made by fungi. The term 'antibiotic' is often used more loosely to include synthetic and semi-synthetic drugs that destroy microorganisms.

First discovered by Alexander Fleming in 1928, penicillin was the first antibiotic to be used to treat infections. Antibiotics have proved highly effective in the treatment of bacterial diseases. Indeed, they are so effective that one in every six prescriptions issued by doctors in the UK each year is for an antibiotic.

How antibiotics work

One way in which antibiotics work is by preventing bacteria from making normal cell walls.

In bacterial cells, as in plant cells, water constantly enters by osmosis (see Topic 3.7). This entry of water would normally cause the cell to burst – a process called **osmotic lysis**. That it doesn't burst is due to the wall that surrounds all bacterial cells. This wall is made of a tough material that is not easily stretched. As water enters the cell by osmosis, the contents expand and push against the cell wall. Being relatively inelastic, the cell wall resists expansion and so halts further entry of water. It thereby prevents osmotic lysis.

Certain antibiotics kill bacteria by preventing them forming cell walls. They inhibit the synthesis and assembly of important peptide cross-linkages in bacterial cell walls. This weakens the walls, making them unable to withstand pressure. As a result they are unable to prevent water entering and so osmotic lysis occurs, killing the bacterium. As these antibiotics inhibit the proper formation of cell walls, they are only effective when bacteria are growing. Penicillin is an antibiotic that works in this way. Viruses have a different covering from bacteria and so are not killed by antibiotics.

Antibiotic resistance

Shortly after the discovery of antibiotics it became apparent that the effectiveness of some antibiotics at killing bacteria was reduced. It was found that these populations of bacteria had developed resistance to antibiotics, such as penicillin. The resistance was due not to a build-up of tolerance to the antibiotic, but to a chance mutation within the bacteria. We saw in Topic 16.1 that a mutation is a change in DNA that results in different characteristics, usually resulting from a change to some protein. In the case of resistance to penicillin, the **mutation** resulted in certain bacteria being able to make a new protein. This new protein was an **enzyme** which broke down the antibiotic penicillin before it was able to kill the bacteria. The enzyme was given the name penicillinase.

It must be stressed that it is not the presence of antibiotics that causes bacteria to mutate. Mutations occur randomly and are very rare.

Figure 1 The use of many antibiotics in hospitals increases the chance of multiple resistance developing in bacteria

Hint

Preventing the formation of cross-linkages in bacterial cell walls is rather like removing the nails or screws from a wooden box. Without the linkages that hold it together any force applied to the box causes it to fall apart.

However, as there are so many bacteria around, the total number of mutations is large. Many of these mutations will be of no advantage to a bacterium. Indeed, most will be harmful, in which case the bacterium will probably die. Very occasionally a mutation will be advantageous. Even then it depends upon the circumstances. For example, a mutation that leads to the production of penicillinase is only an advantage when the bacterium is in the presence of penicillin. If this is the case, then the penicillin will kill all the normal bacteria without penicillinase, but not the mutant type with penicillinase. Only the mutant individual will survive and divide. This means that the bacteria produced from this survivor could be of the mutant type and will therefore be resistant to penicillin. The gene for penicillinase, and hence antibiotic resistance, is passed from one generation to the next, i.e. by **vertical gene transmission**. Consequently the resistant form is selected for rather than the non-resistant form when exposed to penicillin. These penicillin-resistant bacteria therefore gradually predominate in the population. The frequency of the **allele** for penicillin resistance increases in the population.

More significantly, the allele for antibiotic resistance is carried on the small circular loops of DNA called **plasmids**. As we saw in Topic 16.1 these plasmids can be transferred from cell to cell by **conjugation**. Resistance can therefore find its way into other bacterial species by **horizontal gene transmission**. Horizontal gene transmission can lead to certain bacteria accumulating DNA that gives them resistance to a range of antibiotics. These are the so-called 'superbugs'.

New mutations that give bacteria resistance to antibiotics arise randomly all the time. However, the more we use antibiotics, the greater the chance that the mutant bacterium will gain an advantage over the normal variety. In time, and with continued use of an antibiotic, the greater is the chance that the mutant will out-compete and replace the normal variety.

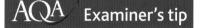

Examiner's tip

Remember that resistance is the result of a chance mutation. Mutations are rare events. If they were common, it is unlikely that any antibiotics would still be effective in treating disease.

Summary questions

1. What is an antibiotic?

2. Some antibiotics prevent the synthesis of cross-linkages in bacterial cell walls. Explain how this may lead to the death of a bacterium.

3. How is antibiotic resistance transferred from species to species?

4. Explain why antibiotic resistance is more likely to develop as more antibiotics are used.

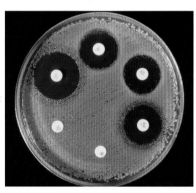

Figure 2 *Antibiotic resistance in* E. coli

Application

Identifying antibiotic-resistant bacteria

To identify which bacterial species have developed resistance to which antibiotics, the species under examination is spread on to a clear nutrient jelly in a dish called a Petri dish. At the same time, small discs, each possessing a different antibiotic, are placed on the jelly. As the bacteria grow they form a cloudy covering over the whole of the dish. The results of one such experiment, with *E. coli*, are shown in Figure 2.

1. To how many antibiotics is *E. coli* resistant? Explain your answer.

2. No bacteria have grown in the clear areas. What is a likely explanation for the absence of any growth?

3. The clear areas around some discs are larger than others. Suggest two possible reasons for this.

16.3 Antibiotic use and resistance

Learning objectives:

▓ How do strains of bacteria emerge that are resistant to many drugs?

▓ What are the implications of using antibiotics frequently?

▓ What are the problems in treating tuberculosis and MRSA?

Specification reference: 3.2.10

To many people, antibiotic resistance may not seem a big issue. Yet to an increasing number of scientists it is viewed as one of the world's most pressing health problems. To illustrate the point, let us look at antibiotic resistance in the treatment of two diseases – tuberculosis and methicillin-resistant *Staphylococcus aureus* (MRSA) infection.

▓ Antibiotic resistance and tuberculosis

We saw in Topic 4.4 that tuberculosis (TB) is a bacterial disease of the lungs. Its treatment involves the use of antibiotics. One problem with all antibiotic treatments for TB is the long period for which the antibiotics must be taken, often for 6–9 months. When individuals are ill, they willingly take the antibiotics as they are keen to recover. The antibiotics initially destroy the least resistant strains of *Mycobacterium* (the bacterium that causes TB). After a number of months the patients feel better because the vast majority of *Mycobacterium* have been killed. The temptation then is for patients to consider themselves cured and to stop taking the antibiotics. This is possibly the worst course of action because the few bacteria that remain are those that are most resistant to the antibiotic. These resistant strains of *Mycobacterium* survive, multiply and spread to others. There is therefore a selection pressure that leads to the development of strains of *Mycobacterium* that do not respond to the antibiotic. These strains can then interchange genes for resistance with other strains, by conjugation (i.e. horizontal gene transmission). It is in this way that multiple-antibiotic-resistant strains of TB have developed. To overcome the problem, a 'cocktail' of three or four antibiotics is used to ensure that at least one will be effective. Health workers often directly observe patients taking these antibiotics in order to ensure that they complete the course of treatment.

Figure 1 *One in every six prescriptions issued by doctors in the UK is for an antibiotic*

■ Antibiotic resistance and MRSA

Many people carry a bacterium belonging to the genus *Staphylococcus* in their throats. *Staphylococcus aureus* is a species that causes only minor symptoms in healthy individuals. If it becomes a major health risk, it can be cleared up with a treatment of antibiotics. MRSA (methicillin-resistant *Staphylococcus aureus*) is the name given to any strain of this bacterium that is resistant to one or more antibiotics. MRSA is especially prevalent in hospitals and can present a particular danger because:

■ people in hospital tend to be older, sicker and weaker than the general population, making them more vulnerable to the infection,

■ many people live close together and are examined by doctors and nurses who have just touched other patients. This is perfect for the **transmission** of infections,

■ many antibiotics are used in hospitals and, as a result, any mutant antibiotic-resistant strain of the bacterium has an advantage over non-mutant strains (see Topic 16.2). With many different antibiotics being used, strains can more easily develop multiple resistance to antibiotics.

MRSA is therefore very difficult to treat, not least because some strains have developed resistance to almost every known antibiotic.

Application and How science works

Implications of antibiotic use

The more widely antibiotics are used, the greater the risk that resistance will develop. Antibiotic resistance is on the increase for a number of reasons:

■ Antibiotics are used to treat minor ailments whose symptoms are trivial and/or short-lived.

■ Antibiotics are sometimes used to treat viral diseases because, although they are ineffective against viruses, they may help prevent the development of secondary bacterial infections to which patients may be vulnerable.

■ Patients do not always complete the course of antibiotics as prescribed.

■ Patients stockpile unused antibiotics from previous prescriptions and then take them later in smaller doses than they should.

■ Doctors accept patients' demands for antibiotic treatments, even when they are not absolutely necessary.

■ Antibiotics are used in the treatment of minor ailments in domesticated animals.

■ Antibiotics are used to prevent disease among intensively reared animals, such as chickens.

■ Antibiotics are used by farmers and companies to reduce disease and hence increase the productivity of animals.

This is an example of How science works (HSW: I and L).

Summary questions

1 Give a reason why a patient might stop taking antibiotics prematurely.

2 Why would patients with tuberculosis be more likely to stop taking antibiotics prematurely than patients with some other diseases?

3 Explain how multiple-drug-resistant strains of bacteria may develop.

4 Why are multiple-drug-resistant strains more likely to arise in hospitals?

Figure 2 *Antibiotics are used to prevent the spread of disease among intensively reared animals, such as chickens*

1. Use your knowledge of adaptation and selection to explain why failure to complete a course of antibiotics can lead to antibiotic resistance.

2. Antibiotics are used to reduce disease in cattle and hence improve milk yields. List the arguments for and against the use of antibiotics in this way.

Application and How science works

A dilemma

A hospital patient is terminally ill with a disease. The doctors, in consultation with the family, have withdrawn treatment as it will no longer cure the patient nor increase life-expectancy. The patient has recently become infected with the bacterium *Clostridium difficile*. The symptoms caused by *C. difficile* include severe diarrhoea. This is causing some discomfort and the embarrassment of the diarrhoea is distressing the patient. The condition can be treated with antibiotics. However *C. difficile* has developed resistance to almost every known antibiotic. There is just one remaining antibiotic that is known to be still effective against it.

1. Using your knowledge of antibiotic resistance, consider the ethical and scientific issues involved here. Then draw up a table listing the arguments both for and against treating this patient with the remaining effective antibiotic. This will help with How science works (HSW: J and L).

17 Biodiversity

17.1 Species diversity

Learning objectives:

- What do we understand by species diversity?
- How is Simpson's Diversity Index used as a measure of species diversity?

Specification reference: 3.2.11

Figure 1 *In a tropical rainforest there is high species diversity*

Figure 2 *In the sub-arctic tundra there is low species diversity*

Throughout this unit we have considered the variety of living organisms. **Biodiversity** is the general term used to describe variety in the living world. It refers to the number and variety of living organisms in a particular area and has three components:

- **Species diversity** refers to the number of different species and the number of individuals of each species within any one **community**.
- **Genetic diversity** refers to the variety of genes possessed by the individuals that make up any one species.
- **Ecosystem diversity** refers to the range of different **habitats** within a particular area.

One measure of biodiversity is species diversity. It has two components:

- the number of different species in a given area
- the proportion of the community that is made up of an individual species.

Two communities may have the same number of species but the proportions of the community made up of each species may differ markedly. For example, a natural meadow and a field of wheat may both have 25 species. However, in the meadow, all 25 species might be equally abundant, whereas, in the wheat field, over 95 per cent of the plants may be a single species of wheat.

⚗ Measuring species diversity

Consider the data shown in Table 1 about two different **habitats**. It does not tell us much about the differences between the two habitats because, in both cases, the total number of species and the total number of individuals are identical. However, if we measure the species diversity, we get a different picture.

Table 1 *Number and types of species found in two different habitats within the same ecosystem*

Species found	Numbers found in habitat X	Numbers found in habitat Y
A	10	3
B	10	5
C	10	2
D	10	36
E	10	4
No. of species	5	5
No. of individuals	50	50

One way of measuring species diversity is to use an index that is calculated as follows:

$$d = \frac{N(N-1)}{\Sigma n(n-1)}$$

Where:

d = species diversity index

N = total number of organisms of all species

n = total number of organisms of each species

Σ = the sum of

To use the index to calculate the species diversity of the two habitats we must first calculate $n\,(n-1)$ for each species in each habitat. We can then calculate the sum of $n(n-1)$ for each species. These calculations are shown in Table 2.

Table 2 *Calculation of $n(n-1)$ and $\Sigma n(n-1)$ for habitats X and Y*

Species	Numbers (n) found in habitat X	$n(n-1)$	Numbers (n) found in habitat Y	$n(n-1)$
A	10	10(9) = **90**	3	3(2) = **6**
B	10	10(9) = **90**	5	5(4) = **20**
C	10	10(9) = **90**	2	2(1) = **2**
D	10	10(9) = **90**	36	36(35) =**1260**
E	10	10(9) = **90**	4	4(3) = **12**
	$\Sigma n(n-1)$	450	$\Sigma n(n-1)$	1300

We can now calculate the species diversity index for each habitat.

Habitat X: $\quad d = \dfrac{50(49)}{450} = \dfrac{2450}{450} = 5.44$

Habitat Y: $\quad d = \dfrac{50(49)}{1300} = \dfrac{2450}{1300} = 1.88$

The higher the value d, the greater is the species diversity. So, in this case, although the total number of species and the total number of individuals are the same in both habitats, the species diversity of habitat X is much greater.

Application

Species diversity and ecosystems

Biodiversity reflects how well an **ecosystem** functions. The higher the species diversity index, the more stable an ecosystem usually is and the less it is affected by climate change. For example, if there is a drought, a community with a high species diversity index is much more likely to have at least one species able to tolerate drought than a community with a low species diversity index. At least some members are therefore likely to survive the drought and maintain the community.

In extreme environments, such as hot deserts, only a few species have the necessary adaptations to survive the harsh conditions. The species diversity index is therefore normally low. This usually results in an unstable ecosystem in which communities are dominated by climatic factors rather than by the organisms within the

Hint

Calculating a species diversity index provides a number that makes it easier to compare the variety in different habitats. It would be so much harder, and less precise, if we had to rely on descriptions of different habitats to make these comparisons.

Summary questions

1 What is meant by species diversity?

2 Table 3 shows the numbers of each of six species of plant found in a salt-marsh community. Calculate the species diversity index for this salt-marsh community using the formula shown earlier. Show your working.

Table 3

Species	Numbers in salt marsh
Salicornia maritima	24
Halimione portulacoides	20
Festuca rubra	7
Aster tripolium	3
Limonium humile	3
Suaeda maritima	1

3 Explain why it is more useful to calculate a species diversity index than just to record the number of species present.

community. In less hostile environments, the species diversity index is normally high. This usually results in a stable ecosystem in which communities are dominated by living organisms rather than climate.

1 Scientists believe that the production of greenhouse gases by human activities is contributing to climate change. Explain why an increase in greenhouse gases is more likely to result in damage to communities with a low species diversity index than communities with a high index.

Key
— Community with low species diversity
— Community with high species diversity
— Environmental change

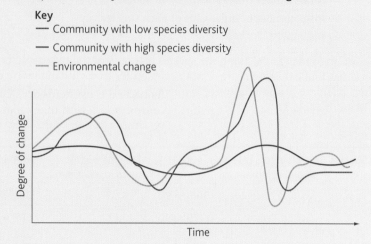

Figure 3

2 The graph in Figure 3 shows the effect of environmental change on the stability and the functioning of ecosystems.

a Describe the relationship between environmental change and the community with a low species diversity index.

b Explain the different responses to environmental change in communities with a low and a high species diversity.

Figure 4 *In harsh environments, like this hot desert, only a few species are adapted to survive the extreme conditions and therefore species diversity is low*

17.2 Species diversity and human activities

Learning objectives:

■ What is the influence of deforestation and the impact of agriculture on species diversity?

Specification reference: 3.2.11

In our efforts to provide enough food for the human population at a low cost, mankind has had a considerable impact on the natural world. This impact has led to a reduction in **biodiversity**. In this topic we will look at how two human activities, agriculture and deforestation, have reduced species diversity.

Impact of agriculture

As natural ecosystems develop over time, they become complex **communities** with many individuals of a large number of different species. In other words, these communities have a high species diversity index. Agricultural **ecosystems** are controlled by humans and are different. We saw in Topic 9.1 that farmers select species for particular qualities that make them more productive. As a result the number of species, and the genetic variety of **alleles** they possess, is reduced to the few that exhibit the desired features. To be economic, the numbers of these desirable species needs to be large. Any particular area can only support a certain amount of **biomass**. If most of the area is taken up by the one species that the farmer considers desirable, it follows that there is a smaller area available for all the other species. These many other species have to compete for what little space and resources are available. Many will not survive this competition. In addition, pesticides are used to exclude these species because they compete for the light, mineral ions, water and food required by the farmed species. The overall effect is a reduction in species diversity. The species diversity index is therefore low in agricultural ecosystems.

Figure 1 *High species diversity in a hay meadow*

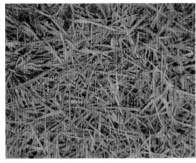

Figure 2 *Low species diversity in a field grown for silage*

Impact of deforestation

Forests are the natural vegetation over much of the Earth. Without human intervention, they would, and once did, cover much of the planet. As forests form many layers between the ground and the tops of the trees, there are numerous habitats available. Many different species are adapted to living in these different habitats and species diversity is therefore high. Indeed, the tropical rainforests have the highest species diversity of any ecosystem. While some deforestation is the result of accidental fires, the vast majority is due to deliberate human actions. Deforestation is the permanent clearing of forests and the conversion of the land to other uses, such as agriculture, grazing, housing and reservoirs. In addition, some forests have been destroyed as a result of man-made pollutants producing acid rain.

The most serious consequence of deforestation is the loss of biodiversity. Some estimates suggest that up to 50 000 species are being lost each year due to deforestation. It is in the tropical rainforests that the loss is greatest. Despite covering only 7 per cent of the Earth's surface, tropical rainforests account for half of all its species. The replacement of these and other forests by agriculture, housing or reservoirs has considerably reduced species diversity. Even where areas are reforested there is still an overall loss of species diversity as the new forests grown for commercial purposes have just a few predominant tree types.

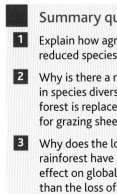

Summary questions

1 Explain how agriculture has reduced species diversity.

2 Why is there a reduction in species diversity when a forest is replaced by grassland for grazing sheep or cattle?

3 Why does the loss of tropical rainforest have a greater effect on global biodiversity than the loss of any other ecosystem?

Figure 3 *Deforestation*

Application and How science works

Human activity and loss of species in the UK

The present rate of species extinction is thought to be between 100 and 1000 times greater than at any time in evolutionary history. The main cause of species loss is the clearance of land in order to grow crops and meet the demand for food from an ever-increasing human population. An area of rainforest roughly the size of the UK is cleared every year. Throughout the world habitats are being lost. Most of this habitat loss has entailed the replacement of natural communities of high species diversity with agricultural ones of low species diversity. The conservation agencies in the UK have made estimates of the percentage of various habitats that have been lost in the UK since 1900. These estimates are shown in Table 1. This is an example of How science works (HSW: I and L).

Figure 4 *Heathland (left) and mixed woodland (right)*

Table 1

Habitat	Habitat loss since 1900/%	Main reason for habitat loss
Hay meadow	95	Conversion to highly productive grass and silage
Chalk grassland	80	Conversion to highly productive grass and silage
Lowland fens and wetlands	50	Drainage and reclamation of land for agriculture
Limestone pavements in England	45	Removal for sale as rockery stone
Lowland heaths on acid soils	40	Conversion to grasslands and commercial forests
Lowland mixed woodland	40	Conversion to commercial conifer plantations and farmland
Hedgerows	30	To make larger fields to accommodate farm machinery

1 There are currently approximately 350 000 km of hedgerow in the UK. How many kilometres were there in 1900?

2 Some lowland mixed woodlands have been replaced by other woodland. Explain how this change might still result in a lower species diversity.

3 Suggest one benefit and one risk associated with the conversion of hay meadows and chalk grasslands to highly productive grass and silage.

4 In what ways might the information in the table be used to inform decision-making on preserving habitats and biodiversity?

5 The European Union gives grants to farmers to replant hedges. Explain how replanting hedges might affect the species diversity found on farms.

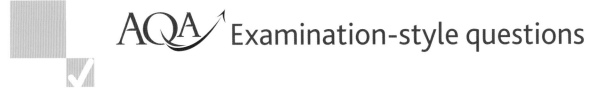

AQA Examination-style questions

Chapter 16 Adaptation and selection

1 *Staphylococcus aureus* is a species of bacteria found in the throat of many people. It can be killed by treatment with antibiotics. MRSA (methicillin-resistant *Staphylococcus aureus*) is the name given to any strain of this bacterium that is resitant to one or more antibiotics.

MRSA infections are more harmful to hospital patients.

(a) Transmission of this infection is more likely in hospitals. Give two reasons why. *(2 marks)*

Figure 1 shows the changes in the number of MRSA infections per 1000 population between January 2003 and December 2006.

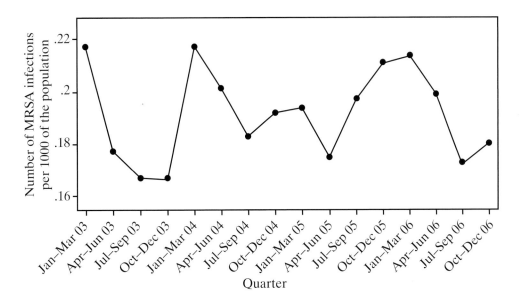

Figure 1

(b) (i) Describe the changes shown in the graph.
    (ii) One reason for the changes shown in the graph is that the bacteria become resistant to an antibiotic. Expain how bacteria can become resistant to an antibiotic. *(6 marks)*

Chapter 17 Biodiversity

1   Lacewings are insects that feed on aphids and mites, which are crop pests. The numbers of six species of lacewings, A to F, were counted on samples of apple and strawberry crops. The results are shown in the table.

Crop	Number of adults of each species of lacewing						Diversity index
	A	B	C	D	E	F	
Strawberry	31	0	3	29	17	1	3.2
Apple	10	1	1	7	0	1	

The diversity index (d) is obtained from the formula

$$d = \frac{N(N-1)}{\Sigma n\,(n-1)}$$

where N is the total number of organisms of all species

and n is the total number of organisms of each species.

(a) Calculate the diversity index for lacewing species in the apple crop and note the figure. Show your working.   *(2 marks)*

(b) Suggest **one** reason why the diversity index for the lacewings is different between the two crops.   *(1 mark)*

AQA, 2004

2   Deforestation often involves clearing large areas of forest for use as agricultural land. Deforestation reduces the diversity index of an area cleared in this way. Explain why.   *(2 marks)*

AQA, 2005

3   The Solomon Islands are situated in the Pacific Ocean. The nearest large land mass is Australia, which is about 1500 km away. The biggest islands are mountainous, with large areas of tropical forest and a wide range of habitats. Some islands have a very high species diversity, and many species are endemic, that is they occur only in the Solomon Islands. The table shows the total number of species on the islands in four vertebrate classes and the percentage which are endemic.

Vertebrate class	Total number of species	Endemic species / %
Mammals	53	36
Birds	223	20
Reptiles	31	13
Amphibians	17	53

(a) How many reptile species are endemic?   *(1 mark)*

(b) Suggest an explanation for the high proportion of endemic species on the Solomon Islands.   *(3 marks)*

AQA, 2004

4   **Figure 1** shows a transect across a sand-dune ecosystem.

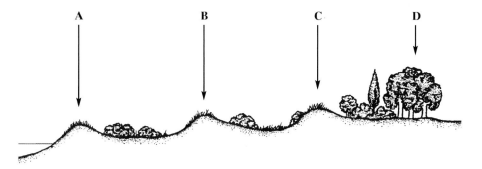

Figure 1

Species	Number of plants in sample
Marram grass	40
Ling	9
Bell heather	4
Gorse	1

The data in the table were obtained from a sample of quadrats taken at position B on the transect. The index of diversity may be calculated from the formula

$$d = \frac{N(N-1)}{\Sigma n\,(n-1)}$$

Where N = total number of organisms of all species

And n = total number of organisms of each species

(a) Use the data in the table to calculate the index of diversity for this sample. Show your working.   *(2 marks)*

(b) Explain why the value of the index of diversity increases along the transect from position **A** to position **D**.   *(1 mark)*

AQA, 2003

5   The table shows the numbers of adult butterflies in two areas of the same tropical forest. In the logged area some trees had been cut down for timber. In the virgin forest no trees had been cut down. The two areas were the same size.

Butterfly species	Logged forest		Virgin forest	
	Number	$n(n-1)$	**Number**	$n(n-1)$
Eurema tiluba	72	5112	19	342
Cirrochroa emalea	43	1806	132	17 292
Partenos sylvia	58	3306	14	182
Neopithecops zalmora	6	30	79	6162
Jamides para	37	1332	38	1406
Total	216	11 586	282	25 384

(a) The index of diversity of a forest can be calculated using the equation

$$d = \frac{N(N-1)}{\Sigma n\,(n-1)}$$

Calculate the index of diversity for the virgin forest. Show your working.   *(2 marks)*

(b) What does the table show about the effects of logging on the butterfly populations?   *(2 marks)*

AQA, 2006

Unit 2 questions: The variety of living organisms

1 Natural woodlands, which once covered 80% of Britain, are stable ecosystems with high levels of diversity. These natural woodlands were dominated by a range of species, such as oak and ash, which lose their leaves in winter. Much of today's woodland consists of evergreen conifer plantations. Conifers are grown for timber. They are planted close together in straight lines. The trees are usually of the same age and the same species.

    (a) Explain why the diversity of animals is higher in natural woodland than in conifer plantations. *(4 marks)*

    (b) The conifers used in plantations are the result of a long period of selection for desirable characteristics. Explain how a programme of selection might affect the variety of alleles in a population. *(4 marks)*

AQA, 2006

2   (a) Yarrow is a herbaceous plant which grows in California at altitudes from 1500 m to 3000 m. The mean height of the stems of plants growing at 3000 m is smaller than that of plants growing at 1500 m. The higher the altitude, the lower the mean temperature. Explain how the lower temperature at high altitude reduces the growth of plants. *(4 marks)*

    (b) The relative contribution of environmental and genetic factors on the growth of the plants was investigated. Samples of young plants were taken and grown outdoors in prepared plots at altitudes of 1500 m and 3000 m.

Altitude at which young plants were collected / m	Mean maximum height of stems of plants / cm	
	Grown at 1500 m	Grown at 3000 m
1500	80.4	35.3
3000	31.5	24.7

    Describe the evidence from the table that the variation in height is:

    (i) partly genetically determined;

    (ii) partly environmentally determined. *(2 marks)*

AQA, 2006

3 **Figure 1** shows part of a DNA molecule in the process of replication.

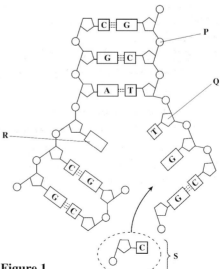

Figure 1

(a) Name parts P, Q,R and S. *(4 marks)*

(b) Which enzyme joins part S to the new DNA strand? *(1 mark)*

(c) During which stage of the cell cycle does DNA replication occur? *(1 mark)*

AQA, 2003

4 **Figure 2** shows the life cycle of a fungus. In favourable environmental conditions the fungus reproduces asexually but, when conditions worsen, sexual reproduction occurs. The advantage of sexual reproduction is that it introduces variation.

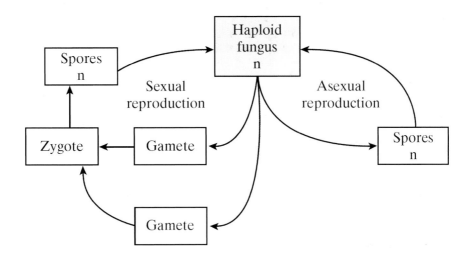

Figure 2

(a) On a copy of the diagram, mark with an X where meiosis occurs. *(1 mark)*

(b) Give **two** ways in which meiosis produces variation. *(2 marks)*

(c) Suggest **one** advantage of sexual reproduction being stimulated by worsening environmental conditions *(1 mark)*

AQA, 2003

5 (a) Describe how water is moved through a plant according to the cohesion–tension hypothesis. *(4 marks)*

(b) The mass of water lost from a plant was investigated. The same plant was used in every treatment and the plant was subjected to identical environmental conditions. In some treatments, the leaves were coated with a type of grease. This grease provides a waterproof barrier. The results of the investigation are given in the table.

Treatment	Mass lost in 5 days / g
No grease applied	10.0
Grease applied only to the upper surface of every leaf	8.7
Grease applied to both surfaces of every leaf	0.1

   (i) What is the advantage of using the same plant in every treatment?

   (ii) Why was it important to keep the environmental conditions constant?

   (iii) What is the evidence that the grease provides a waterproof barrier? *(3 marks)*

(c) (i) Calculate the mass of water lost in 5 days through the upper surface of the leaves.

   (ii) Use your knowledge of leaf structure to explain why less water is lost through the upper surface of leaves than is lost through the lower surface. *(3 marks)*

AQA, 2005

6 **Figure 3** shows some cells from the tissues in a root.

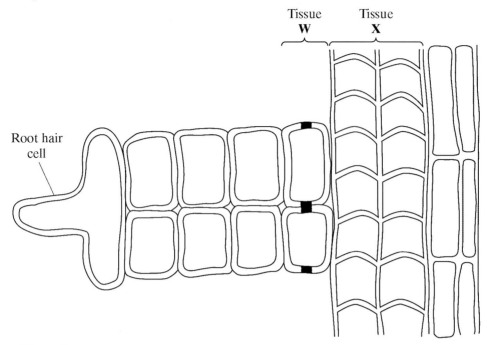

Figure 3

    (a) Name the tissues labelled W and X. *(2 marks)*

    (b) Explain why water moves from the apoplast pathway to the symplast pathway when it reaches the tissue labelled W. *(2 marks)*

AQA, 2005

7 (a) Explain how blood capillaries are adapted for their function of gas exchange. *(4 marks)*

    (b) Describe how haemoglobin is involved in absorbing oxygen in the lungs and transporting it to respiring tissues. *(6 marks)*

AQA, 2003

8 (a) Describe **three** features of all members of the animal kingdom which are absent from all members of the plant kingdom. *(3 marks)*

    (b) *Ensatina eschscholtzi* is a species of salamander, a type of amphibian.

        Copy and complete the table to show the classification of this salamander.

Taxonomic group	Name
Kingdom	Animalia
	Chordata
	Amphibia
	Urodela
	Plethodontidae
Genus	
Species	

(2 marks)

    (c) In California there are different types of *Ensatina eschscholtzi*, each with a characteristic appearance and found in its own area. They are sufficiently different from each other to be classified as subspecies. These may become new species with time.

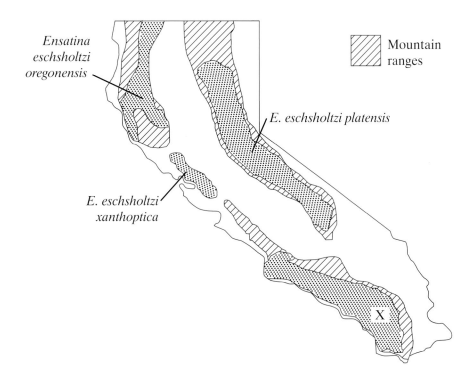

Figure 4

  (i) Suggest **one** way in which scientists could find out whether the salamanders from the area marked X were a different species from those found in other areas.

  (ii) Within each subspecies there is a range of types. Explain the factors that give rise to this variation. *(6 marks)*

AQA, 2003

9   (a) In a hospital laboratory, a sterile Petri dish of nutrient agar was inoculated with bacteria from a patient with a throat infection. Three discs, each of which had been soaked in a different antibiotic, were placed on top of the bacteria. The dish was incubated at 37 °C. **Figure 5** shows the appearance of the dish after incubation.

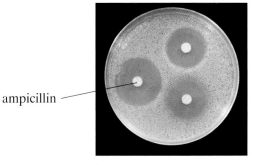

ampicillin

Figure 5

      Explain why there are clear zones around some of the discs containing antibiotic. *(2 marks)*

    (b) It was suggested that ampicillin might be the best antibiotic to treat the patient's throat infection. Give the evidence from the laboratory test to support this suggestion. *(1 mark)*

AQA, 2005

10   Some antibiotics bind with specific receptors in the cell-surface membranes of bacteria. The structure of these receptors is determined genetically. Bacteria can become resistant to an antibiotic because a gene mutation results in an altered receptor.

Explain how resistance to an antibiotic could become widespread in a bacterial population following a gene mutation conferring resistance in just one bacterium. *(5 marks)*

AQA, 2005

Glossary

A

activation energy: energy required to bring about a reaction. The activation energy is lowered by the presence of *enzymes*.

active immunity: resistance to disease resulting from the activities of an individual's own immune system whereby an *antigen* induces plasma cells to produce *antibodies*.

active site: a group of amino acids that makes up the region of an *enzyme* into which the *substrate* fits in order to catalyse a reaction.

active transport: movement of a substance from a region where it is in a low concentration to a region where it is in a high concentration. The process requires the expenditure of *metabolic* energy.

aerobic: connected with the presence of free oxygen. Aerobic respiration requires free oxygen to release energy from glucose. See also *anaerobic*.

allele: one of a number of alternative forms of a *gene*. For example, the gene for the shape of pea seeds has two alleles: one for 'round' and one for 'wrinkled'.

allergen: a normally harmless substance that causes the immune system to produce an immune response. See also *allergy*.

allergy: the response of the immune system to an *allergen*. Examples include hay fever and *asthma*.

antibiotic: a substance produced by living organisms that can destroy or inhibit the growth of microorganisms.

antibiotic resistance: the development in microorganisms of mechanisms that prevent *antibiotics* from killing them.

antibody: a protein produced by *lymphocytes* in response to the presence of the appropriate antigen.

antigen: a molecule that triggers an immune response by *lymphocytes*.

antioxidant: chemical which reduces or prevents *oxidation*. Often used as an additive to prolong the shelf-life of certain foods.

apoplastic pathway: route through the cell walls and intercellular spaces of plants by which water and dissolved substances are transported. See also *symplastic pathway*.

artificial selection: breeding of organisms by human selection of parents/gametes in order to perpetuate certain characteristics and/or to eliminate others.

asthma: a chronic illness in which there is resistance to air flow to the alveoli of the lungs as a result of the airways becoming inflamed due to an allergic response to an *allergen*.

atheroma: fatty deposits in the walls of arteries, often associated with high *cholesterol* levels in the blood.

ATP (adenosine triphosphate): *nucleotide* found in all living organisms, which is produced during respiration and is important in the transfer of energy.

B

B cell (B lymphocyte): type of white blood cell that is produced and matures within the bone marrow. B lymphocytes produce *antibodies* as part of their role in *immunity*. See also *T cell*.

Benedict's test: a simple biochemical reaction to detect the presence of reducing sugars.

biodiversity: the range and variety of genes, species and habitats within a particular region.

biomass: the total mass of living material, normally measured in a specific area over a given period of time.

Biuret test: a simple biochemical reaction to detect the presence of protein.

body mass index (BMI): a person's body mass in kilograms divided by the square of their height in metres.

C

cancer: a disease, resulting from mutations, that leads to uncontrolled cell division and the eventual formation of a group of abnormal cells called a *tumour*, from which cells may break away and form secondary tumours elsewhere in the body.

carcinogen: a chemical, a form of radiation, or other agent that causes *cancer*.

cardiac cycle: a continuous series of events which make up a single heart beat.

cardiac output: the total volume of blood that the heart can pump each minute. It is calculated as the volume of blood pumped at each beat (*stroke volume*) multiplied by the number of heart beats per minute (heart rate).

carrier molecule (carrier protein): a protein on the surface of a cell that helps to transport molecules and ions across plasma membranes.

Casparian strip: a distinctive band of suberin around the endodermal cells of a plant root that prevents water passing into xylem via the cell walls. The water is forced through the living part (*protoplast*) of the endodermal cells.

centrifugation: process of separating out particles of different sizes and densities by spinning them at high speed in a centrifuge.

cholesterol: lipid that is an important component of cell-surface membranes. Excess in the blood can lead to *atheroma*.

chromatid: one of the two copies of a *chromosome* that are joined together by a single centromere prior to cell division.

chromosome: a thread-like structure made of protein and DNA by which hereditary information is physically passed from one generation to the next.

clone: a group of genetically identical cells or organisms formed from a single parent as the result of asexual reproduction or by artificial means.

cohesion: attraction between molecules of the same type. It is important in the movement of water up a plant.

collagen: fibrous protein that is the main constituent of connective tissues such as tendons, cartilage and bone.

community: all the living organisms present in an *ecosystem* at a given time.

complementary DNA: DNA that is made from messenger RNA in a process that is the reverse of normal transcription.

condensation: chemical process in which two molecules combine to form a more complex one with the elimination of a simple substance, usually water. Many biological *polymers*, such as polysaccharides and polypeptides, are formed by condensation. See also *hydrolysis*.

conjugation: the transfer of DNA from one cell to another by means of a thin tube between the two.

continuous variation: variation in which organisms do not fall into distinct categories but show gradations from one extreme to the other.

coronary arteries: arteries that supply blood to the cardiac muscle of the heart.

coronary heart disease (CHD): any condition, e.g. *atheroma* and *thrombosis*, affecting the coronary arteries that supply heart muscle.

correlation: when a change in one variable is reflected by a change in the second variable.

countercurrent system: a mechanism by which the efficiency of exchange between two substances is increased by having them flowing in opposite directions.

covalent bond: type of chemical bond in which two atoms share a pair of *electrons*, one from each atom.

crossing over: the process whereby a *chromatid* breaks during *meiosis* and rejoins to the chromatid of its *homologous chromosome* so that their *alleles* are exchanged.

D

denaturation: permanent changes due to the unravelling of the three-dimensional structure of a protein as a result of factors such as changes in temperature or pH.

diastole: the stage in the *cardiac cycle* when the heart muscle relaxes. See also *systole*.

dicotyledonous plants: any member of the class of flowering plants called Dicotyledonae. Their features include having two seed leaves (cotyledons) and broad leaves.

differentiation: the process by which cells become specialised for different functions.

diffusion: the movement of molecules or ions from a region where they are in high concentration to one where their concentration is lower.

diploid: a term applied to cells in which the nucleus contains two sets of *chromosomes*. See also *haploid*.

discontinuous variation: variation shown when the characters of organisms fall into distinct categories.

E

ecological niche: describes how an organism fits into its environment. It describes what a species is like, where it occurs, how it behaves, its interactions with other species and how it responds to its environment.

ecosystem: all the living and non-living components of a particular area.

electron: negatively charged sub-atomic particle that orbits the positively charged nucleus of all atoms.

emphysema: a disease in which the walls of the alveoli break down, reducing the surface area for gaseous exchange, thereby causing breathlessness in the patient.

enzyme: a protein or RNA that acts as a catalyst and so alters the speed of a biochemical reaction.

epidemiology: the study of the spread of disease and the factors that affect this spread.

eukaryotic cell: a cell that has a membrane-bound nucleus and *chromosomes*. The cell also possesses a variety of other membranous organelles, such as mitochondria and endoplasmic reticulum. See also *prokaryotic cell*.

F

facilitated diffusion: diffusion involving the presence of protein *carrier molecules* to allow the passive movement of substances across plasma membranes.

G

gamete: reproductive (sex) cell that fuses with another gamete during fertilisation.

gene: section of DNA on a *chromosome* coding for one or more polypeptides.

gene pool: the total number of *alleles* in a particular population at a specific time.

H

habitat: the place where an organism normally lives and which is characterised by physical conditions and the types of other organisms present.

haemoglobin: globular protein in blood that readily combines with oxygen to transport it around the body. It comprises four polypeptide chains around an iron-containing haem group.

haploid: term referring to cells that contain only a single copy of each *chromosome*, e.g. the sex cells (*gametes*).

high-density lipoprotein (HDL): a compound of protein and lipid molecules found in blood plasma. It transports cholesterol from other cells to the liver. See also *low-density lipoprotein*.

histamine: substance released on tissue injury that causes dilation of blood vessels.

homologous chromosomes: a pair of *chromosomes*, one maternal and one paternal, that have the same gene *loci* and therefore determine the same features. They are not necessarily identical, however, as individual *alleles* of the same *gene* may vary, e.g. one chromosome may carry the allele for blue eyes, the other the allele for brown eyes. Homologous chromosomes are capable of pairing during *meiosis*.

human genome: the totality of the DNA sequences on the *chromosomes* of a single human cell.

hydrogen bond: chemical bond formed between the positive charge on a hydrogen atom and the negative charge on another atom of an adjacent molecule, e.g. between the hydrogen atom of one water molecule and the oxygen atom of an adjacent water molecule.

hydrolysis: the breaking down of large molecules into smaller ones by the addition of water molecules. See also *condensation*.

I

immunity: the means by which the body protects itself from infection.

interspecific variation: differences between organisms of different species.

intraspecific variation: differences between organisms of the same species.

ion: an atom or group of atoms that has lost or gained one or more *electrons*. Ions therefore have either a positive or negative charge.

ion channel: a passage across a cell-surface membrane made up of a protein that spans the membrane and opens and closes to allow *ions* to pass in and out of the cell.

isotonic: solutions that possess the same concentration of solutes and therefore have the same *water potential*.

isotope: variations of a chemical element that have the same number of protons and *electrons* but different numbers of neutrons. While their chemical properties are similar they differ in mass. One example is carbon which has a relative atomic mass of 12 and an isotope with a relative atomic mass of 14.

K

kinetic energy: energy that an object possesses due to its motion.

L

locus: the position of a gene on a *chromosome*/DNA molecule.

low-density lipoprotein (LDL): a compound containing both protein and lipid molecules that occurs in blood plasma and *lymph*. It carries cholesterol from the liver to other cells in the body. See also *high-density lipoprotein*.

lumen: the hollow cavity inside a tubular structure such as the gut or a *xylem vessel*.

lymph: a slightly milky fluid found in lymph vessels and made up of *tissue fluid*, fats and *lymphocytes*.

lymphocytes: types of white blood cell responsible for the immune response. They become activated in the presence of *antigens*. There are two types: *B lymphocytes* and *T lymphocytes*.

M

meiosis: the type of nuclear division in which the number of *chromosomes* is halved. See also *mitosis*.

mesophyll: tissue found between the two layers of epidermis in a plant leaf comprising an upper layer of *palisade cells* and a lower layer of spongy cells.

metabolism: all the chemical processes that take place in living organisms.

microvilli: tiny finger-like projections from the cell-surface membrane of some animal cells.

middle lamella: layer made up of pectins and other substances found between the walls of adjacent plant cells.

mitosis: the type of nuclear division in which the daughter cells have the same number of *chromosomes* as the parent cell. See also *meiosis*.

monomer: one of many small molecules that combine to form a larger one known as a *polymer*.

mono-unsaturated fatty acid: fatty acid that possesses a carbon chain with a single double bond. See also *polyunsaturated fatty acid*.

mutation: a sudden change in the amount or the arrangement of the genetic material in the cell.

myocardial infarction: otherwise known as a heart attack, results from the interruption of the blood supply to the heart muscle, causing damage to an area of the heart with consequent disruption to its function.

N

nucleotides: complex chemicals made up of an organic base, a sugar and a phosphate. They are the basic units of which the nucleic acids DNA and RNA are made.

O

oral rehydration solution (ORS): means of treating dehydration involving giving, by mouth, a balanced solution of salts and glucose that stimulates the gut to reabsorb water.

osmosis: the passage of water from a region of high *water potential* to a region where its *water potential* is lower, through a partially permeable membrane.

osteoarthritis: degeneration of the cartilage of the joints, causing pain and stiffness of these joints.

oxidation: chemical reaction involving the loss of *electrons*.

P

palisade cells: long, narrow cells, packed with chloroplasts, that are found in the upper region of a leaf and which carry out photosynthesis.

passive immunity: resistance to disease that is acquired from the introduction of *antibodies* from another individual, rather than an individual's own immune system, e.g. across the placenta or in the mother's milk. It is usually short-lived.

pathogen: any microorganism that causes disease.

peptide bond: the chemical bond formed between two amino acids during *condensation*.

phagocytosis: mechanism by which cells engulf particles to form a vesicle or a vacuole.

phospholipid: triglycerides in which one of the three fatty acid molecules is replaced by a phosphate molecule. Phospholipids are important in the structure and functioning of the membranes.

photomicrograph: photograph of an image produced by a microscope.

plasmid: a small circular piece of DNA found in bacterial cells.

plasmodesmata: fine strands of cytoplasm that extend through pores in adjacent plant cell walls and connect the cytoplasm of one cell with another.

plasmolysis: the shrinkage of cytoplasm away from the cell wall that occurs as a plant cell loses water by *osmosis*.

polymer: large molecule made up of repeating smaller molecules (*monomers*).

polymerases: group of enzymes that catalyse the formation of long-chain molecules (*polymers*) from similar basic units (*monomers*).

polyunsaturated fatty acid (PUFA): fatty acid that possesses carbon chains with many double bonds. See also *mono-unsaturated fatty acid*.

primary structure of a protein: the sequence of amino acids that makes up the polypeptides of a protein.

prokaryotic cell: a cell of an organism belonging to the kingdom Prokaryotae that is characterised by lacking a nucleus and membrane-bound organelles. Examples include bacteria. See also *eukaryotic cell*.

protoplast: the living portion of a plant cell, i.e. the nucleus and cytoplasm along with the organelles it contains.

Q

quaternary structure of a protein: a number of polypeptide chains linked together, and sometimes associated with non-protein groups, to form a protein.

R

reduction: chemical process involving the gain of *electrons*.

S

saturated fatty acid: a fatty acid in which there are no double bonds between the carbon atoms.

secondary structure of a protein: the way in which the chain of amino acids of the polypeptides of a protein is folded.

selective breeding: see *artificial selection*.

semi-conservative replication: the means by which DNA makes exact copies of itself by unwinding the double helix so that each chain acts as a template for the next. The new copies therefore possess one original and one new strand of DNA.

serum: clear liquid that is left after blood has clotted and the clot has been removed. It is therefore blood plasma without the clotting factors.

sinoatrial node (SAN): an area of heart muscle in the right atrium that controls and coordinates the contraction of the heart. Also known as the pacemaker.

species: a group of similar organisms that can breed together to produce fertile offspring.

stoma (plural stomata): pore, mostly in the lower epidermis of a leaf, through which gases diffuse in and out of the leaf.

stroke volume: the volume of blood pumped at each ventricular contraction of the heart.

substrate: a substance that is acted on or used by another substance or process. In microbiology, the nutrient medium used to grow microorganisms.

supernatant liquid: the liquid portion of a mixture left at the top of the tube when suspended particles have been separated out at the bottom during *centrifugation*.

symplastic pathway: route through the cytoplasm and *plasmodesmata* of plant cells by which water and dissolved substances are transported. See also *apoplastic pathway*.

systole: the stage in the *cardiac cycle* in which the heart muscle contracts. It occurs in two stages: atrial systole when the atria contract and ventricular systole when the ventricles contact. See also *diastole*.

T

tertiary structure of a protein: the folding of a whole polypeptide chain in a precise way, as determined by the amino acids of which it is composed.

thrombosis: formation of a blood clot within a blood vessel that may lead to a blockage.

tidal volume: the volume of air breathed in and out during a single breath when at rest.

tissue: a group of similar cells organised into a structural unit that serves a particular function.

tissue fluid: fluid that surrounds the cells of the body. Its composition is similar to that of blood plasma except that it lacks proteins. It supplies nutrients to the cells and removes waste products.

T cell (T lymphocyte): type of white blood cell that is produced in the bone marrow but matures in the thymus gland. T lymphocytes coordinate the immune response and kill infected cells. See also *B cell*.

transmission: the transfer of a *pathogen* from one individual to another.

transpiration: evaporation of water from a plant.

triglyceride: an individual lipid molecule made up of a glycerol molecule and three fatty acids.

tumour: a swelling in an organism that is made up of cells that continue to divide in an abnormal way.

turgid: a plant cell that is full of water. Additional entry of water is prevented by the cell wall stopping further expansion of the cell.

U

ultrafiltration: filtration assisted by blood pressure, e.g. in the formation of *tissue fluid*.

unsaturated fatty acid: a fatty acid in which there are one or more double bonds between the carbon atoms.

V

vaccination: the introduction of a vaccine containing appropriate disease *antigens* into the body, by injection or mouth, in order to induce artificial *immunity*.

W

water potential: the pressure created by water molecules. It is the measure of the extent to which a solution gives out water. The greater the number of water molecules present, the higher (less negative) the water potential. Pure water has a water potential of zero.

X

xerophyte: a plant adapted to living in dry conditions.

xylem vessels: dead, hollow, elongated tubes, with lignified side walls and no end walls, that transport water in most plants.

Answers

1.1

1 a microorganism that causes disease

2 Diffusion takes place in these systems so they have a large surface area, are thin, moist and well supplied with blood vessels. This makes it easy for pathogens to attach to and penetrate them.

3 by damaging host tissues; by producing toxins

4 A person with gastroenteritis has vomiting and diarrhoea. Both symptoms mean that the antibiotic is unlikely to remain in the body long enough to be absorbed.

1.2

1 Correlation between the relative risk of lung cancer and the number of cigarettes smoked before stopping; Correlation between the relative risk of lung cancer and the years since giving up smoking.

2 There is no experimental evidence in the data provided to show that smoking causes cancer. Hence there is no causal link between the two variables.

3 the risk of getting lung cancer when compared to a non-smoker

1.3

1 giving up smoking / not starting smoking

2 by lowering blood pressure; by lowering blood cholesterol; by reducing the risk of obesity

3 drink less alcohol, eat more fruit and vegetables, reduce salt intake, eat less red and processed meat, reduce calorie intake if overweight (i.e. body mass index is above 25)

Smoking and lung cancer

1 a 1940–50;   b 1970–80

2 The lines for cigarettes smoked and deaths from lung cancer are a similar shape for both sexes (although separated in time).

3 Any 3 from: an increase in smoking / more air pollution / an overall increase in the population of the UK / any other reasonable answer.

4 Lung cancer develops slowly and so the patient dies many years after it has been first contracted.

Smoking and disease

1 air pollution / inhaled substances (carcinogens), e.g. asbestos at work

2 a positive correlation between the incidence of lung cancer in men and the number of cigarettes smoked

3 It is unlikely that a coincidence would have occurred many times over.

4 No. While the data clearly point to the likelihood that smoking causes lung cancer, they do not provide experimental evidence that specifically links smoking to lung cancer.

5 The experiment that showed that the derivative of benzopyrene caused changes to DNA at precisely the same three points as the mutations of the gene in a cancer cell.

6 This is a single case. The link between early death and lung cancer is about probabilities not certainties. Statistically it is unlikely, but not impossible, for smokers to live to be very old.

2.1

1 a by having a muscular wall;   b by secreting mucus

2 the breakdown of molecules by the addition of water to the bonds that hold these molecules together

3 salivary glands; pancreas

4 Villi and microvilli increase surface area to speed up the absorption of soluble molecules. As the food in the stomach has not yet been broken down into soluble molecules they cannot be absorbed and so villi and microvilli are unnecessary.

2.2

1 Carbon atoms readily link to one another to form a chain.

2 polymer

3 Sugar donates electrons that reduce blue copper(II) sulfate to orange copper(I) oxide.

Semi-quantitative nature of Benedict's test

1 B, E, A, D, C

2 Dry the precipitate in each sample and weigh it. The heavier the precipitate the more reducing sugar was present.

3 Once all the copper(II) sulfate has been reduced to copper(I) oxide, further amounts of reducing sugar cannot make a difference.

2.3

1 a glucose + galactose;   b glucose + fructose;
c glucose only

2 $C_{12}H_{22}O_{11}$ ($C_6H_{12}O_6 + C_6H_{12}O_6 - H_2O$)

3 Enzymes are denatured at higher temperatures and this prevents them functioning / enzymes lower the activation energy required.

2.4

1 α-glucose

2 maltase, sucrase, lactase

3 respiration

4 Carbon dioxide forms as the result of aerobic respiration. Conditions in the large intestine are anaerobic.

2.5

1 peptide bond

2 condensation reaction

3 amino group ($-NH_2$), carboxyl group ($-COOH$), hydrogen atom ($-H$), R group

Protein shape and function

1 It has three polypeptide chains wound together to form a strong, rope-like structure that has strength in the direction of pull of a tendon.

2 It prevents the individual polypeptide chains from sliding past one another and so they gain strength because they act as a single unit.

3 The junctions between adjacent collagen are points of weakness. If they all occurred at the same point in a fibre, this would be a major weak point at which the fibre might break.

2.6

1 a substance that alters the rate of a chemical reaction without undergoing permanent change

2 They are not used up in the reaction and so can be used repeatedly.

3 The changed amino acid may no longer bind to the substrate, which will then not be positioned correctly, if at all, in the active site.

4 The changed amino acid may be one that forms hydrogen bonds with other amino acids. If the new amino acid does not form hydrogen bonds the tertiary structure of the enzyme will change, including the active site, so that the substrate may no longer fit.

2.7

1 To function enzymes must physically collide with their substrate. Lower temperatures decrease the kinetic energy of both enzyme and substrate molecules, which then move around less quickly. They hence collide less often and therefore react less frequently.

2 The heat causes hydrogen and other bonds in the enzyme molecule to break. The tertiary structure of the enzyme molecule changes, as does the active site. The substrate no longer fits the active site.

3 **a** High temperatures denature the enzyme and so they cannot spoil the food;

b Vinegar is very acidic and the low pH will denature the enzymes and so preserve the food;

2.8

1 Competitive inhibitors occupy the active site of an enzyme while non-competitive inhibitors attach to enzyme at a site other than the active site.

2 Increase the substrate concentration. If the degree of inhibition is reduced it is a competitive inhibitor, if it stays the same, it is a non-competitive inhibitor.

Control of metabolic pathways

1 pH / substrate concentration (not temperature)

2 In a metabolic pathway, the product of one reaction acts as the substrate for the next reaction. By having the enzymes in appropriate sequence there is a greater chance of each enzyme coming into contact with its substrate than if the enzymes floating freely in the organelle. This is a more efficient means of producing the end product.

3 **a** it would increase; **b** it would be unchanged

4 Advantage – the level of the end product does not fluctuate with changes in the level of substrate.
Explanation – Non-competitive inhibition occurs at a site on the enzyme other than the active site. Hence it is not affected by the substrate concentration. Therefore, in non-competitive inhibition, changes in the level of substrate do not effect the inhibition of the enzyme, nor the normal level of the end product.
Competitive inhibition involves competition for active sites. In this case the end product needs to compete with the substrate for the active sites of enzyme A. A change in the level of substrate would therefore affect how many end product molecules combine with the active sites. As a result the degree of inhibition would fluctuate and so would the level of the end product.

3.1

1 Magnification is how many times bigger the image is compared to the original object. Resolution is the minimum distance apart that two objects can be in order for them to appear as separate items.

2 200 times

3 10 mm

4 500 nm (0.5 μm)

5 Keep the plants in a cold, isotonic, buffered solution. Break up the cells using a mortar and pestle / homogeniser. Filter the homogenate to remove cell debris. Centrifuge the homogenate at 1000 times gravity and remove the supernatant liquid (leaving nuclei behind in the sediment). Then centrifuge the supernatant liquid at 2000–3000 times gravity. The sediment produced will be rich in chloroplasts.

6 **a** 1.6 μm; **b** 21 nm

7 **a** nuclei; **b** lysosomes;

c mitochondria, lysosomes and ribosomes;

d ribosomes;

3.2

1 The EM uses a beam of electrons that has a much smaller wavelength than light.

2 Electrons are absorbed by the molecules in air and, if present, this would prevent the electrons reaching the specimen.

3 **a** plant cell and bacteria; **b** all of them;

c plant cell, bacterium and virus

4 The preparation of the specimens may not be good enough.

5 The line X–Y is 25 mm (= 25 000 μm) long and represents 5 μm. Magnification is therefore 25 000 μm ÷ 5 μm = 5000 times.

3.3

1 protein synthesis

2 glucose, fructose, galactose

3 **a** mitochondrion; **b** nucleus;

c Golgi apparatus; **d** lysosome

4 **a** mitochondria, nucleus;

b Golgi apparatus, lysosomes;

c rough endoplasmic reticulum / ribosomes, mitochondria / smooth endoplasmic reticulum

3.4

1 **a** triglycerides; **b** glycerol;

c polyunsaturated; **d** two;

e hydrophobic

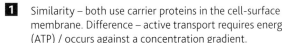

2 triglyceride: 3 fatty acids / no phosphate group / non-polar; phospholipid: 2 fatty acids / 1 phosphate group / hydrophilic 'head' and hydrophobic 'tail'

3 Lipids provide more than twice as much energy as carbohydrate when they are oxidised. If fat is stored, the same amount of energy can be provided for less that half the mass. It is therefore a lighter storage product – a major advantage if the organism is motile.

3.5

1 to control the movement of substances in and out of the cell.

2 hydrophobic tail

3 **a** phospholipid; **b** protein (intrinsic)

4 Any 2 from: lipid-soluble / small in size / have no electrical charge (or if it does, the charge should be opposite to that on the protein channels).

3.6

1 concentration gradient, area over which diffusion takes place and thickness of exchange surface; temperature

2 Facilitated diffusion only occurs at channels on the membrane where there are special protein carrier molecules.

3 There is no external energy used in the process. The only energy used is the in-built (kinetic) energy of the molecules themselves.

Diffusion in action

1 Only lipid-soluble substances diffuse across the phospholipid bilayer easily. Water-soluble substances like glucose diffuse only very slowly.

2 It could increase its surface area with microvilli and it could have more proteins with pores that span the phospholipid bilayer. (Note: the thickness of the cell-surface membranes does not vary to any degree.)

3 **a** increases two times / doubles;

    b no change;

    c decreases four times / it is one quarter;

    d increase two times / doubles; (The CO_2 concentration is irrelevant.)

3.7

1 a membrane that is permeable to water molecules (and a few other small molecules) but not to larger molecules.

2 zero

3 C, D, A, B

Osmosis and plant cells

1 Both cells have a lower water potential than pure water and so water enters them by osmosis. The animal cell is surrounded only by a thin cell-surface membrane and so it swells until it bursts. The plant cell is surrounded by a rigid cellulose cell wall. Assuming the cell is turgid, water cannot enter as the cellulose cell wall prevents the cell expanding and hence it bursting.

2 A = turgid, B = incipient plasmolysis, C = plasmolysed, D = turgid=.

3 solutions A, B and D (all except C).

3.8

1 Similarity – both use carrier proteins in the cell-surface membrane. Difference – active transport requires energy (ATP) / occurs against a concentration gradient.

2 Active transport requires energy in the form of ATP. Mitochondria supply ATP in cells and therefore they are numerous in cells carrying out active transport.

3 Diffusion, at best, can only reabsorb 50% of the glucose lost from the blood. The other 50% will be lost from the body. Active transport can absorb all the glucose, leaving none to be lost from the body.

3.9

1 The beating of the heart ensures that blood rich in glucose is constantly removed from the capillaries of the villi. Muscles in the villi keep the contents of the intestine moving, thus bringing glucose-rich contents in contact with the epithelial cells.

2 Because glucose molecules and sodium ions move into the cells coupled together.

3 **a** active; **b** passive; **c** passive

3.10

1 A = absent; B = present; C = present; D = sometimes; E = sometimes; F = sometimes; G = present; H = present; I = sometimes; J = absent; K = present; L = present; M = absent; N = present

2 Cholera toxin opens chloride channels in the cell-surface membrane of intestinal epithelial cells. Chloride ions flood into the lumen of the intestine. Water potential of epithelial cell rises while that of the lumen falls. Water moves into lumen by osmosis, causing watery stools (diarrhoea).

Transmission of cholera

1 Any 3 from: clean, uncontaminated water supplies / water treatment / chlorination/ proper sanitation and sewage treatment / personal hygiene (washing hands after using the toilet) / proper food hygiene

2 Breast milk does not contain the bacterium that causes cholera (and contains antibodies that provide some resistance to it). Bottle-fed babies are given milk made up with water and this may be contaminated with bacteria that cause cholera.

3 It could prevent the bacterium penetrating the mucus barrier of the intestinal wall and so stop it reaching the epithelial cells.

4 The antibiotic may be digested by enzymes and therefore not function. / The antibiotic may be too large to diffuse across the intestinal epithelium. / Severe diarrhoea is a symptom of cholera. Therefore any antibiotic taken orally may pass through the intestines so rapidly that it is passed out of the body before it can come into contact with the cholera bacterium. Taken via the blood the antibiotic is not digested / does not have to diffuse into the body / can reach the bacterium and kill it.

3.11

1   a   Glucose stimulates the uptake of sodium ions from the intestine and provides energy as it is a respiratory substrate.

    b   The sodium ions replace those lost from the body and encourage the use of the sodium-glucose transporter proteins to absorb more sodium ions.

    c   Boiling the water will kill any diarrhoeal pathogens that would otherwise make the patient's condition worse.

2   Potassium in the banana replaces the potassium ions that have been lost. It also stimulates the appetite and so aids recovery.

3   Banana improves the taste and so makes it easier for children to drink the mixture.

4   Too much glucose might lower the water potential within the intestine to a level below that within the epithelial cells. Water will then pass out of the cells by osmosis, increasing dehydration.

Developing and testing improved oral rehydration packs

1   Each species has different physical and chemical features and therefore may respond differently to the same drug. What is safe for some other animal may be harmful to a human.

2   It acts like a control experiment. Changes in the patients taking the real drug can be compared with patients taking the placebo to see whether they are due to the drug or to some other factor.

3   There is no risk of any deliberate or unwitting bias by the patients. Those knowing they are on the real drug might wrongly attribute changes in their symptoms to the drug.

4.1

1   Any 2 from: humans are large / have a large volume of cells; humans have a high metabolic rate / high body temperature.

2   alveoli, bronchioles, bronchus, trachea

3   The cells produce mucus that traps particles of dirt and bacteria in the air breathed in. The cilia on these cells move this debris up the trachea and into the stomach. The dirt / bacteria could damage / cause infection in the alveoli.

4.2

1 $0.48 \, dm^3$

2 17.14 breaths min^{-1}. Measure the time interval between any two corresponding points on either graph that are at the same phase of the breathing cycle (e.g. two corresponding peaks on the volume graph or two corresponding troughs on the pressure graph). The interval is always 3.5 s. This is the time for one breath. The number of breaths in a minute (60 s) is therefore 60 s ÷ 3.5 s = 17.14.

3   It is essential to first convert all figures to the same units. For example $3000 \, cm^3$ is equal to $3.0 \, dm^3$. From the graph you can calculate that the exhaled volume is $0.48 \, dm^3$ less than the maximum inhaled volume. The exhaled volume is therefore $3.0 - 0.48 = 2.52 \, dm^3$. If working in cm^3, the answer is $2520 \, cm^3$.

4   The muscles of the diaphragm contract, causing it to move downwards. The external intercostals muscles contract, moving the rib cage upwards and outwards. Both actions increase the volume of the lungs. Consequently the pressure in the alveoli of the lungs is reduced.

4.3

1   a   The rate of diffusion is more rapid the shorter the distance across which the gases diffuse.

    b   There is a very large surface area in 600 million alveoli (2 lungs) and this makes diffusion more rapid.

    c   Diffusion is more rapid the greater the concentration gradient. Pumping of blood through capillaries removes oxygen as it diffuses from the alveoli into the blood. The supply of new carbon dioxide as it diffuses out of the blood helps to maintain a concentration gradient that would otherwise disappear as the concentrations equalised.

    d   Red blood cells are flattened against the walls of the capillaries to enable them to pass through. This slows them down, increasing the time for gas exchange and reducing the diffusion pathway, thereby increasing the rate of diffusion.

2   four times greater

4.4

1   The bacteria *Mycobacterium tuberculosis* or *Mycobacterium bovis*.

2   When infected individuals cough, sneeze or talk they project droplets containing the bacterium into the air. Uninfected people who breathe this air may inhale the bacterium which may then infect their lungs.

3   The conditions in which TB is readily transmitted are those associated with poverty. These include poor diet and crowded, damp housing conditions.

4   *M. bovis* causes TB and is found in cattle and the milk they produce. Pasteurisation kills these bacteria and so prevents the milk infecting humans with TB.

Prevention and control of TB

1   Weakening the bacteria means that they are less likely to cause the symptoms of TB.

2   TB is more easily transmitted in overcrowded, poorly ventilated conditions. 'More housing' reduces overcrowding while 'better housing' has adequate ventilation.

3   As some forms of *M. tuberculosis* do not respond to certain drugs, there is a greater chance that, if four are given together, one will be effective.

4   Elderly people are more likely to have less effective immune systems.

4.5

1   a   Asthma – due to constriction of airways, inflamed linings and additional mucus and fluid.

    b   Emphysema – due to loss of elasticity in lungs, making exhaling difficult, and a reduced surface area of the alveoli, leading to patient 'searching' for breath.

    c   Fibrosis – due to reduced lung volume, reduced elasticity of lungs and lengthened diffusion path.

2   **a**   emphysema;   **b**   fibrosis;
     c   emphysema;   **d**   asthma

3   In the emphysematous lung tissue the surface area of the alveoli is reduced / there is a longer diffusion pathway and therefore less oxygen diffuses into the blood. As a result, there is not enough oxygen available for the increased respiration / extra energy (ATP) is needed for strenuous exercise / the elastic recoil in the lungs is reduced, so breathing is more difficult / shallower.

Risk factors for lung disease

1   Any 4 from: smoking / air pollution / genetic make-up / infections / occupation

2   Allow figures in the range 50–60%.

3   two times. Around 80% of non-smokers live to age 70 compared to around 40% of people who smoke more than 25 cigarettes a day.

4   In general terms, she will live longer. More specifically she has a 50% chance of living to be 65 years if she carries on smoking but a 50% chance of living to 80 years if she gives up. Her life expectancy will increase by 10–15 years.

5.1

1   coronary artery

2   **a**   deoxygenated;   **b**   deoxygenated;   **c**   oxygenated

3   pulmonary vein   left atrium   left ventricle   aorta   vena cava   right atrium   right ventricle   pulmonary artery

4   The mixing of oxygenated and deoxygenated blood would result in only partially oxygenated blood reaching the tissues and lungs. This would mean the supply of oxygen to the tissues would be inadequate and there would be a reduced diffusion gradient in the lungs, limiting the rate of oxygen uptake.

5.2

1   left ventricle

2   **a**   true;   **b**   true;   **c**   false;
     d   true;   **e**   false;

3   **a**   atria;   **b**   sinoatrial node;   **c**   bundle of His;

4   Training builds up the muscles of the heart and so the stroke volume increases/ more blood is pumped at each beat. This means that, if the cardiac output is the same, the heart rate / number of beats per minute decreases.

5   One complete cycle takes 0.8 s. Therefore the number of cycles in a minute = 60 ÷ 0.8 = 75. As there is 1 beat per cycle then there are 75 beats in a minute.

5.3

1   **a**   myocardial infarction;   **b**   atheroma;
     c   thrombosis;   **d**   aneurysm

2   the heart must work harder and is therefore prone to failure; an aneurysm may develop, causing a haemorrhage; the artery walls may thicken, restricting blood flow.

A calculated risk

1   Reducing blood pressure – for any given cholesterol level, this will reduce the risk more than giving up smoking, e.g. at 8 mmol dm⁻³ the risk falls from 23% to 15% by giving up smoking but falls to 12% by lowering blood pressure.

2   At 5 mmol dm⁻³, the risk is 5%. At 8 mmol dm⁻³, the risk is 15%. The risk is therefore 15 ÷ 5 = 3 times greater.

3   The man who increases his blood cholesterol level is at greater risk. The risk of the man who starts to smoke increases from 2.5% to 3.5% = +1%. The risk of the man who increases his cholesterol level increases from 2.5% to 5.5% = +3%.

Electrocardiogram

1   A = normal – large peaks and small troughs repeated identically; B = heart attack – less pronounced peaks and smaller troughs repeated in a similar, but not identical, way; C = fibrillation – highly irregular pattern

6.1

1   A specific mechanism distinguishes between different pathogens but responds more slowly than a non-specific mechanism. A non-specific mechanism treats all pathogens in the same way but responds more rapidly than a non-specific mechanism.

2   The lymphocytes that will finally control the pathogen need to build up their numbers and this takes time.

3   The body responds immediately by 'recognising' the pathogen (and by phagocytosis); the delay is in building up numbers of lymphocytes and therefore controlling the pathogen.

How lymphocytes recognise their own cells

1   'Self' refers to the body's own material while 'non-self' refers to material that is foreign to the body.

6.2

1   **a**   epithelial;   **b**   mucus;
     c   (hydrochloric) acid;   **d**   phagocytosis;
     e   phagosome;   **f**   lysosomes

2   The protective covering of the eye, and especially the tear ducts, are potential entry points for pathogens. Lysozyme will break down the cell walls of any bacterial pathogens and so destroy them before they can cause harm.

6.3

1   An organism or substance, usually a protein, that is recognised as foreign by the immune system and therefore stimulates an immune response.

2   Any 2 from: both are types of white blood cell / have a role in immunity / are produced from stem cells

3   T cells mature in the thymus gland while B cells mature in the bone marrow; T cells are involved in cell-mediated immunity while B cells are involved in humoral immunity.

Bird flu

1   H5N1 infects the lungs, leading to a massive production of T cells. Accumulation of these cells may block the airways / fill the alveoli and cause suffocation.

2   Birds carry H5N1 virus. They can fly vast distances across the world in a very short space of time.

6.4

1 In the primary response, the antigens of the pathogen have to be ingested, processed and presented by B cells. T helper cells need to link with the B cells that then clone, some of the cells developing into the plasma cells that produce antibodies. These processes occur consecutively and therefore take time. In the secondary response, memory cells are already present and the only processes are cloning and development into plasma cells that produce antibodies. Fewer processes means a quicker response.

2 Examples of differences include:

Cell-mediated immunity	Humoral immunity
Involves T cells	Involves mostly B cells
No antibodies	Antibodies produced
First stage of immune response	Second stage of immune response after cell mediated stage
Effective through cells	Effective through body fluids

3 rough endoplasmic reticulum – to make and transport the proteins of the antibodies; Golgi apparatus – to sort, process and compile the proteins; mitochondria – to release the energy needed for such massive antibody production

6.5

1 There must be a massive variety of antibodies as each responds to a different antigen, of which there are millions. Only proteins have the diversity of molecular structure to produce millions of different types.

2 An antigen is a molecule that triggers an immune response by lymphocytes while an antibody is the molecule that has a complementary shape to the antigen and is produced in response to it.

Producing monoclonal antibodies

1 to break down the cell-surface membrane allowing B cells and tumour cells to fuse

2 to ensure the B cells and tumour cells repeatedly come into physical contact – essential if they are to fuse

3 because B cells are short-lived and do not divide outside of the body. Tumour cells are long-lived and divide outside the body. Using both of them leads to long-lived B cells that can be grown outside the body.

4 B cells with B cells, and tumour cells with tumour cells.

5 because monoclonal antibodies from mouse tissue will be recognised as foreign (non-self) and will be destroyed by human antibodies if not 'humanised'.

Ethical production and use of monoclonal antibodies

1 The introduction of antibodies into humans could cause a reaction / disease that could be dangerous. The antigen could stimulate an over-response of the immune system.

2 Any accurate response that includes an argument in favour (e.g. removes the risk of healthy volunteers being harmed / terminally ill patients have most to gain and less to lose) and an argument against (e.g. response of terminally ill might be different from those in the early stages of the disease and results therefore could be unreliable / sample size likely to be smaller / not typical).

6.6

1 Active immunity – individuals are stimulated to produce their own antibodies. Immunity is normally long-lasting. Passive immunity – antibodies are introduced from outside rather than being produced by the individual. Immunity is normally only short-lived.

2 The influenza virus displays antigen variability. Its antigens change frequently and so antibodies no longer recognise the virus. New vaccines are required to stimulate the antibodies that complement the new antigens.

3 Any 3 from: HIV infections mean that more people have impaired immune systems / more refugees carrying TB move frequently or live in overcrowded temporary conditions / more mobile population / more elderly people – who often have less effective immune systems.

MMR vaccine

1 the MMR vaccine is given at 12–15 months – the same time as autism symptoms appear.

2 It might: present the findings in an incomplete / biased fashion, ignore unfavourable findings, fund only further research that seems likely to produce the evidence that its seeks rather than investigating all possible outcomes, withdraw funding for research that seems likely to produce unfavourable findings,

7.1

1 mutation, meiosis and fusion of gametes
2 mutation only
3 sampling bias; chance variation.
4 by using random sampling – effectively using a computer to generate sampling sites

7.2

1 a genetic; b environmental; c genetic; d genetic; e environmental; f environmental
2 680

8.1

1 deoxyribose (sugar), phosphate group, organic base
2 Adenine and guanine are longer molecules than thymine and cytosine. The distance between the two phosphate / deoxyribose 'uprights' is constant in the DNA molecule. Pairing adenine and guanine would produce a long 'rung' while pairing thymine and cytosine produces a short 'rung'.
3 The bases are linked by hydrogen bonds. The molecular structures could be such that hydrogen bonds do not form between adenine and cytosine and between guanine and thymine.
4 ACCTCTGA
5 30.1%. If 19.9% is guanine then, as guanine always pairs with cytosine, it also makes up 19.9% of the bases in DNA, so together they make up 39.8%. This means the remaining 60.2% of DNA must be adenine and thymine and, as these also pair, each must make up half of this, i.e. 30.1%.

Unravelling the role of DNA

1 Alternative theories can be explored and investigated. As a result, new facts may emerge and so a new theory is put forward or the existing one is modified. In this way, scientific progress can be made.

2 A suggested explanation of something based on some logical scientific reasoning or idea.

3 The harmful bacteria in the sample could be tested to ensure they were dead, e.g. by seeing if they multiply when grown in ideal conditions. Dead bacteria cannot multiply.

4 The probability of the mutation happening once is very small. The probability of the same mutation occurring each time the experiment is repeated is so minute that it can be discounted.

5 Society will probably be affected by new discoveries and so is entitled to say how they can or cannot be used.

8.2

1 A section of DNA containing coded information for making polypeptides.

2 18

3 A different base might code for a different amino acid. The sequence of amino acids in the polypeptide produced will be different. This change to the primary structure of the protein might result in a different shaped tertiary structure. The enzyme shape will be different and may not fit the substrate. The enzyme-substrate complex cannot be formed and so the enzyme is non-functional.

Features of the triplet code

1 a 5

b the first and last (5th) / the two coded for by the bases TAC

c because some amino acids have up to six different codes, while others have just one triplet code

8.3

1 In prokaryotic cells the DNA is smaller, linear and is not associated with proteins (i.e. does not have chromosomes).

2 It fixes the DNA into position.

3 It is looped and coiled a number of times.

4 a 50 mm (46 chromosomes in every cell);

b 2.3 m (all cells have same quantity of DNA)

8.4

1 haploid because 27 is an odd number. Diploid cells have 2 sets of chromosomes and so their total must be an even number.

2 independent segregation of homologous chromosomes; recombination by crossing over.

3 blue eyes and blood group A, brown eyes and blood group A.

4 Gametes are produced by meiosis. In meiosis, homologous chromosomes pair up. With 63 chromosomes precise pairings are impossible. This prevents meiosis and hence gamete production, making them sterile.

9.1

1 a increase; b decrease; c decrease;
d increase

2 Different DNA – different codes for amino acids – different amino acids – different protein shape – different protein function (e.g. non-functional enzyme) – change in a feature determined by that protein – altered appearance – greater genetic diversity

3 Drop in population numbers due to chance event – few surviving individuals likely to have fewer, less diverse alleles – as population grows its alleles are equally less diverse – reduced genetic diversity.

Ethics of selective breeding in domesticated animals

1 Views of interested parties; technical feasibility; economic factors; safety issues; environmental issues; benefits versus risks, etc.

2 international and national laws / agreements / protocols

3 The process is largely a matter of luck. An organism may possess the desired features, but this does not mean that it will pass these onto the next generation. Equally an organism may possess the genes for the desired features, but it may not exhibit these characteristics and therefore may not be chosen to breed. This means the process is 'imprecise'. It is 'slow' because there will be many 'failures' along the way and it takes many generations to produce organisms that consistently exhibit the desired features. Also the number of offspring produced at each generation is small.

4 There is less genetic diversity. The male might carry a potentially harmful allele that is not apparent or not exhibited by the donor male. This harmful allele may be passed on to hundreds of offspring.

5 Any 2 from: cheaper milk / lower production costs; consistent quality and composition of milk; plentiful supply of milk

6 Any 2 from: the welfare of cattle is at risk / cattle suffer distress / cattle are overworked; cattle are killed at a young age because they are no longer able to produce milk economically; it is unnatural / it interferes with the normal course of nature; it reduces genetic diversity / there is more uniformity / fewer alleles in the population – and potentially valuable alleles / characteristics are lost; cattle that require over-wintering in heated sheds contribute to global warming.

10.1

1 2 pairs of polypeptides (α and β) link to form a spherical molecule. Each polypeptide has a haem group that contains a ferrous (Fe^{2+}) ion

2 Different base sequences in DNA – different amino acid sequences – different tertiary / quaternary structure and shape – different affinities for oxygen

3 If all oxygen molecules were released, there would be none in reserve to supply tissues when they were more active.

4 Carbon monoxide will gradually occupy all the sites on haemoglobin instead of oxygen. No oxygen will be carried to tissues such as the brain. These will cease to respire and to function, making the person lose consciousness.

10.2

1 a 5 kPa; b 90%; c 70% (95% – 25%)

2 a the curve is shifted to the right;

b haemoglobin has become less saturated

3 Exercising muscles release heat, shifting the curve to the right and causing the haemoglobin to release more oxygen to fuel the muscular activity.

Different lives – different haemoglobins: Where you live is important

1 At this partial pressure of oxygen, lugworm haemoglobin is 90% saturated, more than enough to supply sufficient oxygen to the tissues of a relatively inactive organism. Human haemoglobin, by contrast, is only 10% saturated – insufficient to supply enough oxygen to keep tissues alive.

2 The dissociation curve of the lugworm is shifted far to the left. This means it is fully loaded with oxygen even when there is very little available in its environment.

3 'The lugworm is not very active'. This means that it requires less oxygen and therefore what little there is in its burrow when the tide is out is sufficient to supply its needs, Hence it survives

4 Respiration produces carbon dioxide. This builds up in the burrow when the tide is out. If lugworm haemoglobin exhibited the Bohr effect, it would not be able to absorb oxygen when it was present in only very low concentrations in the burrow.

5 The higher part of the beach is uncovered by the tide for a much longer period of time than the lower part. During this longer period all the oxygen in the burrow would be used up and the lugworm might die before the next tide.

6 It is shifted to the left.

Size matters

7 Unloading pressure of human haemoglobin is 5 kPa and of mouse haemoglobin is 9 kPa. Difference = 9 – 5 = 4 kPa.

8 a It unloads more readily.

b Oxygen is more readily released from haemoglobin to the tissues. This helps the tissues to respire more and so produce more heat, which helps to maintain the body temperature of the mouse.

c Even at an oxygen partial pressure of 21 kPa, mouse haemoglobin is still loaded to the maximum with oxygen.

9 Sigmoid-shaped curves, from left to right – elephant, human, shrew – because surface area to volume ratio increases in this order.

Activity counts

10 shifted to the right because this means that oxygen is more readily released to the tissues and so the haemoglobin supplies more oxygen to enable the muscles to respire rapidly.

11 sigmoid-shaped curves, with plaice to the left of mackerel.

12 The temperatures in Antarctic waters are very low. This means respiration rates of cold-blooded groups such as fish are also very low. As respiration needs oxygen, their oxygen requirements are also very low. Without haemoglobin, ice fish must rely on water alone to transport their oxygen. The amount of oxygen dissolved in water, while very little, is still adequate to supply their needs.

10.3

1 starch

2 glycogen

3 α-glucose, β-glucose, starch, cellulose

4 starch, cellulose, glycogen

5 α-glucose

6 cellulose

7 starch, cellulose, glycogen

8 α-glucose, β-glucose

10.4

1 in leaves

2 to carry out photosynthesis

3 thylakoids / grana

4 (cellulose) cell wall; chloroplasts; starch (grains)

Specialised plant cells: The root hair cell

1 thin cell wall, large surface area / long, hair-like extension

2 Osmosis is the passage of water from a region where it has a higher water potential to a region where it has a lower water potential, through a partially permeable membrane.

3 The water potential of the soil solution is higher than that in the vacuole / cytoplasm of the root hair cell. Water therefore moves along a water potential gradient.

4 mitochondria

5 Mitochondria release energy / make ATP during respiration. This energy / ATP is essential for active transport.

Xylem vessels

6 They have thick walls to prevent the vessels collapsing.

7 hollow; elongated

8 Living cells have a cell-surface membrane and cytoplasm, and water movement would be slowed as it crossed this membrane / cytoplasm.

9 Waterproofing

10 Any 1 from: allows the vessel to elongate as the plant grows / uses less material and therefore is less wasteful / uses less material and therefore the plant has lower mass. / allows stems to be flexible.

Other specialised cells

11 a Cell C – possesses chloroplasts

b Cell B – has a very thick cell wall

c Cell A – has a very small / large nucleus / large amount of cytoplasm

11.1

1 TACGATGC

2 because half the original DNA is built into the new DNA strand.

3 The linking together of the new nucleotides could not take place. While the nucleotides would match up to their complementary nucleotides on the original DNA strand, they would not join together to form a new strand.

Evidence for semi-conservative replication

1 the organic bases (adenine, guanine, cytosine and thymine)

2 Each DNA molecule is made up of one strand containing ^{15}N (the original strand) and one strand containing ^{14}N (the new strand). In other words, replication is semi-conservative.

3

4

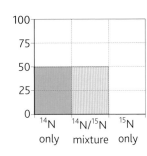

5 75%

11.2

1
a interphase;   b prophase;   c spindle;
d nuclear envelope; e nucleolus;   f metaphase;
g anaphase;   h growth / repair; i growth / repair

Recognising the stages of mitosis

1 A = telophase – chromosomes in two sets, one at each pole; B = prophase – chromosomes visible but randomly arranged; C = interphase – no chromosomes visible; D = metaphase – chromosomes lined up on equator; E = anaphase – chromosomes in two sets, each being drawn towards pole;

2 24 minutes. Number of cells in metaphase ÷ total number of cells observed × time for one cycle (in minutes), i.e. 20 ÷ 1,000 × 1200 = 24

3 11% chromosomes visible in prophase, metaphase, anaphase and telophase (73 + 20 + 9 + 8) ÷ 1,000 × 100

11.3

1 interphase, nuclear division and cell division

2 a 12 hours and 24 hours; b 6–9 hours and 18–21 hours

Cancer and its treatment

1 0.2 million / 200,000

2 50%

3 8.33 times (0.5 ÷ 0.06)

4 More cancer cells are killed because they divide more rapidly than healthy cells and so are more susceptible to the drug.

5 Cancer cells take longer to recover. Cancer cells divide more slowly / rate of mitosis is reduced.

6 One dose of the drug does not kill all the cancer cells. Those that remain continue to divide and build up the number of cancer cells again.

12.1

1 a collection of similar cells aggregated together to perform a specific function

2 An artery is made up of more than one tissue (epithelial, muscle, connective tissues) whereas a blood capillary is made up of only one tissue (epithelial tissue).

3 a organ;   b tissue;
c organ;   d tissue

13.1

1 respiratory gases, nutrients, excretory products and heat

2 0.6

3 Any 3 from: surface area / thickness of cell-surface membrane / permeability of cell-surface membrane to the particular substance / concentration gradient of substance between inside and outside of cell / temperature

Significance of surface area to volume ratio in organisms

1 They are very small and so have a very large surface area to volume ratio.

2 The blue whale has a very small surface area to volume ratio and so loses less heat to the water than it would if it were small.

13.2

1 diffusion over the body surface

2 by having valves that can close spiracles when the insect is inactive

3 Gas exchange requires a thin permeable surface with a large area. Conserving water requires thick, waterproof surfaces with a small area.

4 because it relies on diffusion to bring oxygen to the respiring tissues. If insects were large it would take too long for oxygen to reach the tissues rapidly enough to supply their needs.

Spiracle movements

1 It falls steadily and then remains at the same level

2 Cells use up oxygen during respiration and so it diffuses out of the tracheae and into these cells. With the spiracles closed, no oxygen can diffuse in from the outside to replace it. Ultimately, all the oxygen is used up and so the level ceases to fall.

3 the increasing level of carbon dioxide

4 It helps conserve water because the spiracles are not open continuously and therefore water does not diffuse out continuously

5 It contained more oxygen.

13.3

1 the movement of water and blood in opposite directions across gill lamellae

2 because a steady diffusion gradient is maintained over the whole length of the gill lamellae. Therefore more oxygen diffuses from the water into the blood.

3 Mackerel have more gill lamellae / gill filaments / larger surface area compared to plaice.

4 Less energy is required because the flow does not have to be reversed (important as water is dense and difficult to move)

13.4

1 Any 2 from: no living cell is far from the external air / diffusion takes place in the gas phase / need to avoid excessive water loss / diffuse air through pores in their outer covering (can control the opening and closing of these pores).

2 Any 2 from: insects may create mass air flow – plants never do/ insects have a smaller surface area to volume ratio than plants / insects have special structures (tracheae) along which gases can diffuse – plants do not / insects do not interchange gases between respiration and photosynthesis – plants do.

3 Helps to control water loss by evaporation/transpiration.

Exchange of carbon dioxide

1 respiration

2 photosynthesis

3 At this light intensity the volume of carbon dioxide taken in during photosynthesis is exactly the same as the volume of carbon dioxide given out during respiration.

4 With stomata closed, there is little, if any, gas exchange with the environment. While there will still be some interchange of gases produced by respiration and photosynthesis, neither process can continue indefinitely by relying exclusively on gases produced by the other. Some gases must be obtained from the environment. In the absence of this supply, both photosynthesis and respiration will ultimately cease and the plant will die.

13.5

1 a pulmonary artery; b aorta; c hepatic vein;
d pulmonary vein; e aorta

2 low surface area to volume ratio; a high metabolic rate

3 It increases blood pressure and hence the rate of blood flow to the tissues.

13.6

1 a elastic tissue allows recoil and hence maintains blood pressure / smooth blood flow / constant blood flow;

b muscle can contract, constricting the lumen of the arterioles and therefore controlling the flow of blood into capillaries;

c valves prevent flow of blood back to the tissues and so keep it moving towards the heart / keep blood at low pressure flowing in one direction;

d the wall is very thin, making the diffusion pathway short and exchange of material rapid.

2 a C; b B; c E;
d D; e A

3 hydrostatic pressure (due to pumping of the heart)

4 via the capillaries and via the lymphatic system

Blood flow in various blood vessels

1 Rate of blood flow decreases gradually in the aorta and then very rapidly in the large and small arteries. It remains relatively constant in the arterioles and capillaries before increasing, at an increasing rate, in the venules and veins and vena cava.

2 Contraction of the left ventricle of the heart causes distension of the aorta. The elastic layer in the aorta walls creates a recoil action. There is therefore a series of pulses of increased pressure, each one the result of ventricle contraction.

3 Because the total cross-sectional area is increasing / there is increased frictional resistance from the increasing area of blood vessel wall.

4 Blood flow is slower, allowing more time for metabolic materials to be exchanged.

5 Capillaries have a large surface area and very thin walls (single cell thick) and hence a short diffusion pathway.

13.7

1 Soil solution has a very high water potential, the root hair cell has a lower water potential (due to dissolved sugars, amino acids and ions inside it). Water moves by osmosis from soil solution into the root hair cell.

2 apoplastic pathway takes place in cell walls and symplastic pathway in cytoplasm; apoplastic pathway occurs by cohesion and symplastic pathway by osmosis

3 because endodermal cells have a waterproof band / Casparian strip that prevents the passage of water

4 a passive; b passive;
c passive(the ions are actively transported but the **water** moves passively (osmosis))

5 The root hairs are delicate and may get broken. There may be air pockets rather than soil solution around the roots when transplanting.

13.8

1 a transpiration; b stomata;
c lower / reduced / more negative;
d osmosis; e cohesion;
f increases; g root pressure

Hug a tree

1 at 12.00 hours because this is when water flow is at its maximum. As transpiration creates most of the water flow they are both at a maximum at the same time.

2 Rate of flow increases from a minimum at 00.00 hours to a maximum at 12.00 hours and then decreases to a minimum again at 24.00 hours.

3 As evaporation / transpiration from leaves increases during the morning (due to higher temperature / higher light intensity) it pulls water molecules through the xylem because water molecules are cohesive / stick together. This transpiration pull creates a negative pressure / tension. The greater the rate of transpiration, the greater the water flow. The reverse occurs as transpiration rate decreases during the afternoon and evening.

4 As transpiration increases up to 12.00 hours, so there is a higher tension (negative pressure) in the xylem. This reduces the diameter of the trunk. As transpiration rate decreases, from 12.00 hours to 24.00 hours, the tension in the xylem reduces and the trunk diameter increases again.

5 Transpiration pull is a passive process / does not require energy. Xylem is non-living and so cannot provide energy. Although root cortex and leaf mesophyll cells are living – the movement of water across them uses passive processes, e.g. osmosis, and so continues at least for a while, even though the cells are dead.

13.9

1 Plants photosynthesise and therefore have a large surface area to collect light and stomata through which carbon dioxide diffuses (necessary). Both features lead to a considerable loss of water by transpiration (evil).

2 **a** decreases; **b** increases; **c** increases; **d** increases; **e** increases

3 Any 2 from: high humidity as water vapour cannot escape / still air / darkness – stomata close

Measurement of water using a potometer

1 **a** As xylem is under tension, cutting the shoot in air would lead to air being drawn into the stem, which would stop transport of water up the shoot. Cutting under water means water, rather than air, is drawn in and a continuous column of water is maintained.

  b Sealing prevents air being drawn into the xylem and stopping water flow up it / Sealing prevents water leaking out which would produce an inaccurate result.

2 that all water taken up is transpired

3 Volume of water taken up in one minute: $3.142 \times (0.5 \times 0.5) \times 15.28 = 12.00 \, mm^3$. Volume of water taken up in 1 hour: $12.00 \times 60 = 720 \, mm^3$

4 their surface area / surface area of the leaves

5 An isolated shoot is much smaller than the whole plant / may not be representative of the whole plant / may be damaged when cut.
Conditions in the lab may be different from those in the wild, e.g. less air movement / greater humidity / more light (artificial lighting when dark).

13.10

1 Efficient gas exchange requires a thin, permeable surface with a large area. On land these features can lead to a considerable loss of water by evaporation.

2 waterproof covering to the body / ability to close the openings of the gas-exchange system (stomata and spiracles).

3 Plants photosynthesise and therefore need a large surface area to capture light

4 **a** Water evaporating from the leaf is trapped. The region within the rolled up leaf becomes saturated with water vapour. There is no water potential gradient between the inside and outside of the leaf and so transpiration is considerably reduced.

  b Almost all stomata are on the lower epidermis. This would be exposed to air currents that would reduce the outside humidity. The water potential gradient would be increased and a lot of water vapour would be transpired.

Not only desert plants have problems obtaining water

1 The rain rapidly drains through the sand out of reach of the roots. Sand dunes are usually in windy situations, which reduces humidity and so increases the water potential gradient, leading to increased water loss by transpiration

2 The soil solution is very salty, i.e. it has a very low water potential, making it difficult for root hairs to draw water in by osmosis.

3 because in winter the water in the soil is frozen and therefore cannot be absorbed by osmosis.

4 Being enzyme-controlled, photosynthesis is influenced by temperature. In cold climates enzymes work slowly and this limits the rate of photosynthesis. Therefore there is a reduced need for light as photosynthesis is taking place only slowly. In warm climates, photosynthesis occurs rapidly and therefore a large leaf area is needed to capture sufficient light.

14.1

1 They are similar to one another but different from members of other species. They are capable of breeding to produce offspring which themselves are fertile

2 It is based on evolutionary relationships between organisms and their ancestors; it classifies species into groups using shared characteristics derived from their ancestors; it is arranged in a hierarchy in which groups are contained within larger composite groups with no overlap.

3 1. phylum, 2. class, 3. order, 4. family, 5. *Rana*, 6. species, 7. *temporaria*

The difficulties of defining species

1 Fossil records are normally incomplete and not all features can be observed (there is no biochemical record) and so comparisons between individuals are hard to make. Fossil records can never reveal whether individuals could successfully mate.

2 Species change and evolve over time, sometimes developing into different species. There is considerable variety within a species. Fossil records are incomplete / non-existent. Current classifications only reflect current scientific knowledge and, as this changes, so does the naming and classifying of organisms.

3 During meiosis 1, chromosomes line up across the equator in their homologous pairs. With an odd number of chromosomes, exact pairings are not possible. This prevents meiosis occurring in the normal way.

4 No, it does not. Only fertile female mules are known, so interbreeding (a feature of any species) is impossible. The event is so rare that it can be considered abnormal and it would be wrong to draw conclusions from it. If a mule were a species, it would mean that the parents were the same species – however, donkeys and horses are sufficiently different to be recognised as separate species.

Relationships

1 lizards

2 birds

3 Dinosaurs are extinct but all the other groups are still living and so they are shown extending further along the time line – as far as 'present'.

15.1

1
  a to separate the two complementary strands of the DNA molecule

  b because more complementary bases are joined together and therefore more energy is needed to break the hydrogen bonds linking them

  c the more complementary bases that are joined the more similar are the DNA strands of the two species whose DNA forms the hybrid molecule. The more similar their DNA, the more closely they are related.

2 species 2 and 3 because their amino acid sequences are identical.

New classification of flowering plants

1 mutations

2 Amborellaceae

Establishing relationships

1 chimpanzee, gorilla, orang-utan, lemur, gibbon

2 the chimpanzee and the gorilla because they both show the same % precipitation (95%).

3 the gibbon because it shows only a 3% difference (85–82) in precipitation between itself and the orang-utan. All the other primates show a greater difference.

4 These data suggest that the gibbon is much more closely related to humans than the lemur. The haemoglobin study suggested the lemur was a closer relative. The chimpanzee is shown to be more closely related to humans in the haemoglobin study

5 There are fewer differences between the bases in the gene of a human and that of an orang-utan (29) than there is between the genes of a human and a lemur (48). This suggests that the evolution of humans and lemurs diverged earlier than that of humans and orang-utans, giving more time for the amino acid differences to occur.

6 No, it does not. This study suggests that gorillas (with fewer base differences) are more closely related to humans than chimpanzees. The other studies suggest chimpanzees are more closely related to humans. The position of the orang-utan is the same in all three studies. The position of the lemur is the same as in the immunological study but different from that in the haemoglobin study.

15.2

1 to ensure mating only takes place between members of the same species as only they can produce fertile offspring

2 identification of a mate capable of breeding; formation of a pair bond to raise offspring; synchronisation of mating

3
  a she may be of a different species; she may not be at a fertile stage of her sexual cycle

  b he can court another female who may be receptive and so possibly produce offspring. Continuing to court the first female is likely to be unproductive. Production of offspring is essential to species survival because no individual lives forever.

4 The courtship display that most nearly resembles that of the first species is likely to be the closest evolutionary relative.

Courting mallards

1 so that each can recognise its own species as this increases the probability of successful breeding

2 5 species.

3 because they have a similar sequence (just one element missing for duck C); most of the elements are the same.

4 duck F – the sequence of elements is least like any of the others

5 It signals to the male that she is receptive and prepared to mate.

16.1

1 mutation; the recombination of existing DNA from two individuals

2 a sudden change in the amount or arrangement of DNA that results in different characteristics

3 mutation – change in base sequence of DNA – different amino acid being coded for – different amino acid sequence – different polypeptide – different protein / no protein – the protein is an enzyme – being different / absent it does not catalyse the production of melanin

4 horizontal gene transmission = – transfer of DNA / genes from one species to another; vertical gene transmission = – transfer of DNA / genes within a species from one generation to the next

Discovering conjugation in bacteria

1 Both strains: 1 and 2

2 Neither would be expected to grow

3 Information on how to synthesise the two nutrients that it had previously been unable to synthesise for itself.

4 Any 1 from: mutation (leading to the ability to produce the nutrients they could not previously synthesise) / transformation (acquiring DNA with this information from the medium around it – see topic 8.2) / transduction (via bacteriophages)

16.2

1 a substance produced by a living organism that kills or prevents the growth of other living microorganisms

2 Cross-linkages hold the bacterial cell wall together. Without them the wall is weakened. Water enters the bacterium by osmosis and the bacterium swells. Normally the wall prevents swelling and hence osmosis. When the wall is weakened, it breaks, water continues to enter and the cell bursts – osmotic lysis.

3 by transfer of the gene / DNA for resistance during conjugation , i.e. horizontal gene transmission.

4 When antibiotics are used they only kill the non-resistant bacteria. This reduces competition and makes it easier for the resistant bacteria to survive and so pass on the resistance to subsequent generations and to other species.

Identifying antibiotic-resistant bacteria

1 two – because the bacteria around two of the discs continue to grow normally

2 The antibiotics on the disc have inhibited the growth of the bacteria.

3 The larger clear areas may show that the antibiotic on the disc is more effective at inhibiting bacterial growth or that it diffuses across the jelly more easily.

16.3

1 because they feel better and think they are cured

2 the course of treatment is very long (6–9 months)

3 drug-resistant strains of bacteria exchange DNA by conjugation (horizontal gene transmission) / the bacteria exchange genes for resistance. / some bacterial strains accumulate genes for resistance to many drugs

4 because many different types of antibiotics are used, often in relatively large amounts. This creates a selection pressure favouring multiple resistant strains.

Implications of antibiotic use

1 Individual bacteria have different degrees of antibiotic resistance. The least resistant bacteria are killed first and the most resistant last. If a course of antibiotics is stopped early, the most resistant strains are the ones left. The resistant strains have been selected for survival in preference to the non-resistant strains. These can pass on the genes for resistance by vertical and horizontal transmission. In this way new strains develop that are adapted to resist antibiotics.

2 Arguments might include:

For	Against
• Animals should be protected against disease to prevent possible suffering.	• The more antibiotics are used, the greater the risk of resistant strains predominating. This resistance can be transferred to bacteria causing other disease – including ones affecting humans.
• If antibiotics are not used, productivity will fall and milk prices will rise	
• Milk price rises affect the poor more than the better off – and add to human poverty	• May contribute to the development of multiple drug-resistant strains, making it much harder to treat other, often more severe, animal and human diseases,
• We all welcome cheap milk	• Antibiotics should be reserved for treating animal and human disease – not used to increase profits of companies or incomes of farmers

A dilemma

1 Arguments might include:

For	Against
• Relieving unpleasant symptoms of diarrhoea and the discomfort and distress it is causing.	• Use of antibiotics increases risk of resistance developing.
• People should be able to die with dignity.	• Better to reserve antibiotic use for patients whose lives will be considerably extended by their use or for more dangerous diseases.
• No guarantee that giving the antibiotic will create resistance.	• Sometimes, sadly, some individual sacrifices have to be made for the wider benefit of mankind.
• Without antibiotic, suffering is likely to increase.	• Other drugs / therapies have been withdrawn, so why not this one?

17.1

1 the number of different species and the proportion of each species within a given area / community

2

Species	Numbers in salt marsh	$n(n-1)$
Salicornia maritima	24	24(23) = 552
Halimione portulacoides	20	20(19) = 380
Festuca rubra	7	7(6) = 42
Aster tripolium	3	3(2) = 6
Limonium humile	3	3(2) = 6
Suaeda maritima	1	1(0) = 0
	$\sum n(n-1)$	986

$$d = \frac{58(57)}{986} = \frac{3306}{986} = \text{Answer } 3.35$$

3 It measures both the number of species and the number of individuals. It therefore takes account of species that are only present in small numbers.

Species diversity and ecosystems

1 Greenhouse gases lead to climate change. Communities with a high species diversity index are likely to include at least one species adapted to withstand the change and therefore survive. When the index is low, the community is less likely to include a species adapted to withstand the change and is therefore at greater risk of being damaged.

2 a The community fluctuates in line with environmental change – rising and falling in the same way but a little later in time.

b Communities with a high species diversity are more stable because they have a greater variety of species and therefore are more likely to have species that are adapted to the changed environment. Those with a low species diversity are less stable because they have fewer species and are less likely to include a species adapted to the change.

17.2

1 The few species possessing desirable qualities are selected for and bred. Other species are excluded, as far as possible, by culling or the use of pesticides. Many individuals of a few species = low species diversity.

2 because forests, with their many layers, have many habitats with many different species, i.e. a high species diversity. Grasslands have a single layer, fewer habitats, fewer species and lower species diversity.

3 because tropical rainforests have a greater number and variety of species than any other ecosystem, i.e. the highest species diversity.

Human activity and loss of species in the UK

1 500 000 km (350 000 × 100 ÷ 70)

2 Mixed woodlands comprise many species while the commercial conifer plantations that replace them are largely of a single predominant species

3 Any 1 from each: benefit – cheaper grazing / fodder for animals and hence cheaper food / more efficient food production; risk – loss of species diversity / less stable ecosystem / more fertilizers and pesticides needed

4 It provides evidence to inform and support decision-making. Data show where the most change has occurred and therefore the habitats most at risk. These can be prioritised and measures taken to conserve them, e.g. by giving them special protection. Funds can be directed towards reverting land to its former use, e.g. by grants to farmers to create hay meadows / convert set-aside to woodland / re-establish hedgerows. Helps decision-makers form appropriate rules / legislation to prevent habitat destruction, e.g. ban on drainage of certain sites / rock removal. Informs decisions on planning applications for planting forests / reclaiming land.

5 Hedges provide more habitats / niches / food sources and therefore more species can survive. Species diversity is therefore increased.

Index

Acknowledgements

Photograph Acknowledgements

The authors and publisher are grateful to the following for permission to reproduce photographs and other copyright material in this book.

Alamy/Art Kowalsky: p 228; **Alamy/Celeste Daniels:** p 196; **Alamy/David Fleetham:** p 177; **Alamy/David Levenson:** p 223; **Alamy/Duncan Usher:** p213; **Alamy/FLPA:** p 154 (top); **Alamy/imagebroker:** p 184; **Alamy/Mark J. Barrett:** p 207; **Alamy/Martin Shields:** p 21; **Alamy/Medical-on-line:** p 9 (bottom); **Alamy/Mike Abrahams:** p 81; **Alamy/Natural Visions:** p 155 (bottom); **Alamy/Paul Collis:** p 214; **Alamy/PHOTOTAKE Inc.:** p 9 (top), p 47 (top), p 160; **Alamy/Ron Steiner:** p 155 (top); **Alamy/Worldwide Picture Library:** p 230 (top); **Alamy/WR Publishing:** p 221; **Digital Vision 15 (NT):** p 67; **Digital Vision JA (NT):** p 205 (bottom); **Getty/LWA/Dann Tardif:** p viii; **Glenn and Susan Toole:** p 146 (all), p 154 (bottom), p 200 (both), p 201, p229 (both); **IKON 14 (NT):** p 25 (bottom); **Ingram-INGUFYTH (NT):** p 25 (top & middle); **Oxford Scientific/Bontica:** p 205 (middle); **Oxford Scientific/Carolina Bio. Supply C.:** p 194; **Oxford Scientific/PHOTOTAKE Inc.:** p 4, p 63, p 172, p 191, p 219; **Photodisc 18 (NT):** p 13; **Photodisc 6 (NT):** p 123, p 226 (top), p 230 (middle right); **Science Photo Library:** p 48 (bottom), p 102 (bottom); **Science Photo Library/AJ Photo/Hop Americain:** p 113; **Science Photo Library/Alex Bartel:** p 225; **Science Photo Library/Alfred Pasieka:** p 79, p 109; **Science Photo Library/Andrew Syred:** p 156, p 161; **Science Photo Library/Barbara Strnadova:** p 149 (top); **Science Photo Library/BioPhoto Associates:** p 83 (top), p 83 (bottom), p 139; **Science Photo Library/Bob Gibbons:** p 124 (bottom); **Science Photo Library/BSIP, Fife:** p 149 (bottom); **Science Photo Library/Chris Priest:** p 42; **Science Photo Library/Claude Nuridsany & Marie Perennou:** p 205 (top); **Science Photo Library/CNRI:** p 47 (bottom), p 75 (middle), p 187 (top), p 237; **Science Photo Library/Custom Medical Stock Photo:** p 68; **Science Photo Library/David McCarthy:** p 45 (top right); **Science Photo Library/Don Fawcett:** p 48 (top); **Science Photo Library/Dr Gopal Murti:** p 66, p 108; **Science Photo Library/Dr Jeremy Burgess:** p 110, p 159, p 182; **Science Photo Library/Dr Rob Stepney:** p 111; **Science Photo Library/Eddy Gray:** p 82 (bottom); **Science Photo Library/Eye of Science:** p 3, p 5, p 18, p 102 (top), p 106; **Science Photo Library/Frances Leroy, Biocosmos:** p 150; **Science Photo Library/George D. Lepp:** p 35; **Science Photo Library/George Ranalli:** p 124 (top); **Science Photo Library/GJLP:** p 94; **Science Photo Library/GustoImages:** p 69; **Science Photo Library/J. C. Revy:** p 32, p 59 (right), p136; **Science Photo Library/Jeanne White:** p125; **Science Photo Library/John Durham:** p 222; **Science Photo Library/Leslie J Borg:** p 230 (middle left); **Science Photo Library/K. R. Porter:** p 100: **Science Photo Library/Lowell Georgia:** p 101; **Science Photo Library/Manfred Kage:** p 80; **Science Photo Library/Mauro Fermariello:** p 43 p 44; **Science Photo Library/MedImage:** p 82 (top); **Science Photo Library/Microfield Scientific Ltd.:** p 179; **Science Photo Library/NIBSC:** p 4; **Science Photo Library/Prof. G Gimenez-Martin:**

p 169 (all); **Science Photo Library/Prof. Motta, Correr and Nottola/ Univeristy "La Sapienza", Rome:** p 75 (bottom); **Science Photo Library/ Prof. Motta/G. Macchiarelli/Univeristy "La Sapienza", Rome:** p 91; **Science Photo Library/Prof. P. Motta/Dept. of Anatomy/Univeristy "La Sapienza", Rome:** p 59 (left); **Science Photo Library/Prof. P.M. Motta, G. Macchiarelli, S.A Nottola:** p 95; **Science Photo Library/Simon Fraser:** p 226 (bottom); **Science Photo Library/Steve Gschmeissner:** p 187 (middle); **Science Photo Library/Susumu Nishinaga:** p 45 (middle), **Science Photo Library/Tony Wood:** p 124 (middle); p 187 (bottom); **Science Photo Library/Volker Steger:** p 112.

Every effort has been made to trace and contact all copyright holders and we apologise if any have been overlooked. The publisher will be pleased to make the necessary arrangements at the first opportunity.

We would like to thank Ellie O'Byrne, Carol Usher and Sharon Thorn for their helpful suggestions and hard work, without which this book could not have been produced.

Glenn and Susan Toole